PSYCHIATRIC DISORDERS – NEW FRONTIERS IN AFFECTIVE DISORDERS

Edited by **Dieter Schoepf**

Psychiatric Disorders – New Frontiers in Affective Disorders
http://dx.doi.org/10.5772/2039
Edited by Dieter Schoepf

Contributors

Peter Falkai, Berend Malchow, Andrea Schmitt, Lauren B. Ozbolt, Charles B. Nemeroff, Tom K. Birkenhäger, Henricus G. Ruhé, Carsten Diener, Michèle Wessa, Julia Linke, Larissa Wolkenstein, Martin Hautzinger, Dieter Schoepf, Viola Oertel-Knöchel, Liliane Sayegh, Gustavo Turecki, J. Kim Penberthy, Christopher J. Gioia, Andrea Konig, Aaron M. Martin, Stephanie A. Cockrell, Todd K. Favorite, Todd Vance, , Kayla J. Conrad, Adrie Seldenrijk, Nicole Vogelzangs, Patricia van Oppen, Brenda Penninx, Anneke van Schaik, Susan L. Renes

Published by InTech

Janeza Trdine 9, 51000 Rijeka, Croatia

Copyright © 2013 InTech

Notice

Publishing Process Manager Sandra Bakic
Technical Editor InTech DTP team
Cover InTech Design team

Additional hard copies can be obtained from orders@intechopen.com

Psychiatric Disorders – New Frontiers in Affective Disorders, Edited by Dieter Schoepf
p. cm.
ISBN 978-953-51-1147-4

For EU product safety concerns:
IN TECH d.o.o., Prolaz Marije Krucifikse Kozulić 3, 51000 Rijeka, Croatia,
info@intechopen.com or visit our website at intechopen.com.

Meet the editor

Dr. Dieter Schoepf works at Bonn University in leading position. He has been awarded in 2011 and 2012 as a top expert on depression and bipolar disorder in Germany's largest independent valuation. His main research interest is dedicated to affective disorders and neural mechanisms of change during treatment as well as co-morbidity research. He is a personal trainee of Prof. James P. McCullough and since 2007 the second US-certified CBASP-therapist and supervisor in Germany. He is also founder-member of CBASP-Network.org and its first vice president from 2008-2012. He established the CBASP Centre of Competence since 2006, where he is the principal site investigator of bi-centric and multicentre CBASP studies. In psychotherapy, his special subjects are classical, cognitive, and modern behavioral psychotherapies.

Contents

Preface

Since the turn of the century, our understanding of affective serious mental illness has increased apace. With its onset during early childhood or the crucial period of adolescence, affective disorders often have a significant impact on the (normal) life trajectory, not to mention the effect of those families who have been touched by mental illness. Individuals suffering from affective disorders, such as early-onset major depression, bipolar disorder and schizoaffective disorder, which fall into this rubric, not only have a profile of severe and long-lasting morbidity compared to the general population, they frequently continue to receive less than adequate care - despite the many millions of dollars spent each year on the mentally ill. In addition to recognizing the precise source and environmental commonalities, the combination of biologically orientated investigations into genetic and epigenetic factors, neurochemical and molecular-biological changes in the brain, structural brain and functional neural networking abnormalities, and therapeutic studies have consolidated the current view of a cumulative risk model for the onset and the maintenance of affective disorders.

With respect to causal treatability, affective disorders are characterized by a reduced responsiveness to classical pharmacological and short-term behavioral interventions. The impact of these diseases is - more often than not - pervasive; in up to 30% they develop from an episodic into a chronic or pharmacologic treatment resistant course. Specifically, depression and cognitive impairment usually have a major detrimental effect on personal, social and occupational functioning with marked impairment of dyadic reciprocity, and are associated with considerable personal and healthcare utilisation burden. Therefore the awareness of an urgent need for evidence-based "personalized" approach for chronic and treatment resistant courses is slowly growing in the field of psychiatry. Such approach targets available pharmaceuticals and psychotherapeutic interventions to specific diagnostic subgroups, determines the interplay between psychotherapy and neurobiology, and implements stepped care models of combined treatment models. It can be assumed, that the challenge of an evidence-based "personalized" approach will entail pharmacological progress in the future. Additional advance can be expected from new clinical curiosity combined with pharmacodynamic hypothesis testing. Finally, by the research of the underlying neural mechanisms and the impact of pharmacotherapy and psychotherapy on behavioural and neural network functioning, more is learned about the fundamental processes of learning and memory. The clinical utility of an evidence-based "personalized" approach remains, however, to be evaluated in distinct patient groups.

This book reviews data on affective disorders as applied to a wide range of bio-psycho-social problems and co-morbid mental and somatic disorders. Particular emphasis is put on novel developments for addressing patient concerns in Cognitive-Behavioral Therapy (CBT) as well as on attention to causal mechanisms of behaviour change on the basis of technique adjustment in the Cognitive Behavioral Analysis System of Psychotherapy (CBASP), which represents a highly disorder orientated, theory-driven psychotherapy method from the "third generation" of behaviour therapy models, designed for the outpatient treatment of chronic major depression.

The book is divided into five sections. The focus in each section is put on a different frontier. Inevitable, given the diversity of the contributions, and the fact that some chapters cover more than one frontier, the division is not always optimal. Although the majority of the chapters use – as does the title of the book - the term "affective disorder", the terms "mood disorder" and "affective serious mental illness" are used interchangeably.

The first section of the book covers the neurobiological frontiers in affective disorders, including the role of hypothalamic-pituitary-adrenal (HPA) axis modulation and pharmacological aspects of treatment resistant major depression. In the introduction chapter of the book, Falkei, Malchow and Schmitt present the neurobiological background of affective disorders. Biological data suggest that affective disorders entail a broad spectrum of alterations in different neuronal circuits. Specific findings can be detected on the cellular, molecular and hormonal level favoring a biological based dimensional classification of affective disorders that will help to establish more preventive and cause-related treatments.

In the following chapter, Ozbolt and Nemeroff summarize the key components of the HPA-axis and related therapeutic candidates in affective disorders and post-traumatic stress disorder (PTSD). Innovational findings are discussed in the passage dealing with CRF-1 receptor antagonists that have to be further studied in distinctive subsets of chronically depressed patients and CRF-2 receptor antagonists who should also be studied in future to elucidate their role in an evidenced-based "personalized" approach. Finally, the authors conclude "that HPA-axis related targets that have been found by genetic and genomic screens are potentially interesting but that this field is still very much in its infancy".

In the last chapter of the first section Birkenhäger and Ruhé review the contemporary definitions of treatment resistant depression (TRD). From a pharmacological perspective, hypothetical models show differential actions of antidepressant agents on core symptoms of major depressive disorder. However, the exact cause of treatment resistance of pharmacotherapy in depression is yet not fully understood as well as its epidemiology is still not well known. TRD can be defined as a population of patients with a significant unmet clinical need requiring new treatment options. Since there exists no widely accepted consensus for a guideline around TRD, the utility of currently leading staging models is discussed, which are developed to determine refractoriness. Building on this clinical evidence, three algorithms of several treatment steps for the DSM-IV subtypes of major depression are proposed, i.e. atypical, melancholic, and psychotic.

The second section of the book covers the frontier of translational search for targets to improve treatment. Diener points out that animal and human study emphasize the maladaptive role of aversive events in the development of major depressive disorder. Therefore it is important to investigate in how far alterations of associative learning and learned helplessness causally relate to the (etio-) psychopathology of major depression. His state-of-the-art review on the neural signature of altered associative learning in major depression contributes to develop disorder specific interventions that are based on neuroscientific findings.

In the next chapter, Wessa and Linke review the relevant imaging literature with respect to emotional processes in bipolar disorders. As different brain areas are involved, also findings are reviewed that investigate structural and functional connectivity between these different regions. Then the question is addressed, whether structural and functional abnormalities are more likely to evolve during the course of the illness or rather constitute a vulnerability factor of the disease. Finally, the impact of mood states and psychotropic agents on emotion processing are discussed.

In the last chapter of the second section Wolkenstein and Hautzinger move away from imaging results and instead look for moderator and mediator variables concerning the effectiveness of CBT in unipolar and bipolar disorders. While the core principles of CBT are established, newer research expands the boundaries of the original propositions focussing more on differential approaches to CBT administration and the effects CBT has on the neurobiological substrates of automatic and controlled processing. The chapter serves as a state-of-the art description of a specific area of interest that plays an integral role in the development and execution of clinical trials so that positive and negative results can be validly attributed to the applied interventions. In addition, the chapter has to be considered as a report of promising new frontiers of internet – and telephone delivered CBT.

The third section of the book covers novel psychotherapeutic developments for single- and group CBASP outpatient treatment. Schoepf starts with a chapter that integrates recent advances of exposure therapy with causal mechanisms of behaviour change in CBASP. The CBASP model is based on contemporary learning theory considerations. Associative learning of Pavlovian fear represents the "stimulus input" of chronic major depressive disorder with antecedent dysthymic disorder, accounting for up to 75% of the total number of chronically depressed patients. The transformation of CBASP`s original - one-single session scheduled - Significant Other History (SOH) technique to an exposure based prolonged procedure that he labels "intensified-SOH"

(I-SOH) procedure contains an important technique variable adjustment that significantly contributes to therapeutic improvement in this population. The chapter includes the detailed description of the I-SOH procedure which is carried out in the first treatment phase and the three options to use the - earlier by the Bonn-group defined and applied - three different forms of the Interpersonal Discrimination Exercise in relation to the progress of therapy in the second treatment phase. The represented treatment trajectories over 48 weeks are promising; as early-onset chronically depressed patients are unlikely to remit over time.

Then Oertel-Knöchel and Schoepf present the adaptation of the CBASP to an early-onset chronically depressed female patient - classified prior to treatment as "difficult to treat with a high probability of suicidal behaviour" - who switched into a first hypomanic episode during outpatient treatment. Epidemiological studies assessing the course of unipolar depression within 15 years range indicate that up to 25% of patients diagnosed with non-psychotic major depression converse into bipolar disorder. The here presented single case study shows that "fundamental" and "additional" CBASP interventions that include the disciplined personal involvement of the therapist are successful in reducing acute hypomanic symptoms, increasing the compliance and reducing disease risk as well as falling-back into destructive social behaviour. Especially, the carefully timed self-disclosures during Continuous Performance Responsiveness interventions inhibited maladaptive rule-guided behaviour and counteracted negative interpersonal assumptions in both hypomanic episodes and the inter-episodic phase. The positive course of the treatment leads to the assumption that the implementation of "fundamental" and "additional" interpersonal CBASP strategies in combination with social rhythm interventions has the potential to develop into to a new treatment option for bipolar patients.

In the last chapter of this section Sayegh and Turecki describe a highly structured CBASP group outpatient protocol for (pharmacologic) treatment-resistant chronic major depression, which has first empirical validation from a single arm pilot study published in 2012. While empirical evidence indicates that CBASP is an effective treatment for outpatient treatment, not much is known about its adaptation to a group modality. Treating treatment resistant patients with major depressive disorder in a outpatient group setting has the benefit of being cost-effective and providing in vivo previously avoided interpersonal situations for practicing social skills and role-plays. Patients are admitted to the group modality on a consecutive basis after they are informed of the treatment modalities. In two to four single psychotherapeutic sessions the nature of the disorders chronicity is explained to the patient and the original SOH-exercise is applied to identify the interpersonal domain which is most problematic for the patient before beginning with the group therapy for a two hour session each week. The recent published pilot results are encouraging and support further study of the effectiveness of CBASP group outpatient treatment with a control group.

The fourth section of the book covers co-morbidity frontiers of major depressive disorder. Penberthy and colleagues begin the fourth section with a chapter about an integrative psychosocial approach that investigates CBASP`s effectiveness for reducing both depressive symptoms and alcohol intake for co-occurring chronic major depression and alcohol dependency. They propose that treatment for this population must be personalized to both the underlying interpersonal issues and the specific skill deficits in order to be effective. The applied protocol is currently proved in a pilot study. Although the preliminary results should be interpreted with caution due to a small sample size this patient population seems to be willing to seek and to participate in such extensive and intensive treatment.

Favorite and Vance focus on the use of modified CBASP in the treatment of chronic major depression with co-occurring PTSD. Given the high rate of co-morbidity of both disorders and the significant symptomatic interaction, it is proposed that CBASP with specific adaptations at each stage of the CBASP protocol - by especially adding the significant trauma event to the SOH exercise in the first treatment phase - can provide an active therapeutic environment that has the strength to accommodate a patient's traumatic processed memories and to link these memories to interpersonal avoidance patterns that exacerbate depressive mood. In the here presented feasibility study patients show significant decreases in the symptoms of depression and a reduction of preoperational thinking as well as enhanced formal operational cognitive processes, which may support a shift from avoidant patterns of behaviour, and, in turn, increased capacity for perspective taking and cognitive empathy within the relational environment.

In addition, a modified CBASP group therapy outpatient protocol for this population is currently proofed at several VA Healthcare Systems because of the significant number of treatment refractory veterans who require ongoing mental health care. The promising results of this study are presented by Favorite and Conrad. The outcome criteria focus on the reduction in symptoms of avoidance and hyper-arousal present in both, as well as the reduction in depressive symptoms. It is concluded that the potential benefits of a more transdiagnostic perspective in the adaptation of the CBASP model to patients with chronic depression/PTSD co-morbidities are able to reduce the rate of treatment drop-out and/or treatment refractory outcomes.

In the last chapter of this section Seldenrijk and colleagues shift the focus on depression, vascular conditions and chronicity. Co-morbidity research of overt and subclinical cardiovascular disease (CVD) represents an important target in affective disorders. The lifelong course of early-onset chronic major depression as well as the course of treatment resistant depression place the affected individuals at increased risk for poor general health and associated chronic medical conditions in comparison to the general population. At present the degree, to which patient and provider factors contribute to the fact, that adults with chronic major depression may be less likely to report physical symptoms of CVD, is not clear. Reducing the risk of serious cardiovascular complications during treatment is of extraordinary importance to lessen the burden of avoidable somatic mortality in these patients. Therefore monitoring for CVD and its complications is of utmost relevance to formulate and execute appropriate and successful treatment plans, especially in older chronically depressed patients.

The fifth and last section challenges the stigma of serious mental illness. Rene opens in "a journey through schizophrenia" the door to an important ethical dimension of serious mental illness. The 2006 revised World Medical Association statement on ethical issues concerning patients with mental illness formulates in its preamble that "historically, many societies have regarded individuals with mental illness as a threat to those around them rather than as people in need of support and care. Therefore, in the absence of effective treatment, many individuals with mental illness were confined to asylums for all or part of their lives. The aim of such confinement in these cases was to prevent behaviour that was self-destructive or aggressive toward others". In addition, it is well known but only little published that affected individuals with serious mental illness as well as individuals with mental retardation are at increased risk for becoming physically, emotionally and sexually traumatized during childhood and the crucial period of adolescence. The preamble follows: "at the present time, progress in psychiatric therapy allows for better care of patients with mental illness. Efficacious psychopharmacological and psychotherapeutic treatments – (I add) in combination with an increased communication between researchers and clinicians - can result in patient outcomes ranging from complete alleviation of symptoms to long remissions for patients whose conditions are more serious". With respect to schizophrenia, there are only few famous individuals known because schizophrenia is a psychiatric disorder that typically strikes those affected when they are young, between the ages of 17 to 28. Individuals during this lifespan typically start out their professional lives after completing high school or college. Ms Saks, Associate Dean, Chaired Professor of Law, Psychology, and Psychiatry Behavioral Sciences at the University of Southern California Gould School of Law who additionally supports the rights and interests of children as well as the other presented professionally successful individuals are good counterexamples – hopefully from the perspective of this book for an evidenced-based "personalized" treatment approach that leads in difficult courses of the illness to persisting recovery. Personally I have to say, that when Rene's proposal was accepted for the book I was filled with hope that this form of challenging the stigma of serious mental illness can help us to proactively shape the societies in which we live to become more forgiving and open-minded for mental illness overall. A German official poster - I think of the family ministry and the Lebenshilfe - said a few years ago: "It is always our own decision in what kind of a society we want to live". Pictured were young, elderly and disabled individuals, one boy with Down syndrome.

Dr. Dieter Schoepf
CBASP Centre of Competence, University of Bonn,
Germany

Section 1

Neurobiological Frontiers

Chapter 1

Neurobiological Background of Affective Disorders

Peter Falkai, Berend Malchow and Andrea Schmitt

Additional information is available at the end of the chapter

http://dx.doi.org/10.5772/51801

1. Introduction

Affective disorders, including major depression, mania and bipolar disorder, represent a spectrum of severe psychiatric diseases reflecting a continuum of psychopathological symptoms. Starting in young adulthood and often leading to suicidal ideation, affective disorders are ranking among the most disabling diseases worldwide in terms of the WHO global burden of disease, are socio-economically relevant, severe and prevalent. These diseases lead to enormous social disabilities due to affective and cognitive symptoms [1]. Depression, for example, has a lifetime risk of about 20-25% [2] and, besides suicide, a higher prevalence of the metabolic syndrome including coronary heart disease and diabetes increase mortality [3]. Bipolar disorder with manic episodes, in contrast, has a lifetime prevalence of about 1-5% [4]. However, due to the occurrence of depressive symptoms, the disease may be misdiagnosed - Goldberg et al. [5] could show a hypo-manic or manic episode in 46% in patients with depression.

Despite tremendous efforts, the neurobiological background of affective disorders remains elusive, and due to lacking biomarkers an early diagnosis and reliable prognosis is difficult. Undisputed is a multifactorial etiology with genetic and psychosocial factors such as stress, emotional trauma and viral infections during the vulnerable episodes of brain development. They possibly interact in inducing disease symptoms. Beside neuroendocrinological factors, neurotransmitter disturbances and alterations of signal transduction constitute the basis of structural and functional alterations in neuronal circuits of the brain.

2. Neuroimaging studies in affective diseases

Since the description of the limbic "Papez-circuit of emotion" in the 1930s involving hippocampus, cingulated gyrus, anterior thalamus and hypothalamus, magnetic resonance imaging [6] studies in patients revealed volume deficits in regions relevant for emotion processing, be it amygdala, hippocampus, anterior cingulate gyrus, prefrontal, or orbitofrontal cortex as well as basal ganglia. In bipolar disorder, affective and psychotic symptoms are related to a dysfunction in the prefrontal-subcortical network interacting with limbic regions [7]. Meta-analyses in bipolar disorder indeed show gray matter reductions in the paralimbic regions anterior cingulate cortex and insula, partially overlapping with decreased volumes in schizophrenia and indicating a continuum of the neurobiological background of psychoses [8, 9]. Anterior cingulate dysfunction in bipolar disorder has been strengthened by functional MRI studies, which revealed functional attenuation in the anterior cingulated cortex in patients with bipolar disorder performing cognitive and emotional tasks [10, 11]. Recent meta-analyses of fMRI studies in bipolar disorder show decreased activation of the inferior frontal cortex corresponding to frontal hypoactivity and overactivated hippocampus plus amygdala (limbic hyperactivity), which was consistent across emotional and cognitive tasks and related to the state of mania [12, 13]. Reduced fractional anisotropy nearby the parahippocampal gyrus and anterior cingulate cortex have been identified in diffusion-tensor imaging studies in bipolar disorder and speak for impaired limbic connectivity in neuronal networks [14]. With respect to amygdala size, decreased volumes have only been detected in younger patients and a respective correlation between volume and age has been reported [15, 16]. Contrastingly, schizophrenia patients showed larger ventricles and smaller amygdala volumes compared to bipolar disorder, pointing to a continuum of neurobiological alterations [8].

Compared to patients with bipolar disorder, those with major depressive disorders present decreased rates of white matter hyperintensity, smaller hippocampal and basal ganglia volumes and a decreased corpus callosum area [17, 18]. Along with increased lateral ventricles, smaller volumes of the basal ganglia, hippocampus, thalamus, frontal lobe, orbitofrontal gyrus and gyrus rectus have been detected in major depression [19]. This especially pertained patients during depressive episodes with smaller hippocampal volumes compared to remittend patients [18]. Reduced hippocampal volumes have consistently been reported in patients with major depression and are prominent in patients with recurrent and chronic depression [20]. Shape analysis revealed deformations in the subiculum, CA1 and CA2-3 subfields in the tail of the right hippocampus of patients with first episode of depression [21]. The presence of alterations in first-episode depression is consistent with a neurodevelopmental hypothesis of early stress experience, especially since this region plays a major role in inhibiting stress response [22], providing inhibitory feedback to the hypothalamic-pituitary-adrenal (HPA) axis [23].

3. Synaptic plasticity and stress mediation

Post-mortem investigations reveal reduced density and size of interneurons in cornu ammonis (CA) 2/3 subfield of the hippocampus in bipolar disorder [24]. In the hippocampal subiculum, a decreased density of neuronal dendrites leading to disturbances of microconnectivity and probably representing the basis of the reported volume deficit in bipolar patients has been found [25]. However, the finding of decreased neuropil (dendrites and axons) seems not to be specific for bipolar disorder, as it has also been reported in all hippocampal subfields of patients with major depression showing increased density of neurons and glia cells as a sign of increased packing of the cells. Additionally, in line with the hypothesis of a degenerative process, soma size of pyramidal neurons was decreased [26]. In the prefrontal cortex of patients with major depression, a decrease in cortical thickness goes along with lower densities of neurons and glia cells [27]. In the anterior cingulate cortex, in familial depression and bipolar disorder, decreased glia number has been detected [28]. In both regions, decrease of glia density and neuronal size has been reported [29]. Decreased glia density has also been found in the amygdala of patients with major depression [30]. In animal studies again, chronic stress or repeated administration of glucocorticoids interestingly results in degeneration of hippocampal neurons with decreased soma size and atrophy of dendrites [31, 32]. Stress possibly also influences synaptic plasticity in the prefrontal cortex [33]. Thus the volume loss in brain regions like the hippocampus reported in affective disorders may indeed be mediated by stress-induced glucocorticoid neurotoxicity [34, 35].

Division and differentiation of stem cells to neurons and their migration to the granule cell layer has been demonstrated in the hippocampal dentate gyrus of both humans and adult rodents [36]. Some factors influence this neurogenesis: While blockade of the glutamatergic N-methyl-D-aspartate (NMDA) receptor and adrenalectomy results in increased production of granule neurons, adrenal steroids and NMDA receptor activation diminished neurogenesis [37]. Acute, chronic or prenatal stress, all of them implicated in the pathophysiology of depression [38], have been shown to inhibit proliferation of subgranular neurons [39-42]. Because both, circulating adrenal steroids and glutamate-induced excitatory input to the hippocampus, are enhanced by stress [43, 44], the influence of stressful events on cell proliferation and survival of newly generated neurons may be mediated by these mechanisms [40, 45]. In an animal model of learned helplessness, inescapable stress is leading to downregulation of neurogenesis [46]. Accordingly, antidepressants are known to induce cell proliferation and neurogenesis [46-49].

4. Neurotrophins and the HPA axis

Neurotrophic factors, particulary Brain-Derived Neurotrophic Factor (BDNF) are expressed in the hippocampus and cortex and are involved in neurogenesis and synaptic plasticity such as promotion of survival and differentiation as well as branching of axons and dendrites [50]. In patients with bipolar disorder, reduced hippocampal expression of BDNF has been reported [51] while antidepressants reversed this effect [52]. In blood of depressed patients, including patients with bipolar disorder, BDNF levels have been found to be decreased and correlated to higher depression evaluation scores [53, 54]. Post-mortem studies of the hippocampus in major depression revealed a reduced BDNF immunhistochemistry [51].

To date, beside a genetic vulnerability, stress is widely accepted as risk factor for depression. In animal models, acute or chronic stress decreased BDNF levels in the hippocampus inclusive the dentate gyrus [52]. Along with this hypothesis, stress is known to reduce the branching of hippocampal dendrites [55]. It additionally increases plasma and adrenal corticosterone levels and application of this hormone induces reduced hippocampal BDNF levels, mimicking stress reaction [52]. The major stress system of the body is the HPA axis, a neuroendocrine system involved in the production of the stress hormone cortisol by adrenal glands. In more than 50% of patients with major depression, a dysfunction of the HPA axis with increased basal cortisol levels and dexamethasone non-suppression of cortisol was detected, suggesting abnormal negative feedback system of the HPA axis. Additionally, the production of corticotrophin-releasing hormone (CRH) production is abnormal while pituitary and adrenal sensitivity seem to be intact [56] (figure 1). CRH is produced in the paraventricular nucleus of the hypothalamus in response to psychosocial stress and activates the HPA axis. It is binding in the pituitary gland to induce release of adrenocorticotropine hormone (ACTH), which in turn stimulates the release of cortisol from the adrenal gland. In a negative feedback loop, cortisol binding inhibits CRH and ACTH release, inhibiting the HPA axis [57], but this hormonal feedback is known to be abnormal in depression. In animal models, CRH administration and overexpression induce depression-like behavior, while CRH antagonists have antidepressant properties [58, 59]. Depressed patients with history of childhood abuse have enhanced HPA axis response to psychosocial stress and attenuated adrenocorticotrophin and cortisol response to application of the synthetic corticosteroid dexamethasone [60]. However, individual genetic background influences the incidence of depression in response to psychosocial stress and only a minority of persons exposed to common stressors develops depression [61]. Thus, genes may modulate the association between environmental factors like stress and risk of illness.

5. Genetic findings

Twin, family and adoption studies have shown that major depression is a moderate heritable disease. During the last years, candidate gene and genome-wide association studies (GWAS) have linked common DNA sequence variation, called polymorphisms, to major depression [62-64] and identified novel candidate loci [65]. However, single nucleotide polymorphisms (SNPs) only slightly affect the pathophysiology, and affective disorders seem to be of complex polygenetic origin. With respect to CRH dysfunction, a genetic variation of the corticotropin releasing hormone type 1 receptor (CRHR1) has been found to be associated with decreased HPA axis response to CRH infusion, suggesting to influence this pathophysiology of depression [66]. In addition, negative feedback control on CRH secretion may be impaired due to altered glucocorticoid receptor (GR) function on hippocampal level [67]. A GR polymorphism has also been found to be associated with vulnerability to depression [68]. According to the neurotrophin hypothesis, in patients with depression and healthy controls, smaller hippocampal volumes have been detected in carriers of the BDNF Met66 allele compared to Val/Val homozygotes [69]. These results suggest that a Val66Met polymorphism may possibly predispose to smaller hippocampal volumes and depression, although this topic currently is under debate [70]. An interaction between a 5-HTTLPR serotonin transporter polymorphism and Val66Met BDNF gene variant has been shown to be associated to stress-induced depression [71-73]. Furthermore, depression has been associated with polymorphisms in the glucocorticoid receptor gene NR3C1, the monoamine oxidase A gene, and genes for glycogen synthase kinase-3ß, a neuron-specific neutral amino acid transporter (SLC6A15) as well as group-2 metabotropic glutamate receptor (GRM3) [74, 75].

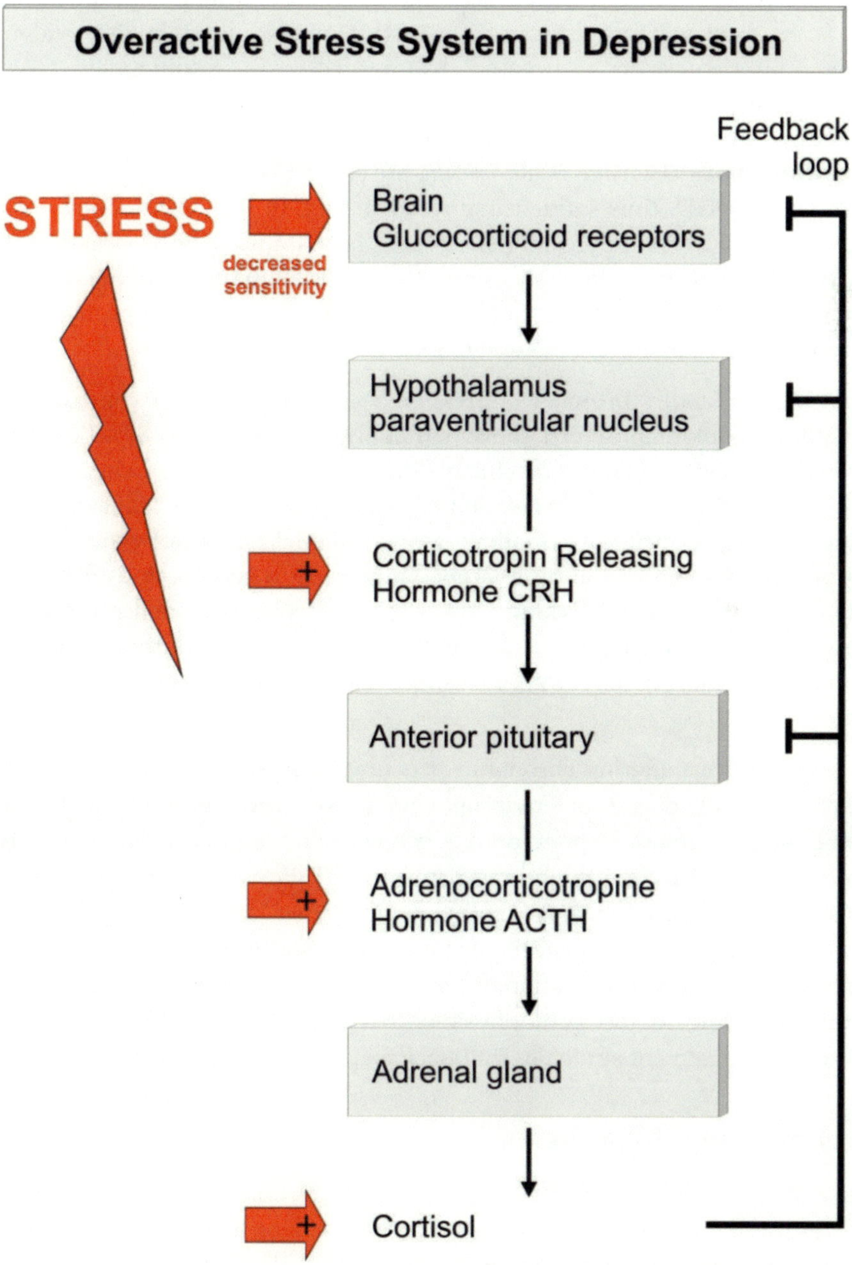

Figure 1.

Several other genes are associated with bipolar disorder inclusive brain-derived neurotrophic factor (BDNF), D-amino acid oxidase activator (DAOA, G72), disrupted in schizophrenia 1 (DISC1), solute carrier family 6 (SLC6A4), tryptophan hydroxylase 2 (TPH2), catechol-O-methyltransferase (COMT), serotonin transporter (5-HTT) [76-81], but there is a large overlap with schizophrenia-associated genes, pointing to a continuum between affective disorders and psychosis. Among the risk variants for bipolar disorder, to date G72 is the most supported locus [76, 82-84]. However, there is also evidence for an association with depression and panic disorder [78, 85]. Additionally, G72 possibly influences a predisposition for affective symptoms in schizophrenia [83]. A further risk gene for bipolar disorder and depression is diacylglycerol kinase (DGKH), showing 10 SNPs to be associated with bipolar disorder while 7 SNPs are associated with unipolar depression and four SNPs with ADHD, thus influencing mood instability [86]. Additionally, a region of both ankyrin 3 (ANK3) and neurocan (NCAN) has been found to be associated with bipolar disorder [65, 87]. A recent meta-analysis revealed association of two SNPs in the serotonin 1A receptor gene with major depression and bipolar disorder and supports the hypothesis of disturbed serotonin neurotransmission in mood disorder [88].

Altogether, the heritability of major depression seems to be meager compared to bipolar disorder and schizophrenia, which show heritability rates of up to 80%. To date, GWAS studies could not identify many reproducible individual gene loci associated with affective disorders [89], but SNPs near exons exhibit a greater probability of replication, supporting an enrichment of reproducible associations near functional regions of genes [90]. However, the confirmation of some loci affords larger samples. In a GWAS study from the GWAS consortium Bipolar Disorder Working Group, in large cohorts evidence for association of CACN1C, an L-type voltage-gated calcium channel has been confirmed [91]. In order to improve methodological quality, new investigations using next-generation sequencing are under way.

Epigenetic mechanisms altering chromatin structure such as histone acetylation and DNA methylation may link effects of environmental factors such as stress to transcriptional regulation of specific genes. Depression-like behavior and antidepressant action have been found to be regulated by epigenetic mechanisms [92]. Besides downregulation of BDNF transcripts, stress increased histone methylation at their corresponding promoters. The antidepressant imipramine reversed the decrease on the mRNA level and increased histone acetylation along with downregulation of histone deacetylase, suggesting an important role in histone remodeling in the pathophysiology and treatment of depression [93]. As a consequence, new treatment strategies influencing epigenetic targets could be developed.

6. Neurotransmitter hypotheses

Selective antidepressant treatment is known to act on the serotonergic and the noradrenergic system. Traditional long-term antidepressant treatment is known to induce increased levels of serotonin from the raphe nuclei [94]. The serotonin hypothesis of depression suggests that decreased serotonin activity increases vulnerability for depression

[95]. The serotonin system originates from the dorsal and medial raphe nuclei in the brainstem infringing on limbic structures such as the hippocampus and amygdala [94]. Reducing serotonin synthesis induces depressive symptoms in healthy probands exposed to uncontrollable stress [96], and increased serotonin release in the hippocampus has been implicated in the mechanisms underlying coping with stress [97]. Serotonin (5-HT) receptors are represented by 5-HT_1 class receptors, being situated pre- and postsynaptically and inhibitory by reduction of adenylate cyclase activity. The 5-HT_2 class excitatory receptors are located predominantly postsynaptically through activation of phospholipase C [94]. 5-HT_{1A} receptors are known to mediate adaption to stress and these receptors located in the hippocampus could attenuate the emotional impact of aversive stimuli, inhibiting the consolidation of stressfull memories [97]. Additionally, 5-HT_{1A} receptors are known to mediate the serotonin-based increase in neurogenesis [98] and induce release of neurotrophic factors [99]. Moreover, serotonin is involved in the regulation of the HPA axis [100]. The downregulation of 5-HT_{1A} receptors in the hippocampus by stressors is corticoid-dependent and reversed by antidepressants [101, 102]. Indeed, patients with depression have reduced 5-HT_{1A} receptor binding as revealed by positron emission tomography (PET) studies [103, 104] plus results of altered receptor number in post-mortem investigations [105, 106].

The noradrenaline system derives from the locus coeruleus and lateral tegmental nuclei. The receptors belong to the excitatory postsynaptic ß-adrenergic, α_1 and inhibitory pre- and postsynaptic α_2 adrenergic categories. They have been shown to be upregulated in post-mortem brains of patients with depression [95, 107], suggesting a primary noradrenaline deficit. Stressors and glucocorticoids persistently activate the noradrenergic system in the locus coeruleus with resulting disrupted responses to brief stimuli [94]. In contrast to the posterior hippocampus, facilitation of noradrenergic transmission in the ventral hippocampus, being involved in emotion and anxiety [108, 109], seems to protect against stress effects [110]. Moreover, the noradrenaline system closely interacts with serotonin, facilitating serotonin neurotransmission in the hippocampus and amygdala [97] thus providing a therapeutic target for antidepressant drugs such as noradrenaline reuptake inhibitors [111]. Dopamine is another monoamine proposed to play a role in mood disorder since the mesolimbic dopamine reward circuit originating from the ventral tegmental area is associated with rewarding effects of food, sex and drug abuse. A dopaminergic deficit may contribute to anhedonia reduced motivation and energy level in patients with depression and may represent a target for the development of new therapeutic strategies [112]. It is expected that reuptake inhibitors for all three catecholamines (serotonin, noradrenaline, dopamine) can produce greater efficacy than traditional antidepressants [113].

It has been shown that 5-HT depletion alone does not induce mood symptoms, but an interaction with glutamate may be responsible for developing affective disorders. Additionally, noradrenaline is involved in release and uptake of glutamate [114]. Glutamate is the principal excitatory, γ-aminobutyric acid (GABA) the predominant inhibitory neurotransmitter in the brain, both occupying at least 50% of the synapses. Besides regulating synaptic plasticity, they closely interact with the HPA axis. In depression, an overactive glutamate system and hypoactive GABA system has been suggested [115]. Elevated levels of glutamine/glutamate have been shown in MR-spectroscopy (MRS) studies in the frontal and occipital cortex as well as in basal ganglia of patients with depression. In the anterior cingulate cortex, reduced levels have been reported in depression, while in bipolar disorder with acute mania, glutamate/glutamine levels were increased [28]. These findings are consistent with glutamatergic overactivity in acute mania. However, medication effects may contribute to the findings in mood disorder. In medication-free depressed patients, GABA levels have been found to be reduced in the occipital and anterior cingulate cortex as well as prefrontal cortex [115]. In clinical studies, agonists at the glycine site of the glutamatergic N-methyl-D-aspartate (NMDA) receptor as well as inhibitors of the glycine transporter elevating glycine levels have been found to exert antidepressant properties. But also antagonists at the NMDA receptor like ketamine induce a presynaptic release of glutamate, which in turn activates glutamatergic α-amino-3-hydroxy-5-methyl-isoxazole-4-propionic acid (AMPA) receptors act as antidepressants [116-118]. Novel potential therapeutic drugs affecting the glutamate system are under investigation, such as modulators of AMPA receptors, NMDA receptor subunit NR2B, metabotropic glutamate receptors, glutamate transporter EAAT2, and N-acetyl-L-cysteine which is a precursor of the NMDA receptor activating antioxidant glutathione [117, 119].

7. Findings on the molecular level

The above described neurotransmitters are known to modulate gene transcription and protein synthesis [120]. Proteomic studies in the frontal cortex and nucleus accumbens of depressed patients revealed altered expression of Dihydropyrimidinase-related protein 2 (DPYSL2), regulating neuronal development, migration and differentiation as well as differential expression of aldolase C (ALDOC), which plays a major role in glucose and energy metabolism [121]. In the dorsolateral prefrontal cortex, proteomic profiles and a phosphoproteomic approach showed differences in proteins associated with synaptic transmission and cellular architecture [122] [123]. In bipolar disorder, dysregulation of DPYSL2 and glial fibrillary acid protein (GFAP) along with tubulin subunits suggest cytoskeletal dysfunction and altered brain development [121].

Genome-wide gene expression studies in bipolar disorder unearthed a high correlation of expression changes also observed in schizophrenia such as decreased oligodendrocyte and myelination related genes, as well as deregulation of mitochondrial energy metabolism, oxidative phosphorylation, synapse-related and mitochondrial genes [124, 125]. In depressed patients, alterations of genes involved in neurodevelopment, signal transduction, cell communication and myelination have been reported. Additionally, genes encoding for the glutamate and serotonin system have been found to be altered in bipolar disorder and depression [125]. Moreover, in mood disorder, alterations of BDNF and subunits of glutamate receptors and the GABA synthesizing enzyme GAD have been detected to be differentially regulated [126]. In a previous laser-capture microdissection study of the locus coeruleus, Bernard [127] found alterations of the glutamate-, astroglia- and growth factor related genes in depression, but not in bipolar disorder, suggesting differential processes in both disorders. In the frontal cortex of patients with major depression, increased apoptosis stress and upregulation of pro-and anti-inflammatory cytokines have been detected [128] which differs from findings in schizophrenia [129]. Interestingly, in an animal study, chronic stress affected expression of genes involved in brain development, morphogenesis and synaptic transmission in the dentate gyrus of the hippocampus, which is involved in neurogenesis [130]. Modulation of these stress effects may lead to development of new therapeutic strategies for mood disorder.

8. Conclusion

Overall, mood disorder entails a broad spectrum of alterations in specific neuronal circuits. Despite overlapping findings in patients with major depression, bipolar disorder and even schizophrenia, pointing to a neurobiological continuum of the diagnostic spectrum of psychoses, specific findings can be detected on the cellular, molecular and hormonal level. Besides genetics, environmental factors like acute or chronic stress are known to account for the pathophysiology of the named disorders. New treatment strategies involving several neurotransmitter systems are under way and may improve outcome. However, preventive and cause-related treatments based on molecular findings plus animal studies of environmental and genetic factors should be developed to increase efficacy and prevent burden of severe psychiatric diseases.

Author details

Peter Falkai and Andrea Schmitt
Department of Psychiatry and Psychotherapy, Ludwig-Maximilians-University Munich, Munich, Germany

Berend Malchow
Department of Psychiatry and Psychotherapy, Ludwig-Maximilians-University Munich, Munich, Germany
Department of Psychiatry and Psychotherapy, University of Göttingen, Göttingen, Germany

9. References

[1] Menken M, Munsat TL, Toole JF. The global burden of disease study: implications for neurology. Archives of neurology. 2000;57(3):418-20. Epub 2000/03/14.
[2] Kessler RC, Berglund P, Demler O, Jin R, Merikangas KR, Walters EE. Lifetime prevalence and age-of-onset distributions of DSM-IV disorders in the National Comorbidity Survey Replication. Arch Gen Psychiatry. 2005;62(6):593-602. Epub 2005/06/09.
[3] Evans DL, Charney DS, Lewis L, Golden RN, Gorman JM, Krishnan KR, et al. Mood disorders in the medically ill: scientific review and recommendations. Biol Psychiatry. 2005;58(3):175-89. Epub 2005/08/09.

[4] Baldessarini RJ. Treatment research in bipolar disorder: issues and recommendations. CNS drugs. 2002;16(11):721-9. Epub 2002/10/18.

[5] Goldberg JF, Harrow M, Whiteside JE. Risk for bipolar illness in patients initially hospitalized for unipolar depression. Am J Psychiatry. 2001;158(8):1265-70. Epub 2001/08/02.

[6] Leweke FM, Giuffrida A, Wurster U, Emrich HM, Piomelli D. Elevated endogenous cannabinoids in schizophrenia. Neuroreport. 1999;10(8):1665-9. Epub 1999/09/29.

[7] Strakowski SM, Delbello MP, Adler CM. The functional neuroanatomy of bipolar disorder: a review of neuroimaging findings. Mol Psychiatry. 2005;10(1):105-16. Epub 2004/09/02.

[8] Ellison-Wright I, Bullmore E. Anatomy of bipolar disorder and schizophrenia: a meta-analysis. Schizophr Res. 2010;117(1):1-12. Epub 2010/01/15.

[9] De Peri L, Crescini A, Deste G, Fusar-Poli P, Sacchetti E, Vita A. Brain structural abnormalities at the onset of schizophrenia and bipolar disorder: a meta-analysis of controlled magnetic resonance imaging studies. Curr Pharm Des. 2012;18(4):486-94. Epub 2012/01/14.

[10] Gruber SA, Rogowska J, Yurgelun-Todd DA. Decreased activation of the anterior cingulate in bipolar patients: an fMRI study. J Affect Disord. 2004;82(2):191-201. Epub 2004/10/19.

[11] Lennox BR, Jacob R, Calder AJ, Lupson V, Bullmore ET. Behavioural and neurocognitive responses to sad facial affect are attenuated in patients with mania. Psychol Med. 2004;34(5):795-802. Epub 2004/10/27.

[12] Chen CH, Suckling J, Lennox BR, Ooi C, Bullmore ET. A quantitative meta-analysis of fMRI studies in bipolar disorder. Bipolar Disord. 2011;13(1):1-15. Epub 2011/02/16.

[13] Kupferschmidt DA, Zakzanis KK. Toward a functional neuroanatomical signature of bipolar disorder: quantitative evidence from the neuroimaging literature. Psychiatry Res. 2011;193(2):71-9. Epub 2011/06/17.

[14] Vederine FE, Wessa M, Leboyer M, Houenou J. A meta-analysis of whole-brain diffusion tensor imaging studies in bipolar disorder. Prog Neuropsychopharmacol Biol Psychiatry. 2011;35(8):1820-6. Epub 2011/06/01.

[15] Usher J, Leucht S, Falkai P, Scherk H. Correlation between amygdala volume and age in bipolar disorder - a systematic review and meta-analysis of structural MRI studies. Psychiatry Res. 2010;182(1):1-8. Epub 2010/03/17.

[16] Pfeifer JC, Welge J, Strakowski SM, Adler CM, DelBello MP. Meta-analysis of amygdala volumes in children and adolescents with bipolar disorder. J Am Acad Child Adolesc Psychiatry. 2008;47(11):1289-98. Epub 2008/10/02.

[17] Arnone D, McIntosh AM, Chandra P, Ebmeier KP. Meta-analysis of magnetic resonance imaging studies of the corpus callosum in bipolar disorder. Acta Psychiatr Scand. 2008;118(5):357-62. Epub 2008/07/23.

[18] Kempton MJ, Salvador Z, Munafo MR, Geddes JR, Simmons A, Frangou S, et al. Structural neuroimaging studies in major depressive disorder. Meta-analysis and comparison with bipolar disorder. Arch Gen Psychiatry. 2011;68(7):675-90. Epub 2011/07/06.

[19] Arnone D, McIntosh AM, Ebmeier KP, Munafo MR, Anderson IM. Magnetic resonance imaging studies in unipolar depression: systematic review and meta-regression analyses. Eur Neuropsychopharmacol. 2012;22(1):1-16. Epub 2011/07/05.

[20] Cole J, Costafreda SG, McGuffin P, Fu CH. Hippocampal atrophy in first episode depression: a meta-analysis of magnetic resonance imaging studies. J Affect Disord. 2011;134(1-3):483-7. Epub 2011/07/13.

[21] Cole J, Toga AW, Hojatkashani C, Thompson P, Costafreda SG, Cleare AJ, et al. Subregional hippocampal deformations in major depressive disorder. J Affect Disord. 2010;126(1-2):272-7. Epub 2010/04/16.

[22] McEwen BS, Magarinos AM. Stress and hippocampal plasticity: implications for the pathophysiology of affective disorders. Hum Psychopharmacol. 2001;16(S1):S7-S19. Epub 2002/10/31.

[23] Fanselow MS. Contextual fear, gestalt memories, and the hippocampus. Behav Brain Res. 2000;110(1-2):73-81. Epub 2000/05/10.

[24] Knable MB, Barci BM, Webster MJ, Meador-Woodruff J, Torrey EF. Molecular abnormalities of the hippocampus in severe psychiatric illness: postmortem findings from the Stanley Neuropathology Consortium. Mol Psychiatry. 2004;9(6):609-20, 544. Epub 2004/01/07.

[25] Rosoklija G, Toomayan G, Ellis SP, Keilp J, Mann JJ, Latov N, et al. Structural abnormalities of subicular dendrites in subjects with schizophrenia and mood disorders: preliminary findings. Arch Gen Psychiatry. 2000;57(4):349-56. Epub 2000/04/18.

[26] Stockmeier CA, Mahajan GJ, Konick LC, Overholser JC, Jurjus GJ, Meltzer HY, et al. Cellular changes in the postmortem hippocampus in major depression. Biol Psychiatry. 2004;56(9):640-50. Epub 2004/11/04.

[27] Rajkowska G, Miguel-Hidalgo JJ, Wei J, Dilley G, Pittman SD, Meltzer HY, et al. Morphometric evidence for neuronal and glial prefrontal cell pathology in major depression. Biol Psychiatry. 1999;45(9):1085-98. Epub 1999/05/20.

[28] Ongur D, Jensen JE, Prescot AP, Stork C, Lundy M, Cohen BM, et al. Abnormal glutamatergic neurotransmission and neuronal-glial interactions in acute mania. Biol Psychiatry. 2008;64(8):718-26. Epub 2008/07/08.

[29] Cotter D, Mackay D, Landau S, Kerwin R, Everall I. Reduced glial cell density and neuronal size in the anterior cingulate cortex in major depressive disorder. Arch Gen Psychiatry. 2001;58(6):545-53. Epub 2001/06/29.

[30] Bowley MP, Drevets WC, Ongur D, Price JL. Low glial numbers in the amygdala in major depressive disorder. Biol Psychiatry. 2002;52(5):404-12. Epub 2002/09/21.

[31] Watanabe Y, Gould E, Cameron HA, Daniels DC, McEwen BS. Phenytoin prevents stress- and corticosterone-induced atrophy of CA3 pyramidal neurons. Hippocampus. 1992;2(4):431-5. Epub 1992/10/01.

[32] Sapolsky RM, Uno H, Rebert CS, Finch CE. Hippocampal damage associated with prolonged glucocorticoid exposure in primates. J Neurosci. 1990;10(9):2897-902. Epub 1990/09/01.

[33] Rajkowska G. Postmortem studies in mood disorders indicate altered numbers of neurons and glial cells. Biol Psychiatry. 2000;48(8):766-77. Epub 2000/11/07.
[34] Arango C, Kirkpatrick B, Koenig J. At issue: stress, hippocampal neuronal turnover, and neuropsychiatric disorders. Schizophr Bull. 2001;27(3):477-80. Epub 2001/10/13.
[35] Frodl T, O'Keane V. How does the brain deal with cumulative stress? A review with focus on developmental stress, HPA axis function and hippocampal structure in humans. Neurobiol Dis. 2012. Epub 2012/03/20.
[36] Cameron HA, McKay RD. Restoring production of hippocampal neurons in old age. Nat Neurosci. 1999;2(10):894-7. Epub 1999/09/24.
[37] Cameron HA, Tanapat P, Gould E. Adrenal steroids and N-methyl-D-aspartate receptor activation regulate neurogenesis in the dentate gyrus of adult rats through a common pathway. Neuroscience. 1998;82(2):349-54. Epub 1998/02/18.
[38] Rayen I, van den Hove DL, Prickaerts J, Steinbusch HW, Pawluski JL. Fluoxetine during development reverses the effects of prenatal stress on depressive-like behavior and hippocampal neurogenesis in adolescence. PloS one. 2011;6(9):e24003. Epub 2011/09/14.
[39] Gould E, McEwen BS, Tanapat P, Galea LA, Fuchs E. Neurogenesis in the dentate gyrus of the adult tree shrew is regulated by psychosocial stress and NMDA receptor activation. J Neurosci. 1997;17(7):2492-8. Epub 1997/04/01.
[40] Gould E, Tanapat P. Stress and hippocampal neurogenesis. Biol Psychiatry. 1999;46(11):1472-9. Epub 1999/12/22.
[41] Tanapat P, Galea LA, Gould E. Stress inhibits the proliferation of granule cell precursors in the developing dentate gyrus. International journal of developmental neuroscience : the official journal of the International Society for Developmental Neuroscience. 1998;16(3-4):235-9. Epub 1998/10/24.
[42] Duman RS. Depression: a case of neuronal life and death? Biol Psychiatry. 2004;56(3):140-5. Epub 2004/07/24.
[43] Krugers HJ, Koolhaas JM, Bohus B, Korf J. A single social stress-experience alters glutamate receptor-binding in rat hippocampal CA3 area. Neurosci Lett. 1993;154(1-2):73-7. Epub 1993/05/14.
[44] Moghaddam B, Bolinao ML, Stein-Behrens B, Sapolsky R. Glucocorticoids mediate the stress-induced extracellular accumulation of glutamate. Brain Res. 1994;655(1-2):251-4. Epub 1994/08/29.
[45] Czeh B, Welt T, Fischer AK, Erhardt A, Schmitt W, Muller MB, et al. Chronic psychosocial stress and concomitant repetitive transcranial magnetic stimulation: effects on stress hormone levels and adult hippocampal neurogenesis. Biol Psychiatry. 2002;52(11):1057-65. Epub 2002/12/04.
[46] Malberg JE, Duman RS. Cell proliferation in adult hippocampus is decreased by inescapable stress: reversal by fluoxetine treatment. Neuropsychopharmacology. 2003;28(9):1562-71. Epub 2003/07/03.
[47] Manev H, Uz T, Smalheiser NR, Manev R. Antidepressants alter cell proliferation in the adult brain in vivo and in neural cultures in vitro. European journal of pharmacology. 2001;411(1-2):67-70. Epub 2001/01/04.

[48] Coyle JT, Duman RS. Finding the intracellular signaling pathways affected by mood disorder treatments. Neuron. 2003;38(2):157-60. Epub 2003/04/30.
[49] Encinas JM, Vaahtokari A, Enikolopov G. Fluoxetine targets early progenitor cells in the adult brain. Proc Natl Acad Sci U S A. 2006;103(21):8233-8. Epub 2006/05/17.
[50] Zigova T, Pencea V, Betarbet R, Wiegand SJ, Alexander C, Bakay RA, et al. Neuronal progenitor cells of the neonatal subventricular zone differentiate and disperse following transplantation into the adult rat striatum. Cell transplantation. 1998;7(2):137-56. Epub 1998/05/20.
[51] Dunham JS, Deakin JF, Miyajima F, Payton A, Toro CT. Expression of hippocampal brain-derived neurotrophic factor and its receptors in Stanley consortium brains. J Psychiatr Res. 2009;43(14):1175-84. Epub 2009/04/21.
[52] Neto FL, Borges G, Torres-Sanchez S, Mico JA, Berrocoso E. Neurotrophins role in depression neurobiology: a review of basic and clinical evidence. Current neuropharmacology. 2011;9(4):530-52. Epub 2012/06/02.
[53] Brunoni AR, Lopes M, Fregni F. A systematic review and meta-analysis of clinical studies on major depression and BDNF levels: implications for the role of neuroplasticity in depression. Int J Neuropsychopharmacol. 2008;11(8):1169-80. Epub 2008/08/30.
[54] Gorgulu Y, Caliyurt O. Rapid antidepressant effects of sleep deprivation therapy correlates with serum BDNF changes in major depression. Brain research bulletin. 2009;80(3):158-62. Epub 2009/07/07.
[55] Magarinos AM, Li CJ, Gal Toth J, Bath KG, Jing D, Lee FS, et al. Effect of brain-derived neurotrophic factor haploinsufficiency on stress-induced remodeling of hippocampal neurons. Hippocampus. 2011;21(3):253-64. Epub 2010/01/23.
[56] Palazidou E. The neurobiology of depression. Br Med Bull. 2012;101:127-45. Epub 2012/02/16.
[57] Bogdan R, Nikolova YS, Pizzagalli DA. Neurogenetics of depression: A focus on reward processing and stress sensitivity. Neurobiol Dis. 2012. Epub 2012/06/05.
[58] Hauger RL, Risbrough V, Brauns O, Dautzenberg FM. Corticotropin releasing factor (CRF) receptor signaling in the central nervous system: new molecular targets. CNS & neurological disorders drug targets. 2006;5(4):453-79. Epub 2006/08/22.
[59] Zieba B, Grzegorzewska M, Branski P, Domin H, Wieronska JM, Hess G, et al. The behavioural and electrophysiological effects of CRF in rat frontal cortex. Neuropeptides. 2008;42(5-6):513-23. Epub 2008/07/12.
[60] Heim C, Newport DJ, Heit S, Graham YP, Wilcox M, Bonsall R, et al. Pituitary-adrenal and autonomic responses to stress in women after sexual and physical abuse in childhood. Jama. 2000;284(5):592-7. Epub 2000/08/05.
[61] Keers R, Uher R. Gene-environment interaction in major depression and antidepressant treatment response. Current psychiatry reports. 2012;14(2):129-37. Epub 2011/12/27.
[62] Caspi A, Sugden K, Moffitt TE, Taylor A, Craig IW, Harrington H, et al. Influence of life stress on depression: moderation by a polymorphism in the 5-HTT gene. Science. 2003;301(5631):386-9. Epub 2003/07/19.

[63] Levinson DF. The genetics of depression: a review. Biol Psychiatry. 2006;60(2):84-92. Epub 2005/11/23.

[64] Sullivan PF, de Geus EJ, Willemsen G, James MR, Smit JH, Zandbelt T, et al. Genome-wide association for major depressive disorder: a possible role for the presynaptic protein piccolo. Mol Psychiatry. 2009;14(4):359-75. Epub 2008/12/10.

[65] Cichon S, Muhleisen TW, Degenhardt FA, Mattheisen M, Miro X, Strohmaier J, et al. Genome-wide association study identifies genetic variation in neurocan as a susceptibility factor for bipolar disorder. American journal of human genetics. 2011;88(3):372-81. Epub 2011/03/01.

[66] Ressler KJ, Bradley B, Mercer KB, Deveau TC, Smith AK, Gillespie CF, et al. Polymorphisms in CRHR1 and the serotonin transporter loci: gene x gene x environment interactions on depressive symptoms. Am J Med Genet B Neuropsychiatr Genet. 2010;153B(3):812-24. Epub 2009/12/24.

[67] Claes S. Glucocorticoid receptor polymorphisms in major depression. Ann N Y Acad Sci. 2009;1179:216-28. Epub 2009/11/13.

[68] Lahti J, Raikkonen K, Bruce S, Heinonen K, Pesonen AK, Rautanen A, et al. Glucocorticoid receptor gene haplotype predicts increased risk of hospital admission for depressive disorders in the Helsinki birth cohort study. J Psychiatr Res. 2011;45(9):1160-4. Epub 2011/04/12.

[69] Frodl T, Schule C, Schmitt G, Born C, Baghai T, Zill P, et al. Association of the brain-derived neurotrophic factor Val66Met polymorphism with reduced hippocampal volumes in major depression. Arch Gen Psychiatry. 2007;64(4):410-6. Epub 2007/04/04.

[70] Yulug B, Ozan E, Kilic E. Brain-derived neurotrophic factor polymorphism as a genetic risk for depression? A short review of the literature. J Neuropsychiatry Clin Neurosci. 2010;22(1):123 E5-6. Epub 2010/02/18.

[71] Aguilera M, Arias B, Wichers M, Barrantes-Vidal N, Moya J, Villa H, et al. Early adversity and 5-HTT/BDNF genes: new evidence of gene-environment interactions on depressive symptoms in a general population. Psychol Med. 2009;39(9):1425-32. Epub 2009/02/14.

[72] Wichers M, Kenis G, Jacobs N, Mengelers R, Derom C, Vlietinck R, et al. The BDNF Val(66)Met x 5-HTTLPR x child adversity interaction and depressive symptoms: An attempt at replication. Am J Med Genet B Neuropsychiatr Genet. 2008;147B(1):120-3. Epub 2007/06/21.

[73] Golimbet V, Alfimova M, Korovaitseva G, Abramova LI, Kaled VG. Emotional distress in parents of psychotic patients is modified by serotonin transporter gene (5-HTTLPR)--brain-derived neurotrophic factor gene interactions. The Spanish journal of psychology. 2009;12(2):696-706. Epub 2009/11/11.

[74] Kohli MA, Lucae S, Saemann PG, Schmidt MV, Demirkan A, Hek K, et al. The neuronal transporter gene SLC6A15 confers risk to major depression. Neuron. 2011;70(2):252-65. Epub 2011/04/28.

[75] Kupfer DJ, Frank E, Phillips ML. Major depressive disorder: new clinical, neurobiological, and treatment perspectives. Lancet. 2012;379(9820):1045-55. Epub 2011/12/23.

[76] Schumacher J, Jamra RA, Freudenberg J, Becker T, Ohlraun S, Otte AC, et al. Examination of G72 and D-amino-acid oxidase as genetic risk factors for schizophrenia and bipolar affective disorder. Mol Psychiatry. 2004;9(2):203-7. Epub 2004/02/18.

[77] Maier W, Hofgen B, Zobel A, Rietschel M. Genetic models of schizophrenia and bipolar disorder: overlapping inheritance or discrete genotypes? Eur Arch Psychiatry Clin Neurosci. 2005;255(3):159-66. Epub 2005/07/05.

[78] Rietschel M, Beckmann L, Strohmaier J, Georgi A, Karpushova A, Schirmbeck F, et al. G72 and its association with major depression and neuroticism in large population-based groups from Germany. Am J Psychiatry. 2008;165(6):753-62. Epub 2008/03/19.

[79] Barnett JH, Smoller JW. The genetics of bipolar disorder. Neuroscience. 2009;164(1):331-43. Epub 2009/04/11.

[80] Dutt A, McDonald C, Dempster E, Prata D, Shaikh M, Williams I, et al. The effect of COMT, BDNF, 5-HTT, NRG1 and DTNBP1 genes on hippocampal and lateral ventricular volume in psychosis. Psychol Med. 2009;39(11):1783-97. Epub 2009/07/04.

[81] Purcell SM, Wray NR, Stone JL, Visscher PM, O'Donovan MC, Sullivan PF, et al. Common polygenic variation contributes to risk of schizophrenia and bipolar disorder. Nature. 2009;460(7256):748-52. Epub 2009/07/03.

[82] Fallin MD, Lasseter VK, Avramopoulos D, Nicodemus KK, Wolyniec PS, McGrath JA, et al. Bipolar I disorder and schizophrenia: a 440-single-nucleotide polymorphism screen of 64 candidate genes among Ashkenazi Jewish case-parent trios. American journal of human genetics. 2005;77(6):918-36. Epub 2005/12/29.

[83] Williams NM, Green EK, Macgregor S, Dwyer S, Norton N, Williams H, et al. Variation at the DAOA/G30 locus influences susceptibility to major mood episodes but not psychosis in schizophrenia and bipolar disorder. Arch Gen Psychiatry. 2006;63(4):366-73. Epub 2006/04/06.

[84] Prata D, Breen G, Osborne S, Munro J, St Clair D, Collier D. Association of DAO and G72(DAOA)/G30 genes with bipolar affective disorder. Am J Med Genet B Neuropsychiatr Genet. 2008;147B(6):914-7. Epub 2008/01/01.

[85] Schumacher J, Abou Jamra R, Becker T, Klopp N, Franke P, Jacob C, et al. Investigation of the DAOA/G30 locus in panic disorder. Mol Psychiatry. 2005;10(5):428-9. Epub 2004/10/13.

[86] Weber H, Kittel-Schneider S, Gessner A, Domschke K, Neuner M, Jacob CP, et al. Cross-disorder analysis of bipolar risk genes: further evidence of DGKH as a risk gene for bipolar disorder, but also unipolar depression and adult ADHD. Neuropsychopharmacology. 2011;36(10):2076-85. Epub 2011/06/10.

[87] Ferreira MA, O'Donovan MC, Meng YA, Jones IR, Ruderfer DM, Jones L, et al. Collaborative genome-wide association analysis supports a role for ANK3 and CACNA1C in bipolar disorder. Nature genetics. 2008;40(9):1056-8. Epub 2008/08/20.

[88] Kishi T, Yoshimura R, Fukuo Y, Okochi T, Matsunaga S, Umene-Nakano W, et al. The serotonin 1A receptor gene confer susceptibility to mood disorders: results from an extended meta-analysis of patients with major depression and bipolar disorder. Eur Arch Psychiatry Clin Neurosci. 2012. Epub 2012/07/04.

[89] Scott LJ, Muglia P, Kong XQ, Guan W, Flickinger M, Upmanyu R, et al. Genome-wide association and meta-analysis of bipolar disorder in individuals of European ancestry. Proc Natl Acad Sci U S A. 2009;106(18):7501-6. Epub 2009/05/07.

[90] Smith EN, Koller DL, Panganiban C, Szelinger S, Zhang P, Badner JA, et al. Genome-wide association of bipolar disorder suggests an enrichment of replicable associations in regions near genes. PLoS genetics. 2011;7(6):e1002134. Epub 2011/07/09.

[91] Sklar P, Ripke S, Scott LJ, Andreassen OA, Cichon S, Craddock N, et al. Large-scale genome-wide association analysis of bipolar disorder identifies a new susceptibility locus near ODZ4. Nature genetics. 2011;43(10):977-83. Epub 2011/09/20.

[92] Sun H, Kennedy PJ, Nestler EJ. Epigenetics of the Depressed Brain: Role of Histone Acetylation and Methylation. Neuropsychopharmacology. 2012. Epub 2012/06/14.

[93] Tsankova NM, Berton O, Renthal W, Kumar A, Neve RL, Nestler EJ. Sustained hippocampal chromatin regulation in a mouse model of depression and antidepressant action. Nat Neurosci. 2006;9(4):519-25. Epub 2006/02/28.

[94] Ressler KJ, Nemeroff CB. Role of serotonergic and noradrenergic systems in the pathophysiology of depression and anxiety disorders. Depress Anxiety. 2000;12 Suppl 1:2-19. Epub 2000/12/01.

[95] Mann JJ. Role of the serotonergic system in the pathogenesis of major depression and suicidal behavior. Neuropsychopharmacology. 1999;21(2 Suppl):99S-105S. Epub 1999/08/05.

[96] Richell RA, Deakin JF, Anderson IM. Effect of acute tryptophan depletion on the response to controllable and uncontrollable noise stress. Biol Psychiatry. 2005;57(3):295-300. Epub 2005/02/05.

[97] Joca SR, Ferreira FR, Guimaraes FS. Modulation of stress consequences by hippocampal monoaminergic, glutamatergic and nitrergic neurotransmitter systems. Stress. 2007;10(3):227-49. Epub 2007/07/07.

[98] Banasr M, Hery M, Printemps R, Daszuta A. Serotonin-induced increases in adult cell proliferation and neurogenesis are mediated through different and common 5-HT receptor subtypes in the dentate gyrus and the subventricular zone. Neuropsychopharmacology. 2004;29(3):450-60. Epub 2004/02/12.

[99] Galter D, Unsicker K. Sequential activation of the 5-HT1(A) serotonin receptor and TrkB induces the serotonergic neuronal phenotype. Molecular and cellular neurosciences. 2000;15(5):446-55. Epub 2000/06/02.

[100] Feldman S, Weidenfeld J. Glucocorticoid receptor antagonists in the hippocampus modify the negative feedback following neural stimuli. Brain Res. 1999;821(1):33-7. Epub 1999/03/05.

[101] Neumaier JF, Sexton TJ, Hamblin MW, Beck SG. Corticosteroids regulate 5-HT(1A) but not 5-HT(1B) receptor mRNA in rat hippocampus. Brain research Molecular brain research. 2000;82(1-2):65-73. Epub 2000/10/24.

[102] Bijak M, Zahorodna A, Tokarski K. Opposite effects of antidepressants and corticosterone on the sensitivity of hippocampal CA1 neurons to 5-HT1A and 5-HT4 receptor activation. Naunyn-Schmiedeberg's archives of pharmacology. 2001;363(5):491-8. Epub 2001/06/01.

[103] Drevets WC, Frank E, Price JC, Kupfer DJ, Greer PJ, Mathis C. Serotonin type-1A receptor imaging in depression. Nuclear medicine and biology. 2000;27(5):499-507. Epub 2000/08/30.

[104] Sargent PA, Kjaer KH, Bench CJ, Rabiner EA, Messa C, Meyer J, et al. Brain serotonin1A receptor binding measured by positron emission tomography with [11C]WAY-100635: effects of depression and antidepressant treatment. Arch Gen Psychiatry. 2000;57(2):174-80. Epub 2000/02/09.

[105] Cheetham SC, Crompton MR, Katona CL, Horton RW. Brain 5-HT1 binding sites in depressed suicides. Psychopharmacology (Berl). 1990;102(4):544-8. Epub 1990/01/01.

[106] Stockmeier CA, Shapiro LA, Dilley GE, Kolli TN, Friedman L, Rajkowska G. Increase in serotonin-1A autoreceptors in the midbrain of suicide victims with major depression-postmortem evidence for decreased serotonin activity. J Neurosci. 1998;18(18):7394-401. Epub 1998/09/16.

[107] Meana JJ, Barturen F, Garcia-Sevilla JA. Alpha 2-adrenoceptors in the brain of suicide victims: increased receptor density associated with major depression. Biol Psychiatry. 1992;31(5):471-90. Epub 1992/03/01.

[108] Bannerman DM, Rawlins JN, McHugh SB, Deacon RM, Yee BK, Bast T, et al. Regional dissociations within the hippocampus--memory and anxiety. Neurosci Biobehav Rev. 2004;28(3):273-83. Epub 2004/07/01.

[109] Bertoglio LJ, Joca SR, Guimaraes FS. Further evidence that anxiety and memory are regionally dissociated within the hippocampus. Behav Brain Res. 2006;175(1):183-8. Epub 2006/09/26.

[110] Petty F, Sherman AD. Regional aspects of the prevention of learned helplessness by desipramine. Life sciences. 1980;26(17):1447-52. Epub 1980/04/28.

[111] Dell'Osso B, Palazzo MC, Oldani L, Altamura AC. The noradrenergic action in antidepressant treatments: pharmacological and clinical aspects. CNS Neurosci Ther. 2011;17(6):723-32. Epub 2010/12/16.

[112] Nestler EJ, Carlezon WA, Jr. The mesolimbic dopamine reward circuit in depression. Biol Psychiatry. 2006;59(12):1151-9. Epub 2006/03/29.

[113] Prins J, Olivier B, Korte SM. Triple reuptake inhibitors for treating subtypes of major depressive disorder: the monoamine hypothesis revisited. Expert opinion on investigational drugs. 2011;20(8):1107-30. Epub 2011/06/21.

[114] Drago A, Crisafulli C, Sidoti A, Serretti A. The molecular interaction between the glutamatergic, noradrenergic, dopaminergic and serotoninergic systems informs a detailed genetic perspective on depressive phenotypes. Prog Neurobiol. 2011;94(4):418-60. Epub 2011/07/05.

[115] Gao SF, Bao AM. Corticotropin-releasing hormone, glutamate, and gamma-aminobutyric acid in depression. The Neuroscientist : a review journal bringing neurobiology, neurology and psychiatry. 2011;17(1):124-44. Epub 2010/03/20.

[116] Maeng S, Zarate CA, Jr. The role of glutamate in mood disorders: results from the ketamine in major depression study and the presumed cellular mechanism underlying its antidepressant effects. Current psychiatry reports. 2007;9(6):467-74. Epub 2008/01/29.

[117] Hashimoto K. Emerging role of glutamate in the pathophysiology of major depressive disorder. Brain Res Rev. 2009;61(2):105-23. Epub 2009/06/02.

[118] Kugaya A, Sanacora G. Beyond monoamines: glutamatergic function in mood disorders. CNS Spectr. 2005;10(10):808-19. Epub 2006/01/10.

[119] Skolnick P, Popik P, Trullas R. Glutamate-based antidepressants: 20 years on. Trends Pharmacol Sci. 2009;30(11):563-9. Epub 2009/10/20.

[120] Kalia M. Neurobiological basis of depression: an update. Metabolism: clinical and experimental. 2005;54(5 Suppl 1):24-7. Epub 2005/05/07.

[121] Martins-de-Souza D, Harris LW, Guest PC, Turck CW, Bahn S. The role of proteomics in depression research. Eur Arch Psychiatry Clin Neurosci. 2010;260(6):499-506. Epub 2009/12/10.

[122] Martins-de-Souza D. Comprehending depression through proteomics. Int J Neuropsychopharmacol. 2012:1-2. Epub 2012/06/22.

[123] Martins-de-Souza D, Guest PC, Vanattou-Saifoudine N, Rahmoune H, Bahn S. Phosphoproteomic differences in major depressive disorder postmortem brains indicate effects on synaptic function. Eur Arch Psychiatry Clin Neurosci. 2012. Epub 2012/02/22.

[124] Lopez de Lara C, Jaitovich-Groisman I, Cruceanu C, Mamdani F, Lebel V, Yerko V, et al. Implication of synapse-related genes in bipolar disorder by linkage and gene expression analyses. Int J Neuropsychopharmacol. 2010;13(10):1397-410. Epub 2010/07/30.

[125] Sequeira A, Turecki G. Genome wide gene expression studies in mood disorders. Omics : a journal of integrative biology. 2006;10(4):444-54. Epub 2007/01/20.

[126] Kim S, Webster MJ. The stanley neuropathology consortium integrative database: a novel, web-based tool for exploring neuropathological markers in psychiatric disorders and the biological processes associated with abnormalities of those markers. Neuropsychopharmacology. 2010;35(2):473-82. Epub 2009/10/16.

[127] Bernard R, Kerman IA, Thompson RC, Jones EG, Bunney WE, Barchas JD, et al. Altered expression of glutamate signaling, growth factor, and glia genes in the locus coeruleus of patients with major depression. Mol Psychiatry. 2011;16(6):634-46. Epub 2010/04/14.

[128] Shelton RC, Claiborne J, Sidoryk-Wegrzynowicz M, Reddy R, Aschner M, Lewis DA, et al. Altered expression of genes involved in inflammation and apoptosis in frontal cortex in major depression. Mol Psychiatry. 2011;16(7):751-62. Epub 2010/05/19.

[129] Schmitt A, Leonardi-Essmann F, Durrenberger PF, Parlapani E, Schneider-Axmann T, Spanagel R, et al. Regulation of immune-modulatory genes in left superior temporal cortex of schizophrenia patients: a genome-wide microarray study. World J Biol Psychiatry. 2011;12(3):201-15. Epub 2010/11/26.

[130] Datson NA, Speksnijder N, Mayer JL, Steenbergen PJ, Korobko O, Goeman J, et al. The transcriptional response to chronic stress and glucocorticoid receptor blockade in the hippocampal dentate gyrus. Hippocampus. 2012;22(2):359-71. Epub 2010/12/25.

Chapter 2

HPA Axis Modulation in the Treatment of Mood Disorders

Lauren B. Ozbolt and Charles B. Nemeroff

Additional information is available at the end of the chapter

http://dx.doi.org/10.5772/51600

1. Introduction

1.1. The Hypothalamic-Pituitary-Adrenal (HPA) axis

The primary regulator of the mammalian stress response is the hypothalamic-pituitary-adrenal (HPA) axis. Corticotrophin-releasing factor (CRF), a 41 amino-acid containing neuropeptide, is the major physiological mediator of the HPA axis. CRF is synthesized in parvocellular neurons of the hypothalamic paraventricular nucleus (PVN). These neurons project to the median eminence where CRF, together with arginine vasopressin (AVP), is released into the hypothalamic-hypophyseal portal circulation to act on corticotrophs of the anterior pituitary. Activation of these cells, leads to the synthesis and release of adrenocorticotrophic (ACTH) hormone. ACTH is released into systemic circulation and acts on the adrenal cortex resulting in the synthesis and secretion of cortisol. Cortisol, the main glucocorticoid in primates, mobilizes energy stores in response to a threat. Additionally, cortisol regulates the release of CRF, AVP and ACTH through negative feedback via glucocorticoid receptors in the hypothalamus and pituitary mineralcorticoid receptors in the hippocampus.

CRF, first isolated by Vale *et al.* in 1981, is released in response to stress not only in the hypothalamus but in other subcortical regions as well, including the central amygdala (CeA) [1]. Although hypothalamic CRF release occurs in response to all types of stress, the central amygdale (CeA) CRF is believed to mediate a large proportion of the emotional component of stress. CRF release produces multiple effects in the body including alterations in metabolic rate, changes in sympathetic output, modulation of emotional state and regulation of appetite and reproductive status [2-5]. A great deal of evidence suggests that CRF coordinates the endocrine, autonomic, immune and behavioral responses to stress. Adaptation to acute verses chronic stress also appears to play a significant role. Chronic stress is associated with a number of health conditions including heart disease, infertility and mood disorders [6].

CRF binds to a family of CRF receptors, of which two have been identified in humans, CRF 1 and CRF 2. Both receptors are 7-transmembrane G-protein coupled receptors that share a 70% sequence homology. The CRF 1 receptor, first cloned in 1993, contains 415 amino acids and is widely expressed throughout the CNS. It is thought to be the receptor mediating the direct action of CRF on the HPA axis. Additionally, the CRF 1 receptor is highly expressed in the cerebellum, hippocampus, amydala, pituitary and throughout the cerebral cortex. The CRF 2 receptor is structurally similar to the CRF 1 receptor with a few noticeable differences. The CRF 2 receptor is poorly expressed in the anterior pituitary, but is highly expressed in the CNS lateral septum, ventromedial nucleus of the hypothalamus, the cerebral cortex, olfactory bulb, amygdala, dorsal raphae nuclei and bed nucleus of stria terminalis.

Although CRF was the first endogenous ligand described to act upon the CRF receptors, others have subsequently been identified. CRF binds to the CRF 1 receptor and is thought to act on the corticotrophs regulating HPA activity. CRF is expressed both peripherally as well as in the CNS with highest expression in the hypothalamus, amygdala, cerebral cortex and septum. Urocortin 1, a 40 amino acid peptide sharing 45 % homology to human CRF, has high affinity to both the CRF 1 and CRF 2 receptors [6]. Urocortin 1 is found in highest concentration in the Edinger-Westphal nucleus and the hypothalamus but overall, its expression is more widespread peripherally in the GI tract, testes, heart, thymus, spleen and kidney. Urocortin 2 (stresscopin-related peptide), a 38 amino acid peptide, has a high affinity for the CRF 2 receptor suggesting that it may be a primary ligand. Urocortin 2 is found in highest concentration within the hypothalamus, locus ceruleus and brain stem nuclei. Urocortin 3 (stresscopin), a 38 amino acid peptide with 40% homology to Urocortin 2, also appears to be selective for the CRF 2 receptor and is mainly expressed in the amygdala, hippocampus and brainstem [6]. The HPA system is further regulated by the CRF binding protein (CRBP), which binds to CRF and Urocortin 1 in the extracellular fluid and plasma thus sequestering them and preventing CRF receptor binding. Interestingly, Urocortin 2 and 3 have little affinity for CRFBP and therefore may be regulated through a different mechanism. In general, activation of CRF receptors by either CRF or Urocortins leads to a G protein coupled activation of adenylate cyclase , cAMP production and c-fos activation in most cell types, though co-activation of additional pathways have been reported [144]. In corticotrophs, CRF binds to CRF 1 receptors causing co-activation of both calcium pathways and protein kinase A (PKA) pathways leading to phosphorylation of extracellular regulated kinases (ERK) 1 and 2. It is notable that injections of CRF into limbic areas does not lead to ERK phorphorylation which suggest that other downstream responses may regulate extrahypothalamic sites.

2. The HPA axis in mood disorders

There is much evidence demonstrating that components of the HPA axis play a role in the pathogenesis of affective disorders including depression. One notable early study was performed by D.J. McClure and colleagues in 1966 in which he demonstrated increased cortisol levels in the urine of depressed patients [7-8]. Later studies have confirmed these results and extended the findings by documenting that MDD patients have increased cortisol concentrations in the urine, blood and cerebrospinal fluid (CSF). This elevation in cortisol generally occurs immediately preceding or during the onset of mood symptoms. However, hypercortisolemia is considered a state rather than a trait marker for depression and thus lacks specificity as a biomarker for risks for mood disorders [9-13].

In addition to cortisol, other HPA hormones have been found to be dysregulated in depression and chronic stress. CRF, ACTH and AVP have consistently shown dysregulation in mood disorders. In 1984, Nemeroff et al. reported an increase in CRF concentrations in CSF of untreated depressed patients, which has been confirmed in a number of studies [14-16]. CRF signaling is overactive in major depressive disorder, both in regards to HPA and extrahypothalamic function [145]. Laboratory animal studies that utilize brain-region specific microinjections of CRF have shown behavior responses reminiscent of major depression in humans including increased anxiety, changes in slow wave sleep, anhedonia, decreased appetite and diminished libido. Elevated cerebrospinal fluid (CSF) concentrations of CRF are observed in many MDD patients, thought to reflect hyperactivity of the hypothalamic and extrahypothalmic CRF producing regions [20]. Examination of post-mortem tissue of depressed subjects reveals increased CRF mRNA expression in the PVN, locus ceruleus and prefrontal cortex, a finding that supports CRF hyperactivity. Autoradiographic studies reveal a 23% decrease in CRF 1 receptor binding sites within the frontal cortex of suicide victims [17-18], reflecting a downregulation of the system most likely secondary to chronically high levels of CRF. It is hypothesized that downregulation of CRF receptors is deleterious to the disease pathophysiology in depression because negative feedback regulation likely occurs in the brain. Thus without feedback inhibition, there is an inability to shut off the HPA axis, including CRF overproduction in both the hypothalamus and other regions such as the central amydgala. Further evidence for hyperactivity of CRF containing circuits in depression is provided by several studies that have revealed that patients in the recovery stages of MDD who maintain elevated CSF CRF concentrations despite their euthymic state are predisposed to early relapse of depression. Similarly patients who exhibit improvement in depression symptoms without concurrent normalization of the DEX/CRF response are more likely to relapse [26]. Currently available antidepressants, while exerting their primary pharmacological effect on monoamine systems, also reduce HPA responsiveness. Treatment of depressed patients with a selective serotonin reuptake inhibitor (SSRI) and electroconvulsive therapy (ECT) leads to reductions in CSF CRF concentrations. This data is concordant with the hypothesis that CRF/HPA axis normalization is associated with symptom resolution.

Although CSF CRF levels are often elevated in depressed patients, it is not a reliable biomarker for mood disorders [20]. The CRF stimulation test is a more accurate measure of HPA axis activity than CSF CRF concentrations in part because the latter represent contributions of both hypothalamic and extrahypothalamic circuits. In the CRF stimulation test, intravenously administered CRF (which does not enter the CNS) elevates plasma ACTH and cortisol concentrations by stimulating the CRF 1 receptors in the anterior pituitary. In normal patients, ACTH and cortisol concentrations increase predictably. MDD patients as a group demonstrate a blunted ACTH response in this test, most likely due to chronic CRF hypersecretion and negative feedback and cortisol hypersecretion at the pituitary corticotrophs [21-23]. Another even more sensitive test of HPA axis activity is the DEX-CRF test [24-25]. In this test, dexamethasone (DEX) is administered the evening before CRF. In normal controls without depression, DEX suppresses ACTH and cortisol secretion via negative feedback to the pituitary. In MDD patients, feedback inhibition is blunted by the presence of elevated cortisol, therefore little suppression takes place and ACTH levels remain high. CRF administered to healthy patients the next morning will show little or no increase CRF or ACTH due to the effect of DEX suppression. On the contrary in MDD patients, DEX does not suppress ACTH secretion and ACTH and cortisol levels increase. This suggests that both CRF overexpression and glucocorticoid insensitivity contribute to the hyperactivity of the HPA in depression. The sensitivity of the DEX-CRF test can predict 90% of MDD patients correctly and can even have utility in identifying asymptomatic remitted patients who continue to exhibit HPA axis dysfunction and are at risk for relapse [26].

A second line of research that supports the link between HPA axis dysfunction and depression is found in studies that associate early life stressors with subsequent changes in neuroendocrine function. A series of clinical studies suggest that childhood trauma in humans is associated with sensitization of the HPA axis, glucocorticoid resistance, increased CRF activity, immune activation and reduced hippocampal volume, closely paralleling the neuroendocrine features of depression.[40-41]. Early life stressors, such as child abuse and neglect, influence CRF neuronal activity and HPA functioning during development and lower the individual's threshold to develop depression. Heim et al. reported that depressed women with and without childhood abuse and nondepressed women with childhood abuse exhibited blunted cortisol responses in a standard ACTH stimulation test [40-41]. Decreased cortisol response under conditions of chronic stress might result in a relative lack of cortisol regulation at the CNS level. Upon further stress, such women may then repeatedly hypersecrete CRF, eventually resulting in pituitary CRF receptor downregulation and symptoms of depression through CRF effects on extra-hypothalamic circuits. The hippocampus is critically involved in the control of the HPA axis as well as explicit memory and contextual aspects of fear conditioning. Stress and glucocorticoid overexposure have adverse effects on the CA3 region of the hippocampus resulting in loss of dendritic spines, reduction in branching and impairments in neurogenesis [35,143]. Furthermore, patients with MDD and PTSD exhibit decreased hippocampal volumes. Heim et al. found that the left hippocampus was 18% smaller than in non-abused depressed women and 15% smaller than non-abused controls. It appears that a smaller hippocampal volume in major depression is associated with childhood trauma and is not observed in depressed patients without such trauma, paralleling neuroendocrine findings. [39-41]

Genetic studies focusing on single nucleotide polymorphisms (SNPs) in the CRF system have shown susceptibility or resilience to developing depression as well as variation in response rates to antidepressants. Multiple studies have examined the effect of SNPs in the CRF system. Binder et al. described an association of SNPs within the CRF system and remission and response rates to antidepressant treatment in the STAR*D sample [57]. A genetic variant within the corticotrophin releasing hormone binding protein (CRHBP) locus affects response to citalopram in African American and Hispanic patients, suggesting a role for this gene and the CRF system in antidepressant treatment response. Van Rossum et al. described carriers of a rare polymorphism in the glucocorticoid receptor gene ER22/23EK as demonstrating a more robust response to antidepressants. Ressler et al. reported that variants in the serotonin transporter-linked polymorphic region (5-HTTLPR) interacts with CRF 1 receptor gene (CRHR1) and child abuse to predict current adult depressive symptoms (i.e. gene x gene x environment) [145]. These data indicate that individuals carrying the risk alleles in both genes exhibited clinically relevant depressive symptoms at less severe levels of child abuse than individuals with no or only one of the risk alleles. Heim et al. scrutinized variations of the CRHR1 gene and the development of depression in childhood trauma. The allele rs110402 SNP was associated with decreased symptoms of depression among male subjects exposed to moderate-severe childhood abuse exposure, whereas this protective effect is not observed in female subjects with childhood abuse exposure.

3. Non-mood related effects of HPA-axis hyperactivity

HPA axis hyperactivity can have a significant impact on an individual's physical health aside from the effects directly related to mood disorders. Although we will not review this literature because it is not a focus of this chapter, such adverse effects often additionally complicate mood disorders. Clinical studies indicate that the prevalence of depression in patients with cardiovascular disease can be as high as 1 in 3 [27-28]. Chronic mood disorders are a risk factor as threatening as high fat diets or cigarette smoking to cardiovascular health. Depressed patients often suffer higher rates of cardiovascular disease, perhaps due in part to chronic dysregulation of the HPA axis. It is therefore of major importance that modulators of the HPA axis may be advantageous not only in regards to treatment of mood disorders, but for their potential to diminish the systemic effects of depression including heart disease, obesity, osteoporosis and immune system dysfunction.[6]

4. Modulation of the HPA axis as a therapeutic strategy to treat mood disorders

Based upon the preponderance of data linking HPA axis hyperactivity to mood disorders, it is reasonable to assume that CRF/ACTH/cortisol and their receptors are pathologically involved in the neurobiology of depression. Taking this into consideration, efforts have been made to identify critical components of the HPA axis a properly designed drug could exert a therapeutic action. One of the most promising targets in recent years has been the CRF receptors. CRF receptors are G protein coupled receptors which are present in humans in two forms, CRF 1 and CRF 2. The CRF 1 receptor exists in multiple isoforms (ie. CFR 1a-CRF 1h) with the CRF 1a subtype being the best known and most functional isoform. The CRF 1 receptor is predominantly located in the CNS and controls HPA axis activity. [2, 29] The CRF 2 receptor has three known functional subtypes in humans (ie. CRF 2a, CRF 2b,

CRF 2c). The CRF 2 receptor has a higher affinity for Urocortins than CRF, and is thought to mediate the peripheral effects of stress [4]. When considering a modulator, it is interesting to speculate on both receptor subtypes, but in actuality, therapeutic development has focused solely on the CRF 1 receptor. Antagonism of the CRF1 receptor should theoretically decrease basal and stress induced increases in HPA axis activity, reduce the health-related side effects of depression and improve the treatment of mood disorders. The most convincing data supporting CRF 1 receptor antagonists comes from animal models. CRF1 receptor knockout mice demonstrate a large reduction in ACTH, decreased stress-induced glucocorticoid secretion and reduced anxiety [30-32]. There have been several attempts to develop clinically useful CRF 1 receptor antagonists to treat mood disorders, with minimal success. It is important to note that in terms of mood and anxiety symptoms, CRF 1 receptor antagonists are believed to act on extrahypothalamic/extrapituitary sites. This has been well documented in preclinical studies. In fact the CRF1 receptor antagonists exhibit anxiolytic and antidepressant effects even in hypophysectomized animals [33-34].

Antidepressant-induced HPA axis normalization may be attributable to some improvement in depressive symptoms. Currently available antidepressants reduce the overall responsiveness of the HPA axis and the activity of hypothalamic and extrahypothalamic CRF neurons. This is supported by the fact that chronic antidepressant administration results in reductions in CRF mRNA expression and CRF concentrations [143]. In laboratory animal studies, these changes followed depressive symptom resolution supporting the hypothesis that normalization of CRF transmission plays a vital role in the mechanism of action of antidepressants. In rats treated with the antidepressant tianeptine (approved in Europe for depression and anxiety), decreased CRF concentrations were noted in the rat hypothalamus, as well as decreased ACTH concentrations in the anterior pituitary. Numerous connections between the neuropeptide circuit and the CNS monoamine system suggest that elevations in CRF activity might alter monoamine signaling. For example reserpine, an agent that causes monoamine depletion and depression in vulnerable individuals, also increases CRF release from the rat hypothalamus and posterior pituitary [143].

During a depressive episode, hypersecretion of CRF in the CNS likely increases locus cerulous (LC) activity through a CeA-LC connection. Reciprocal noradrenergic projections from the LC to the amygdala activate CRF-containing cells [19]. Elevated noradrenergic transmission in depression may indirectly contribute to symptoms secondary to increased activity of CeA CRF. Noradrenergic neurons from the LC also project to the dorsal raphe nucleus (DRN) to increase serotonergic activity and project back from the DRN to decrease noradrenergic firing. [143] One hypothesized mechanism of action of SSRIs is that by increasing serotonin availability, SSRIs subsequently decrease activation of the LC and in turn decrease amygdalar activation of CRF. Additional animal studies have shown that chronic imipramine and desipramine administration in rats increases CRF binding in the CNS as well as other brain regions. Such increases in the density of CRF 1 receptor binding sites are likely secondary to antidepressant induced reductions in CRF-ergic activity. Furthermore, chronic administration of venlafaxine has been shown to reduce hypothalamic

CRF responsiveness to stress as well as blocking stress-induced elevations in CRF mRNA expression in the PVN [143].

5. CRF1 receptor antagonists in mood and anxiety disorders

Since Vale first isolated CRF in 1981, CRF receptor antagonists have been sought for the treatment of not only depression but for anxiety, addiction and irritable bowel syndrome [1]. In 2000, Zobel et al. published the first small clinical trial of a CRF1 receptor antagonist for the treatment of mood disorders [35]. In this open-label trial, doses of R-121919 were titrated up to 80 mg and produced an antidepressant effect equivalent to the SSRI paroxetine. There was no decrease in basal plasma ACTH or cortisol levels, which lessened concern that CRF 1 receptor antagonists might produce a state of adrenal insufficiency. To date, there are more than 28 clinical trials in the peer reviewed literature that address the potential utility of CRF 1 receptor antagonists for the treatment of anxiety and mood disorders [4].

Animal models have repeatedly shown that non-peptide CRF 1 receptor antagonists produce anxiolytic effects in rodents. For example, these agents have been shown to reduce conditioned fear, shock-induced freezing, defensive burying behavior, acoustic startle response and anxiety-like effects from neonatal isolation [4]. Positive findings in animal models include a few notable studies. In 2004, Nielsen et al. demonstrated that treatment with DMP696 and R121919 reduced forced swim immobility (a genetic model of depression) in mice [146]. Similarly Chaki et al. showed that olfactory bulbectomized rats, a putative model of depression, reduced hyperemotionality when treated with R278995 [147]. Improvement in coat appearance and reversed reductions in hippocampal neurogenesis were found in mice chronically treated with antalarmin or SSR125543A [4]. Unfortunately several animal studies produced negative findings in regards to screening tests for antidepressant activity. Jutkiewicz et al. found that CP-154526 and R121919 failed to reduce swim immobility in rats [148]. Similarly, acute treatment with CP-154526 which was initially reported to produce antidepressant-like effects in the learned helplessness paradigm was later found to be unsubstantiated [4]. A potential explanation for these mixed findings is that CRF 1 antagonists might only exhibit antidepressant properties in certain animal models or particular endophenotypes. Support for this explanation is found in studies that show CRF 1 antagonists differentially reduce anxiety behaviors in high anxiety models and reduce ethanol intake in dependence models rather than in healthy animals.

Paralleling the mixed results in animal models, many of the better-powered clinical trials have been disappointing by revealing a lack of efficacy for CRF1 receptor antagonists in patients with MDD. A 6-week randomized, placebo controlled trial in 2005 compared CP-316,311 to placebo and sertraline in 128 patients with major depressive disorder. The trial, however, was terminated early due to no significant antidepressant effect of the CRF1 antagonist compared to placebo [36-37]. In the largest study to date (n=260), Coric et al. conducted an 8-week multicenter, randomized, double-blind, placebo-controlled clinical trial with Pexacerfont (BMS-562,086) for generalized anxiety disorder. No significant anxiolytic effect was observed compared to placebo though the comparator in the study, escitalopram, was efficacious [38-39]. It is important to note that these studies have not used narrowly defined patient sub-types such as psychotic, anxious or atypical depression, but instead have utilized the broader MDD inclusion criterion. Considering the fact that there is overwhelming evidence that CRF is hypersecreted in depressed patients with a history of childhood abuse and neglect, a clinical trial of CRF1 receptor antagonism in this discrete subset of patients with major depression would be of considerable interest [40-45].

Despite the above listed shortcomings, several pharmaceutical companies have developed viable clinical candidates. Several CRF 1 antagonists from different pharmaceutical companies have entered clinical trials since December 2004. Due to promising results with R121919 during an open-label Phase IIa trial, clinical anticipation has been high. However, R121919 development was discontinued shortly thereafter secondary to elevation of liver enzymes. Despite major efforts to the contrary, no subsequent CRF 1 antagonist has successfully completed a definitive Phase III trial. Currently, the number of additional CRF 1 antagonists that are undergoing or have completed efficacy trials is two for social anxiety disorder (GSK561679, GW876008), and three for depression (GSK561679, GW876008 and Pexacerfont) [4]. Apparently the results from these trials in the treatment of anxiety and depression have been uniformly negative.

6. CRF-2 receptor antagonists in the treatment of mood disorders

CRF 2 receptor knockout mice have revealed inconsistent findings in regards to anxiolytic behaviors and sensitivity to stress [48-51]. Several studies to date suggest a contribution of the CRF2 receptor to HPA axis regulation and mood disorders. There is evidence that the CRF 2 receptor helps to modulate the duration of the HPA response to stress. By blocking the CRF 2 receptors in humans, the HPA axis response could potentially be more quickly terminated after a stressful event. To date, there are no studies examining early attenuation of the HPA axis following stressful situations. The best candidates for CRF 2 receptor antagonists at this time are antisauvagine-30, astressin-2B and K41498, all of which are peptide based and thus have limited therapeutic efficacy [46-52].

7. CRF binding protein

The CRF binding protein (CRF-BP) is a 37-kDa glycoprotein which is present in interstitial spaces and plasma. Its primary function is to bind CRF and Urocortin 1 to reduce their bioavailability and prevent binding to the CRF receptors [53-54]. To our knowledge, CRF-BP has received little attention as a novel therapeutic target for drug development and treatment of mood disorders despite its regulatory function in the HPA system [56]. Binder et al. studied patients from the STAR*D sample and found a SNP within the CRHBP locus (rs10473984) that was significantly associated with glucocorticoid-receptor resistance and higher HPA axis hormone levels [57]. This SNP significantly reduced both remission and reduction in depressive symptoms in response to citalopram. In a study of post-mortem brain tissue of bipolar and schizophrenic patients, CRF-BP mRNA expression was found to be decreased possibly indicating increased CRF availability [55]. It is important to note that some evidence exists that increasing CRF-BP could potentially modulate the HPA axis. It is feasible to propose that by increasing the CRF-BP (i.e. through administration, genetic up-regulation, microRNA targeting) and decreasing the bioavailability of CRF, HPA hyperactivity may be attenuated [58-59].

8. Arginine vasopressin 1b receptors

Arginine vasopressin (AVP) is a peptide hormone produced in the both the magnocellular and parvocellular neurons in the hypothalamus but released through two different mechanisms. AVP produced by the magnocellular neurons travels through the infundibulum to the posterior pituitary where it is stored until release. AVP synthesized by the parvocellular neurons is released into the median eminence and travels via hypophyseal portal circulation to the anterior pituitary where it stimulates corticotrophs. The primary function of AVP is to regulate extracellular fluid volume via its action on the V2 receptors (V2R) located on the renal collecting ducts; thus absorbing water and decreasing urine formation.

AVP and AVP receptor activation, however, can produce a number of CNS and peripheral effects and have been postulated to play a role in mood disorders [60-61]. AVP that is released from the parvocellular neurons travels to the anterior pituitary to act on AVP1b receptors and enhances the release of CRF and ACTH. This pathway has the potential to be a modulation point in the treatment of mood disorders. For example, SSR149415, a potent and selective AVP1b receptor antagonist has been proposed as a novel antidepressant and has been tested in clinical trials for the treatment of major depression. However, the clinical trial was discontinued in 2008 for undisclosed reasons [62, 62]. A great deal of interest still surrounds AVP 1b receptor antagonist development with future compounds possibly acting in synergistic ways with CRF 1 antagonist.

9. Anti-glucocorticoid therapy for mood disorders

Hyperactivity of the HPA axis has been repeatedly demonstrated in patients with psychotic depression. Early studies have shown that patients with psychotic depression have high rates of dexamethasone nonsuppression in the DST and abnormal diurnal fluctuations of cortisol [64-65]. It has been hypothesized that high concentrations of cortisol in psychotic depression lead to hyperactivity of dopamine neurons thus worsening the psychosis [66]. Adopting this hypothesis, it is feasible that one therapeutic modality in the treatment of psychotic depression would involve using agents that block the synthesis of cortisol. Several types of anticortisol agents have been investigated in psychiatric disorders. These include cortisol synthesis inhibitors (ie. ketoconazole, metyrapone, aminogluthethamide), CRF receptor antagonists and glucocorticoid receptor antagonists such as mifepristone. Ketoconazole, an antifungal agent, has been used in clinical trials with varying amounts of success. For example, Wolkowitz et al. found that ketoconazole was associated with significant antidepressant effects in patients with depression and baseline hypercortisolemia [149]. While the majority of studies have suggested that cortisol synthesis inhibitors have antidepressant benefits, conclusions are limited due to small sample sizes. Complicating the issues further are the potential side effects of ketoconazole administration which include decreased androgen and aldosterone synthesis, nausea, vomiting and occasionally hypoadrenalism and hepatotoxicity.

The brain is an important target organ for corticosteroids. Both high-affinity mineralocorticoid receptor (MR) and lower affinity glucocorticoid receptor (GR) are highly expressed in specific brain regions including the CA1 hippocampus, dentate gyrus and basolateral amygdala [64]. Through an interplay with other stress hormones (CRF and norepinephrine), corticosteroids alter neuronal activity and play a key role in attention, vigilance, memory and behavioral adaption. Cortisol is similar in structure to the sex steroid progesterone as well as the potent progesterone antagonist, mifepristone (RU486). Mifepristone has a high affinity for progesterone and glucocorticord receptors. It is primarily used in the gynecological treatment of endometriosis, as contraceptive and for various progesterone sensitive tumors. It was recently FDA approved for the treatment of Cushing's syndrome. Mifepristone has the added advantages of having little to no effect on estrogen, monoamine, histamine, muscarinic or mineralocorticoid receptors. It appears to be well tolerated and has not been associated with adrenal insufficiency or heptatotoxicity. At high doses mifepristone antagonizes GRs, but not MRs, and there is considerable evidence that it has efficiency in the management of psychotic depression [67-72]. Van der Lely et al. first reported the psychotropic effects of mifepristone in 1991 citing a substantial resolution of psychosis and depression in 2 patients with Cushing Syndrome [150]. A possible mechanism of action for mifepristone is through potent antagonism of GRs, MRs are up-regulated, thus enhancing HPA feedback regulation. Several clinical trials have used mifepristone in the treatment of depressive disorders [73-74]. Murphy *et al.* completed an open label study of mifepristone 200mg/day in four nonpsychotic patients with chronic depression. Patients were treated for eight weeks with 3 out of 4 reporting improvements in depression as measured by the Hamilton Rating Scale for Depression (HAM D) score [67]. Due to the fact that psychotic depression exhibits the most consistent HPA dysregulation, Belanoff et al. examined the psychotrophic effects of mifepristone in a group of five patients with psychotic depression. In a double blind, crossover design, patients were treated for four days with mifepristone 600mg/day or placebo. All five patients showed substantial improvement in depression and 4 out of 5 experienced an improvement in psychosis [75-76]. As a follow up, this same group studied 30 additional patients with psychotic depression and used mifepristone in doses of 50, 600 or 1200mg/day for 7 days. Of the groups treated with 600+ mg/day, 30% had a decrease in psychotic symptoms as measured by the Brief Psychiatric Rating Scale (BPRS) [75-76]. Subsequent larger clinical trials, with 221, 258 and 443 patient cohorts were treated with placebo or mifepristone (doses 300-1200 mg/day) over 7 days. Results revealed a correlation between mifepristone plasma concentrations and clinical improvement, which persisted for several weeks after mifepristone discontinuation [68, 69, 72, 77-79].

Since mifepristone has significant and potentially deleterious side effects associated with its affinity for the progesterone receptor, the development of more selective GR antagonists is of great interest. There have been reports of RU-43044, CORT-108297 and RU-43044 as possible candidates for selective GR antagonism. [80-84]

10. Glucocorticoid and mineralcorticoid receptor activation in the treatment of non-psychotic and anxious mood disorders

HPA axis feedback both in the brain and in the pituitary is achieved via cortisol activation of mineralcorticoid receptors (MR) and glucocorticoid receptors (GR). As noted above, the MRs have approximately ten times the affinity for circulating cortisol than the GRs. Thus, the GRs will only be occupied when the MRs are saturated. HPA feedback primarily occurs first at MRs in the hippocampus and then as cortisol levels increase further, GR are activated for additional feedback inhibition [85].

Due to the fact that non-psychotic patients tend to have an overactivity of the HPA axis with elevated cortisol levels, the MR feedback regulation system is likely already saturated thus making MRs a poor modulation point for therapeutic intervention. The GR system, due to its lower rate of activation and broader receptor distribution, makes a much better target for therapy. Traditionally, mood disorder patients display poor feedback regulation of the HPA axis via GRs [86-87]. Clinical studies have revealed polymorphisms of GRs and related molecules that are present in some mood disorders [88].

Several GR and MR specific agonists have been developed for potential treatment in mood disorders. The central idea of these agonists is to use them to potentiate the feedback inhibition of CRF and ACTH release thus reducing HPA axis tone. Endogenous glucocorticoids could serve as potential candidates due to their long plasma half life and penetration of the blood-brain barrier. Synthetic analogs of endogenous glucocorticoids (ie. dexamethasone and prednisone) may also serve as viable options. Dexamethasone (DEX) is a potent synthetic GR agonist that is 25 times more potent than cortisol [89]. Its main clinical use is for the treatment of various inflammatory syndromes. Arana et al. conducted a number of trials using DEX for the treatment of depression and bipolar disorder. In one of the studies 37 patients were treated for a 2 week period with DEX treatment showing superiority to placebo in reducing depressive symptoms [90-91].

DEX has also been studied for the treatment of anxiety disorders including PTSD. Several clinical studies have shown that patients with PTSD have lower cortisol levels, elevated CSF CRF levels and are more sensitive than normal volunteers to DEX suppression [42, 92]. Due to their low cortisol level and reduced capacity for GR feedback inhibition, administration of DEX could be helpful to regulate HPA activity in these patients. Early studies involving DEX treatment in a cohort of PTSD patients, one in combat veterans and the other in sexually abused adolescents, demonstrated reductions in ACTH levels after DEX administration [93-94]. In 2011, Jovanovic et al. examined the effects of DEX on fear-potentiated startle (FPS) in 33 PTSD patients and 67 controls [95]. DEX administration was associated with reduced fear potentiated startle and was correlated with cortisol levels. Further studies need to be performed to examine if GR or MR agonists are playing a role in HPA axis regulation or is their beneficial effect due to extra-endocrine CNS effects.

Unfortunately the use of DEX, prednisone or other glucocorticoids is not without its limitations. Side effects including depression, mania, psychosis and delirium have all been reported even after a single dose [96]. Additionally, high dose corticosteroid administration increases the incidence of depression, anxiety and hypomania in medically ill patients [97-108].

11. FKBP5 as a genetically-linked HPA axis therapeutic target

A number of HPA axis genes have been identified and are speculated to play a role in the initiation of mood disorders [109-135]. It is therefore likely that genetic polymorphisms that affect the function of these genes may modulate an individual's response to treatment. For example, FKBP5 (a.k.a. FKBP51, FK506 binding protein 51, hsp58) is an immunophilin that works with hsp90 to regulate glucocorticoid receptor sensitivity has been genetically linked to anxiety, depression and PTSD [136, 137]. Briefly, hsp90 (along with numerous other proteins) act in the cell to assist with protein folding. Hsp90 action is supported by co-chaperones in the cell as well, one of these being FKBP5. In GR containing cells, hsp90 and FKBP5 both bind to the GR as chaperones during protein folding and maturation [137-139]. When the GR is bound with hsp90 and FKBP5, it becomes less sensitive to the presence of cortisol. Thus over expression of FKBP5 produces a significant reduction in cortisol action at GRs [137-140]. Additionally, FKBP5 is upregulated by GR activation, suggesting that FKBP5 is an intracellular negative feedback protein [141-142]. Therefore, it is not surprising that FKBP5 polymorphisms have been shown to be associated with a variety of mood disorders [136, 137]. The development of selective FKBP5 antagonists might be useful to reduce the FKBP5 desensitizing effects on GRs and allow feedback inhibition of HPA axis tone.

12. Conclusions and expert opinion

This chapter outlines a number of different components of the HPA axis that represent attractive targets to treat mood disorders. The strongest therapeutic candidates, and the ones most directly linked to the HPA axis, are glucocorticoid receptor antagonists for depression and agonists for PTSD. It is interesting to note, that mifeprisotne (GR antagonist) and dexamethasone (a GR agonist) are presently available and FDA approved for other indications. Clinical trials with these two compounds for psychotic depression and PTSD are ongoing.

CRF1 receptor antagonists need to be more carefully evaluated in distinctive subsets of depressed patients, (ie. MDD with a history of child abuse or neglect) who exhibit chronically elevated CRF, ACTH and cortisol levels. The CRF2 receptor antagonists should also be further studied to more elucidate their role in therapeutic treatment of mood disorders. Finally, targets that have been found by genetic and genomic screens, such as FKBP5, are potentially interesting but this field is still very much in its infancy.

Author details

Lauren B. Ozbolt and Charles B. Nemeroff
Department of Psychiatry and Behavioral Sciences,
University of Miami Leonard M. Miller School of Medicine, Florida

13. References

[1] W. Vale, J. Spiess, C. Rivier and J. Rivier, *Science*, 1981, 213, 1394-1397.
[2] L. Arborelius, M. J. Owens, P. M. Plotsky and C. B. Nemeroff, *The Journal of Endocrinology*, 1999, 160, 1-12.
[3] X. F. Li, A. M. Knox and K. T. O'Byrne, *Brain Res.*, 2010, 1364, 153-163.
[4] E. P. Zorrilla, Y. Tache and G. F. Koob, *Trends Pharmacol. Sci.*, 2003, 24, 421-427.
[5] E. G. Lowery and T. E. Thiele, *CNS Neurol. Disord. Drug Targets*, 2010, 9, 77-86.
[6] E. B. Binder and C. B. Nemeroff, *Mol. Psychiatry*, 2010, 15, 574-588.
[7] D. H. Henneman, M. D. Altschule and R. M. Goncz, *A.M.A. Archives of Internal Medicine*, 1955, 95, 241-246.
[8] D. J. McClure, *J. Psychosom. Res.*, 1966, 10, 189-195.
[9] C. F. Gillespie and C. B. Nemeroff, *Psychosom. Med.*, 2005, 67 Suppl 1, S26-28.
[10] D. G. Baker, S. A. West, W. E. Nicholson, N. N. Ekhator, J. W. Kasckow, K. K. Hill, A. B. Bruce, D. N. Orth and T. D. Geracioti, Jr., *The American Journal of Psychiatry*, 1999, 156, 585- 588.
[11] J. D. Bremner, J. Licinio, A. Darnell, J. H. Krystal, M. J. Owens, S. M. Southwick, C. B. Nemeroff and D. S. Charney, *The American Journal of Psychiatry*, 1997, 154, 624-629.
[12] C. M. Banki, G. Bissette, M. Arato, L. O'Connor and C. B. Nemeroff, *The American Journal of Psychiatry*, 1987, 144, 873-877.
[13] D. A. Axelson, P. M. Doraiswamy, W. M. McDonald, O. B. Boyko, L. A. Tupler, L. J. Patterson, C. B. Nemeroff, E. H. Ellinwood, Jr. and K. R. Krishnan, *Psychiatry Res.*, 1993, 47, 163-173.
[14] C. B. Nemeroff, E. Widerlov, G. Bissette, H. Walleus, I. Karlsson, K. Eklund, C. D. Kilts, P. T. Loosen and W. Vale, *Science*, 1984, 226, 1342-1344.
[15] L. L. Carpenter, A. R. Tyrka, C. J. McDougle, R. T. Malison, M. J. Owens, C. B. Nemeroff and L. H. Price, *Neuropsychopharmacology*, 2004, 29, 777-784.
[16] M. D. Fossey, R. B. Lydiard, J. C. Ballenger, M. T. Laraia, G. Bissette and C. B. Nemeroff, *Biol. Psychiatry*, 1996, 39, 703-707.
[17] C. B. Nemeroff, M. J. Owens, G. Bissette, A. C. Andorn and M. Stanley, *Arch. Gen. Psychiatry*, 1988, 45, 577-579.
[18] Z. Merali, L. Du, P. Hrdina, M. Palkovits, G. Faludi, M. O. Poulter and H. Anisman, *The Journal of neuroscience*, 2004, 24, 1478-1485.

[19] E. I. Flandreau, K. J. Ressler, M. J. Owens and C. B. Nemeroff, *Psychoneuroendocrinology*, 2011.

[20] C. Stetler and G. E. Miller, *Psychosom. Med.*, 2011, 73, 114-126.

[21] C. Heim, D. J. Newport, R. Bonsall, A. H. Miller and C. B. Nemeroff, *The American Journal of Psychiatry*, 2001, 158, 575-581.

[22] C. B. Nemeroff, K. R. Krishnan, D. Reed, R. Leder, C. Beam and N. R. Dunnick, *Arch. Gen. Psychiatry*, 1992, 49, 384-387.

[23] C. Heim and C. B. Nemeroff, *Biol. Psychiatry*, 1999, 46, 1509-1522.

[24] E. Holsboer-Trachsler, R. Stohler and M. Hatzinger, *Psychiatry Res.*, 1991, 38, 163-171.

[25] F. Holsboer, *J. Affect. Disord.*, 2001, 62, 77-91.

[26] A. W. Zobel, A. Yassouridis, R. M. Frieboes and F. Holsboer, *The American journal of psychiatry*, 1999, 156, 949-951.

[27] G. N. Neigh, K. Karelina, N. Zhang, E. R. Glasper, M. J. Owens, P. M. Plotsky, C. B. Nemeroff and A. C. Devries, *Journal of cerebral blood flow and metabolism*, 2009, 29, 1673-1682.

[28] M. A. Whooley, *JAMA : the journal of the American Medical Association*, 2006, 295, 2874-2881.

[29] J. B. Regard, I. T. Sato and S. R. Coughlin, *Cell*, 2008, 135, 561-571.

[30] P. Timpl, R. Spanagel, I. Sillaber, A. Kresse, J. M. Reul, G. K. Stalla, V. Blanquet, T. Steckler, F. Holsboer and W. Wurst, *Nat. Genet.*, 1998, 19, 162-166. 24

[31] J. H. Kehne and C. K. Cain, *Pharmacol. Ther.*, 2010, 128, 460-487.

[32] D. A. Gutman, M. J. Owens, K. V. Thrivikraman and C. B. Nemeroff, *Neuropharmacology*, 2011, 60, 1135-1141.

[33] G. F. Koob, *Brain Res.*, 2009, 1293, 61-75.

[34] M. Eaves, K. Thatcher-Britton, J. Rivier, W. Vale and G. F. Koob, *Peptides*, 1985, 6, 923-926.

[35] A. W. Zobel, T. Nickel, H. E. Kunzel, N. Ackl, A. Sonntag, M. Ising and F. Holsboer, *J. Psychiatr. Res.*, 2000, 34, 171-181.

[36] M. Ising, U. S. Zimmermann, H. E. Kunzel, M. Uhr, A. C. Foster, S. M. Learned-Coughlin, F. Holsboer and D. E. Grigoriadis, *Neuropsychopharmacology*, 2007, 32, 1941-1949.

[37] B. Binneman, D. Feltner, S. Kolluri, Y. Shi, R. Qiu and T. Stiger, *The American journal of psychiatry*, 2008, 165, 617-620.

[38] V. Coric, H. H. Feldman, D. A. Oren, A. Shekhar, J. Pultz, R. C. Dockens, X. Wu, K. A. Gentile, S. P. Huang, E. Emison, T. Delmonte, B. B. D'Souza, D. L. Zimbroff, J. A. Grebb, A. W. Goddard and E. G. Stock, *Depress. Anxiety*, 2010, 27, 417-425.

[39] C. S. Hubbard, J. S. Labus, J. Bueller, J. Stains, B. Suyenobu, G. E. Dukes, D. L. Kelleher, K. Tillisch, B. D. Naliboff and E. A. Mayer, *The Journal of neuroscience*, 2011, 31, 12491-12500.

[40] C. Heim, D. J. Newport, S. Heit, Y. P. Graham, M. Wilcox, R. Bonsall, A. H. Miller and C. B. Nemeroff, *The Journal of the American Medical Association*, 2000, 284, 592-597.

[41] C. Heim, T. Mletzko, D. Purselle, D. L. Musselman and C. B. Nemeroff, *Biol. Psychiatry*, 2008, 63, 398-405.

[42] C. B. Nemeroff, J. D. Bremner, E. B. Foa, H. S. Mayberg, C. S. North and M. B. Stein, *J. Psychiatr. Res.*, 2006, 40, 1-21.

[43] A. B. Amstadter, N. R. Nugent, B. Z. Yang, A. Miller, R. Siburian, P. Moorjani, S. Haddad, A. Basu, J. Fagerness, G. Saxe, J. W. Smoller and K. C. Koenen, *Dis. Markers*, 2011, 30, 89-99. 44. G. Polanczyk, A. Caspi, B. Williams, T. S. Price, A. Danese, K. Sugden, R. Uher, R. Poulton and T. E. Moffitt, *Arch. Gen. Psychiatry*, 2009, 66, 978-985.

[44] A. C. Chen, N. Manz, Y. Tang, M. Rangaswamy, L. Almasy, S. Kuperman, J. Nurnberger, Jr., S. J. O'Connor, H. J. Edenberg, M. A. Schuckit, J. Tischfield, T. Foroud, L. J. Bierut, J. Rohrbaugh, J. P. Rice, A. Goate, V. Hesselbrock and B. Porjesz, *Alcohol. Clin. Exp. Res.*, 2010, 34, 988-996.

[45] R. Ciccocioppo, D. R. Gehlert, A. Ryabinin, S. Kaur, A. Cippitelli, A. Thorsell, A. D. Le, P. A. Hipskind, C. Hamdouchi, J. Lu, E. J. Hembre, J. Cramer, M. Song, D. McKinzie, M. Morin, D. Economidou, S. Stopponi, N. Cannella, S. Braconi, M. Kallupi, G. de Guglielmo, M. Massi, D. T. George, J. Gilman, J. Hersh, J. T. Tauscher, S. P. Hunt, D. Hommer and M. Heilig, *Alcohol*, 2009, 43, 491-498.

[46] M. Heilig and M. Egli, *Pharmacol. Ther.*, 2006, 111, 855-876.

[47] S. C. Coste, R. A. Kesterson, K. A. Heldwein, S. L. Stevens, A. D. Heard, J. H. Hollis, S. E. Murray, J. K. Hill, G. A. Pantely, A. R. Hohimer, D. C. Hatton, T. J. Phillips, D. A. Finn, M. J. Low, M. B. Rittenberg, P. Stenzel and M. P. Stenzel-Poore, *Nat. Genet.*, 2000, 24, 403-409.

[48] T. L. Bale, R. Picetti, A. Contarino, G. F. Koob, W. W. Vale and K. F. Lee, *The Journal of Neuroscience*, 2002, 22, 193-199.

[49] T. Kishimoto, J. Radulovic, M. Radulovic, C. R. Lin, C. Schrick, F. Hooshmand, O. Hermanson, M. G. Rosenfeld and J. Spiess, *Nat. Genet.*, 2000, 24, 415-419.

[50] R. Gerlai, *Trends Neurosci.*, 1996, 19, 177-181.

[51] R. L. Hauger, V. Risbrough, O. Brauns and F. M. Dautzenberg, *CNS Neurol. Disord. Drug Targets*, 2006, 5, 453-479.

[52] D. N. Orth and C. D. Mount, *Biochem. Biophys. Res. Commun.*, 1987, 143, 411-417.

[53] E. Potter, D. P. Behan, W. H. Fischer, E. A. Linton, P. J. Lowry and W. W. Vale, *Nature*, 1991,349, 423-426.

[54] R. J. Herringa, P. H. Roseboom and N. H. Kalin, *Neuropsychopharmacology*, 2006, 31, 1822-1831.25

[55] A. J. Rush, M. Fava, S. R. Wisniewski, P. W. Lavori, M. H. Trivedi, H. A. Sackeim, M. E. Thase, A. A. Nierenberg, F. M. Quitkin, T. M. Kashner, D. J. Kupfer, J. F. Rosenbaum, J. Alpert, J. W. Stewart, P. J. McGrath, M. M. Biggs, K. Shores-Wilson, B. D. Lebowitz, L. Ritz and G. Niederehe, *Control. Clin. Trials*, 2004, 25, 119-142.

[56] E. B. Binder, M. J. Owens, W. Liu, T. C. Deveau, A. J. Rush, M. H. Trivedi, M. Fava, B. Bradley, K. J. Ressler and C. B. Nemeroff, *Arch. Gen. Psychiatry*, 2010, 67, 369-379.

[57] R. J. Herringa, S. A. Nanda, D. T. Hsu, P. H. Roseboom and N. H. Kalin, *Brain Res. Mol. Brain Res.*, 2004, 131, 17-25.

[58] M. A. Faghihi and C. Wahlestedt, *Nat. Rev. Mol. Cell Biol.*, 2009, 10, 637-643.

[59] S. Rotzinger, D. A. Lovejoy and L. A. Tan, *Peptides*, 2010, 31, 736-756.

[60] C. Murgatroyd, A. V. Patchev, Y. Wu, V. Micale, Y. Bockmuhl, D. Fischer, F. Holsboer, C. T.Wotjak, O. F. Almeida and D. Spengler, *Nat. Neurosci.*, 2009, 12, 1559-1566.
[61] A. Holmes, M. Heilig, N. M. Rupniak, T. Steckler and G. Griebel, *Trends Pharmacol. Sci.*,2003, 24, 580-588.
[62] C. Serradeil-Le Gal, J. Wagnon, 3rd, B. Tonnerre, R. Roux, G. Garcia, G. Griebel and A.Aulombard, *CNS drug reviews*, 2005, 11, 53-68.
[63] D. L. Evans, G. B. Burnett and C. B. Nemeroff, *The American Journal of Psychiatry*, 1983, 140,586-589.
[64] J. C. Nelson and J. M. Davis, *The American Journal of Psychiatry*, 1997, 154, 1497-1503.
[65] A. F. Schatzberg, A. J. Rothschild, P. J. Langlais, E. D. Bird and J. O. Cole, *J. Psychiatr. Res.*,1985, 19, 57-64.
[66] B. E. Murphy, D. Filipini and A. M. Ghadirian, *Journal of Psychiatry & Neuroscience : JPN*,1993, 18, 209-213.
[67] C. DeBattista, J. Belanoff, S. Glass, A. Khan, R. L. Horne, C. Blasey, L. L. Carpenter and G.Alva, *Biol. Psychiatry*, 2006, 60, 1343-1349.
[68] A. H. Young, P. Gallagher, S. Watson, D. Del-Estal, B. M. Owen and I. N. Ferrier,*Neuropsychopharmacology : official publication of the American College ofNeuropsychopharmacology*, 2004, 29, 1538-1545.
[69] C. B. Nemeroff, *Hum. Psychopharmacol.*, 2002, 17 Suppl 1, S13-16.
[70] K. R. Krishnan, D. Reed, W. H. Wilson, W. B. Saunders, J. C. Ritchie, C. B. Nemeroff and B.J. Carroll, *Prog. Neuropsychopharmacol. Biol. Psychiatry*, 1992, 16, 913-920.
[71] C. M. Blasey, T. S. Block, J. K. Belanoff and R. L. Roe, *J. Clin. Psychopharmacol.*, 2011, 31,436-440.
[72] C. G. Bachmann, A. C. Linthorst, F. Holsboer and J. M. Reul, *Neuropsychopharmacology*, 2003, 28, 1056-1067.
[73] L. K. Nieman, G. P. Chrousos, C. Kellner, I. M. Spitz, B. C. Nisula, G. B. Cutler, G. R. Merriam,C. W. Bardin and D. L. Loriaux, *The Journal of Clinical Endocrinology and Metabolism*, 1985,61, 536-540.
[74] J. K. Belanoff, B. H. Flores, M. Kalezhan, B. Sund and A. F. Schatzberg, *J. Clin.Psychopharmacol.*, 2001, 21, 516-521.
[75] J. K. Belanoff, A. J. Rothschild, F. Cassidy, C. DeBattista, E. E. Baulieu, C. Schold and A. F.Schatzberg, *Biol. Psychiatry*, 2002, 52, 386-392.
[76] G. M. Simpson, A. El Sheshai, N. Loza, S. J. Kingsbury, M. Fayek, A. Rady and W. Fawzy,*The Journal of clinical psychiatry*, 2005, 66, 598-602.
[77] B. H. Flores, H. Kenna, J. Keller, H. B. Solvason and A. F. Schatzberg,*Neuropsychopharmacology*, 2006, 31, 628-636.79. C. M. Blasey, C. Debattista, R. Roe, T. Block and J. K. Belanoff, *Contemp. Clin. Trials*, 2009,30, 284-288.
[78] Y. Ago, S. Arikawa, M. Yata, K. Yano, M. Abe, K. Takuma and T. Matsuda,*Neuropharmacology*, 2008, 55, 1355-1363.26
[79] T. Asagami, J. K. Belanoff, J. Azuma, C. M. Blasey, R. D. Clark and P. S. Tsao, *Journal ofNutrition and Metabolism*, 2011, 2011, 235389.
[80] Q. Y. Li, M. Zhang, T. M. Hallis, T. A. Derosier, J. M. Yue, Y. Ye, D. E. Mais and M. W. Wang,*Biochem. Biophys. Res. Commun.*, 2010, 391, 1531-1536.

[81] A. R. Brown, M. Bosies, H. Cameron, J. Clark, A. Cowley, M. Craighead, M. A. Elmore, A.Firth, R. Goodwin, S. Goutcher, E. Grant, M. Grassie, S. J. Grove, N. M. Hamilton, H.Hampson, A. Hillier, K. K. Ho, M. Kiczun, C. Kingsbury, S. G. Kultgen, P. T. Littlewood, S. J.Lusher, S. Macdonald, L. McIntosh, T. McIntyre, A. Mistry, J. R. Morphy, O. Nimz, M.Ohlmeyer, J. Pick, Z. Rankovic, B. Sherborne, A. Smith, M. Speake, G. Spinks, F. Thomson,L. Watson and M. Weston, *Bioorg. Med. Chem. Lett.*, 2011, 21, 137-140.

[82] J. Rimland, A. Dunne, S. S. Hunjan, R. Sasse, I. Uings, D. Montanari, M. Caivano, P. Shah, D.Standing, D. Gray, D. Brown, W. Cairns, R. Trump, P. W. Smith, N. Bertheleme, P.D'Alessandro, S. Gul, M. Vimal, D. N. Smith and S. P. Watson, *Bioorg. Med. Chem. Lett.*,2010, 20, 2340-2343.

[83] J. G. Tasker and J. P. Herman, *Stress*, 2011, 14, 398-406.

[84] G. N. Neigh and C. B. Nemeroff, *Trends in Endocrinology and Metabolism: TEM*, 2006, 17,124-125.

[85] S. Ridder, S. Chourbaji, R. Hellweg, A. Urani, C. Zacher, W. Schmid, M. Zink, H. Hortnagl, H.Flor, F. A. Henn, G. Schutz and P. Gass, *The Journal of neuroscience*, 2005, 25, 6243-6250.

[86] S. Claes, *Ann. N. Y. Acad. Sci.*, 2009, 1179, 216-228.

[87] E. W. Boland, *Ann. Rheum. Dis.*, 1958, 17, 376-382.

[88] D. J. McClure and R. A. Cleghorn, *Can. Psychiatr. Assoc. J.*, 1968, 13, 477-488.

[89] G. W. Arana, A. B. Santos, M. T. Laraia, S. McLeod-Bryant, M. D. Beale, L. J. Rames, J. M.Roberts, J. K. Dias and M. Molloy, *The American journal of psychiatry*, 1995, 152, 265-267.

[90] K. Handwerger, *Harv. Rev. Psychiatry*, 2009, 17, 184-205.

[91] C. S. de Kloet, E. Vermetten, C. J. Heijnen, E. Geuze, E. G. Lentjes and H. G. Westenberg,*Psychoneuroendocrinology*, 2007, 32, 215-226.

[92] F. Duval, M. A. Crocq, M. S. Guillon, M. C. Mokrani, J. Monreal, P. Bailey and J. P. Macher,*Psychoneuroendocrinology*, 2004, 29, 1281-1289.

[93] T. Jovanovic, J. E. Phifer, K. Sicking, T. Weiss, S. D. Norrholm, B. Bradley and K. J. Ressler,*Psychoneuroendocrinology*, 2011.

[94] D. A. Lewis and R. E. Smith, *J. Affect. Disord.*, 1983, 5, 319-332.

[95] D. Naber, P. Sand and B. Heigl, *Psychoneuroendocrinology*, 1996, 21, 25-31.

[96] E. S. Brown, T. Suppes, D. A. Khan and T. J. Carmody, 3rd, *J. Clin. Psychopharmacol.*, 2002,22, 55-61.

[97] E. S. Brown, *Ann. N. Y. Acad. Sci.*, 2009, 1179, 41-55.

[98] R. Caceda, B. Kinkead and C. B. Nemeroff, *Int. Rev. Neurobiol.*, 2007, 78, 327-376.

[99] M. P. Curran and D. M. Robinson, *Drugs*, 2009, 69, 1853-1878.

[100] V. Madaan and D. R. Wilson, *Drug News Perspect.*, 2009, 22, 319-324.

[101] I. Karagiannides and C. Pothoulakis, *Current opinion in endocrinology, diabetes, and obesity*,2009, 16, 47-52.

[102] P. E. Holtzheimer, 3rd and C. B. Nemeroff, *NeuroRx*, 2006, 3, 42-56.

[103] G. G. Nussdorfer and L. K. Malendowicz, *Peptides*, 1998, 19, 949-968.

[104] M. Hamke, I. Herpfer, K. Lieb, C. Wandelt and B. L. Fiebich, *Brain Res.*, 2006, 1102, 135-144.

[105] J. J. Rakofsky, P. E. Holtzheimer and C. B. Nemeroff, *Curr. Opin. Chem. Biol.*, 2009, 13, 291-302.

[106] M. S. Kramer, N. Cutler, J. Feighner, R. Shrivastava, J. Carman, J. J. Sramek, S. A. Reines,G. Liu, D. Snavely, E. Wyatt-Knowles, J. J. Hale, S. G. Mills, M. MacCoss, C. J. Swain, T.Harrison, R. G. Hill, F. Hefti, E. M. Scolnick, M. A. Cascieri, G. G. Chicchi, S. Sadowski, A. R.Williams, L. Hewson, D. Smith, E. J. Carlson, R. J. Hargreaves and N. M. Rupniak, *Science*,1998, 281, 1640-1645.27

[107] M. S. Kramer, A. Winokur, J. Kelsey, S. H. Preskorn, A. J. Rothschild, D. Snavely, K. Ghosh,W. A. Ball, S. A. Reines, D. Munjack, J. T. Apter, L. Cunningham, M. Kling, M. Bari, A. Getsonand Y. Lee, *Neuropsychopharmacology*, 2004, 29, 385-392.

[108] M. Keller, S. Montgomery, W. Ball, M. Morrison, D. Snavely, G. Liu, R. Hargreaves, J. Hietala,C. Lines, K. Beebe and S. Reines, *Biol. Psychiatry*, 2006, 59, 216-223.

[109] T. Furmark, L. Appel, A. Michelgard, K. Wahlstedt, F. Ahs, S. Zancan, E. Jacobsson, K. Flyckt,M. Grohp, M. Bergstrom, E. M. Pich, L. G. Nilsson, M. Bani, B. Langstrom and M. Fredrikson,*Biol. Psychiatry*, 2005, 58, 132-142.

[110] J. Tauscher, W. Kielbasa, S. Iyengar, F. Vandenhende, X. Peng, D. Mozley, D. R. Gehlert andG. Marek, *European neuropsychopharmacology : the journal of the European College ofNeuropsychopharmacology*, 2010, 20, 80-87.

[111] S. J. Mathew, M. Vythilingam, J. W. Murrough, C. A. Zarate, Jr., A. Feder, D. A. Luckenbaugh,B. Kinkead, M. K. Parides, D. G. Trist, M. S. Bani, P. U. Bettica, E. M. Ratti and D. S. Charney,*European Neuropsychopharmacology*, 2011, 21, 221-229.

[112] S. C. Huang and V. L. Korlipara, *Expert opinion on therapeutic patents*, 2010, 20, 1019-1045.

[113] Y. Fujimura, F. Yasuno, A. Farris, J. S. Liow, M. Geraci, W. Drevets, D. S. Pine, S. Ghose, A.Lerner, R. Hargreaves, H. D. Burns, C. Morse, V. W. Pike and R. B. Innis, *Biol. Psychiatry*,2009, 66, 94-97.

[114] M. A. Rosenkranz, *Psychol. Bull.*, 2007, 133, 1007-1037.

[115] T. J. Sajdyk, A. Shekhar and D. R. Gehlert, *Neuropeptides*, 2004, 38, 225-234.

[116] K. A. Paschos, S. Veletza and E. Chatzaki, *CNS drugs*, 2009, 23, 755-772.

[117] S. P. Brothers and C. Wahlestedt, *EMBO Mol. Med.*, 2010, 2, 429-439.

[118] J. C. Morales-Medina, Y. Dumont and R. Quirion, *Brain Res.*, 2010, 1314, 194-205.

[119] T. Karl and H. Herzog, *Peptides*, 2007, 28, 326-333.

[120] J. P. Redrobe, Y. Dumont and R. Quirion, *Life Sci.*, 2002, 71, 2921-2937.

[121] S. P. Brothers, S. A. Saldanha, T. P. Spicer, M. Cameron, B. A. Mercer, P. Chase, P.McDonald, C. Wahlestedt and P. S. Hodder, *Mol. Pharmacol.*, 2010, 77, 46-57.

[122] A. Holmes, J. W. Kinney, C. C. Wrenn, Q. Li, R. J. Yang, L. Ma, J. Vishwanath, M. C.Saavedra, C. E. Innerfield, A. S. Jacoby, J. Shine, T. P. Iismaa and J. N. Crawley,*Neuropsychopharmacology*, 2003, 28, 1031-1044.

[123] K. Mitsukawa, X. Lu and T. Bartfai, *Cellular and molecular life sciences : CMLS*, 2008, 65,1796-1805.

[124] U. Sollenberg, T. Bartfai and U. Langel, *Neuropeptides*, 2005, 39, 161-163.

[125] K. Saar, A. M. Mazarati, R. Mahlapuu, G. Hallnemo, U. Soomets, K. Kilk, S. Hellberg, M.Pooga, B. R. Tolf, T. S. Shi, T. Hokfelt, C. Wasterlain, T. Bartfai and U. Langel, *Proc. Natl.Acad. Sci. U. S. A.*, 2002, 99, 7136-7141.

[126] T. Bartfai, X. Lu, H. Badie-Mahdavi, A. M. Barr, A. Mazarati, X. Y. Hua, T. Yaksh, G.Haberhauer, S. C. Ceide, L. Trembleau, L. Somogyi, L. Krock and J. Rebek, Jr., *Proc. Natl.Acad. Sci. U. S. A.*, 2004, 101, 10470-10475.

[127] A. Floren, U. Sollenberg, L. Lundstrom, M. Zorko, J. Stojan, M. Budihna, M. Wheatley, N. P.Martin, K. Kilk, A. Mazarati, T. Bartfai, M. Lindgren and U. Langel, *Neuropeptides*, 2005, 39,547-558.

[128] S. C. Ceide, L. Trembleau, G. Haberhauer, L. Somogyi, X. Lu, T. Bartfai and J. Rebek, Jr.,*Proc. Natl. Acad. Sci. U. S. A.*, 2004, 101, 16727-16732.

[129] R. M. Karlsson and A. Holmes, *Amino Acids*, 2006, 31, 231-239.

[130] J. D. Coplan, C. G. Abdallah, J. Kaufman, J. Gelernter, E. L. Smith, T. D. Perera, A. J. Dwork,A. Kaffman, J. M. Gorman, L. A. Rosenblum, M. J. Owens and C. B. Nemeroff,*Psychoneuroendocrinology*, 2011, 36, 289-293.28

[131] D. van West, J. Del-Favero, Y. Aulchenko, P. Oswald, D. Souery, T. Forsgren, S. Sluijs, S. Bel-Kacem, R. Adolfsson, J. Mendlewicz, C. Van Duijn, D. Deboutte, C. Van Broeckhoven and S. Claes, *Mol. Psychiatry*, 2004, 9, 287-292.

[132] D. Mehta and E. B. Binder, *Neuropharmacology*, 2011.

[133] R. H. Derijk, *Neuroimmunomodulation*, 2009, 16, 340-352.

[134] E. B. Binder, R. G. Bradley, W. Liu, M. P. Epstein, T. C. Deveau, K. B. Mercer, Y. Tang, C. F.Gillespie, C. M. Heim, C. B. Nemeroff, A. C. Schwartz, J. F. Cubells and K. J. Ressler, *JAMA :the journal of the American Medical Association*, 2008, 299, 1291-1305.

[135] E. B. Binder, *Psychoneuroendocrinology*, 2009, 34 Suppl 1, S186-195.

[136] J. J. Siekierka, S. H. Hung, M. Poe, C. S. Lin and N. H. Sigal, *Nature*, 1989, 341, 755-757.

[137] G. M. Wochnik, J. Ruegg, G. A. Abel, U. Schmidt, F. Holsboer and T. Rein, *The Journal of biological chemistry*, 2005, 280, 4609-4616.

[138] W. B. Denny, D. L. Valentine, P. D. Reynolds, D. F. Smith and J. G. Scammell, *Endocrinology*, 2000, 141, 4107-4113.

[139] H. Vermeer, B. I. Hendriks-Stegeman, B. van der Burg, S. C. van Buul-Offers and M. Jansen,*The Journal of clinical endocrinology and metabolism*, 2003, 88, 277-284.

[140] G. Wiederrecht, S. Hung, H. K. Chan, A. Marcy, M. Martin, J. Calaycay, D. Boulton, N. Sigal, R. L. Kincaid and J. J. Siekierka, *The Journal of Biological Chemistry*, 1992, 267, 21753-21760.

[141] E.L. Martin and C.B. Nemeroff, *Psychiatric Annals*, 2008, 38:4, 260-265.

[142] R.B. Lloyd and C.B.Nemeroff, *Current Topics in Medicinal Chemistry*, 2011, 11, 608-617.

[143] K.J. Ressler, B. Bradley, K.B. Mercer, T.C. Deveau, A.K. Smith, C.F. Gillespie, C.B. Nemeroff, J.F. Cubells, E.B.Binder, *American Journal of Medical Genetics*, 2009, 153B: 812-824.

[144] D.M. Nielsen, D.M. *Eur. Journal Pharmacology*. 2004, 499, 135-146.

[145] S.Chaki et al. *Eur. Journal Pharmacology*. 2004, 485, 145-158.

[146] E.M. Jukiewicz. *Psychopharmacology*. 2005, 180, 215-223.

[147] O. M. Wolkowitz et al. Biol. Psychiatry. 1999, 45, 1070-1074.

[148] A.J. Van der Lely et al. *Annuals of Internal Medicine*. 1991, 114, 143-144.

Chapter 3

The Pharmacological Frontiers in Treatment Resistant Major Depression*

Tom K. Birkenhäger and Henricus G. Ruhé

Additional information is available at the end of the chapter

http://dx.doi.org/10.5772/53224

1. Introduction

Major depressive disorder (MDD) is a major burden for society, with a year-prevalence of 5% in the adult population. Usually MDD is treated with psychotherapy or serotonergic and noradrenergic antidepressants. With the first antidepressant, often a Selective Serotonin Reuptake Inhibitor (SSRI), 30-40% of patients achieve symptomatic remission. This rate increases to 67% after ≥4 trials with different classes of antidepressants (Rush et al., 2006). However, non-response (<50% improvement of symptom-severity) occurs frequently and is associated with prolonged suffering by patients and their family members, but also prolonged hospitalisations and increased suicide-rates.

2. Treatment resistant depression

Non-response to more classes of antidepressants is referred to as treatment resistant (or refractory) depression (TRD). TRD is not the same as chronic depression, as a properly treated patient might prove to be treatment resistant within 6 months, while patients suffering from chronic depression have often been undertreated or were non-adherent (also referred to as 'pseudo-TRD'). In addition, when TRD is considered, a re-evaluation of the patient might reveal unrecognized other axis I disorders (e.g. anxiety and substance abuse disorders), somatic diagnoses or bipolar disorder (Berlim and Turecki 2007a).

Inconsistencies in definitions of TRD impair exact estimations of the prevalence of TRD (Nemeroff 2007), but estimations range between 15-30% of patients. Also, inconsistent definitions diminish transparency in the field of clinical trials to identify the most efficacious next-step treatments, and impair reliable comparisons or meta-analyses of results from next-

* Parts of this chapter have been published previously in an adapted form in chapter 8 of "Keuzecriteria voor antidepressiva" (criteria for choosing an antidepressant), edited by Verkes R.J. & Ruhé H.G.

step studies (Ruhé et al., 2006). Nevertheless, TRD is considered as the main cause of chronic depression with enduring hospitalizations, work-absenteeism and suicides. Therefore, TRD is responsible for the majority of direct and indirect costs of MDD (Beekman and van Marwijk, 2008).

2.1. Definitions of TRD

A systematic review of definitions of TRD used in clinical trials (Berlim and Turecki 2007b) identified six different definitions of TRD, ranging from non-response to one antidepressant (for ≤4 weeks) to a failure to respond to multiple adequate (in terms of duration and dosage) trials of different classes of antidepressants and electroconvulsive therapy (ECT).

Unfortunately, none of the definitions has been properly operationalized, nor systematically investigated. For these definitions, it was most often not stated explicitly whether previous treatments were considered to determine TRD when these had been applied during the *current* or also during *any previous* episode. Furthermore, TRD-assessment was often unspecified regarding the adequacy and duration of previous antidepressant treatments, assessed retrospectively (based on patient-recall only), with occasional assessment of previous non-response by clinical global impression or validated rating scales. All definitions of TRD only focused on previous pharmacological treatment, leaving out psychological treatments like cognitive behavioural therapy (CBT) or interpersonal therapy (IPT).

In summary, Berlim et al. (2007) defined TRD as an episode of MDD which has not improved after at least two adequate trials of different classes of antidepressants, which is supported by the deteriorating chances of response after the second antidepressant observed in STAR*D (Rush et al., 2006;Ruhe et al., 2006). This definition assumes that treatment with drugs from the same class of antidepressants are less effective than successive treatments that apply a between class switch. There is very little evidence that actually supports this notion (Ruhe et al., 2006; Papakostas et al., 2008).

Berlim et al. (2007) suggested that consequent and international use of this definition would improve understanding of research findings and communication between investigators and clinicians. The European Medicines Agency (EMEA) revised their definition of TRD, stating that a "clinically relevant TRD is a current episode of depressive disorder which has not benefited from at least two adequate trials of antidepressant compounds of different mechanism of action" (Committee for medicinal product for human use (CHMP) 2009). This definition will define TRD for clinical registration studies of (new) antidepressant agents, especially to license next-step treatments. It will also exclude the inclusion of partial responders, and increase homogeneity of study-populations. Nevertheless, it should be taken into consideration that any definition of TRD is based on clinical parameters/outcomes, while it does not address underlying pathophysiology.

2.2. TRD as a dimensional concept; staging methods

The above definitions of TRD imply a dichotomy, which does not acknowledge the clinical impression of a more dimensional nature of TRD (Berlim and Turecki 2007a). Therefore, a staging model for TRD appears more appropriate. Such a model should be able to classify patients according to their level of resistance to treatment for MDD, predict chances of future remission and guide clinical treatment selection. Like in oncology (Fagiolini and Kupfer 2003), in the future, psychopathological and biological markers for staging of TRD might be useful to better predict the course and prognosis of the disease. Several clinical variables might influence the development or level of TRD: duration of the episode, depression subtype, depression severity, and psychiatric and/or somatic co-morbidity (Berlim and Turecki 2007b).

We recently systematically reviewed the literature to identify staging models for TRD and compared these models regarding predictive utility (possibility to discriminate different levels of treatment response in relation to unresponsiveness to subsequent treatments) and reliability (adequacy of staging between and within raters) (Ruhe et al, 2012). Several staging methods have been developed: the the Antidepressant Treatment History Form (Sackeim, et al.,1990), the Thase and Rush Model (TRSM) (Thase and Rush, 1997), the European Staging Model (Souery et al.,1999), the Massachusetts General Hospital Staging model (Fava 2003) and the Maudsley Staging Model (MSM) (Fekadu et al., 2009a; Fekadu et al., 2009b), but to date, no staging model has been widely accepted.

With these models, an evolution from single antidepressant adequacy ratings, towards a multidimensional and more continuous scored staging model occurred over time, while also illness characteristics (severity and duration) have been introduced. The operationalization criteria for these models improved over time. The scoring of different treatment strategies (between/within class switching, augmentation/combination) changed according to the existing evidence. Over time, efforts to validate models improved as well.

The most comprehensive clinical staging/profiling model for TRD is the MSM, which was validated as measure for treatment resistance as well (Fekadu et al., 2009a; Fekadu et al., 2009b). The MSM summarizes the actual stage of TRD in a single score, varying between 3 and 15. Staging of TRD can also be presented in 3 ordinal categories: mild (scores = 3-6), moderate (scores = 7-10) and severe (scores = 11-15). The predictive utility of the MSM was tested by using prospective data (average treatment duration 26±16 weeks) from case notes (N=88) from all patients discharged from a specialized TRD-inpatient unit (Fekadu et al., 2009a). With logistic regression the MSM and its components (number of medications, duration of presenting episode, and severity of illness) were associated with failure to achieve remission (Hamilton Depression Rating Scale (21-items) ≥11) at discharge. Furthermore, variations of the MSM were examined by the introduction of additional items.

Duration, severity and treatment were independently associated with non-remission at discharge (OR: 2.27 (1.4-3.8), 2.14 (1.1-4.3) and 1.43 (1.1-2.0) respectively), as was the total MSM-score (OR 1.67 (1.3-2.2)). The MSM correctly predicted treatment resistance in 85.5% of the cases. A second study tested whether this model predicted clinical outcome after a longer follow-up (Fekadu et al., 2009b) . For this purpose, 62 patients (Fekadu et al., 2009b) were followed-up (median follow-up 29.5 months (IQR 19.0-52.5 months)). Of the patients, 21% remained depressed continuously, while 37.7% remained depressed for ≥50% of the follow-up. Higher MSM scores were found to predict the persistence of a depressive episode throughout follow-up (OR = 2.01 (1.1-3.5), p= 0.015), and the presence of a depressive episode for ≥50% of time (OR 2.11 (1,3-3.6), p = .005). In contrast with the MSM, the TRSM also predicted future non-response, albeit worse than the MSM, but the TRSM failed to predict long-term clinical outcome.

3. Treatment options for treatment resistant depression

Regardless of the initial choice of antidepressant, about 30% to 50% of patients with MDD do not achieve full remission to adequately performed first-line treatment (Fava and Davidson, 1996). Several treatment strategies have been proposed for patients not responding sufficiently to monotherapy with an antidepressant. The strategies which are most commonly used are: 1) switching to a new antidepressant, either from within the same pharmacologic class or from a different class, 2) augmenting the antidepressant with other agents to enhance antidepressant efficacy, 3) combining 2 antidepressants from different classes, and 4) combining the antidepressant with depression-specific psychotherapy (Fava and Davidson, 1996). Potential benefits of switching are: this strategy is heuristically clear, because of less side effects compliance may be better than with augmentation/combination. Possible disadvantages of switching are: loss of partial response, and withdrawal symptoms (Papakostas, 2009). Potential benefits of augmentation/combination: therapeutic effect of the first drug is preserved, and augmentation may lead to a faster response. Possible disadvantages of combination/augmentation: more adverse effects, lower compliance, and the risk of possible drug interactions (Papkostas, 2009)

Currently, there is no consensus about which strategy should be favored for nonresponding patients, since until now no randomized clinical trials have been conducted to answer this question (Spijker and Nolen, 2010). Some authors argued in favor of augmentation strategies, instead of switching, because there is no need for a washout period between antidepressants and possible partial response to the antidepressant is maintained. Indeed, patients who have had some response may be reluctant to risk a loss of that improvement, and in this situation, augmentation may be beneficial. When effective, benefits of augmentation can be observed rapidly. In this chapter we will discuss three different augmentation strategies: Lithium augmentation, T3 augmentation, and The augmentation of atypical antipsychotics.

3.1. Switching

If a patient fails to respond to treatment with an antidepressant (usually an SSRI), an obvious strategy would be to switch to another antidepressant. A review by Ruhé et al. (2006) found 23 open studies and 8 randomized studies, often conducted in heterogeneous patient samples and with considerable variation in methodological standards. The response rates of the switch studies varied between 12 and 86%. No clear-cut advantage of switching between classes of antidepressants compared with switching within the same class emerged. Switching to venlafaxine showed a modest and clinically equivocal benefit over switching between SSRIs with a number needed to treat = 13. This difference increased when the largest and methodologically poorest study was omitted (NNT=10). After a first SSRI, the majority of open studies reveal that switching to any of the current classes of antidepressants leads to a response rate of about 50%. However, in the randomized but unblinded STAR*D study the response rate after switching was lower; 26.8%, which may have been due to the inclusion of a higher proportion of patients with a chronic course of depression, a lower socioeconomic status and more somatic and psychiatric comorbidity (Rush et al., 2006). The level of treatment resistance was inversely correlated with outcome in the switch studies (Ruhé et al., 2006; Rush et al., 2006).

3.2. Combination

Combination treatment involves prescription of two different antidepressants at the same time. By combining two different antidepressants treatment may be more effective since different neurotransmitter systems can be influenced. Several studies have shown that combination treatment may be superior to antidepressant monotherapy. Blier et al. (2010) showed that three combination therapies (fluoxetine+mirtazapine, venlafaxine+mirtazapine, bupropion+mirtazapine) were all superior to fluoxetine monotherapy. In an earlier study, Blier et al. (2009) found that the combination of mirtazapine and paroxetine was more effective than mirtazapine or paroxetine as monotherapy. In the STAR*D study a combination of citalopram and bupropion showed a significant larger decrease of the Inventory of Depressive Symptoms (IDS) than a citalopram-buspiron combination, but the difference in the number of patients attaining remission was not significantly different (Gilmer et al., 2008). The co-med study (Rush et al., 2011) compared escitalopram-placebo with both an escitalopram-bupropion combination, and a venlafaxine-mirtazapine combination in a single-bind randomized study. In this study similar response and remission rates were found both after 12 weeks and 7 months of treatment for all three treatment conditions. When trying to explain why the Blier et al (2010) study found combination therapy superior to monotherapy, while the co-med study did not, Rush et al. noted that in their study only a small proportion of patients had melancholic features (20%), and the majority suffered from chronic depression. In the study by Blier et al. (2010) the majority of patients had melancholic features and lthe proportion of patients with a chronic course of depression was less. In conclusion, combining two different antidepressants may be useful, but this strategy has not been studied in specific subgroups of depressed patients, and it has not been compared with other strategies, i.e. lithium addition or non-selective MAOIs.

3.3. Augmentation

3.3.1. Lithium augmentation

Lithium has been used to augment the efficacy of antidepressant medications for about 30 years. The first study to test the efficacy of this augmentation strategy in patients with major depression was performed by de Montigny et al. (1981). The authors observed a rapid response, within 48 hours, when lithium was added to the ongoing antidepressant treatment of patients who had not responded to at least 3 weeks of treatment with tricyclic antidepressants (TCAs). The efficacy of the augmentation and its rapid response has led to relatively many studies concerning lithium augmentation. It has been well established in controlled trials that approximately one-half of all patients with treatment-refractory depression respond when lithium is added to their ongoing antidepressant treatment. The level of evidence for the efficacy of lithium augmentation is higher than that for other augmentation strategies (Fava and Davidson, 1996). Therefore, lithium augmentation should be considered a first-line treatment strategy in patients with major depression that does not sufficiently respond to standard antidepressant treatment. There are clues that lithium augmentation to TCAs has a higher efficacy than lithium added to modern antidepressants (Bruijn et al., 1998; Birkenhäger et al., 2004). However, lithium may also augment the therapeutic effects of SSRIs and venlafaxine. Whether lithium augmentation is effective for specific subtypes of major depression is unclear. The presence of melancholic features might be related to a higher efficacy of lithium augmentation: in the STAR*D study the efficacy of lithium addition appeared to be very low in a patient population, of which 12% fulfilled criteria for major depression with melancholic features (Nierenberg et al, 2006). In another study in depressed inpatients showing a high efficacy of lithium augmentation, 88% of the patients suffered from major depression with melancholic features (Bruijn et al., 1998). Whether or not patients with bipolar depression show a superior response to lithium augmentation is unknown.

The efficacy of lithium augmentation in depressed patients with psychotic features has been studied scarcely. In a small (n=15) open study, 60% of the patients achieved full remission during four weeks of lithium augmentation (Birkenhäger et al., 2009). Although the effect of lithium augmentation may appear during the first week of treatment, for other patients the effect becomes apparent within 2-6 weeks. The target lithium level should be at least 0.5 mmol/l, while levels of 0.6-0.8 mmol/l are recommended.In patients who respond to lithium augmentation, both lithium and the antidepressant should be continued for at least 12 months, with therapeutic plasma levels.

3.3.2. T3 augmentation

The thyroid gland produces two hormones, triiodothyronine (T3) and levothyroxine (T4). T4 is the main hormone secreted by the thyroid, a large proportion of T4 is converted to T3 in peripheral tissues in order to perform its physiological function. T3 has been used in combination with antidepressants (mostly TCAs) in three different ways: A. during the first week of treatment with an antidepressant with the purpose of acceleration of the antidepressant effect; B. in combination with an antidepressant throughout the antidepressant trial, with the purpose of enhancement of the antidepressant effect; C. as additional treatment after apparent nonresponse to antidepressant monotherapy: T3 augmentation. In this chapter we will focus on C.T3 augmentation for refractory depression.

Triiodothyronine (T3) was first used in the treatment of depression in 1958. Early studies used T3 with TCAs to accelerate the response to TCAs. A meta analysis of six double-blind, placebo-controlled studies (125 patients total) of T3 acceleration of tricyclics by Altshuler et al. (2001) was positive, as shown by d=0.58. Furthermore, a significant gender effect was observed, with women responding more robustly than men. By definition, these were short-term studies of 2 to 3 weeks, and no study investigated the option of continuing T3 once antidepressant response was achieved. Several placebo-controlled studies confirmed a more rapid effect in patients treated with both TCAs and T3 compared with TCA monotherapy.

Several open studies suggested that the augmentation of T3 to an ongoing treatment with TCAs leads to a response in a substantial proportion of patients with refractory depression. Aronson et al. (1996) performed a meta-analysis of 8 clinical trials of T3 augmentation comprising a total of 292 patients. The duration of T3 addition varied from 10 days to 6 weeks and the daily dose T3 was between 20 and 50 microgram. Patients receiving T3 were twice as likely to respond as controls, the NNT was 3. Aronson et al. (1996) concluded that T3 augmentation is an effective and safe method of increasing response in patients refractory to TCAs. However, most of the studies included in this meta-analysis had methodological flaws. When the authors restricted their analysis to 4 randomized double-blind studies, the effect of T3 augmentation was not significant any more.

Recently, a number of studies have examined the addition of triiodothyronine to selective serotonin reuptake inhibitors (SSRIs) in non-responders, but the data are more limited than with TCAs. A review by Cooper-Kazaz and Lerer (2008) found that there were insufficient data for a meta-analysis but that a positive trend was revealed when the available double- and single-blind studies were analyzed, response to T3 augmentation amounted to 40%. Papakostas et al. (2009) performed a meta-analysis which only included three double-blind, randomized, placebo-controlled studies. This analysis found response rates of 64.6% for SSRIs + T3 versus 58.5% for SSRI monotherapy, this difference was not significant.

The Sequenced treatment Alternatives to Relieve Depression (STAR*D) study compared SSRI augmentation with either lithium or T3 during 12 weeks in 142 depressed outpatients, who were refractory to treatment with citalopram and a second step (either augmentation with bupropion, buspirone or cognitive therapy or switching to a second antidepressant). This study revealed no statistical difference in efficacy between the treatments (Nierenberg et al., 2006). T3 was tolerated better and adherence was higher. However, remission rates were surprisingly low: 16% for lithium addition and 25% for T3 augmentation, respectively.

In conclusion, T3 augmentation, given at a daily dose of 25-50 microgram, is effective for patients who failed to respond to treatment with a TCA. Compared with lithium addition, the efficacy of T3 addition is established less firmly. It is unknown how long continuation treatment with T3 is necessary, following response to T3 augmentation.

3.4. Augmentation with atypical antipsychotics

First generation antipsychotics have been used to treat MDD, but extrapyramidal side effects and the risk of tardive dyskinesia limited the use of these agents. Since 1999 several case reports and open studies appeared, concerning the use of atypical antipsychotics as adjunctive treatment in patients with insufficient response to treatment with an SSRI, also/especially in non-psychotic patients. Following these case series, a number of double-blind, placebo-controlled augmentation trials have been conducted. A recent meta-analysis by Nelson and Papakostas (2009) comprised sixteen double-blind studies. The following atypical antipsychotics were used in these 16 studies: quetiapine, olanzapine(both 5 studies), risperidone and aripiperazole (both 3 studies). The duration of the addition with the antipsychotics varied from 4-12 weeks, the majority of the studies investigated effects over 6-8 weeks. The meta-analysis by Nelson and Papakostas (2009) analyzes the efficacy of each of the antipsychotics separately. Olanzapine, quetiapine, riperidone and aripiperazole augmentation appeared to be superior to placebo addition. The effect of olanzapine addition was relatively small, with an Odds Ratio (OR) of 1.39. For the other antipsychotics the ORs varied between 1.63-2.00. With regard to the sixteen double-blind studies, included in this meta-analysis, it is remarkable that only a minority shows a statistically significant effect compared to placebo (six of sixteen studies). In four studies this failure to find a difference may have been caused by the fact that these studies were small. However, these figures suggest that the effect of augmentation with atypical antipsychotics is relatively small. Furthermore, Nelson and Papakostas (2009) find signs indicating publication bias. An unanswered question regarding the effect of augmentation with atypical antipsychotics: is it merely an effect on anxiety and sleep disturbance, or does this augmentation also has an effect on 'core symptoms' of MDD (depressed mood, psychomotor retardation, diurnal variation, weight loss)? Another unanswered question is whether augmentation with atypical antipsychotics is more effective than switching antidepressants.

It is unknown how long continuation treatment with both the antidepressant and the atypical antipsychotic is necessary, following response to augmentation with an antipsychotic.

4. Algorithms to treat major depressive disorder

4.1. Why using an algorithm?

Although MDD is considered to have a favourable prognosis, remission rates in controlled studies are considerably less than 50%. Insufficient response to antidepressant treatment is often caused by inadequately performed pharmacotherapy, i.e., suboptimal dosage or suboptimal duration of treatment. Since residual symptomatology carries a high risk of relapse during continuation treatment and, subsequently, a chronic course of depression, full remission should be the aim of treatment (Thase and Rush, 1997). Therefore, both inadequate treatment and actual treatment resistance constitute major problems in the management of patients with major depression. The use of a systematic treatment algorithm may decrease the variance and increase the appropriateness of antidepressant treatment and, therefore, improve outcome. Only a few studies compared the efficacy of a treatment algorithm with treatment as usual (TAU). The only prospective randomized trial (Bauer et al., 2009) found a higher remission rate in the algorithm-treated sample (54% versus 39% in the TAU sample).

4.2. The algorithm in the Dutch multidisciplinary guideline for MDD

The algorithm proposed in the most recent version of the Dutch multidisciplinary guideline for depression consists of five subsequent steps. Since antidepressants are effective in moderate to severe major depression, and in both primary and secondary care (psychiatric outpatients) there is no clear difference in efficacy between antidepressants, SSRIs, SNRIs, mirtazapine, bupropion and TCAs are good options as first antidepressant treatment. SSRIs are the most frequently used antidepressants in the first treatment step. If there is insufficient response after 6-10 weeks of treatment, the second step is to switch to another antidepressant. There is a slight preference for switching from an SSRI to a TCA or venlafaxine, although switching from one SSRI to another is also possible. Lithium augmentation has the strongest evidence in treatment resistant depression, but because of its potential poorer tolerability, lithium augmentation is chosen as third step. Most of the evidence for lithium augmentation concerns augmentation of a TCA. The fourth step consists of switching to a non-selective MAOI (preferentially tranylcypromine). Although the evidence for ECT is strong, ECT is sometimes not acceptable to patients, and its availability is limited. Therefore, ECT is the fifth step in this algorithm (Spijker and Nolen, 2010).

4.3. One algorithm?

Is it appropriate to use one algorithm for a very heterogeneous illness like major depression? Some of the treatment steps prove to be effective in one subtype of MDD whereas they appear less effective in another. Therefore we propose three different algorithms, after distinguishing three subtypes of major depression, based on the DSM-IV criteria for melancholic and psychotic features. The specific treatment steps in the algorithms are selected, when proven effective for the subtype of major depression.

4.4. Algorithm 1: Major depression without psychotic or melancholic features

Considerations: SSRIs, SNRIS, mirtazapine, bupropion, TCAs, interpersonal psychotherapy (IPT) and cognitive behavioural therapy (CBT) all appear to be effective. The efficacy of lithium augmentation is doubtful: lithium augmentation appeared to be ineffective in the third step of the STAR*D study (Nierenberg et al., 2006). This lack of efficacy could be explained by the fact that lithium levels were determined in only 50% of the patients and 50% of the lithium levels were low. An alternative explanation for the poor result is the very low prevalence of melancholic features in this patient sample (12%). Lithium augmentation appeared to be very effective in a study concerning depressed inpatients; of whom 88% had melancholic features. Non-selective MAOIs can be effective regardless of the presence of melancholic features. ECT has a higher efficacy in patients with melancholic depression, compared with patients without melancholic features. These considerations result in the following algorithm:

Step 1. SSRI or another modern antidepressant
Step 2. a second SSRI or another modern antidepressant

Step 3. a TCA
Step 4. a non-selective MAOI (preferentially tranylcypromine)

The addition of IPT or CBT can be considered with every step.

4.5. Algorithm 2: Major depression with melancholic features

Considerations: Treatment with SSRIs or other modern antidepressants (with the exception of venlafaxine) appears to be less effective than treatment with a TCA. SSRIs are less effective than TCAs or venlafaxine in depressed inpatients. This difference in efficacy may be explained by a higher compliance in inpatients, but it can also be due to a higher presence of melancholic features among inpatients compared with outpatients. Lithium augmentation to TCAs is (very) effective in patients with melancholic features. Lithium augmentation to venlafaxine has never been the subject of a double-blind study, but may possibly be effective, based on open studies. Non-selective MAO inhibitors may be effective, whereas the efficacy of ECT is high. Both CBT and IPT appear to be less effective in melancholic depression as opposed to non-melancholic depression. These considerations result in the following algorithm:

Step 1. a TCA or venlafaxine
Step 2. Lithium addition to a TCA
Step 3. a non-selective MAOI (preferentially tranylcypromine)
Step 4. ECT

Depending on the patient's condition, step 3 and 4 can be switched.

4.6. Algorithm 3: Major depression with psychotic features

Considerations: Monotherapy with a TCA is not effective according to studies from the US, while European studies found TCAs as monotherapy to be effective for psychotic depression. Whether a combination of a TCA and an antipsychotic is superior to TCA monotherapy is unclear. A Combination of venlafaxine and quetiapine proved to be superior to venlafaxine monotherapy. Treatment with lithium addition has been studied scarcely in psychotic depression, but possibly it may be effective. The efficacy of non-selective MAOIs in psychotic depression is unknown. Treatment with ECT is very effective. These consideration results in the following algorithm:

Step 1. TCA with/without an antipsychotic OR venlafaxine + quetiapine
Step 2. If Step 1 was TCA, add an antipsychotic. If Step 1 was venlafaxine switch to a TCA
Step 3. Lithium addition to a TCA
Step 4. ECT

ECT may be performed prior to step 4, especially for patients in a critical condition.

5. Conclusion

Treatment-resistant depression is a major health issue, since major depression is a prevalent disorder and remission is not easily attained. Futhermore, treatment-resistance appears to be difficult to define. In this chapter, we discuss several staging methods for treatment-resistant depression. With regard to treatment options for patients who fail to respond to the first antidepressant, these consist of switching antidepressants, combining antidepressants, and augmentation strategies. Optimisation of antidepressant treatment can be achieved by applying those treatment strategies as an algorithm. In the Dutch multidisciplinary guideline for depression one standard algorithm is proposed, without considering the (limited) evidence that various subtypes of major depression respond differently to specific treatment steps. Therefore, we propose three algorithms, which are based on the limited evidence regarding the efficacy of several treatment steps for a specific subtype of major depression.

6. Summary

In the first part of the chapter various definitions of treatment resistant (refractory) depression (TRD) are reviewed. We conclude that there is no consensus regarding the operational criteria for TRD. For TRD, five different staging models have been developed to determine a staging level of refractoriness: the Antidepressant Treatment History Form, the Thase and Rush Staging model, the Massachusetts General Hospital Staging Model, the European Staging Model and the Maudsley Staging Model. The utility of these models will be discussed.

The second part of the chapter focuses on treatment options for TRD. Apart from switching the antidepressant, various augmentation strategies are currently applied for refractory depression, e.g. lithium addition, triiodothyronine addition and the addition of second generation antipsychotics. The advantages of these strategies will be discussed.

Finally, we will discuss the use of treatment algorithms. The algorithm for the pharmacological treatment of major depression of the Dutch multidisciplinary guidelines for depression is presented. The five subsequent steps of this algorithm (treatment with an antidepressant, switching to another antidepressant, lithium addition, switching to an MAO inhibitor, electroconvulsive therapy) will be discussed and a proposal for three different algorithms will be presented, depending on the presence or absence of melancholic and psychotic features will be discussed, as well as alternative strategies for the pharmacological treatment of TRD, which are not (yet) included in the algorithms.

Author details

Tom K. Birkenhäger**
Dept. of Psychiatry, Erasmus Medical Center, CA Rotterdam, The Netherlands

Henricus G. Ruhé
Program for Mood and Anxiety Disorders. Dept. of Psychiatry, University Medical Center Groningen, The Netherlands
Program for Mood Disorders, Dept. of Psychiatry Academic Medical Center, Amsterdam, The Netherlands

** Corresponding Author

7. References

[1] Altshuler ll, Bauer M, Frye MA, Gitlin MJ, Mintz J, Szuba MP, Leight Kl, Whybrow PC (2001) Does thyroid supplementation accelerate tricyclic antidepressant response? a review and meta-analysis. Am J Psychiatry 158: 1617-1622.

[2] Aronson R, Offman HJ, Joffe RT, Naylor D (1996) Triiodothyronine augmentation in the treatment of refractory depression. Arch Gen Psychiatry 53: 842-848.

[3] Bauer M, Forsthoff A, Baethge C, Adli M, Berghofer A, Dopfmer S, Bschor T (2003) Lithium augmentation in refractory depression-update 2002. Eur Arch Psychiatry Clin Neurosci 253: 132-139.

[4] Beekman AT, Marwijk HWv (2008): Epidemiologie van depressie. In Huyser J, Schene AH, Sabbe B, Spinhoven Ph, editors. *Handboek depressieve stoornissen*. Utrecht: De Tijdstroom, pp 13-25.

[5] Berlim MT, Turecki G (2007a): Definition, assessment, and staging of treatment-resistant refractory major depression: a review of current concepts and methods. *Can J Psychiatry* 52: 46-54.

[6] Berlim MT, Turecki G (2007b): What is the meaning of treatment resistant/refractory major depression (TRD)? A systematic review of current randomized trials. *Eur Neuropsychopharmacol* 17: 696-707.

[7] Birkenhager TK, van den Broek WW, Mulder PG, Bruijn JA, Moleman P (2004). Comparison of two-phase treatment with imipramineor fluvoxamine, both followed by lithium addition, in inpatients with major depressive disorder. Am J Psychiatry 161: 2060-2065.

[8] Birkenhager TK, van den Broek WW, Wijkstra J, Bruijn JA, van Os E, Boks M, Verkes RJ, Janzing JG, Nolen WA (2009). Treatment of unipolar psychotic depression . An open study of lithium addition in refractory psychotic depression. J Clin Psychopharmacol 29: 513-515.

[9] Blier P, Gobbi G, Turcotte JE, de Montigny C, Boucher N, Hebert C, Debonnel G (2009) Mirtazapine and paroxetine in major depression: a comparison of monotherapy versus their combination from treatment initiation. Eur Neuropsychopharmacol 19: 457-465.

[10] Blier P, Ward HE, Tremblay P, Laberge L, Hebert C, Bergeron R (2010) Combination of antidepressant medications from treatment inititation for major depressive disorder: a double-blind randomized study. Am J Psychiatry 167:281-288.

[11] Bruijn JA, Moleman P, Mulder PG, van den Broek WW (1998) Comparison of 2 treatment strategies for depressed inpatients: imipramine and lithium addition or mirtazapine and lithium addition. J Clin Psychiatry 59: 657-663.

[12] Committee for medicinal product for human use (CHMP). Concept paper on the need for revision of note for guidance on clinical investigation of medicinal products in the treatment of depression with regard to treatment resistant depression. 2009. Ref Type: Data File

[13] Cooper-Kazaz R, Lerer B (2008) Efficacy and safety of triiodothyronine supplementation in patients with major depressive disorder treated with specific serotonin reuptake inhibitors. Int J Neuropsychopharmacol 11: 685-699.

[14] Fagiolini A, Kupfer DJ (2003): Is treatment-resistant depression a unique subtype of depression? *Biol Psychiatry* 53: 640-648.

[15] Fava M (2003): Diagnosis and definition of treatment-resistant depression. *Biol Psychiatry* 53: 649-659.

[16] Fava M, Davidson KG (1996) Definition and epidemiology of treatment-resistant depression. Psychiatr Clin North Am 19: 179-200.

[17] Fekadu A, Wooderson S, Donaldson C, Markopoulou K, Masterson B, Poon L et al (2009): A multidimensional tool to quantify treatment resistance in depression: the Maudsley staging method. *J Clin Psychiatry* 70: 177-184.

[18] Fekadu A, Wooderson SC, Markopoulou K, Cleare AJ (2009): The Maudsley Staging Method for treatment-resistant depression: prediction of longer-term outcome and persistence of symptoms. *J Clin Psychiatry* 70: 952-957.

[19] Gilmer WS, Gollan JK, Wisniewski SR, Holand RH, Trivedi MH, Miyahara S, Fleck J, Thase ME, Alpert JE, Nierenberg AA, Warden D, Fava M, Rush AJ (2008) Does the duration of index episode affect the treatment outcome of major depressive disorder? A STAR*D report. J Clin Psychiatry 69: 1246-1256.

[20] de Montigny C, Grunberg F, Mayer A, Deschenes JP (1981) Lithium induces rapid relief in tricyclic antidepressant drug non-responders. Br J Psychiatry 138: 252-256.

[21] Nelson JC, Papakostas GI (2009) Atypical antipsychotic augmentation in major depressive disorder: a meta-analysis of placebo-controlled randomized trials. Am J Psychiatry 166: 980-991.

[22] Nemeroff CB (2007): Prevalence and management of treatment-resistant depression. *J Clin Psychiatry* 68 Suppl 8: 17-25.

[23] Nierenberg AA, Fava M, Trivedi MH, Wisniewski SR, Thase ME, McGrath PJ, Alpert JE, Warden D, Luther JF, Niederehe G, Lebowitz B, Shores-Wison K, Rush AJ (2006) A comparison of lithium and T3 augmentation following two failed medication treatments for depression: a STAR*D report. Am J Psychiatry 163: 1519-1530.

[24] Papakostas GI (2009) Managing partial response or nonresponse: Switching, augmentation and combination startegies for major depressive disorder. J Clin Psychiatry 70 Suppl 6: 16-25.

[25] Papakostas GI, Fava M, Thase ME (2008): Treatment of SSRI-resistant depression: a meta-analysis comparing within- versus across-class switches. *Biol Psychiatry* 63: 699-704.

[26] Ruhe HG, Huyser J, Swinkels JA, Schene AH (2006): Switching antidepressants after a first selective serotonin reuptake inhibitor in major depressive disorder: a systematic review. *J Clin Psychiatry* 67: 1836-1855.

[27] Ruhe HG, van Rooijen G, Spijker J, Peeters FP, Schene AH (2012): Staging methods for treatment resistant depression. A systematic review. *J Affect Disord* 137: 35-45.

[28] Rush AJ, Trivedi MH, Stewart JW, Nierenberg AA, Fava M, Kurian BT, Warden D, Morris DW, Luther JF, Husain MM, Cook IA, Shelton RC, Lesser IM, Korstein SG, Wisniewski SR (2011) Combining medications to enhance depression outcomes (CO-MED): acute and long-term outcomes of a single-blind randomized study. Am J Psychiatry 168: 689-701.

[29] Rush AJ, Trivedi MH, Wisniewski SR, Nierenberg AA, Stewart JW, Warden D et al (2006): Acute and longer-term outcomes in depressed outpatients requiring one or several treatment steps: a STAR*D report. *Am J Psychiatry* 163: 1905-1917.

[30] Sackeim HA, Prudic J, Devanand DP, Decina P, Kerr B, Malitz S (1990): The impact of medication resistance and continuation pharmacotherapy on relapse following response to electroconvulsive therapy in major depression. *J Clin Psychopharmacol* 10: 96-104.

[31] Souery D, Amsterdam J, de Montigny C., Lecrubier Y, Montgomery S, Lipp O et al (1999): Treatment resistant depression: methodological overview and operational criteria. *Eur Neuropsychopharmacol* 9: 83-91.

[32] Spijker J, Nolen WA (2010) An algorithm for the pharmacoligical treatment of depression. Acta Psychiatr Scand 121: 180-189.

[33] Thase ME, Rush AJ (1997): When at first you don't succeed: sequential strategies for antidepressant nonresponders. *J Clin Psychiatry* 58 Suppl 13: 23-29.

Section 2

Translational Search for Targets to Improve Treatment

Chapter 4

Altered Associative Learning and Learned Helplessness in Major Depression

Carsten Diener

Additional information is available at the end of the chapter

http://dx.doi.org/10.5772/51787

1. Introduction

Major depressive disorder (MDD) is a highly prevalent and recurrent disorder. Recent epidemiological studies have shown that up to 16% of the general population will suffer from at least one clinical episode of depression in their lifetime with women being affected more frequently than men (for a review, see [1]). The World Health Organization considers depressive disorders as one of the leading causes of disease worldwide, accounting for about 4.4% of total disability adjusted life years (DALY; [2]). Longitudinal studies indicate that up to 85% of depressed patients suffer from multiple episodes [3], and that 15-20% of episodes take a chronic course [4]. However, a unitary model providing axiomatic factors related to the development and maintenance of depression has not been established so far, what is most likely due to substantial heterogeneity in the etiology and symptomatology of depressive syndromes [5].

This chapter aims to provide a selective review of evidence on how alterations in associative learning relate to the (etio-) psychopathology of depression in the context of widely accepted models of the disorder.

2. Models of depression

The literature on the development and maintenance of MDD is characterized by several lines of research that have highlighted alterations on different levels (i.e., cognitive-emotional, behavioral, and psychophysiological) to be relevant for the understanding of depression. Cognitive models of depression focus on alterations in human information processing by investigating attributional style and other cognitive variables, recently also including rumination. Behavioral and neurobiological models of depression dominantly refer to animal models of depression such as chronic stress or learned helplessness to investigate behavioral, endocrinological, and molecular characteristics of depression-like behaviors. Meanwhile, recent neuroimaging studies in humans aim to isolate specific structural and functional alterations in the brain associated with dysfunctions of emotion, motivation, and cognition in depression.

The current diagnosis of depressive disorders according to recent versions of the Diagnostic and Statistical Manual of Mental Disorders (DSM-IV) [6] and the International Statistical Classification of Diseases and Health Related Problems (ICD-10) [7] exclusively refer to the presence of decisive symptoms including depressed mood and anhedonia in a given time period. Although these nosological classification systems allow for objective diagnosis of and communication about depression, the neuropsychopathological signature of the disorder as proposed by depression models is not leading for the diagnosis. As a consequence, current depression diagnosis and research on the psychological and psychophysiological correlates of depression do not inevitable fall into place.

2.1. Cognitive models of depression

Cognitive theories of depression are among the most prominent models of depression. The two most influential cognitive theories, Beck's schema theory and the reformulated hopelessness theory by Abramson and colleagues (cf., [8]), point to the role of maladaptive self-schemata and negative inferential style for the onset, course, and outcome of depression. Prospective studies have shown that negative attributional styles and dysfunctional attitudes predict the onset of depressed mood and symptoms [9]. Parallel research strategies using experimental paradigms from cognitive psychology found depression to be associated with excessive attending to negative stimuli, fast recall of negative memories, over-generalized recall of autobiographical experiences, and a tendency for negative judgments on hypothetical and real-life experiences (e.g., [10]).

A third line of research deals with cognitive processes of affect regulation that might predict recovery from or worsening of depressed mood. In this context, the response styles theory by Nolen-Hoeksema [11] addresses the role of perseverative self-focused rumination versus distraction from negative mood for the exacerbation, maintenance, and discontinuation of depressed states. Ruminative responses are defined as thoughts and behaviors that comprise passively focusing one's attention on one's depressive symptoms, and repetitively thinking about possible causes and consequences of these symptoms. Distractive coping is defined as actively turning one's attention away from one's symptoms to pleasant or neutral thoughts and actions. There is strong evidence from laboratory and observational studies with nonclinical samples for the proposed predictions of response styles, particularly rumination, on the severity and duration of depressed mood. Self-reported rumination is associated with depression severity [12-14] and experimentally induced rumination prolongs dysphoric mood, enhances negatively biased memories, and impairs interpersonal and complex problem solving, while induced distraction predicts the decline of depressed mood [15]. Furthermore, a ruminative response style was found to predict future levels of depressed mood, even after controlling for baseline levels of depression (e.g., [11, 13-14]). High trait rumination scores in currently and past depressed subjects point to the role of a ruminative style as a potential vulnerability factor for depression [16-17].

These findings generally support the hypothesis that depressed individuals suffer from two dominant cognitive biases [18]: First, depressed individuals show increased attention for negative information; and second, they show extensive self-referential processing concerning the (negative) appraisal of stimuli and experiences.

2.2. Behavioral and neurobiological models of depression

Animal models of depression have dominantly focused on paradigms such as chronic mild stress or learned helplessness to induce depression-like behavior in unselected strains of animals or in animals bred for susceptibility to stress. When exposing animals to inescapable shocks or chronic mild stress they show subsequent impairments in active escape responses and a reduction in responsiveness to rewards as well as distinct neuroendocrinological changes [19-21]. These models in addition to lesion studies in animals [22] have generated many hypotheses about the neurobiological mechanisms involved in depression [23]. In parallel, proposed alterations in candidate regions and neural networks, assumed to play a major role in depression, have been found in neuroimaging studies in humans. Besides structural alterations mainly in terms of reduced grey-matter volumes in fronto-limbic regions [22], functional alterations in frontal regions, including the anterior cingulate cortex, and limbic structures, such as the amygdala and hippocampus, have been detected in prominent functional imaging studies. Recently, functional alterations in striatal structures (nucleus accumbens, caudate, putamen) have been related to altered reward and loss processing in depression [24]. Meta-analytic findings [25] emphasize that depression is characterized by predominantly reduced activity in the rostral anterior cingulate cortex and anterior insula, which is linked to altered salience processing of emotional and cognitive stimuli. In addition, hypersensitivity to negative information and reduced executive functioning seem substantially associated with a lack of prefrontal control in terms of both exaggerated frontal hypo- and hyperactivity. Functional alterations in striatal regions seem closely related to biased valence processing in MDD with a hemispheric dissociation depicting right-sided hypoactivity to positive and left-sided hyperactivity to negative stimuli. Moreover, increased activation in an extended medial prefrontal network during self-referential processing was found in depressed individuals [26].

Thus, biased information processing in depression as proposed by cognitive models of the disorder obviously correlate with partly specific neurofunctional alterations in depressed individuals. Several lines of evidence point to medial prefrontal, limbic, and striato-pallido-thalamic regions to be critically involved in the pathophysiology of MDD [27]. However, it needs to be mentioned that rather heterogeneous than homogeneous results for multiple cortical and subcortical regions characterize the current state on functional neuroimaging findings in major depression [25].

2.3. Integrative diathesis-stress models of depression

In attempting to understand how alterations on the emotional-cognitive and neurophysiological dimension emerge, diathesis-stress models generally postulate that both biological and environmental factors affect the development of psychological disorders, including depression [28]. The basic assumption is that stress activates a diathesis in turn transforming the predisposition or vulnerability for a disorder into the presence of the disorder. During the long history of this general model, the concepts for vulnerability and stress have notably changed. Importantly, although multiple events might be universally termed as stressful (e.g., the death of a significant person), the experience of stress is assumed to be dependent on the individual's appraisal of negative events. Likewise, the concept of vulnerability – initially focusing on heritable and biological factors – has been enriched by including psychological factors, such as cognitive and interpersonal variables [28]. As a consequence, the rigorous distinction between external (stressors) and internal (vulnerability) factors has been abandoned in support of an interactive perspective. That is, the diathesis is assumed to influence the way in which individuals deal with life events and thus with stressors to which they are exposed [29]. Empirical studies found a significant association between adverse life events encountered during development [30-31] as well as adulthood [32-34] and increased diathesis for depression. Major adverse life events related to depression seem to involve experiences of threat, loss, and humiliation [32, 35]. Therefore, changes in behavior that occur as a result of such experiences, i.e. learning to cope with negative events, may become central for the understanding of depression.

3. Associative learning and depression

About a century ago, Thorndike [36] proposed that learning reinforces the formation of connections or associations between stimuli and responses, whenever a response is followed by a positive outcome (law of effect). In parallel, Pavlov [37] found that repeated pairings of a neutral stimulus (e.g., a ringing bell) with an unconditioned stimulus (e.g., food pellets) qualify the neutral stimulus to trigger (almost) identical physiological reactions as the unconditioned stimulus. That is, the unconditioned reaction (in this case: salivation), which was initially only released by the unconditioned stimulus, came elicited by the neutral stimulus. In conditioning terminology: The neutral stimulus became a conditioned stimulus triggering a conditioned reaction (for reviews, see [38-39]). Consequently, Pavlovian condition is traditionally conceptualized as learning through "stimulus substitution". The influential Rescorla-Wagner model of conditioning, however, rejects the classical notion on how Pavlovian conditioning is working: "Pavlovian conditioning is not the shifting of a response from one stimulus to another. Instead, conditioning involves the learning of relations among events that are complexly represented, a learning that can be exhibited in various ways" [40]. Thus, modern Pavlovian thinking highlights the information that one stimulus gives about another and that organisms adjust their Pavlovian associations for their internal representation of the world. This implies that associative learning advances only to the extent to which a reinforcer is unpredicted (in terms of producing a prediction error) and slows progressively as the reinforcer becomes more predicted. Therefore, learning is assumed to be driven by changes in the expectations about salient events such as rewards and punishments [41].

Dysfunctional associative learning in terms of both instrumental (operant, Thorndikean) and respondent (Pavlovian) conditioning has been related to the development and maintenance of depression. Most remarkably, altered associative learning seems particularly linked to enhanced sensitivity for negative events and impaired responsiveness to positive stimuli in depression [42-43].

3.1. Altered aversive instrumental conditioning and learned helplessness in depression

Learning from the consequences of one's own behavior is central to instrumental conditioning. Against the background of cognitive theories proposing that depression is associated with negative attitudes and assumptions, depressed individuals are suggested to show increased sensitivity for negative outcomes and feedback. In addition to depressed mood, anhedonia is one of the core symptoms of depression and depict the loss of interest in originally rewarding or enjoyable activities. Thus, reduced responsiveness to positive outcomes should be evident in depression as well.

Numerous cognitive tasks have been applied to elucidate the neuropsychological profile of depression [10]. Some of these tasks provide direct information about performance accuracy and depressed individuals have been found to show biased responding to negative feedback in terms of a "catastrophic response to perceived failure" [44]: When depressed individuals make a mistake, their subsequent performance deteriorated considerably. In addition, depressed individuals showed such impairment when objected to false negative feedback in tasks known to be dependent on the integrity of the neural affective loop circuitry [45-46]. It has been concluded that failure feedback can exert its influence on cognitive performance by altering the attentive focus toward increased negative focussing on the self, and that this attentional shift might decrease the cognitive resources available for the task [45]. These findings suggest that depressed individuals are in particular vulnerable to negative feedback, what might constitute a major etiological factor for the disorder. However, the question why depressed individuals show altered responding to errors and negative feedback can not be answered by means of neuropsychological tests. To this end, experimental paradigms which manipulate psychological variables related to negative events are mandatory. This was done in paradigms investigating learned helplessness.

Incidentally found in animals [47-48], learned helplessness gives an explanation for the observation that exposure to inescapable aversive events leads to a subsequent deficit in escape or avoidance behavior. Mirroring instrumental learning theory, which proposes that subjects learn that their behavior controls reinforcement, learned helplessness proposes that subjects learn that their behavior cannot control reinforcement [49]. In contrast to animal research, however, few studies have used the original (triadic) experimental design to investigate learned helplessness in humans [50]. Moreover, most of these studies did not assess the neural correlates of learned helpless behaviors and they were often conducted in healthy individuals or analogue subjects rather than clinically depressed patients.

3.1.1. From learned helplessness to hopelessness depression

To evaluate learned helplessness findings in humans, it is important to bear in mind the methodological procedure of the original animal paradigm (cf. [51]). In the original protocol, animals were first subjected to aversive respondent conditioning, in which a light was repeatedly paired with electric footshocks, while the animals were restrained in a Pavlovian harness. Subsequently the majority of animals (but not all) failed to learn to escape or avoid footshocks in a shuttlebox. Further experimental variations found the light unnecessary for this effect, and evidenced the inescapable and unavoidable shocks as the causative agent. Groups exposed to unescapable and unavoidable shocks versus escapable and yoked inescapable shocks have been compared. To this end, shocks were applied at the same time (frequency) and for the same intensity in the animals that could escape and their yoked partners. The shocks terminated when the animals which had the possibility to escape made an instrumental response (i.e., hitting a panel). Importantly, hitting the panel had no consequences in the yoked animal group: Aversive shocks were inescapable, and only animals receiving yoked inescapable shocks showed a subsequent learning deficit. Thus, uncontrollability over the aversive shocks was proposed as key variable in producing later failure to learn and consequently termed as learned helplessness (for a critical discussion on the term learned helplessness versus interference, see [52]).

According to these experimental results, two fundamental components are essential for the investigation of learned helplessness: First, it is crucial to show that indeed uncontrollability over aversive events is the driving force of learned helplessness. This implies a comparison between conditions in which subjects were exposed to uncontrollable, relative to exactly equal controllable stressors. Second, in the original procedure, subjects received uncontrollable stressors in a different arrangement (Pavlovian harness) than the one which was used to test for learned helplessness effects (shuttlebox). Therefore, learned helplessness includes trans-situationality as part of the original definition [51]. Moreover, the fully established triadic design includes a control group, which is naïve to aversive stimulation. That is, both the escape and yoked group have identical aversive stimulation as compared to the naïve group, but uncontrollability over aversive electrical stimulation is only present in the yoked group. As a well replicated finding, the naïve group shows a comparable level of escape behavior as the escape group and thus learned helplessness effects can be attributed to the loss of control over aversive events in the yoked group (cf. [53]).

Possible consequences of stressor uncontrollability range from cognitive, motivational, and emotional alterations [54] to neuroendocrinological as well as functional and structural brain changes [55] that are in line with core features of depression. However, it is noteworthy that learned helplessness was initially not conceptualized to provide an animal model of depression or any other psychopathological condition [51]. Nevertheless, there is an obvious analogy to emotional, motivational, and cognitive complains of depressed individuals: Increased negative emotions, reduced motivation, and reduced cognitive abilities to establish adaptive behavior to cope with stressors. Thus, it is reasonable to assume that if individuals learn that their behavior cannot control aversive events, negative emotionality becomes persistent and the motivation to actively manipulate stressful situations decreases in line with reduced awareness for potentially changed contingencies between own behavioral responses and environmental events. In addition, based on the trans-situational nature of the learned helplessness paradigm, learned helpless behavior is assumed to generalize across contexts with also future events being expected as uncontrollable.

Experimental studies in healthy humans widely validated learned helplessness results from animal research. By translating the general experimental procedure into human laboratory protocols, several aversive stimuli have been employed, such as electric and heat shocks, loud noise, and challenging cognitive tasks. In such a way learned helplessness effects were demonstrated for reduced escape behavior to aversive stimuli and reduced performance on cognitive tasks in healthy humans (for a review, see [56]). However, studies which focussed on the generalization of learned helplessness did not always show unambiguous results [57]. Moreover, it remains an open question as to which extent these experimental findings can be transferred to real-life settings. In addition to the assumption that repeated exposure to uncontrollable aversive events might increase generalization of learned helpless behavior, it has been proposed that generalized learned helplessness is dependent on the strength of aversive outcomes. That is, generalized learned helplessness is more likely to occur when the outcome is highly aversive, or when a highly desired outcome is not reachable by the individual [56]. Uncontrollable adverse life events, such as loss and humiliation might have the potential to induce long-lasting learned helplessness effects. At least such life events have been found to predict depressive episodes [58]. However, independent of whether negative events are objectively controllable or not, the manner of how individuals attribute the causes of negative events seems essential. This cognitive aspect was addressed in the revised learned helplessness theory [56]. Based on social attribution theory [59], revised learned helplessness theory proposes that individuals attribute causes on several dimensions: internal/external, stable/unstable, and global/specific. Hence, highly internal, stable, and global attributions for negative outcomes would relate to low self-esteem and helplessness depression. Moreover, a subsequent reformulation – the hopelessness theory of depression – suggests that latent attributional diatheses combined with stressors produce a specific subtype of depression, i.e. hopelessness depression [8, 60]. This subtype of depression is characterized by dispositional negative expectations that desired outcomes will never occur and that one's own behavior is not effective for realizing desired outcomes (hopelessness).

Taken together, original learned helplessness theory proposed uncontrollability over aversive events, which in conditioning terminology depicts noncontingency between behavioral responses and reinforcement, as key variable for subsequent deficits in instrumental learning. The learned helplessness effect involves emotional, motivational, and cognitive characteristics obviously mirroring constituent parts of depressive symptomatology. Refined learned helplessness theory subsequently focussed on negative self-referential attributional style as a prerequisite for depressogenic behavior. Finally, the hopelessness theory of depression proposed a subtype of depression to be fundamentally related to habitual negative expectations about the self and outcomes (hopelessness). Thus, bringing the original assumptions of learned helplessness to clinical depression provoked a change in meaning for the causal importance of uncontrollability. In contrast to the original finding that uncontrollability over aversive events results in depression-like emotional, motivational, and cognitive alterations, the hopelessness theory of depression treats learned helplessness (caused by uncontrollability) not as a cause but as a necessary, however, not sufficient component of generalized hopelessness. Beside other critical issues, this conceptual development was mainly driven by the question whether or not learned helplessness does generalize across contexts in humans. Both revised learned helplessness and hopelessness theory suggest additional cognitive variables (causal attribution, negative inferential style) to be necessary for generalization.

Taking account of cognitive variables for the understanding of depression is beyond dispute. However, proposed effects of these variables have been obtained mainly by means of psychometric questionnaires which measure, e.g., inferential and response style [61] and hopelessness [62]. In addition to this approach and in the context of learned helplessness theory, it is desirable to have more direct data on cognitive mechanisms and related brain functioning when individuals are confronted with aversive events. Surprisingly few studies have addressed this topic.

3.1.2. Neural correlates of uncontrollability over aversive events in humans

Alterations in neural activation related to uncontrollability over aversive stimulation have been investigated by means of electroencephalography (EEG), functional magnetic resonance imaging (fMRI), and positron emission tomography (PET).

Seminal EEG studies [63-64] used a change from an escape to an uncontrollability paradigm in healthy individuals to assess variations in slow cortical potentials (SCP) and especially the post-imperative negative variation (PINV) related to controllability versus uncontrollability over aversive stimuli. In an S1-S2 reaction paradigm, participants received two different warning stimuli that signaled either a neutral tone or an aversive noise. Participants could avoid the aversive noise by a motor response in the first half of the experiment. Control was withdrawn in the second half of the experiment without prior warning and subjects unexpectedly could no longer avoid aversive stimulation. The main finding was an increase of the PINV over frontal recording sites during the uncontrollability condition independent of the amount of aversive stimulation per se. Subsequent studies confirmed increased PINV magnitudes to be sensitively related to unpredictable changes in response outcome contingencies [65] in support of the notion that the PINV reflects contingency reappraisal of formerly learned response outcome associations [64]. However, one major methodological aspect distinguishes paradigms for the investigation of the PINV as an electrophysiological index of altered information processing related to loss of control from paradigms used to investigate learned helplessness: Original PINV paradigms started with a condition in which subjects were able to control aversive stimulation followed by a condition of loss of control. This is exactly in reversed order as compared to learned helplessness studies. Against this background, a recent EEG study [66] expanded the traditional PINV paradigm. In this study, a modified forewarned (S1-S2) reaction paradigm was presented to three groups. The S1 always signaled subjects to prepare for the imperative stimulus (S2). In case of aversive stimulation, a short electrical shock was applied to the index finger of the non-dominant hand following S2. During blocks of control, correct button presses to the imperative stimulus avoided electrical stimulation. During uncontrollability, participants received electrical stimuli in randomized order in half of the trials irrespective of their behavioral responses (response outcome noncontingency). One group started with a waiting block followed by a block of uncontrollability and a final block of control. The authors called this group the learned helplessness group, since active conditions started with uncontrollability followed by controllability. The experience of uncontrollability was assumed to result in enhanced PINV magnitudes in the following condition of control. As a learned helplessness effect enhanced PINV magnitudes should reflect enhanced response outcome contingency processing (ambiguity) in a condition where aversive stimulation is objectively controllable. For validation, a second group was introduced, which also started with a waiting block, however, followed by two successive blocks of control. In contrast to the learned helplessness group, this group received constant control and was expected not to show PINV alterations during the final block of control. In addition, the study investigated a third group, which initially received a block of control, followed by a block of loss of control and a final block of restitution of control. This group was assumed to show immunization against learned helplessness, as human [67] and animal studies [68] found that initially experienced escapable shocks which were followed by inescapable shocks do diminish learned helplessness effects. Compared to the constant control group, the learned helplessness as well as the immunization group showed enhanced frontal PINV magnitudes during the second block (uncontrollability). This finding indicates that prior contingency learning (immunization group) does not affect the immediate impact of stressor uncontrollability. However, during the final block where all groups were able to control aversive electrical stimulation, only the learned helplessness group showed enhanced PINV magnitudes. These results are in line with the assumption that uncontrollability over aversive events alters subsequent instrumental learning when control is reestablished. Moreover, the experience of control prior to loss of control seems to protect against biased information processing during restitution of control.

These findings expand on previous results for SCP changes in healthy individuals during blocks of solvable (control) followed by blocks of unsolvable (loss of control) items of a reasoning task [69-70]. Low resolution electromagnetic tomography (LORETA; [71]) of these data found activation in Brodmann area (BA) 24 in the anterior cingulate cortex (ACC) significantly associated with the processing of uncontrollability. Source localization analysis of the PINV by means of sLORETA [72] also identified BA 24 in the anterior cingulate cortex as a core region for PINV generation [73] (see Figure 1). A recent review [74] of neuroimaging studies for this region suggest that negative affect, pain, and cognitive control is processed in this area, which is located in the anterior midcingulate cortex (aMCC). The aMCC is proposed to constitute a central relay or hub node which links information about reinforcers to motor centres responsible for expressing affect and executing aversively motivated instrumental behaviors. In the context of uncontrollability over aversive stimuli, a fMRI study also found increased activity in several brain regions (secondary somatosensory cortex and insula) including the ACC when a heat pain stimulus was perceived as uncontrollable [75]. Therefore the ACC and especially the aMCC might represent a cardinal region for the processing of instrumental contingencies related to (un)controllability over aversive events. However, a PET study [76] did not find alterations in ACC activity linked to the processing of solvable versus unsolvable items in a reasoning task. This study discovered increases in regional cerebral blood flow in the hippocampus and decreases in the mammillary bodies during solvable items. Subsequent unsolvable items were associated with decreases in hippocampal regions and increases in the mammillary bodies and the amygdalae. Therefore and in addition to the proposed key role of the aMCC, subcortical limbic areas in concert with other frontal, temporal and parietal areas seem to be engaged in resolving instrumental conflicts during uncontrollability over aversive stimulation [73].

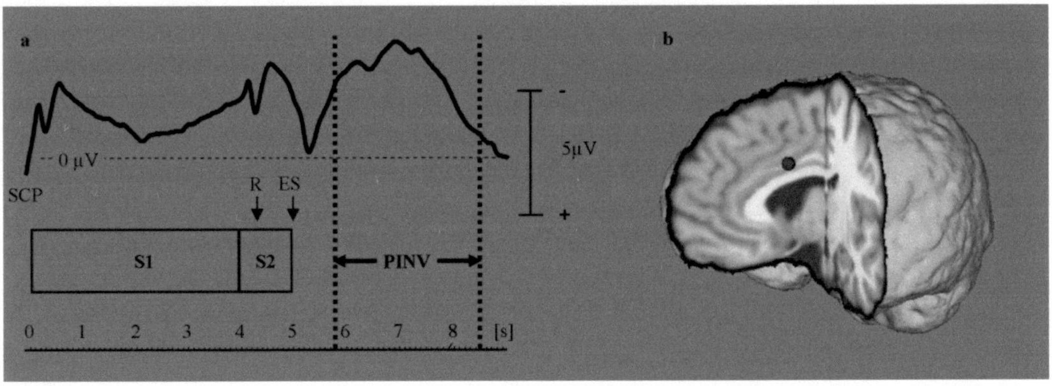

Figure 1. (a) Averaged slow cortical potential (SCP) showing the post-imperative negative variation (PINV) in the post-S2 interval during a S1 (warning stimulus) S2 (imperative stimulus) paradigm used in [66, 77-79], R: reaction (button press), ES: (potential) electrical stimulation; (b) Source localization analysis of the PINV showed BA 24 in the anterior midcingulate cortex as key region for PINV generation [73] (the centre of mass location (5,5,30) from [73] is shown as a red sphere on the standard Colin brain).

3.1.3. Neural correlates of uncontrollability over aversive events in depressed individuals

Neural correlates of altered instrumental learning related to learned helplessness in depressed individuals have been investigated solely by means of EEG studies which focussed on the PINV. In comparison to healthy individuals both anhedonic individuals [80] and depressed patients [81] have been found to show enhanced PINV magnitudes when aversive stimulation was uncontrollable or when control was restricted. These findings suggest that depression is associated with increased vulnerability to uncontrollable aversive events. By using the modified S1-S2 reaction paradigm, which includes successive conditions of control, loss of control, and restitution of control, it was demonstrated that depressed individuals show enhanced frontal PINV magnitudes during both loss of control and restitution of control [77]. Most remarkably and consistent with learned helplessness theory, the experience of uncontrollability seems to bias subsequent cortical processing in depressed individuals during a condition, where control over aversive stimulation is objectively reestablished. In addition, depressed individuals in this study showed enhanced ratings of helplessness in the restitution of control condition. Moreover, increased habitual symptom-focused and self-focused rumination were significantly linked to frontal PINV magnitudes during restitution of control in depressed individuals. For the first time, these results suggest a substantial relation between cognitive vulnerability markers of depression (rumination) and altered psychophysiological functioning during instrumental learning in depressed individuals. These results were confirmed in a follow-up study (T2) taking place six months after the initial assessment (T1) [79]. Alterations in PINV magnitudes were related to concurrent depression levels in patients, and when controlling for depression severity group differences in PINV magnitudes diminished. The authors concluded that PINV alterations wax and wane in parallel to the extent of depression severity. As frontal PINV magnitudes at T1 were not predictive for the amount of depressive symptoms or diagnostic status at T2 when baseline symptom levels were controlled, it was concluded that PINV alterations in depression represent a state rather than a trait marker of the disorder.

In summary, these findings clearly indicate that depressed subjects are especially vulnerable to perceived uncontrollability over aversive events and that it is reasonable to speculate that brain regions found in healthy subjects being related to the processing of uncontrollability show altered functioning in depression. Evidence converge that the aMCC is substantially involved in the processing of stressor uncontrollability and its consequences, highlighting this region as relevant for both learned helplessness effects and the state of helplessness in depression.

3.2. Appetitive (respondent and operant) conditioning in healthy and depressed individuals

Besides enhanced susceptibility to uncontrollable negative events, depression is typically characterized by marked anhedonia. Behavioral models emphasize that loss over environmental reinforcement is linked to reduced reward-related behavior in depression [82]. A deficient instrumental response to appetitive contingencies has also been proposed by animal models of depression [83]. In humans, anhedonia seems to be linked to dysfunctions in mesocorticolimbic dopaminergic projections from the ventral tegmental area to the dorsal and ventral striatum (including the nucleus accumbens), amygdala and hippocampus, anterior cingulate (including the subgenual portion), and ventral prefrontal cortex; circuits known to be related to the processing of reward [84-85]. In addition, the orbitofrontal cortex is involved in reward-related decision processes [86]. While functional abnormalities in these regions have been identified in depressed patients [87-90], few studies have examined specific deficits in reward processing in depression and underlying neural alterations.

In neuropsychological tests, depressed individuals show delayed responses to positive stimuli in affective signal detection tasks and a reduced positive attentional bias during facial expression identification [91-94]. In a fMRI study with medicated depressed patients, anhedonia was found to be linked to increased activation in the ventromedial prefrontal cortex and to reduced striatal activity in response to happy faces, suggesting that prefrontal activation might compensate for reduced striatal activation [95]. Healthy but not depressed individuals showed bilaterally increased activity in the fusiform gyrus and the right putamen to expressions of increasing happiness, while depressed individuals showed increased activity in the left putamen, left parahippocampal, right fusiform gyrus and amygdala to expressions of increasing sadness [96]. Another fMRI study used a dopaminergic probe to directly stimulate the human reward system [97]. Depressed individuals showed hypersensitive behavioral responses to the rewarding effects of d-amphetamine in line with altered brain activity in the ventrolateral prefrontal cortex, the orbitofrontal cortex, the caudate, and the putamen.

As noted above, modern theories of associative learning emphasize the fundamental role of predictions (and surprise) in both Pavlovian and instrumental conditioning [39, 86]. The prediction error denotes the discrepancy between a received reinforcer and its prediction. Learning is proportional to the prediction error and reaches its asymptote when the prediction error approaches zero after several learning trials. In humans, a number of fMRI studies (cf. [98]) have investigated reward-prediction. By means of probabilistic tasks in which individuals learn to make a choice that gives monetary gains or avoids losses, it has been found that short-term reward prediction is positively correlated with activation in the caudate and ventral striatum and the lateral orbito-frontal cortex, while longer-term reward prediction is positively correlated with activation in the dorsolateral prefrontal cortex and the inferior parietal cortex. The ACC was found to be involved in monetary gambles with high versus low monetary risk. However, gain versus loss outcomes seem to activate medial frontal areas and the ventral striatum including the nucleus accumbens. A fMRI study in healthy individuals [99] found the nucleus accumbens proportionally activated to the magnitude of anticipated gains, whereas the medial prefrontal cortex showed activation changes in relation to the probability of anticipated gains. Similarly, activation of striatal regions has been found to reflect differences in magnitude and probability of reward and also medial prefrontal cortex activation seem to vary with the probability of reward [100]. In addition, it was shown that activation in the caudate and ventral striatum is positively correlated with behavioral indices of reward learning and that the caudate displays increased activation in early stages of learning. Moreover, it was shown that activation in the ventral striatum is positively correlated with prediction error signals during both Pavlovian and instrumental conditioning [101]. Furthermore, the ventral striatum was found to respond to a conditioned stimulus which predicts reward delivery and seems to be characterized by a strong outcome-related response when reward is delivered unexpectedly or a decrease in activity when an expected reward is omitted. In addition, linear increases of activation were observed in the nucleus accumbens with increasing reward probabilities [102].

Yacubian and colleagues [103] were the first to use a gambling task with different gain and loss magnitudes and probabilities. Only gain-related predictions and associated prediction errors were found to be expressed in the ventral striatum, while loss-related predictions and related prediction errors were localized in the amygdala. Therefore, the authors proposed two dissociable value systems for gains and losses and suggested that the ventral striatum generates value predictions to which actual outcomes were compared, while the amygdala predicts possible losses and compares these predictions against actual outcomes.

Recent studies in depression research used variations of the monetary incentive delay paradigm to investigate neural similarities and disparities between the anticipation and receipt of reward and punishment [24, 104]. In this paradigm, trials start with the presentation of a cue which indicates a potential outcome (win/loss) followed by an imperative stimulus to which subjects have to respond with a button press. After the motor response subjects receive feedback about their actual outcome (win/loss). This protocol allows differentiating between anticipatory neural responses (in the time interval between the presentation of the cue and the imperative stimulus) and neural responses related to the presentation of the outcome (win/loss feedback). During anticipation motivational processes (wanting) are assumed to be linked to outcome-predicting cues, whereas during the outcome phase emotional responses (liking) may dominate neural responsivity, in turn providing reinforcers to foster learning about the relationship between cues and outcomes. Depressed individuals have been found to show reduced activity in fronto-striatal regions during both reward anticipation [105-106] and outcome [24, 104], suggesting that dysfunctional incentive processing in MDD is particularly linked to functional alterations in fronto-striatal regions. However, neuroimaging studies have also found intact responsivity in the ventral striatum including the nucleus accumbens [24] and enhanced anterior cingulate cortex activity [104] during reward anticipation. In addition, increased frontal activity but reduced activity in the caudate was found during the anticipation and receipt of reward in medication-free depressed adolescents [107]. Euthymic patients were found not to show fronto-striatal hypoactivity during the anticipation and receipt of reward [108]. Moreover, only few studies have investigated reward-related prediction error signaling in depression. Their results are equivocal with studies showing enhanced activity in prefrontal, striatal and ventral tegmental areas coding reward-associated prediction errors [109-111] but also reduced prediction error signaling over time in the ventral striatum and the dorsal ACC in depressed individuals [110].

Therefore and although reduced reward processing in depression seem substantially associated with anhedonia, the neural signature of reduced reward responsiveness in MDD is still a puzzling topic. Direct and indirect evidence point to fronto-striatal regions to be substantially involved during both the expectation and receipt of positive outcomes. However, further studies are clearly needed to validate these findings. Despite differences in sample characteristics, future studies may additionally focus on the interaction of brain regions involved in altered reward processing in MDD to further elucidate the current heterogeneity of findings.

4. Conclusions

In summary, recent neuroimaging results clearly demonstrate (a) increased sensitivity of depressed individuals to loss of control during instrumental conditioning, subsequently (b) causing biased information processing of actually controllable aversive events. This dysfunctional learning mechanism, which is (c) linked to negative self-referential cognition (rumination), represents (d) a valid state marker of the disorder. Brain regions of interest for altered instrumental learning in MDD seem to include (e) the anterior cingulate (in particular the aMCC), prefrontal regions, and limbic structures (amygdala, hippocampus). From a respondent perspective, alterations in associative learning mechanisms were evident (f) already during the anticipation of positive (rewarding) outcomes, most probably associated (g) with reduced prefrontal, striatal, and limbic activation for positive outcomes and (h) altered prediction error signaling in the ventral striatum and the ACC. However and as mentioned above, the latter findings need further validation in future neuroimaging studies.

Cognitive models of depression substantially benefit from current findings on altered associative learning mechanisms in MDD. Clinical interventions based on cognitive models such as cognitive behavioral therapy emphasize cognitive restructuring and behavioral activation for the treatment of depression. Increasing knowledge about the psychophysiological correlates of altered associative learning in MDD may result in focussing on interventions helping individuals suffering from MDD to experience controllability and hedonia. Future pre/post treatment studies should make use of neuroimaging methods to demonstrate treatment-specific effects of such tailored interventions on the neurobiological level. Moreover, recent approaches with neurofeedback showed the feasibility of brain self-regulation to upregulate brain areas involved in the generation of positive emotions in depressed patients [112]. Neurofeedback as a holistic approach that overcomes bio-psychological dualisms has fascinating advantages especially in the case of depression: By the use of operant learning mechanisms patients experience successful self-regulation of their own brain activity.

Author details

Carsten Diener

Department of Cognitive and Clinical Neuroscience, Central Institute of Mental Health, Medical Faculty Mannheim, University of Heidelberg, Mannheim, Germany

Acknowledgement

This work was supported by the Deutsche Forschungsgemeinschaft (SFB 636/D4). The author gratefully acknowledges the contribution of Christine Kuehner, Bettina Ubl, and Herta Flor and the valuable assistance of Veronika Thomas for the preparation of this chapter.

5. References

[1] Richards D. Prevalence and clinical course of depression: a review. Clin Psychol Rev 2011;31(7) 1117-25.

[2] Ustun TB, Ayuso-Mateos JL, Chatterji S, Mathers C, Murray CJ. Global burden of depressive disorders in the year 2000. Br J Psychiatry 2004;184 386-92.

[3] Keller MB, Boland RJ. Implications of failing to achieve successful long-term maintenance treatment of recurrent unipolar major depression. Biol Psychiatry 1998;44(5) 348-60.

[4] Angst J. Major depression in 1998: are we providing optimal therapy? J Clin Psychiatry 1999;60(Suppl 6) 5-9.

[5] Harald B, Gordon P. Meta-review of depressive subtyping models. J Affect Disord 2012;139(2) 126-40.

[6] American Psychiatric Association. Diagnostic and Statistical Manual of Mental Disorders. 4 ed. Washington DC: Author; 1994.

[7] World Health Organisation. International Statistical Classification of Diseases and Health Related Problems. Geneva: Author; 2004.

[8] Abramson LY, Alloy LB, Hankin BL, Haeffel GJ, MacCoon DG, Gibb BE. Cognitive vulnerability-stress models of depression in a self-regulatory and psychobiological context. In: Gotlib IH, Hammen CL. (eds.) Handbook of depression. New York: Guilford Press; 2002. p.268-94.

[9] Alloy LB, Abramson LY, Hogan ME, Whitehouse WG, Rose DT, Robinson MS, et al. The Temple-Wisconsin Cognitive Vulnerability to Depression Project: lifetime history of axis I psychopathology in individuals at high and low cognitive risk for depression. J Abnorm Psychol 2000;109(3) 403-18.

[10] Elliott R. The neuropsychological profile in unipolar depression. Trends Cogn Sci 1998;2(11) 447-54.

[11] Nolen-Hoeksema S. The role of rumination in depressive disorders and mixed anxiety/depressive symptoms. J Abnorm Psychol 2000;109(3) 504-11.

[12] Nolen-Hoeksema S, Parker LE, Larson J. Ruminative coping with depressed mood following loss. J Pers Soc Psychol 1994;67(1) 92-104.

[13] Nolen-Hoeksema S, Larson J, Grayson C. Explaining the gender difference in depressive symptoms. J Pers Soc Psychol 1999;77(5) 1061-72.

[14] Kuehner C, Weber I. Responses to depression in unipolar depressed patients: an investigation of Nolen-Hoeksema's response styles theory. Psychol Med 1999;29(6) 1323-33.
[15] Lyubomirsky S, Tucker KL, Caldwell ND, Berg K. Why ruminators are poor problem solvers: clues from the phenomenology of dysphoric rumination. J Pers Soc Psychol 1999;77(5) 1041-60.
[16] Roberts JE, Gilboa E, Gotlib IH. Ruminative response style and vulnerability to episodes of dysphoria: Gender, neuroticism, and episode duration. Cognitive Ther Res 1998;22(4) 401-23.
[17] Kuehner C, Huffziger S. Response styles to depressed mood affect the long-term course of psychosocial functioning in depressed patients. J Affect Disord 2012;136(3) 627-33.
[18] Clark DA, Beck AT., editors. Scientific Foundations of Cognitive Theory and Therapy of Depression. New York: John Wiley & Sons; 1999.
[19] Henn FA, Vollmayr B. Stress models of depression: forming genetically vulnerable strains. Neurosci Biobehav Rev 2005;29(4-5) 799-804.
[20] Vollmayr B, Mahlstedt MM, Henn FA. Neurogenesis and depression: what animal models tell us about the link. Eur Arch Psychiatry Clin Neurosci 2007;257(5)300-3.
[21] Holsboer F. The corticosteroid receptor hypothesis of depression. Neuropsychopharmacology 2000;23(5) 477-501.
[22] Price JL, Drevets WC. Neurocircuitry of mood disorders. Neuropsychopharmacology 2010;35(1) 192-216.
[23] Krishnan V, Nestler EJ. The molecular neurobiology of depression. Nature 2008;455(7215) 894-902.
[24] Pizzagalli DA, Holmes AJ, Dillon DG, Goetz EL, Birk JL, Bogdan R, et al. Reduced caudate and nucleus accumbens response to rewards in unmedicated individuals with major depressive disorder. Am J Psychiatry 2009;166(6) 702-10.
[25] Diener C, Kuehner C, Brusniak W, Ubl B, Wessa M, Flor H. A meta-analysis of neurofunctional imaging studies of emotion and cognition in major depression. Neuroimage 2012;61(3) 677-85.
[26] Lemogne C, le Bastard G, Mayberg H, Volle E, Bergouignan L, Lehericy S, et al. In search of the depressive self: extended medial prefrontal network during self-referential processing in major depression. Soc Cogn Affect Neurosci 2009;4(3) 305-12.
[27] Drevets WC, Price JL, Furey ML. Brain structural and functional abnormalities in mood disorders: implications for neurocircuitry models of depression. Brain Struct Funct 2008;213(1-2) 93-118.
[28] Monroe SM, Simons AD. Diathesis-stress theories in the context of life stress research: implications for the depressive disorders. Psychol Bull 1991;110(3) 406-25.
[29] Ingram RE, Luxton DD. Vulnerability-Stress Models. In: Hankin BL, Abela JRZ. (eds.) Development of psychopathology: A vulnerability-stress perspective. Thousand Oaks: Sage Publications, Inc.; 2005. p.32-46.

[30] Green JG, McLaughlin KA, Berglund PA, Gruber MJ, Sampson NA, Zaslavsky AM, et al. Childhood adversities and adult psychiatric disorders in the national comorbidity survey replication I: associations with first onset of DSM-IV disorders. Arch Gen Psychiatry 2010;67(2) 113-23.
[31] Kessler RC, McLaughlin KA, Green JG, Gruber MJ, Sampson NA, Zaslavsky AM, et al. Childhood adversities and adult psychopathology in the WHO World Mental Health Surveys. Br J Psychiatry 2010;197(5) 378-85.
[32] Brown GW, Harris TO, Hepworth C. Loss, humiliation and entrapment among women developing depression: a patient and non-patient comparison. Psychol Med 1995;25(1) 7-21.
[33] Kendler KS, Gardner CO. Dependent stressful life events and prior depressive episodes in the prediction of major depression: the problem of causal inference in psychiatric epidemiology. Arch Gen Psychiatry 2010;67(11) 1120-7.
[34] Kendler KS, Gardner CO, Prescott CA. Toward a comprehensive developmental model for major depression in women. Am J Psychiatry 2002;159(7) 1133-45.
[35] Monroe SM, Reid MW. Gene-environment interactions in depression research: genetic polymorphisms and life-stress polyprocedures. Psychol Sci 2008;19(10) 947-56.
[36] Thorndike EL. Animal intelligence: Experimental studies. New York: MacMillan; 1911.
[37] Pavlov IP. Conditioned reflexes.An investigation of the physiological activity of the cerebral cortex. London: Oxford University Press; 1927.
[38] Wasserman EA, Miller RR. What's elementary about associative learning? Annu Rev Psychol 1997;48 573-607.
[39] Pearce JM, Bouton ME. Theories of associative learning in animals. Annu Rev Psychol 2001;52 111-39.
[40] Rescorla RA. Pavlovian conditioning. It's not what you think it is. Am Psychol 1988;43(3) 151-60.
[41] Schultz W, Dayan P, Montague PR. A neural substrate of prediction and reward. Science;275(5306) 1593-9.
[42] Martin-Soelch C, Linthicum J, Ernst M. Appetitive conditioning: neural bases and implications for psychopathology. Neurosci Biobehav Rev 2007;31(3) 426-40.
[43] Chase HW, Frank MJ, Michael A, Bullmore ET, Sahakian BJ, Robbins TW. Approach and avoidance learning in patients with major depression and healthy controls: relation to anhedonia. Psychol Med 2010;40(3) 433-40.
[44] Beats BC, Sahakian BJ, Levy R. Cognitive performance in tests sensitive to frontal lobe dysfunction in the elderly depressed. Psychol Med 1996;26(3) 591-603.
[45] Murphy FC, Michael A, Robbins TW, Sahakian BJ. Neuropsychological impairment in patients with major depressive disorder: the effects of feedback on task performance. Psychol Med 2003;33(3) 455-67.
[46] Evers EA, Cools R, Clark L, van der Veen FM, Jolles J, Sahakian BJ, et al. Serotonergic modulation of prefrontal cortex during negative feedback in probabilistic reversal learning. Neuropsychopharmacology 2005;30(6) 1138-47.

[47] Solomon RL, Turner LH. Discriminative classical conditioning under curare can later control discriminative avoidance responses in normal state. Science 1960;132 1499-500.
[48] Overmier JB, Leaf RC. Effects of discriminative Pavlovian fear conditioning upon previously or subsequently acquired avoidance responding. J Comp Physiol Psychol 1965;60(2) 213-7.
[49] Seligman MEP, Maier SF, Solomon RL. Unpredictable and uncontrollable aversive events. In: Brush FR. (ed.) Aversive Conditioning and Learning. New York: Academic Press; 1971. p.347–400.
[50] Pryce CR, Seifritz E. A translational research framework for enhanced validity of mouse models of psychopathological states in depression. Psychoneuroendocrinology 2011;36(3) 308-29.
[51] Maier SF, Watkins LR. Stressor controllability and learned helplessness: the roles of the dorsal raphe nucleus, serotonin, and corticotropin-releasing factor. Neurosci Biobehav Rev 2005;29(4-5) 829-41.
[52] Anisman H, Merali Z. Rodent models of depression: learned helplessness induced in mice. Curr Protoc Neurosci 2001;Chapter 8:Unit 8.10C.
[53] Pryce CR, Azzinnari D, Spinelli S, Seifritz E, Tegethoff M, Meinlschmidt G. Helplessness: a systematic translational review of theory and evidence for its relevance to understanding and treating depression. Pharmacol Ther 2011;132(3) 242-67.
[54] Maier SF, Seligman, MEP. Learned helplessness: theory and evidence. Journal of Experimental Psychology: General 1976;105(1) 3-46.
[55] Breier A, Albus M, Pickar D, Zahn TP, Wolkowitz OM, Paul SM. Controllable and uncontrollable stress in humans: alterations in mood and neuroendocrine and psychophysiological function. Am J Psychiatry 1987;144(11) 1419-25.
[56] Abramson LY, Seligman ME, Teasdale JD. Learned helplessness in humans: critique and reformulation. J Abnorm Psychol 1978;87(1) 49-74.
[57] Miller IW, Norman WH. Learned helplessness in humans: a review and attribution theory model. Psychological Bulletin 1979;86 93-118.
[58] Kendler KS, Hettema JM, Butera F, Gardner CO, Prescott CA. Life event dimensions of loss, humiliation, entrapment, and danger in the prediction of onsets of major depression and generalized anxiety. Arch Gen Psychiatry 2003;60(8) 789-96.
[59] Heider F. The Psychology of Interpersonal Relations. New York: Wiley; 1958.
[60] Spangler DL, Simons AD, Monroe SM, Thase ME. Evaluating the hopelessness model of depression: diathesis-stress and symptom components. J Abnorm Psychol 1993;102(4) 592-600.
[61] Nolen-Hoeksema S. The response styles theory. In: Papageorgiou C, Wells A. (eds.) Depressive rumination: nature, theory, and treatment of negative thinking in depression. New York: Wiley; 2004. p.107-23.
[62] Beck AT, Steer RA. Manual for the Beck Hopelessness Scale. San Antonio, Texas: Psychological Corporation; 1988.

[63] Rockstroh B, Elbert T, Lutzenberger W, Birbaumer N. Slow cortical potentials under conditions of uncontrollability. Psychophysiology 1979;16(4) 374-80.

[64] Elbert T, Rockstroh B, Lutzenberger W, Birbaumer N. Slow brain potentials after withdrawal of control. Arch Psychiatr Nervenkr 1982;232(3) 201-14.

[65] Kathmann N, Jonitz L, Engel RR. Cognitive determinants of the postimperative negative variation. Psychophysiology 1990;27(3) 256-63.

[66] Diener C, Struve M, Balz N, Kuehner C, Flor H. Exposure to uncontrollable stress and the postimperative negative variation (PINV): prior control matters. Biol Psychol 2009;80(2) 189-95.

[67] Seligman MEP, Maier SF. Failure to escape traumatic shock. J Exp Psychol 1967;74(1) 1-9.

[68] Dyck DG, Breen LJ. Learned helplessness, immunization and importance of task in humans. Psychological Reports 1978;43 315-21.

[69] Fretska E, Bauer H, Leodolter M, Leodolter U. Loss of control and negative emotions: a cortical slow potential topography study. Int J Psychophysiol 1999;33(2) 127-41.

[70] Bauer H, Pripfl J, Lamm C, Prainsack C, Taylor N. Functional neuroanatomy of learned helplessness. Neuroimage 2003;20(2) 927-39.

[71] Pascual-Marqui RD, Michel CM, Lehmann D. Low resolution electromagnetic tomography: a new method for localizing electrical activity in the brain. Int J Psychophysiol 1994;18(1) 49-65.

[72] Pascual-Marqui RD. Standardized low-resolution brain electromagnetic tomography (sLORETA): technical details. Methods Find Exp Clin Pharmacol 2002;24D 5-12.

[73] Diener C, Kuehner C, Flor H. Loss of control during instrumental learning: a source localization study. Neuroimage 2010;50(2) 717-26.

[74] Shackman AJ, Salomons TV, Slagter HA, Fox AS, Winter JJ, Davidson RJ. The integration of negative affect, pain and cognitive control in the cingulate cortex. Nat Rev Neurosci 2011;12(3) 154-67.

[75] Salomons TV, Johnstone T, Backonja MM, Davidson RJ. Perceived controllability modulates the neural response to pain. J Neurosci 2004;24(32) 7199-203.

[76] Schneider F, Gur RE, Alavi A, Seligman ME, Mozley LH, Smith RJ, et al. Cerebral blood flow changes in limbic regions induced by unsolvable anagram tasks. Am J Psychiatry 1996;153(2) 206-12.

[77] Diener C, Kuehner C, Brusniak W, Struve M, Flor H. Effects of stressor controllability on psychophysiological, cognitive and behavioural responses in patients with major depression and dysthymia. Psychol Med 2009;39(1) 77-86.

[78] Diener C, Kuehner C, Flor H. Loss of control during instrumental learning: a source localization study. Neuroimage 2010;50(2) 717-26.

[79] Kuehner C, Diener C, Ubl B, Flor H. Reproducibility and predictive value of the post-imperative negative variation during aversive instrumental learning in depression. Psychol Med 2011;41(4) 890-2.

[80] Lutzenberger W, Elbert T, Rockstroh B, Birbaumer N, Stegagno L. Slow cortical potentials in subjects with high or low scores on questionnaire measuring physical anhedonia and body image distortion. Psychophysiology 1981;18(4) 371-80.

[81] Bolz J, Giedke H. Controllability of an aversive stimulus in depressed patients and health controls: a study using slow brain potentials. Bioligical Psychiatry 1981;16(5) 441-52.

[82] Lewinsohn PM. A behavioral approach to depression. In: Friedman RJ, Katz MM. (eds.) The psychology of depression: contemporary theory and research. Washington, D.C.: Winston-Wiley; 1974. p.157-78.

[83] Anisman H, Matheson K. Stress, depression, and anhedonia: caveats concerning animal models. Neurosci Biobehav Rev 2005;29(4-5) 525-46.

[84] Bressan RA, Crippa JA. The role of dopamine in reward and pleasure behaviour - review of data from preclinical research. Acta Psychiatr Scand Suppl 2005(427) 14-21.

[85] Nestler EJ, Carlezon WA, Jr. The mesolimbic dopamine reward circuit in depression. Biol Psychiatry 2006;59(12) 1151-9.

[86] Schultz W. Behavioral theories and the neurophysiology of reward. Annu Rev Psychol 2006;57 87-115.

[87] Drevets WC. Neuroimaging and neuropathological studies of depression: implications for the cognitive-emotional features of mood disorders. Curr Opin Neurobiol 2001;11(2) 240-9.

[88] Mayberg HS. Positron emission tomography imaging in depression: a neural systems perspective. Neuroimaging Clin N Am 2003;13(4) 805-15.

[89] Hasler G, Drevets WC, Manji HK, Charney DS. Discovering endophenotypes for major depression. Neuropsychopharmacology 2004;29(10) 1765-81.

[90] Must A, Szabo Z, Bodi N, Szasz A, Janka Z, Keri S. Sensitivity to reward and punishment and the prefrontal cortex in major depression. J Affect Disord 2006;90(2-3) 209-15.

[91] Erickson K, Drevets WC, Clark L, Cannon DM, Bain EE, Zarate CA, Jr., et al. Mood-congruent bias in affective go/no-go performance of unmedicated patients with major depressive disorder. Am J Psychiatry 2005;162(11) 2171-3.

[92] Joormann J, Gotlib IH. Selective attention to emotional faces following recovery from depression. J Abnorm Psychol 2007;116(1) 80-5.

[93] Phillips ML, Drevets WC, Rauch SL, Lane R. Neurobiology of emotion perception II: Implications for major psychiatric disorders. Biol Psychiatry 2003;54(5) 515-28.

[94] Pizzagalli DA, Jahn AL, O'Shea JP. Toward an objective characterization of an anhedonic phenotype: a signal-detection approach. Biol Psychiatry 2005;57(4) 319-27.

[95] Keedwell PA, Andrew C, Williams SC, Brammer MJ, Phillips ML. A double dissociation of ventromedial prefrontal cortical responses to sad and happy stimuli in depressed and healthy individuals. Biol Psychiatry 2005;58(6) 495-503.

[96] Surguladze S, Brammer MJ, Keedwell P, Giampietro V, Young AW, Travis MJ, et al. A differential pattern of neural response toward sad versus happy facial expressions in major depressive disorder. Biol Psychiatry 2005;57(3) 201-9.

[97] Tremblay LK, Naranjo CA, Graham SJ, Herrmann N, Mayberg HS, Hevenor S, et al. Functional neuroanatomical substrates of altered reward processing in major depressive disorder revealed by a dopaminergic probe. Arch Gen Psychiatry 2005;62(11) 1228-36.

[98] Knutson B, Cooper JC. Functional magnetic resonance imaging of reward prediction. Curr Opin Neurol 2005;18(4) 411-7.

[99] Knutson B, Taylor J, Kaufman M, Peterson R, Glover G. Distributed neural representation of expected value. J Neurosci 2005;25(19) 4806-12.

[100] Tobler PN, O'Doherty JP, Dolan RJ, Schultz W. Reward value coding distinct from risk attitude-related uncertainty coding in human reward systems. J Neurophysiol 2007;97(2) 1621-32.

[101] O'Doherty J, Dayan P, Schultz J, Deichmann R, Friston K, Dolan RJ. Dissociable roles of ventral and dorsal striatum in instrumental conditioning. Science 2004;304(5669) 452-4.

[102] Abler B, Walter H, Erk S, Kammerer H, Spitzer M. Prediction error as a linear function of reward probability is coded in human nucleus accumbens. Neuroimage 2006;31(2) 790-5.

[103] Yacubian J, Glascher J, Schroeder K, Sommer T, Braus DF, Buchel C. Dissociable systems for gain- and loss-related value predictions and errors of prediction in the human brain. J Neurosci 2006;26(37) 9530-7.

[104] Knutson B, Bhanji JP, Cooney RE, Atlas LY, Gotlib IH. Neural responses to monetary incentives in major depression. Biol Psychiatry 2008;63(7) 686-92.

[105] Smoski MJ, Felder J, Bizzell J, Green SR, Ernst M, Lynch TR, et al. fMRI of alterations in reward selection, anticipation, and feedback in major depressive disorder. J Affect Disord 2009;118(1-3) 69-78.

[106] Stoy M, Schlagenhauf F, Sterzer P, Bermpohl F, Hagele C, Suchotzki K, et al. Hyporeactivity of ventral striatum towards incentive stimuli in unmedicated depressed patients normalizes after treatment with escitalopram. J Psychopharmacol 2012;26(5) 677-88.

[107] Forbes EE, Phillips ML, Silk JS, Ryan ND, Dahl RE. Neural systems of threat processing in adolescents: role of pubertal maturation and relation to measures of negative affect. Dev Neuropsychol 2011;36(4) 429-52.

[108] Dichter GS, Kozink RV, McClernon FJ, Smoski MJ. Remitted major depression is characterized by reward network hyperactivation during reward anticipation and hypoactivation during reward outcomes. J Affect Disord 2012;136(3) 1126–1134

[109] Steele JD, Meyer M, Ebmeier KP. Neural predictive error signal correlates with depressive illness severity in a game paradigm. Neuroimage 2004;23(1) 269-80.

[110] Kumar P, Waiter G, Ahearn T, Milders M, Reid I, Steele JD. Abnormal temporal difference reward-learning signals in major depression. Brain 2008;131(8) 2084-93.

[111] Gradin VB, Kumar P, Waiter G, Ahearn T, Stickle C, Milders M, et al. Expected value and prediction error abnormalities in depression and schizophrenia. Brain 2011;134(6) 1751-64.

[112] Linden DE, Habes I, Johnston SJ, Linden S, Tatineni R, Subramanian L, et al. Real-time self-regulation of emotion networks in patients with depression. PLoS One 2012;7(6) e38115.

Chapter 5

Emotional and Motivational Processes in Bipolar Disorder: A Neural Network Perspective

Michèle Wessa and Julia Linke

Additional information is available at the end of the chapter

http://dx.doi.org/10.5772/51890

1. Introduction

Recurrent prominent mood swings are the most obvious characteristic of bipolar disorder. Thus it is not surprising that models of bipolar disorder emphasize the importance of disturbed emotion processing for the pathogenesis of this disorder. More precisely, models of bipolar disorder focus on abnormal unconscious and conscious evaluation of events (appraisal) relevant to the elicitation and regulation of emotions [1]. The close link between emotion and motivation has received less attention but appears equally important in bipolar disorder as evaluation of stimuli as appetitive (reward) or aversive (punishment) facilitates either approach or avoidance motivation and behavior [2]. Abnormal approach and avoidance behavior is observed in bipolar disorder patients in the manic and depressive states. During mania, patients seek rewarding outcomes more intensively despite potential negative consequences leading to such symptoms as an increase in goal-directed activity (at work, at school, or sexually) and excessive involvement in pleasurable activities. On the contrary, during depression, patients anticipate punishment rather than reward explaining why they show markedly diminished interest in almost all activities.

Despite these theoretical and clinical considerations, brain research in bipolar disorder has mainly focused on automatic emotional responses through the application of paradigms that use emotionally evocative stimuli like faces and words to elicit emotion during passive viewing, action choices, and facilitation or inhibition of responses. Most studies assess the activity of relevant brain regions using functional magnetic resonance imaging (fMRI) [3, 4], a technique that takes advantage of the different magnetic properties of oxygenated and deoxygenated blood. Measurement of this blood-oxygenated-level-dependent (BOLD) contrast reflects hemodynamic metabolic changes associated with neural activation, offering an indirect and complex representation of underlying neural processes [5, 6].

Based on the results of these studies, an imbalance between the activity of 'core emotional' brain regions and brain areas associated with both emotion and cognition has been proposed to underlie bipolar symptoms. Ventrally located 'core emotional' brain regions like the amygdala, the striatum, the orbitofrontal cortex, the subgenual and ventral anterior cingulate cortex, and the ventromedial prefrontal cortex are thought to be hyper-active in bipolar disorder, whereas regions belonging to the extended emotional and cognitive control network like the hippocampus, the anterior insula, the dorsal prefrontal cortex, and the posterior cingulate cortex are assumed to be hypo-active [7, 8]. Although the simplicity of this model is rather intriguing, one has to consider that each of these regions is itself a complex area that is connected to other regions forming different networks involved in numerous not exclusively emotional processes. In other words, each of these regions that showed abnormal activity in response to emotionally relevant stimuli in bipolar disorder patients is involved in multiple cognitive and emotional processes like emotion elicitation, emotion regulation, and motivation, which are carried out by several of these regions [9].

In the present chapter, we will review imaging literature examining both emotional and motivational processes as they are tightly linked psychological processes that represent two sides of the same coin. Whereas the focus on emotion implies a certain state of feeling, emphasis of motivation relates to a certain state of goal, pursuit like the achievement of pleasant feelings and the avoidance of unpleasant feelings. Imaging literature examining emotional processes in bipolar disorder will be reviewed, focusing on different stages of emotion processing (early emotional processes, elicitation of an emotional response, emotion regulation). Review of motivational processes will center on anticipation of positive and negative consequences and the delivery of these consequences. We will discuss volumetric alterations in relevant brain areas and we will also describe findings, which examine structural connectivity between these regions. Next we will address the question whether functional and structural abnormalities related to disturbed emotion and motivation processing in bipolar disorder are more likely to evolve during the course of the disease or rather constitute a vulnerability factor for bipolar disorder. We will also discuss current knowledge about the effects of mood states and psychotropic medication on emotional and motivational processes in bipolar disorder.

2. Emotional processes

Various theoretical accounts agree that emotion processing includes different mechanisms that vary with respect to the involvement of attentional and cognitive resources. In more detail, these mechanisms comprise a pre-attentive stage, attention allocation, sensory perception, transient and automatic emotional responses, experience and expression of emotion, higher-level appraisal of emotional stimuli, and finally the regulation of emotions [10]. From an experimental and clinical neuroscience perspective, it is important to make a distinction between these sub-processes in order to be able to validly characterize disturbed or maladaptive processes into psychopathologies. In this chapter, we will roughly divide these mechanisms into (1) early emotional processing, (2) emotional responses including transient, automatic responses and the subjective emotional experience, and (3) expression of emotion and emotion regulation (see Figure 1).

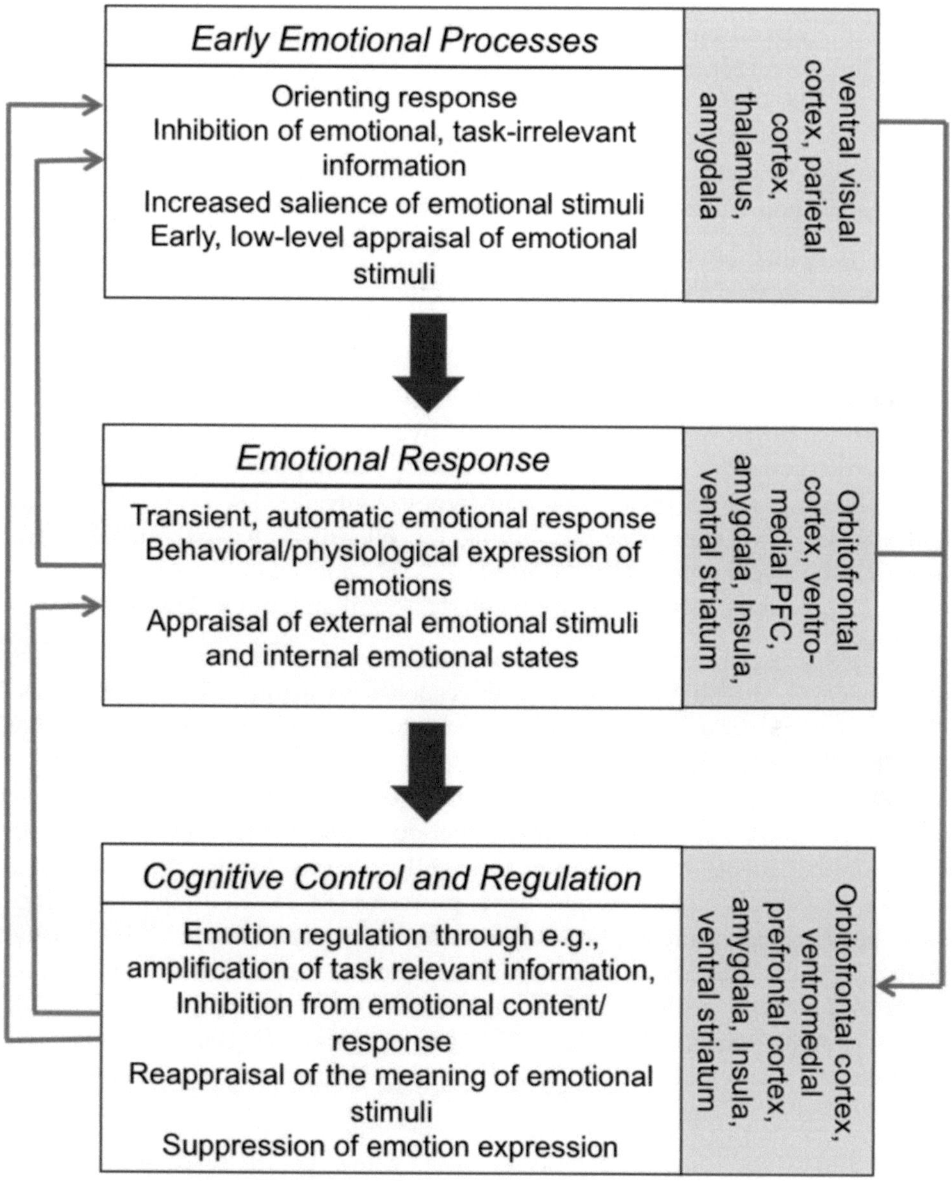

Figure 1. Schematic outline of the steps involved in emotional processing

2.1. Early emotional processes

Early emotional processes refer to the attribution of salience to motivationally relevant stimuli and the allocation of attentional resources to these stimuli. These processes are known to rely on the amygdala, thalamus, prefrontal cortex, parietal cortex, and visual processing areas [9, 11, 12]. In bipolar disorder, the identification of disturbances in neural networks during these early stages of emotional processing is complicated by general attention deficits. Applying the Stroop color-word selective attention task, blunted activation in the ventral prefrontal cortex [13-16], anterior cingulate cortex [17], and parietal cortex [15] has been reported for bipolar disorder patients compared to healthy controls. Reduced activation in the anterior cingulate cortex and the parietal cortex has also been reported during high attentional control during a n-back task [18]. Furthermore, manic bipolar disorder patients displayed stable amygdala hyper-activation and striatal and thalamic deactivation during sustained attention compared to healthy persons [19].

In contrast to 'pure' attentional tasks where bipolar disorder patients showed hypo-activation of the ventral prefrontal cortex, the anterior cingulate cortex, and the parietal cortex in response to non-emotional targets, studies examining attention to non-emotional targets while emotional distractors are presented have produced rather conflicting results in bipolar disorder patients. In response to emotional distractors, the medial orbitofrontal and medial prefrontal cortex were hyper- [20-22] and hypoactive [21, 23] in euthymic and manic bipolar disorder patients. Similar hyper- [18, 20, 24] and hypo-activity [25] of the anterior cingulate cortex as well as hyper- [18] and hypo-activity [21, 26, 27] of the dorsolateral prefrontal cortex have been observed during the presentation of emotional distractors. Furthermore, the hyper-activity of the insula [20, 21] and posterior regions such as the precuneus [20], parietal cortex [18], and posterior cingulate cortex [21] have occasionally been reported.

More consistently, striatal hyper-activity in response to emotional distractor, has been observed in euthymic bipolar disorder patients using various tasks such as an emotional go/no go task [20], an emotional Stroop task [28], an emotional n-back paradigm [18], and a task asking participants to direct attention to non-emotional aspects (age, gender) of emotional faces [22, 26, 27]. Furthermore, hyper-activation of the amygdala in euthymic bipolar disorder patients has also been frequently reported using different paradigms, testing the influence of emotion on attentional processes [18, 21, 24, 28, 29]. However, there have also been reports of no alterations in amygdala activity [27, 30] and hypo-activity of amygdala [23]. Interestingly, several authors reported reduced connectivity between the amygdala and various regions such as the dorsal anterior cingulate cortex [18], the perigenual anterior cingulate cortex [31], the posterior cingulate cortex, and the parahippocampal cortex [32] – all implicated in 'pure' attentional deficits of bipolar disorder patients.

Thus, in contrast to 'pure' attentional tasks associated with hypo-activity of frontal and parietal brain regions in bipolar disorder patients, attention allocation on non-emotional targets in the presence of emotional distractors is not clearly associated with hypo- or hyper-activity of the frontal and parietal areas. Inconsistencies concerning the activity of the frontal and parietal brain regions during attention allocation on non-emotional targets might be related to reduced connectivity between these regions and the amygdala, which was reported to be rather hyperactive during attention allocation on non-emotional targets. As most results stem from studies investigating euthymic bipolar disorder patients, reports of hyper-activity of frontal and parietal brain regions might point towards a compensatory mechanism meant to down-regulate subcortical structures. Further, striatal hyper-activation during attention allocation on non-emotional targets was the most robust finding. Although this has not been investigated so far, altered connectivity between the striatum and frontal brain regions might also be of importance during attention allocation on non-emotional targets.

With regard to emotional targets of attention, studies have produced very discrepant results. When pediatric bipolar patients were asked to direct their attention towards emotional aspects of emotional faces, either hyper-activation of the amygdala [30] or no alterations in amygdala activity [33, 34] were observed. Furthermore, hypo-activation in the prefrontal cortex and the anterior cingulate cortex and hyper-activation in the right precuneus and the fusiform gyrus were reported [21]. Using an emotional go/no go task, enhanced response of the ventral prefrontal cortex to emotional targets was reported for manic bipolar disorder patients [35].

Some of the discrepancies described above are likely due to methodological variety as studies used paradigms addressing different psychological processes such as selective attention [21, 22, 26, 27, 30, 33, 34] and executive functions involving attention such as response inhibition [20, 35], set-shifting [28], and working memory [18] corresponding to different neural circuits. Furthermore, studies varied with respect to emotional valence of distractors – some used only negative and neutral distractors [23], whereas others applied positive, negative and neutral distractors [18, 20, 28, 30, 35]. In addition, bipolar disorder patients in different mood states were examined. Further, conflicting results might also be due to effects of psychotropic medication. However, this influence was not tested in three of the studies reviewed above [20, 28, 35], whereas others ruled out the possibility that psychotropic medication confounded the results [18, 22, 23, 27, 29-31, 33]. However, Hassel and colleagues (2009) showed that increased medication load was associated with decreased activity of the dorsolateral prefrontal cortex while directing attention away from fearful faces and increased activity of the ventral striatum while focusing attention away from the emotional content of happy faces.

In summary, it seems very interesting that although 'pure' attentional deficits in bipolar disorder seem to be related to hypo-activity in the ventral prefrontal cortex and anterior cingulate cortex, this pattern is likely to be reversed to hyper-activation in both structures in the presence of emotional distractors. On a cautious note, first results indicate that this change might be related to altered connectivity of these structures with the amygdala [18, 31], which showed hyper-activation in response to emotional distractors. As the striatum displayed rather robust hyper-activity in the presence of emotional distractors, altered connectivity between the striatum and frontal brain regions might also be of relevance and needs to be investigated in the future. Nevertheless, existing results underline that there is not one disturbed network in bipolar disorder, but that the task-dependent interaction between networks is of great interest and relevance.

Future studies should compare patients in different symptomatic states. This seems especially interesting, as it has been suggested that both mood states of bipolar disorder are associated with a mood- congruent attentional bias. And indeed, some behavioral studies have reported a mood-congruent attentional bias in manic and depressed bipolar patients [36, 37] that might even persist during remission [38-40]. Although, there are also reports indicating a mood-congruent cognitive bias only for depressed bipolar patients [41] and mood-incongruent bias in manic and depressed patients [42].

2.2. Affective response and evaluation

With respect to the emotional response and appraisal of emotional stimuli, studies on bipolar disorder have mostly focused on the recognition of emotions and the reaction to emotional stimuli. As previous studies have demonstrated that neural responses to emotional stimuli are dependent upon the nature of the task performed during stimulus presentation and the valence of the emotional material used [43-46], we will review the existing literature grouped according to the involvement of cognitive processes and appraisal and valence of emotional stimuli.

Firstly, we will present results from passive viewing tasks instructing the participants to view the stimuli without drawing any cognitive interference. Independent of the valence of the emotional stimuli used, this task is known to activate networks involving the medial prefrontal cortex and the anterior cingulate cortex [44]. Secondly, results from affect matching tasks demanding to choose one out of two pictures matching the emotional valence of a target picture will be reviewed. This is a perceptual task with rather low involvement of cognitive appraisal known to activate the amygdala, the thalamus, and the fusiform gyrus [43]. Finally, evidence derived from affect recognition tasks asking participants to label emotional pictures will be discussed. In contrast to the other two paradigms, this task involves cognitive appraisal and was shown to deactivate the amygdala and to activate the prefrontal and temporal cortices [43, 45, 46]. For this task, we will differentiate between different emotional valence such as happiness, sadness, fear, and disgust.

2.2.1. Passive viewing

Bipolar disorder patients display hypo-activation of the ventrolateral prefrontal cortex during mania [47, 48], euthymia [49], and depression [48, 50] when passively viewing pictures of negative emotional valence. With regard to the amygdala, hyper-activation during mania [51], euthymia [49], depression [50] and in a mixed sample [52] have been reported. However, hypo-activation during mania and euthymia [48], and no alterations during mania [47] have also been reported. Further reports include increased activity of the anterior cingulate during mania when viewing fearful faces [47], euthymia when viewing angry and happy faces [49], and in a mixed sample when viewing happy faces [53]. Also, striatal hyper-activity during mania when viewing fearful faces [47] and in a mixed sample when viewing happy faces [53] was observed. Hyper-activation of the prefrontal cortex, superior temporal gyrus, thalamus, and hypothalamus when viewing pictures of negative valence and increased activity of the prefrontal cortex, superior temporal gyrus, fusiform gyrus, parahippocampal gyrus, and thalamus when viewing pictures of positive valence have been reported in depressed bipolar disorder patients [50]. Unfortunately, none of the studies using passive viewing of emotional pictures in bipolar disorder patients examined the effects of psychotropic medication. Nevertheless, hypo-activation of the ventrolateral orbitofrontal cortex is a very robust finding in bipolar disorder patients during passive viewing of emotional stimuli. In addition, hyper-activation of the anterior cingulate cortex and the striatum have been frequently and consistently reported across mood states.

2.2.2. *Face matching tasks*

Interestingly, both manic [54, 55] and depressed [56] patients showed hypo-activation of the ventrolateral prefrontal cortex during this task, but during euthymia, hyper-activation of the lateral prefrontal cortex was observed, although anticonvulsants showed some normalizing effect [57]. When manic bipolar disorder patients were asked to match facial expressions, they displayed hyper-activation of the amygdala [54, 55]. Euthymic patients did not show any hyper-activation of the amygdala, which might be attributed to antidepressants [57]. Furthermore, increased activity of the thalamus and the ventral anterior cingulate cortex during mania [55], and increased activity of the dorsolateral prefrontal cortex during depression [56] have been observed. However, as only four studies used this paradigm to investigate bipolar disorder patients, it is difficult to draw any clear and valid conclusions. Although the possible influence of psychotropic medication has not been frequently tested, hypo-activation of the ventrolateral prefrontal cortex has been repeatedly shown across mood states during this task [54-56].

2.2.3. *Affect recognition tasks*

When asked to recognize happy facial expressions, neuronal activity in manic [36], euthymic [58], and depressive [58] bipolar disorder patients did not differ from controls. However, others reported hypo-activation of the parahippocampal gyrus during euthymia [59] and depression [60] but hyper-connectivity between parahippocampal gyrus and subgenual anterior cingulate cortex during euthymia [59]. Further, depressed bipolar disorder patients showed hyper-activity of the striatum, ventral prefrontal cortex [42, 60], superior frontal gyrus, middle temporal gyrus, visual cortex, thalamus, and dorsal and posterior cingulate gyrus [42], and they showed hypo-activation of the thalamus and amygdala [60] while recognizing positive affect. Thus, altered activation during appraisal of positive stimuli appears to be rather state dependent in bipolar disorder.

When asked to recognize sad facial expressions, manic bipolar disorder patients showed hyper-activity in the posterior cingulate cortex, nucleus caudate, posterior insula, temporal cortex [36], and fusiform gyrus [42], but they showed hypo-activation in the subgenual anterior cingulate and parahippocampal gyrus [36]. Euthymic bipolar disorder patients displayed hypo-activation in the prefrontal and cingulate cortex but hyper-activation in the parahippocampal gyrus [61]. Depressed bipolar disorder patients showed increased activity of the amygdala [58, 59], hippocampus, and ventral prefrontal cortex [60] but decreased activation of the orbitofrontal cortex, putamen, and dorsolateral prefrontal cortex [60].

Further, connectivity between the amygdala and the orbitofrontal cortex was increased in depressed bipolar disorder patients during recognition of a sad facial expression [62]. However, no altered brain activation was also reported for euthymic [58] and depressed [42] bipolar disorder patients. Similarly to reports concerning appraisal of happiness, altered brain activation in response to appraisal of sadness also seems to be rather state dependent.

When labeling fearful facial expression, manic, euthymic, and depressed bipolar disorder patients showed hyper-activation of the parahippocampal gyrus and the temporal cortex [42, 63]. Further, hyper-activity of the prefrontal cortex, nucleus caudate, putamen, thalamus, and brainstem was observed during mania and depression [42]. There are also reports of increased activity in the amygdala in depressed bipolar disorder patients [58, 60] and hyper-activity of the hippocampus, the parietal cortex, and lingual cortex as well as hypo-activity of the precentral gyrus in euthymic bipolar disorder patients [63]. However, no alterations were also reported for manic [36] and euthymic [58] bipolar disorder patients. Comparable to reports for happy and sad affect, altered brain activation in response to fear appraisal seems to be rather state dependent in bipolar disorder except, potentially, hyper-activation of the parahippocampal gyrus, which has been reported to be hyper-active across mood states.

Labeling disgust has only been investigated in euthymic bipolar disorder patients. Disgust appraisal was reported to be associated with increased activity of the nucleus caudate, hippocampus [64], occipital cortex, and lingual cortex [63]. Furthermore, hypo-activity of the prefrontal cortex [63, 64], anterior cingulate cortex, thalamus [64], insula, fusiform gyrus, and precuneus was observed [63].

Studies combining different emotions during data analysis also showed rather heterogeneous results of hyper-activity in the orbitofrontal cortex and in the nucleus caudate during mania [65], and hyper-activity of the amygdala, hippocampus, orbitofrontal cortex, and insula during euthymia [65]. Further, in a sample of mixed states, hyper-activation of the dorsolateral prefrontal cortex, ventrolateral prefrontal cortex, insula, and superior temporal gyrus when labeling negative pictures also occurred [66]. When recognizing positive pictures, hyper-activation of the medial prefrontal cortex, anterior cingulate cortex, nucleus caudate, thalamus, and precuneus was observed [66].

Regarding appraisal of affective stimuli, no clear pattern of hyper- and / or hypo-activation has emerged so far. Reports are especially inconsistent for frontal brain regions. During all mood states, hyper-activity of the prefrontal brain regions [42, 55, 65] but also no altered activity in the prefrontal cortex [36, 58, 59, 62, 67] has been reported. Furthermore, there are also reports of hypo-activity in the prefrontal cortex during mania and euthymia [55, 63, 64]. When ignoring the valence of the emotional stimuli, hyper-activation of the striatum [36, 42, 64-66] and amygdala [55, 58, 59, 65] are most consistently found across mood states. However, one has to keep in mind that many studies also reported no activation differences for the striatum [55, 58, 59, 62, 63, 67] and amygdala [36, 42, 62, 63, 67].

In part, medication effects might explain heterogeneity of the results. Unfortunately, many authors did not test whether there was a significant influence of psychotropic medication

[36, 42, 55, 63, 64, 66]. Whereas some studies ruled out such influence [59, 65, 67], others reported negative correlation between medication load and amygdala activation [58] and an influence of psychotropic medication on the functional connectivity between the amygdala and orbitofrontal cortex [62] during labeling of sad affect.

2.2.4. Summary

Interestingly, when tasks like passive viewing and stimulus matching, which do not explicitly ask for appraisal of emotional stimuli, are used, hypo-activity of the ventrolateral prefrontal cortex independent of the emotional valence of the stimuli is consistently observed across mood states. Furthermore, abnormal activity of the anterior cingulate cortex has been frequently reported for 'appraisal-free' tasks, although it seems that hypo- or hyper-activity of this region is more related to current mood state and psychotropic medication. However, when using affect recognition tasks, which ask for appraisal of emotional stimuli, a different picture evolves. In case of appraisal, which always implicates a certain personal relevance, hyper-activity of the ventral striatum is the most robust finding across mood states. Although altered activity of the prefrontal brain regions, parahippocampus / hippocampus, insula, and thalamus has also be repeatedly observed, it seems to depend on mood states and medication. It is also important to note that, independent of the mood state, hyper-activation of the amygdala has been consistently observed during both 'appraisal-free' and 'appraisal-demanding' tasks.

2.3. Emotion regulation

The inability to effectively regulate emotions within an adequate range and to adapt to the respective context has been proposed to be at the core of bipolar disorder [1, 8]. Until now, however, neural correlates of voluntary emotion regulation have not been investigated in bipolar disorder. One major problem in emotion regulation research in general is a very heterogeneous conceptualization of emotion regulation and, consequently, diverse operationalization in experimental research.

According to Gross and Thompson (2007), emotion regulation refers to the process of increasing or decreasing current affect. Such a process may occur consciously or unconsciously on a continuum from effortless and automatic (unconscious) to effortful and controlled regulation (conscious). Within their model of emotion regulation, the authors [68] differentiate five types of emotion regulation strategies which can be broadly divided into (1) antecedent-focused strategies, occurring before full-blown emotional responses are elicited (situation selection, situation modification, attentional deployment, and cognitive change), and (2) response-focused strategies, occurring after emotional responses are generated (response modulation). In experimental emotion regulation, research focus has been placed on the investigation of a few strategies, particularly on distraction as an example for attentional deployment, on reappraisal as an example for cognitive change, and on suppression as an example for response modulation. Whereas distraction refers to redirecting attention away from the emotional features of the situation to different, potentially non-emotional aspects of the situation, reappraisal refers to changing the meaning of a situation or how we think about a situation in order to alter its emotional significance.

In a way, some of the studies reviewed in the section of early emotional processes might also be considered to have examined deployment of attention as participants were asked to ignore emotional distractors and focus on the task. These studies most consistently showed hyper-activity of the striatum and the amygdala during distraction, yet there is a difference between emotional distractors presented during a cognitive task and conscious perception of an emotional stimulus followed by the 'decision' to redirect attention in order to prevent in depth processing of this stimulus.

Recently, our research group completed a study on the neural correlates of two different voluntary emotion regulation strategies, namely distraction and reappraisal in patients with bipolar-I disorder (unpublished manuscript). Bipolar disorder patients showed impaired down-regulation of amygdala activity in response to positive and negative stimuli during reappraisal when compared to healthy controls, but not during distraction. This impaired amygdala down-regulation was mediated by a relatively reduced negative connectivity between the amygdala and the lateral orbitofrontal cortex. These first results concerning emotion regulation mechanisms in bipolar disorder underline the importance of appraisal mechanisms for understanding emotional disturbances in bipolar disorder. However, more studies are needed to draw further conclusions.

2.4. Summary

In summary, consideration of appraisal might be essential in understanding altered brain activation in response to emotional stimuli in bipolar disorder. If the task does not ask for appraisal of the emotional stimuli but allows emotional content without assigning any meaning to it (passive viewing: "just look what is there"; face matching: "compare whether you see the same"), hypo-activity of the ventrolateral prefrontal cortex is observed independent of the emotional valence of the stimuli or the current mood state. However, as soon as the task labels the emotional content as important with either a positive (affect recognition: "correct labeling of emotion means mastering the task") or negative (emotional distractors: "affect is an information that might prevent the person from mastering the task") connotation, hyper-activity of the striatum implicated in learning and evaluation [69] is the most consistent finding across mood states. Further, in case of negative appraisal, the ventral prefrontal cortex known to encode behavioral significance [70] and the anterior cingulate cortex shown to process choice predictions and prediction errors [71] have been reported to be rather hyper-active. In contrast, positive appraisal of emotional content is not clearly associated with hyper- or hypoactivation of ventral prefrontal structures or anterior cingulate cortex.

Interestingly, hyper-activation of the amygdala has been reported during both 'appraisal-free' and 'appraisal-demanding' tasks independent of the mood state. Further, euthymic bipolar disorder patients also showed hyper-activation of amygdala activity during reappraisal of positive and negative stimuli. Further, there are several reports of altered functional connectivity between the amygdala and various regions such as the lateral orbitofrontal cortex [62], the dorsal anterior cingulate cortex [18], the perigenual anterior cingulate cortex [31], the posterior cingulate cortex, and the parahippocampal cortex [32], which itself has been shown to be differentially connected to the subgenual anterior cingulate cortex in bipolar disorder [59]. However, only a few studies have examined functional connectivity during emotion processing in bipolar disorder, so definite conclusions cannot be drawn.

It would be interesting to see the results of a meta-analysis that considers the proposed differentiation between 'appraisal-free' and 'appraisal-demanding' tasks. To date, meta-analyses included tasks using emotional stimuli irrespective of the task given to the patients. Results of recent meta-analyses consistently showed hypo-activation of the ventrolateral prefrontal cortex during emotional processes [72-74]. Further, meta-analyses showed hyper-activity of the parahippocampal gyrus [72-74], striatum [73, 74], and amygdala [72, 73] in bipolar disorder patients compared to healthy controls. However, a recent review on emotion processing and regulation in bipolar disorder concluded that amygdala activation is rather likely to vary as a function of mood state [75].

These results have already been incorporated in a 'condensed' neurobiological model of bipolar disorder suggesting that impaired prefrontal-limbic modulation in two networks: (1) a network originating in the ventrolateral prefrontal cortex and (2) a network starting from ventromedial prefrontal cortex underlies bipolar disorder [76]. Both networks are thought to be similarly organized, building iterative feedback loops that process information and modulate activity of the amygdala, the ventral striatum, and the thalamus. Whereas the first network is assumed to be involved in the modulation of external emotional cues such as emotional faces, the second network supposedly regulates internal emotional states [77, 78]. Although the simplicity of this hypothesis is rather intriguing, it remains unclear how complex processes of appraisal and reappraisal might be integrated in this model. Further, this model does not account for motivational aspects of the bipolar symptomatology.

3. Motivational processes

In general, motivation is defined as the process of initiating, controlling, and maintaining behavior with the goal of maximizing pleasant outcomes [79; see Figure 2]. Thus, motivation has been closely linked to the human reward network [80], whose key structures are the midbrain dopamine neurons, the ventral striatum representing reward anticipation [81], the orbitofrontal cortex embodying the value of possible outcomes, and the anterior cingulate cortex coding the value of actions to guide future behavior [71]. However, information about the incentive value alone is not sufficient to actually receive the reward but must be combined with planning, decision-making, troubleshooting, learning, and the overcoming of strong habitual responses. Consequently, other structures, including the dorsolateral prefrontal cortex guiding the allocation of attentional resources and the learning of stimulus-response contingencies [71], the habenula and the amygdala involved in the devaluation of previously rewarding stimuli [82, 83], and the thalamus integrating information about reward from different brain areas are involved in motivation regulation [80].

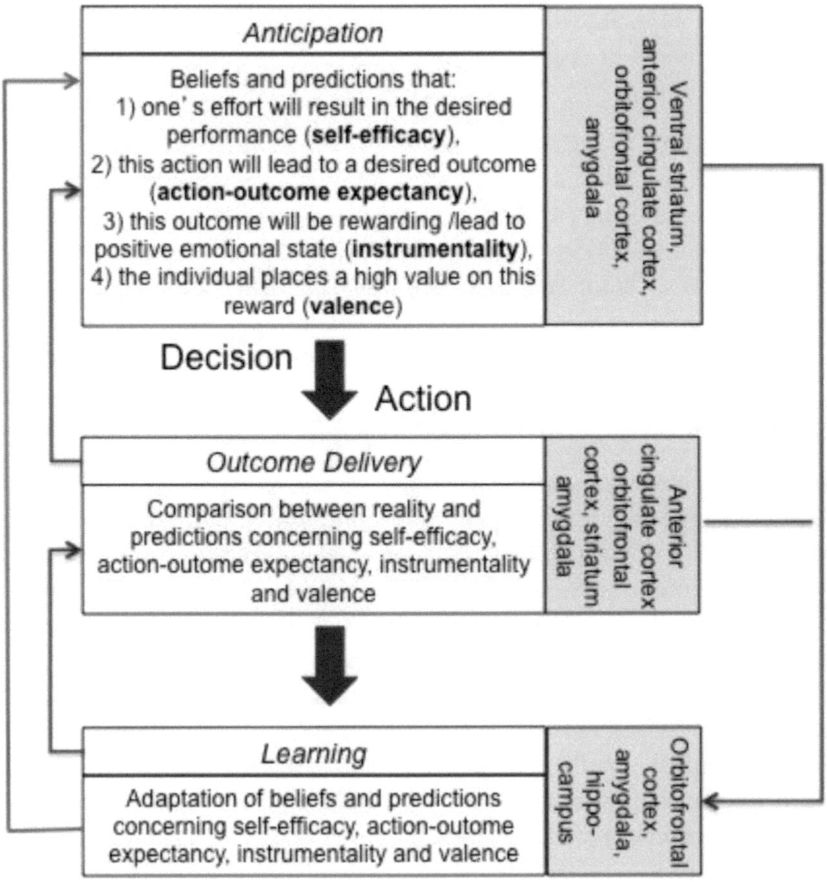

Figure 2. Schematic outline of the steps involved in motivational processing

Most of the structures comprising neurobiological models of bipolar disorder are innervated by dopaminergic projections ascending from the ventral tegmental area to the mesolimbic system, including the ventral striatum, the amygdala, and the hippocampus, as well as the mesocortical system, which includes, among others, the dorsomedial prefrontal cortex, the anterior cingulate cortex, and the orbitofrontal cortex [84]. These dopamine-irrigated structures are the neural correlate of the behavioral activation system, which mediates individual differences in sensitivity and reactivity to appetitive stimuli. High behavioral activation system sensitivity is associated with enhanced appetitive stimuli processing and approach-motivation as well as the diminished processing of aversive stimuli. However, the behavioral activation system might also facilitate active avoidance when safety is perceived as a reward and aggression when reward acquisition is blocked [85]. Thus, hypersensitivity of the behavioral activation system refers to extreme reactions of this system in response to motivationally relevant stimuli also depending on the pre-event state of the behavioral activation system [2, 84, 86]. Extreme fluctuations in activation and deactivation of the behavioral activation system are then reflected in such bipolar symptoms as "excessive involvement in pleasurable activities that have a high potential for painful consequences e.g., engaging in unrestrained buying sprees, sexual indiscretions, or foolish business investments" during mania and "markedly diminished ... pleasure in all, or almost all, activities" during depression [87].

Whereas the reaction to primary emotional stimuli such as fear, anger, disgust, and happiness has been extensively investigated in bipolar disorder patients, neuroimaging studies on reward processes and motivation in patients with bipolar disorder are extremely rare, although altered reward processing has recently been hypothesized to represent an important mechanism of the alternating phases of mania and depression [88]. On a behavioral level, a reduced and delayed response bias towards more frequently rewarded stimuli was reported in euthymic patients with bipolar disorder [89]. In addition, previous studies have shown that euthymic bipolar disorder patients need more time when the consequence of a decision leads to reward or punishment [90-92]. This might indicate a general deficit in responding to motivationally relevant stimuli in bipolar disorder patients.

3.1. Anticipation of positive and negative consequences

In general, anticipation of positive consequences (reward) has been linked to the concept of incentive motivation [93]. The most important brain structures involved in the anticipation of reward are dopaminergic and include midbrain regions (substantia nigra, ventral tegmental area) projecting to the striatum (nucleus caudatus, putamen, nucleus accumbens) and the frontal cortex [94, 95].

To date, only three studies have examined the anticipation of positive and negative consequences in bipolar disorder patients. During a delayed-incentive paradigm, no differences were observed in a small sample of twelve manic patients in response to expected rewards compared to healthy controls and schizophrenic patients [96]. In a second study, manic patients showed increased activation of the orbitofrontal cortex when expecting increasing gain and decreased responses of the orbitofrontal cortex when expecting increasing loss, which normalized in a subsample of seven patients after remission [97]. In the third study, greater activation in the right ventral striatum and the right lateral orbitofrontal cortex was observed in euthymic bipolar disorder patients compared to healthy controls during reward anticipation. However, no significant group differences were observed during anticipation of loss [98]. All studies tested whether results were influenced by psychotropic medication, but this was not the case.

As there are only a few studies with conflicting results, no definite conclusions can be drawn. However, first evidence suggests that the orbitofrontal cortex is especially relevant for alterations in reward anticipation in bipolar disorder.

3.2. Delivery of positive and negative consequences

Similarly, only a few studies have investigated the neural correlates of reward and punishment delivery. During a delayed-incentive paradigm, manic patients showed significantly decreased activation of the nucleus accumbens in response to the receipt or omission of expected rewards, which was interpreted as deficits in prediction error processing [96]. However, other studies have failed to replicate this result in a different sample of manic patients [97]. Errors made during a behavioural task with changing reward contingencies correlated negatively with activity in orbitofrontal and striatal brain regions in bipolar disorder patients when measured during a separate language-processing task [99]. In addition, increased activation in the frontal polar region close to the orbitofrontal cortex was reported in manic patients during reward processing [100]. However, in euthymic pediatric bipolar disorder patients applying the same task with changing reward contingencies, increased activation in parietal and frontal brain regions, but not in the orbitofrontal cortex, have been reported [101]. Further, adding more inconsistency, a study comparing a small sample of twelve depressed bipolar disorder patients to healthy controls observed no difference in neuronal activations during the same task [102]. Furthermore, decreased activation of the ventral prefrontal cortex and increased activation of the anterior cingulate cortex in response to the receipt of reward during a gambling task were reported for euthymic bipolar disorder patients [103]. In a recent study of our group, greater activation in response to reward and decreased deactivation in response to reversal of reward contingencies were observed in the medial orbitofrontal cortex in euthymic bipolar patients [104]. Further, activation of the amygdala in response to reversal of reward contingencies was increased. In response to reward, there was a significant negative correlation between medication and amygdala activation in bipolar disorder patients. Heightened activation of the medial orbitofrontal cortex and the amygdala during wins was interpreted as heightened sensitivity toward reward, whereas greater activation of the amygdala and reduced deactivation of the medial orbitofrontal cortex during rule reversal was suggested to represent an attenuated prediction error signal. Interestingly, heightened reward sensitivity and reduced prediction error signal, as coded by the medial orbitofrontal cortex, was significantly correlated with the score of the behavioral activation system scale, lending further support to the behavioral system dysregulation model [2]. Last but not least, increased activity in the lateral orbitofrontal cortex, the dorsal anterior cingulate cortex, and the putamen in response to changing reward contingencies was also observed; it was suggested that this might represent a compensatory mechanism that aids in suppressing previously rewarded responses, thus allowing adequate performance during euthymia [104]. Interestingly, despite the significant negative correlation between amygdala response and psychotropic medication observed by Linke and coworkers (2012), no influence of psychotropic medication on brain responses upon delivery of reward or punishment have been observed in other studies [96, 97, 99, 101].

To sum up, in bipolar disorder, the orbitofrontal cortex seems to react differently upon delivery and omission of reward in a way that suggests a heightened reward sensitivity and deficient prediction error signal of this brain structure, which might even be a vulnerability factor for bipolar disorder. Furthermore, other key structures of the human reward system, namely the ventral striatum, the anterior cingulate cortex, and amygdala, seem to react differently upon reward delivery in bipolar disorder patients compared to healthy controls. However, the connection between these alterations needs to be investigated in more depth in the future.

3.3. Summary

In patients with bipolar disorder and individuals with an increased risk to develop bipolar disorder, reward anticipation and reward delivery seems to elicit a more pronounced response in the orbitofrontal cortex, which is known to code the positive value an individual places on rewards [71]. Furthermore, if a previously rewarding stimulus has lost its rewarding properties, it will still be more likely to elicit a response in the medial OFC, similar to the response upon reward in euthymic bipolar disorder patients and high-risk individuals. This combination of heightened reward sensitivity and attenuated prediction-error signals in response to changing reward contingencies might facilitate the pursuit of immediate rewards despite the negative consequences in the medium or long term. Further, increased motivation to approach rewarding, or at least formerly rewarding, stimuli is likely to be present before the onset of bipolar disorder and could therefore be a vulnerability factor for this disease.

4. Structural alterations in networks associated with emotion and motivation

4.1. Gray matter alterations

In bipolar disorder, regional abnormalities of gray matter volume have been reported for all regions involved in the described emotional and motivational networks. But, as most studies have been performed on heterogeneous samples with respect to illness subtype, medication status, comorbidity, and mood state, they have produced conflicting findings.

Results have been especially inconsistent for the ventral striatum, the amygdala, the anterior cingulate cortex, the thalamus, and the hippocampus. Studies have reported larger caudate volumes in males [105] and in both affected and unaffected monozygotic bipolar twins [106] compared to controls. However, other studies have found no differences in the caudate of bipolar disorder patients [107-113] or decreased caudate volume [114]. Similarly, putamen enlargement was reported [112, 115, 116], but other studies found no differences in the putamen [105, 107, 113] or decreased volume [117]. Studies also showed reduced volume in the nucleus accumbens [118, 119]. With respect to the amygdala, findings indicate an enlargement of this structure [120-124], but reductions of amygdala volume have also been reported [118, 125-129]. There were also frequent reports of enlargement of the anterior cingulate cortex [130-133]; however, other studies found volume reductions of the anterior cingulate cortex [134]. Studies reported increased volume of the thalamus [123, 131], while others showed no differences [108] or reduced volume of the thalamus [119, 135]. Regarding the hippocampus, some studies reported increased volume [136] as well as decreased volume [119, 137]. By contrast, reports of gray matter abnormalities for dorsolateral prefrontal cortex [118, 134, 138-140] and the habenula [141] have been infrequent but show a more consistent pattern of reduced volume. For the orbitofrontal cortex, decreased volume [117, 134, 142] and neuronal size reduction [143] have been reported, in addition to no alterations [144].

Interestingly, there has been evidence suggesting that abnormal gray matter volumes in the amygdala, hippocampus, thalamus, anterior cingulate cortex, and orbitofrontal cortex are not pervasive characteristics of bipolar disorder but may instead be associated with specific clinical features. Mood-stabilizers, such as lithium, were shown to increase the gray matter volume of the amygdala, hippocampus, and anterior cingulate cortex in bipolar disorder [116, 145-149]. In contrast, antipsychotics and anticonvulsants do not seem to influence gray matter volume of structures involved in emotional and motivational processes [150]. In addition, a longer duration of illness has been associated with increased gray matter in the basal ganglia, the anterior cingulate cortex, and the amygdala [146] as well as loss of hippocampal gray matter [151]. Further, depressive episodes have been associated with gray matter density increases in the orbitofrontal cortex and gray matter density decreases in the prefrontal cortex and anterior cingulate cortex [152].

Based solely on the empirical evidence reviewed above, it is difficult to draw conclusions about potential morphological alterations associated with emotional and motivational circuits as there is either insufficient data on volumetric alterations (habenula, dorsolateral prefrontal cortex) or the results are too heterogenic (striatum, amygdala, thalamus, hippocampus, and orbitofrontal cortex). However, on an important note, a meta-analysis of gray matter alterations in bipolar disorder revealed gray matter reductions in the rostral anterior cingulate cortex [146], which, in addition, seems to be specific to bipolar disorder but not schizophrenia [153]. Hence, gray matter loss in the anterior cingulate cortex, which was also shown in a recent meta-analysis [74], might be the most promising correlate of aberrant emotional and motivational processes emerging from volumetric studies of gray matter alterations.

4.2. White matter alterations

The different gray matter regions constituting networks related to emotional and motivational processes are connected through white matter, which is composed of axons. Deviation from normal axonal organization can be investigated using diffusion tensor imaging, a technique that quantifies the restricted diffusion of water in white matter through scalars, such as fractional anisotropy (FA). Fractional anisotropy is known to be positively correlated with the directionality and coherence of white matter bundles [154]. Although studies of bipolar disorder using diffusion tensor imaging lag behind other psychiatric diseases such as schizophrenia, the existing body of evidence strongly suggests that the loss of white matter integrity in fronto-limbic and cortical-striatal-thalamic circuits is a biological vulnerability factor for bipolar disorder [155]. In more detail, it has been hypothesized that impaired development of white matter, such as altered prefrontal pruning, leads to decreased connectivity within emotional and motivational networks. This is further thought to result in impaired top-down and bottom-up modulation of prefrontal-limbic circuits eventually leading to symptoms of bipolar disorder [76, 156].

With regard to motivation, the integrity of the anterior corpus callosum providing interhemispheric connections between the left and right ventral prefrontal cortex and the anterior limb of the internal capsule, which contains fibers interconnecting the thalamus, striatum, amygdala, hippocampus, anterior cingulate cortex, orbitofrontal cortex, and dorsolateral prefrontal cortex [157, 158], seems to be of particular relevance. In more detail, risky decision-making has been shown to be negatively correlated with the integrity in the corpus callosum [159-161] and the integrity of the anterior limb of the internal capsule [162]. Interestingly, pathological gambling was also negatively related to the integrity of the anterior limb of the internal capsule itself and the uncinate fasciculus [163]. On an important note, the integrity of the uncinate fasciulus is also positively associated with recognition of fearful facial expression [164], harm avoidance [165], and neuroticism [166], pointing towards its relevance for emotional processes.

During depression, mania, and euthymia, reduced white matter integrity, especially in the anterior corpus callosum in children and adolescents [167-170] as well as in adults [171-177] suffering from bipolar disorder, has been described. Interestingly, a normalizing effect of lithium on the volume of the corpus callosum has been observed [178], and a study of euthymic bipolar disorder patients even reported increased integrity of the corpus callosum [179]. Furthermore, all but one [180] tractography study showed reduced white matter integrity in the anterior thalamic radiation [181-183], which passes through the anterior limb of the internal capsule [184] in depressed, euthymic, and manic patients. In line, reduced white matter integrity in the anterior limb of the internal capsule has also been repeatedly observed in bipolar patients [173, 185, 186]. Similar, reduced integrity of the uncinate fasciculus, which interconnects the amygdala with the orbitofrontal cortex and the anterior cingulate cortex [187], has also been frequently observed in depressed and euthymic bipolar disorder patients [173, 180, 182, 183, 188, 189]. Although, increased white matter integrity and increased number of fibers have also been reported for the uncinate fasciculus [180, 190]. On an important note, the integrity of the uncinate fasciculus was shown to influence functional coupling between the anterior cingulate cortex and the amygdala [31]. Reports of reduced white matter integrity of the orbitofrontal cortex [191, 192], which were shown to be related to impulsivity and suicide attempts [12], are of further interest for the understanding of neurobiological underpinnings of emotional and motivation processes in bipolar disorder.

The effect of psychotropic medication on white matter integrity has been less thoroughly investigated than its influence on gray matter integrity. There are some studies stating that psychotropic medication such as lithium, antidepressants, or antipsychotics do not affect the corpus callosum [167, 173, 176, 177, 179, 192-195], although thickening of the corpus callosum has also been observed after lithium treatment [196]. Similarly, the white matter integrity of the anterior limb of the internal capsule and the uncinate fasciculus were not influenced by psychotropic medication [173, 180, 183].

Based on the empirical findings reviewed above, we conclude that white matter tracts connecting emotional and motivational circuits are disturbed in bipolar disorder. Thus it is very likely that this reduced structural connectivity underlies functional alterations, particularly in the orbitofrontal cortex and amygdala, and emotional and motivational symptoms in bipolar disorder. However, to date, association between impaired white matter integrity in the corpus callosum, the anterior limb of the internal capsule, or the uncinate fasciculus and altered early emotional processes, disturbed generation of an emotional response, or emotional and motivational dysregulation has not been shown.

5. The chicken or the egg

So far, empirical data provide evidence that bipolar disorder is a disorder of emotion and motivation. Furthermore, disturbances in these tightly linked but distinct psychological processes are related to impairments in similar neural networks involving prefrontal brain regions such as the orbitofrontal cortex and the anterior cingulate cortex and subcortical structures like the amygdala and the ventral striatum. However, it appears that neural networks associated with emotional and motivational disturbances in bipolar disorder are not uniformly hypo- or hyperactive. Instead, the ongoing psychological process (e.g. early emotional processes, emotion regulation, motivation) and the current mood state crucially interact with neural activation patterns. In addition, psychotropic medication was also repeatedly reported to influence the neural correlates of emotional and motivational processes in bipolar disorder on a structural and functional level (for review see [197]). Therefore, it is difficult to distinguish whether the neural abnormalities in emotional and motivational networks represent biological vulnerability factors for bipolar disorder or a consequence of the disease. Despite the lack of longitudinal studies, this issue might in part be clarified by studies examining healthy persons at high risk of developing bipolar disorder, such as first-degree relatives of patients with bipolar disorder.

5.1. Early emotional processes

Using the emotional Stroop task on a behavioral level, an increased emotional interference effect that was specifically associated to disease-related words was reported for first-degree relatives of bipolar disorder patients compared to healthy controls [198], whereas the 'regular' Stroop task did not reveal any deficits in relatives of bipolar disorder patients [198, 199]. However, on a neural level, relatives of bipolar disorder patients displayed reduced activity in the parietal cortex; unaffected relatives also displayed this reduced activity in the nucleus caudate during the Stroop task [15]. In addition, relatives also showed significantly reduced functional connectivity between the ventrolateral prefrontal cortex and the insula compared to healthy controls during the Stroop task [200]. On a descriptive level, connectivity between the ventrolateral prefrontal cortex and the ventral anterior cingulate cortex appeared to be weaker in relatives. Further, connectivity between the ventrolateral prefrontal cortex and the nucleus caudatus appeared weaker in relatives suffering from major depression but not in healthy relatives of bipolar disorder patients, who showed a negative coupling between ventrolateral prefrontal cortex and dorsolateral prefrontal cortex, which was absent in healthy controls and was interpreted as a compensational mechanism [200]. Interestingly, when directing attention away from fearful and happy faces, hyper-activation of the amygdala, the medial prefrontal cortex, and by trend also of the putamen but only during presentation of fearful faces as distractors was also reported in adolescent relatives of bipolar disorder patients [22]. Despite the interesting results of this first imaging study examining early emotional processes in relatives of bipolar disorder patients, no conclusions can be drawn concerning the question whether abnormal early emotional processes constitute a vulnerability or a consequence of bipolar disorder. Thus, future studies should examine these processes in relatives of bipolar disorder patients preferably using imaging techniques.

5.2. Affective response and evaluation

Fortunately, the generation of an emotional response has been studied more extensively in relatives of bipolar disorder patients. On a behavioral level, relatives of bipolar disorder patients showed significant deficits in recognizing and labeling emotional faces correctly [201-203], yet no difference in emotional responsiveness operationalized by choosing the emotion that would best fit the description of a real-life situation was observed [203]. While rating their fear of fearful faces, unaffected subjects at-risk for bipolar disorder exhibited amygdala hyperactivity [204]. After induction of a sad mood, siblings of bipolar disorder patients showed hyper-activity in the dorsal anterior cingulate cortex and the anterior insula but hypo-activation in the orbitofrontal cortex [205]. Interestingly, siblings also showed hyper-activity in the medial prefrontal cortex, which distinguished this group from bipolar disorder patients and was hence interpreted as protective compensatory mechanism [205]. It is difficult to draw any conclusions based on the existing evidence as both imaging studies in relatives of bipolar disorder used very different paradigms – rating of emotion intensity and mood induction through recall of autobiographical life events. Thus, inconsistencies are likely to be related to different experimental operationalization. Further studies are, therefore, needed examining the neurobiological correlates of affective response and evaluation in relatives of bipolar disorder patients.

5.3. Emotion regulation

Similar to early emotional processes, emotion regulation has been rarely studied in first-degree relatives of bipolar disorder. One behavioral study investigated the use of different emotion regulation strategies and reported more frequent use of maladaptive strategies such as catastrophizing and self-blame among relatives, which correlated with higher scores in measures of depression, anxiety, and hypomanic personality [206]. Concerning the mechanisms underlying this preference of mal-adaptive emotion regulation strategies, our workgroup recently observed impaired down-regulation of amygdala activity in response to positive and negative stimuli during reappraisal, but not during distraction in first-degree relatives of bipolar disorder patients, when compared to healthy controls (unpublished manuscript). Similar to the results already reported for bipolar disorder patients, this impaired amygdala down-regulation was mediated by a relatively reduced negative connectivity between the amygdala and the lateral orbitofrontal cortex. These results are the first evidence that deficits in emotion regulation through reappraisal might be a vulnerability marker for bipolar disorder. The underlying neural mechanisms include impaired control of amygdala reactivity in response to emotional stimuli and dysfunctional connectivity of the amygdala and regulatory control regions in the orbitofrontal cortex. Such impaired functional connectivity might result from impaired white matter development disturbing fronto-limbic circuits [76, 207].

Thus, reports of aberrant emotion regulation in first-degree relatives of bipolar disorder patients need to be replicated and imaging studies investigating the neural basis of these alterations are warranted.

5.4. Motivation

To the best of our knowledge, anticipation of reward or punishment has not been studied so far in healthy individuals to develop bipolar disorder. However, there is one study investigating the neural responses to the delivery of reward and punishment in healthy first-degree relatives of bipolar disorder patients. Similar to bipolar disorder patients, the authors observed greater activation in response to reward in the medial prefrontal cortex and the amygdala, which was interpreted as heightened reward sensitivity [104]. Further, in response to negative feedback, which was followed by a change in behavior (reversal of reward contingencies), decreased deactivation in the medial orbitofrontal cortex and increased activation in the amygdala was observed, which is thought to represent an attenuated prediction error signal. This attenuated prediction error signal was particularly pronounced during negative feedback that was not followed by a behavioral change. It was speculated that this might be the underlying mechanism of a behavior frequently observed in manic bipolar patients: the pursuit of immediate rewards despite negative consequences because on a neural level, they are not coded as punishment. Furthermore, heightened reward sensitivity and reduced prediction error signal as coded by the medial orbitofrontal cortex were significantly correlated with the score of the behavioral activation system scale in the healthy relatives of bipolar disorder patients.

Although results need to be replicated, existing empirical evidence from bipolar disorder patients and their relatives suggests that hyper-activation of the amygdala and the medial orbitofrontal cortex in the context of motivational processes constitute a vulnerability for bipolar disorder. This idea is further supported by another study that showed increased amygdala activation in response to reward in carriers of the risk allele of *CACNA1C* rs1006737, a genome-wide supported risk variant for bipolar disorder [208].

5.5. Gray matter alterations in networks associated with emotional and motivational processes

Similar to the results in bipolar disorder patients, the literature is very inconsistent with respect to alterations of gray matter volume in relatives of bipolar disorder patients. Although gray matter reduction in the anterior cingulate cortex appeared to be the most robust finding in bipolar disorder patients [146], the picture is less clear in their relatives as there are both reports of reduced volume [209] and no volumetric alterations [210, 211]. Other cortical regions, which were investigated in relatives of bipolar disorder patients, are the medial prefrontal cortex where the volume was found to be reduced [212] and the insula with conflicting results of decreased [212] and increased volume [213, 214].

The literature also remains inconsistent for subcortical structures. Comparable to patient data, there is also evidence of decreased caudate volume in relatives of bipolar disorder patients [209, 215]. However, increased volume [106] and no alterations [216] in caudate volume have also been reported. Whereas there seem to be no volumetric alterations in the amygdala of relatives of patients with bipolar disorder [217, 218], there are reports of reduced hippocampal volume [218] and also reports of no apparent alterations in the hippocampus [217]. Furthermore, one study observed reduced thalamic volumes in relatives of bipolar disorder patients [215].

Due to the heterogeneity of the gray matter alterations in bipolar disorder patients and their unaffected relatives, no final conclusion whether alterations are the cause or the consequence of the disease can be drawn. However, considering the variance of the obtained results, it seems more likely that gray matter alterations are more related to certain endophenotypes like altered early emotional processes, impulsivity, working-memory, or reward processing than the illness itself. If at all, the volume of the anterior cingulate cortex seems to be the most promising candidate for a vulnerability factor of bipolar disorder.

5.6. White matter alterations in networks associated with emotional and motivational processes

Similar to the results obtained in patients, decreased integrity of the corpus callosum was also reported for adult and adolescent first-degree relatives of patients with bipolar disorder [186, 219, 220], although others observed no differences in the corpus callosum of relatives of bipolar disorder patients [193, 196]. Also corresponding to the abnormalities reported in patients, unaffected relatives displayed reduced integrity of the internal capsule [186, 220], even though not all research groups replicated this finding [185]. Interestingly, white matter integrity in the anterior limb of the internal capsule was also inversely related to cyclothymic temperament [220]. To date, we are not aware of any study replicating the finding of decreased integrity of the uncinate fasciculus observed in bipolar disorder patients in unaffected relatives of bipolar disorder patients.

The empirical findings of reduced inter-hemispheric and prefrontal-subcortical connectivity in children, adolescents, and adults that are independent of the current mood state and are also observable in unaffected first-degree relatives of bipolar disorder patients support the hypothesis that impaired development in white matter precedes functional alterations in networks relevant for emotion and motivation. Although causality still needs to be proven, there is notable evidence suggesting that impaired white matter integrity in the corpus callosum, the anterior limb of the internal capsule, and the uncinate fasciculus might be biological vulnerability factors of bipolar disorder. However, enthusiasm for this assumption has been limited by the fact that reductions of white matter integrity, especially of the corpus callosum [221-228], the anterior limb of the internal capsule, and the uncinate fasciculus, have also been reported for schizophrenia and unipolar depression [173, 183, 229-233]. Thus, reported white matter abnormalities might not be a vulnerability specific to bipolar disorder, but they seem linked to clinical features like impulsivity, psychosis, and depressive mood as well. Consequently, impaired development of inter-hemispheric and prefrontal-subcortical connectivity seems to be a necessary but not a sufficient condition for the development of bipolar disorder.

5.7. Summary

Supporting the view that impaired white matter development in early life might precede the onset of bipolar disorder [76], reduced white matter integrity in the corpus callosum and the anterior limb of the internal capsule was observed in children, adolescents, and adults suffering from bipolar disorder as well as in unaffected first-degree relatives of bipolar disorder patients. Further, it has been hypothesized that the impaired development of white matter results in impaired prefrontal-limbic modulation in two networks comprising either the ventrolateral or ventromedial prefrontal cortex as well as the amygdala, ventral striatum, and thalamus [76]. And, indeed, hyper-activation of the amygdala has also been observed during early emotional processes [22], generation of an affective response [204], emotion regulation (unpublished manuscript of our group), and motivational processes [104] in unaffected relatives. Thus, we conclude that both impaired white matter of the corpus callosum and the anterior limb of the internal capsule likely disturb fronto-limbic feedback- and feedforward-loops, leading to hyper-activity of the amygdala that precede bipolar symptoms. Further, abnormalities in prefrontal brain regions such as hyper-activity of the medial prefrontal cortex in response to emotional distractors [22] and sad mood [205], hyper-activity of the anterior cingulate cortex [205], hyper-activity of the orbitofrontal cortex in response to reward and omission of reward [104], and reduced functional connectivity between the lateral orbitofrontal cortex and the amygdala (unpublished manuscript of our group) have been observed. However, results are rather inconsistent, implying that these abnormalities might be either protective [205] or risk factors [104]. However, it might be of great interest to examine potential alterations in frontal brain regions in more detail in unaffected relatives. This is especially true as white matter alterations were shown to be not specific for a certain mental disorder, raising the question which neurobiological alterations make the difference between uni- and bipolar affective disorder or bipolar disorder and schizophrenia. However, we like to emphasize that these reflections are rather speculative and that more studies examining emotional and motivational processes in relatives of bipolar disorder patients as well as longitudinal studies are warranted in order to definitely clarify the question which neurobiological abnormalities are risks or consequences of the disease.

6. Conclusion and future perspectives

The interpretation of the above-reviewed results is hampered by a large heterogeneity of results, which is likely to arise from the investigation of heterogenic samples with respect to (1) current symptomatic states, (2) main diagnosis of bipolar I, bipolar II, or bipolar spectrum disorder, (3) psychotropic medication, and (4) life time as well as current psychiatric comorbidities. In the past years, authors started to investigate effects of psychotropic medication more regularly and it seems that functional magnetic resonance imaging and diffusion tensor imaging is rather not influenced by medication [150]. However, the effect of current symptomatology and especially of comorbidity has not been investigated in depth. Thus, future research should address how current symptomatology and comorbidity influences emotional and motivational processes. Further, it would be of great interest to compare patients of bipolar I, bipolar II, and bipolar spectrum disorder.

Despite all heterogeneity, the presented synopsis of empirical results on the neural underpinnings of emotional and motivational processes in bipolar disorder show that bipolar disorder clearly is a disorder of emotion and motivation. As Figure 3 shows, these two psychological processes are closely interrelated and cannot be separated when studying the psychological and neurobiological mechanisms underlying bipolar disorder. This notion is underlined by the fact that emotional and motivational disturbances in bipolar disorder partly share one neural basis. Several structures that are part of the emotion-motivation circuit (ventral prefrontal/orbitofrontal cortex, dorsolateral prefrontal cortex, anterior cingulate cortex, parietal cortex, amygdala, striatum, thalamus, hippocampus) show deviant activation patterns in bipolar patients compared to healthy controls; however, the direction of deviance (hyper- or hypo-activity) depends on the underlying ongoing psychological process. One example is the ventral prefrontal/orbitofrontal cortex: this structure appears to be (1) hypo-active during passive perception of emotions without being asked to actively deal with the emotional content (e.g., correct labeling of emotion) and (2) hyper-active during reward anticipation and reward delivery. From a systems neuroscience perspective, bipolar disorder might therefore be well described on the basis of a neural network dysfunction mainly originating from the amygdala and the ventral prefrontal/orbitofrontal cortex [76]. However, from a psychological and psychotherapeutic perspective, the reviewed results also imply that the underlying psychological processes are the crucial determinants of neural dysfunctions on the one side and of bipolar symptoms during mania and depression on the other. Integrating the systems neuroscience and psychological perspective suggest that alterations in the described emotional and motivational processes, for example, through psychotherapy would accordingly result in neural changes. Thus, in the case of successful therapy, behavioral modifications should result in normalization of disturbed functioning of the emotion-motivation brain network. Consequently, research on modifications of emotional and motivational processes in bipolar patients with neuroimaging methods would be worthwhile and timely.

Finally, although existing data clearly show that a neural network of several brain structures and not single structures on their own forms the pathophysiological basis of bipolar disorder symptoms, more studies on altered functional connectivity during emotion and motivation processing combined with and related to measures of structural connectivity are warranted.

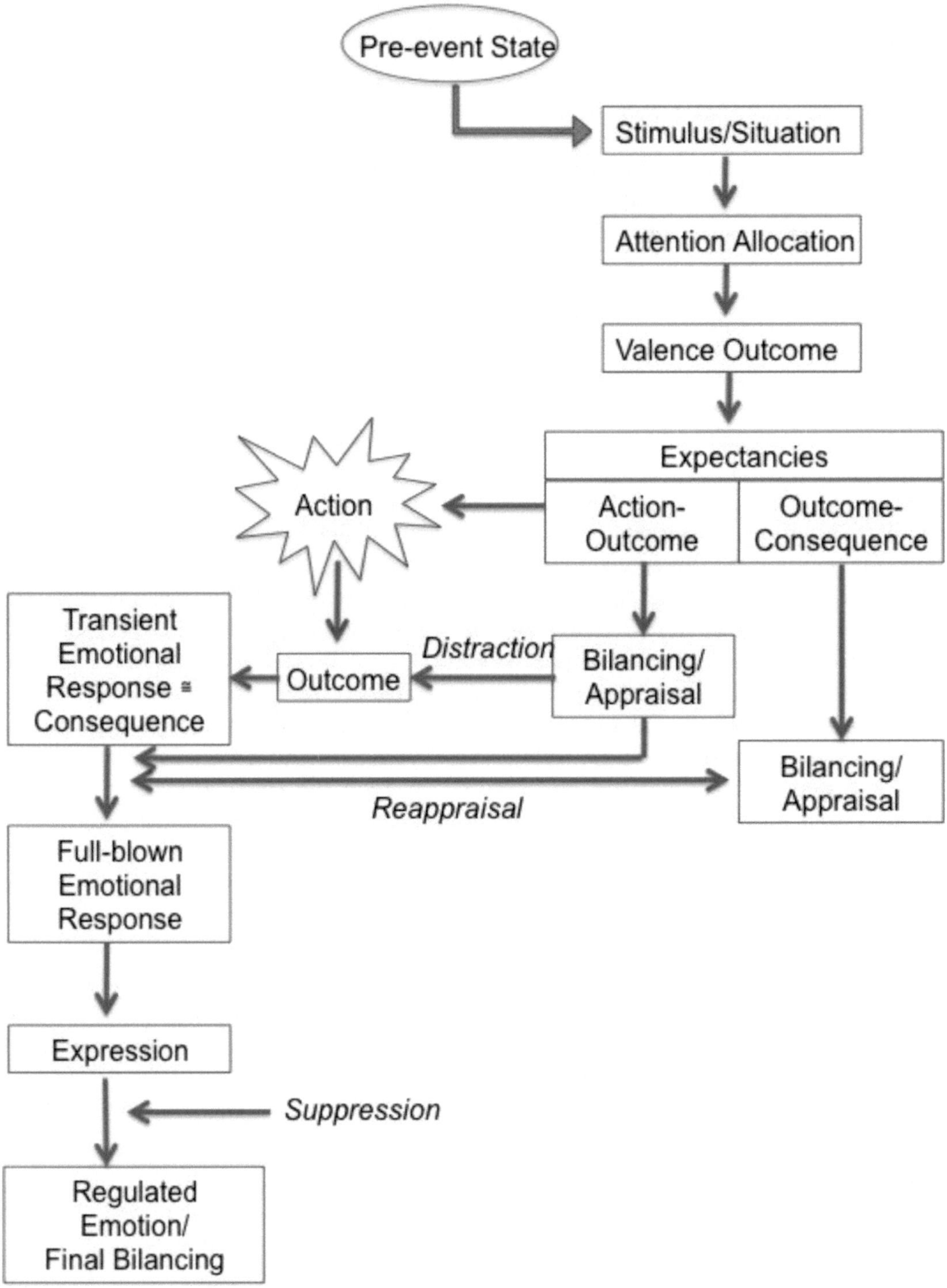

Figure 3. Schematic outline of emotion-motivation interaction

Author details

Michèle Wessa and Julia Linke

Section for Experimental Psychopathology and Neuroimaging, Department of General Psychiatry, Center of Psychosocial Medicine, Heidelberg University, Germany

Acknowledgement

We thoroughly thank Tracy Netemeyer for language editing.

7. References

[1] Phillips ML, Ladouceur CD, Drevets WC. A neural model of voluntary and automatic emotion regulation: implications for understanding the pathophysiology and neurodevelopment of bipolar disorder. Mol Psychiatry. 2008;13(9):829, 33-57.

[2] Alloy LB, Abramson LY. The Role of the Behavioral Approach System (BAS) in Bipolar Spectrum Disorders. Curr Dir Psychol Sci. 2010;19(3):189-94. Epub 2010/07/08.

[3] Ogawa S, Lee TM, Kay AR, Tank DW. Brain magnetic resonance imaging with contrast dependent on blood oxygenation. Proc Natl Acad Sci U S A. 1990;87(24):9868-72. Epub 1990/12/01.

[4] Ogawa S, Lee TM, Nayak AS, Glynn P. Oxygenation-sensitive contrast in magnetic resonance image of rodent brain at high magnetic fields. Magn Reson Med. 1990;14(1):68-78. Epub 1990/04/01.

[5] Logothetis NK, Pfeuffer J. On the nature of the BOLD fMRI contrast mechanism. Magn Reson Imaging. 2004;22(10):1517-31. Epub 2005/02/15.

[6] Logothetis NK. What we can do and what we cannot do with fMRI. Nature. 2008;453(7197):869-78. Epub 2008/06/13.

[7] Keener MT, Phillips ML. Neuroimaging in bipolar disorder: a critical review of current findings. Current Psychiatry Reports. 2007;9(6):512-20.

[8] Phillips M, Drevets W, Rauch S, Lane R. Neurobiology of emotion perception II: Implications for major psychiatric disorders. Biol Psychiatry. 2003;54(5):515-28.

[9] Fox RK, Currie SL, Evans J, Wright TL, Tobler L, Phelps B, et al. Hepatitis C virus infection among prisoners in the California state correctional system. Clin Infect Dis. 2005;41(2):177-86. Epub 2005/06/29.

[10] Wessa M, Linke J. Emotional processing in bipolar disorder: behavioural and neuroimaging findings. Int Rev Psychiatry. 2009;21(4):357-67. Epub 2009/01/01.

[11] Anderson AK, Phelps EA. Is the human amygdala critical for the subjective experience of emotion? Evidence of intact dispositional affect in patients with amygdala lesions. J Cogn Neurosci. 2002;14(5):709-20. Epub 2002/08/09.

[12] Vuilleumier P. How brains beware: neural mechanisms of emotional attention. Trends Cogn Sci. 2005;9(12):585-94. Epub 2005/11/18.

[13] Blumberg HP, Leung HC, Skudlarski P, Lacadie CM, Fredericks CA, Harris BC, et al. A functional magnetic resonance imaging study of bipolar disorder: state- and trait-related dysfunction in ventral prefrontal cortices. Arch Gen Psychiatry. 2003;60(6):601-9.

[14] Kronhaus DM, Lawrence NS, Williams AM, Frangou S, Brammer MJ, Williams SC, et al. Stroop performance in bipolar disorder: further evidence for abnormalities in the ventral prefrontal cortex. Bipolar Disord. 2006;8(1):28-39.

[15] Pompei F, Jogia J, Tatarelli R, Girardi P, Rubia K, Kumari V, et al. Familial and disease specific abnormalities in the neural correlates of the Stroop Task in Bipolar Disorder. Neuroimage. 2011;56(3):1677-84. Epub 2011/03/01.

[16] Strakowski SM, Adler CM, Holland SK, Mills NP, DelBello MP, Eliassen JC. Abnormal FMRI brain activation in euthymic bipolar disorder patients during a counting Stroop interference task. Am J Psychiatry. 2005;162(9):1697-705.

[17] Phelps J. Prenatal PAH exposure causes genetic changes in newborns. Environmental health perspectives. 2005;113(4):A237. Epub 2005/04/15.

[18] Mullin BC, Perlman SB, Versace A, de Almeida JR, Labarbara EJ, Klein C, et al. An fMRI study of attentional control in the context of emotional distracters in euthymic adults with bipolar disorder. Psychiatry Res. 2012;201(3):196-205. Epub 2012/04/19.

[19] Fleck DE, Eliassen JC, Durling M, Lamy M, Adler CM, DelBello MP, et al. Functional MRI of sustained attention in bipolar mania. Mol Psychiatry. 2012;17(3):325-36. Epub 2010/10/27.

[20] Wessa M, Houenou J, Paillere-Martinot ML, Berthoz S, Artiges E, Leboyer M, et al. Fronto-striatal overactivation in euthymic bipolar patients during an emotional go/nogo task. Am J Psychiatry. 2007;164(4):638-46.

[21] Pavuluri MN, Passarotti AM, Harral EM, Sweeney JA. An fMRI study of the neural correlates of incidental versus directed emotion processing in pediatric bipolar disorder. Journal of the American Academy of Child Adolescent Psychiatry. 2009;48(3):308-19.

[22] Surguladze SA, Marshall N, Schulze K, Hall MH, Walshe M, Bramon E, et al. Exaggerated neural response to emotional faces in patients with bipolar disorder and their first-degree relatives. Neuroimage. 2010;53(1):58-64.

[23] Strakowski SM, Eliassen JC, Lamy M, Cerullo MA, Allendorfer JB, Madore M, et al. Functional magnetic resonance imaging brain activation in bipolar mania: evidence for disruption of the ventrolateral prefrontal-amygdala emotional pathway. Biol Psychiatry. 2011;69(4):381-8. Epub 2010/11/06.

[24] Pavuluri MN, O'Connor MM, Harral EM, Sweeney JA. An fMRI study of the interface between affective and cognitive neural circuitry in pediatric bipolar disorder. Psychiatry Res. 2008;162(3):244-55. Epub 2008/02/26.

[25] Shah MP, Wang F, Kalmar JH, Chepenik LG, Tie K, Pittman B, et al. Role of variation in the serotonin transporter protein gene (SLC6A4) in trait disturbances in the ventral anterior cingulate in bipolar disorder. Neuropsychopharmacology. 2009;34(5):1301-10.

[26] Hassel S, Almeida JR, Frank E, Versace A, Nau SA, Klein CR, et al. Prefrontal cortical and striatal activity to happy and fear faces in bipolar disorder is associated with comorbid substance abuse and eating disorder. J Affect Disord. 2009;118(1-3):19-27.

[27] Hassel S, Almeida JR, Kerr N, Nau S, Ladouceur CD, Fissell K, et al. Elevated striatal and decreased dorsolateral prefrontal cortical activity in response to emotional stimuli in euthymic bipolar disorder: no associations with psychotropic medication load. Bipolar Disord. 2008;10(8):916-27.

[28] Malhi GS, Lagopoulos J, Sachdev PS, Ivanovski B, Shnier R. An emotional Stroop functional MRI study of euthymic bipolar disorder. Bipolar Disord. 2005;7 Suppl 5:58-69. Epub 2005/10/18.

[29] Kalmar JH, Wang F, Chepenik LG, Womer FY, Jones MM, Pittman B, et al. Relation between amygdala structure and function in adolescents with bipolar disorder. J Am Acad Child Adolesc Psychiatry. 2009;48(6):636-42.

[30] Rich BA, Vinton DT, Roberson-Nay R, Hommer RE, Berghorst LH, McClure EB, et al. Limbic hyperactivation during processing of neutral facial expressions in children with bipolar disorder. Proc Natl Acad Sci U S A. 2006;103(23):8900-5.

[31] Wang F, Kalmar JH, He Y, Jackowski M, Chepenik LG, Edmiston EE, et al. Functional and structural connectivity between the perigenual anterior cingulate and amygdala in bipolar disorder. Biol Psychiatry. 2009;66(5):516-21.

[32] Rich BA, Fromm SJ, Berghorst LH, Dickstein DP, Brotman MA, Pine DS, et al. Neural connectivity in children with bipolar disorder: impairment in the face emotion processing circuit. J Child Psychol Psychiatry. 2008;49(1):88-96.

[33] Brotman MA, Rich BA, Guyer AE, Lunsford JR, Horsey SE, Reising MM, et al. Amygdala activation during emotion processing of neutral faces in children with severe mood dysregulation versus ADHD or bipolar disorder. Am J Psychiatry. 2010;167(1):61-9.

[34] Liu X, Akula N, Skup M, Brotman MA, Leibenluft E, McMahon FJ. A genome-wide association study of amygdala activation in youths with and without bipolar disorder. J Am Acad Child Adolesc Psychiatry. 2010;49(1):33-41. Epub 2010/03/11.

[35] Elliott R, Ogilvie A, Rubinsztein JS, Calderon G, Dolan RJ, Sahakian BJ. Abnormal ventral frontal response during performance of an affective go/no go task in patients with mania. Biol Psychiatry. 2004;55(12):1163-70.

[36] Lennox BR, Jacob, R., Calder, A.J., Lupson, V., Bullmore, E.T. Behavioural and neurocognitive responses to sad facial affect are attenuated in patients with mania. Psychological Medicine. 2004;34:795 - 8ß2.

[37] Murphy FC, Rubinsztein JS, Michael A, Rogers RD, Robbins TW, Paykel ES, et al. Decision-making cognition in mania and depression. Psychological Medicine. 2001;31:679-93.

[38] Jongen EM, Smulders FT, Ranson SM, Arts BM, Krabbendam L. Attentional bias and general orienting processes in bipolar disorder. J Behav Ther Exp Psychiatry. 2007;38(2):168-83.

[39] Todd RM, Cunningham WA, Anderson AK, Thompson E. Affect-biased attention as emotion regulation. Trends Cogn Sci. 2012;16(7):365-72. Epub 2012/06/22.

[40] Linke J, Sonnekes C, Wessa M. Sensitivity to positive and negative feedback in euthymic patients with bipolar I disorder: the last episode makes the difference. Bipolar Disord. 2011;13(7-8):638-50. Epub 2011/11/17.

[41] Farb NA, Anderson AK, Segal ZV. The mindful brain and emotion regulation in mood disorders. Can J Psychiatry. 2012;57(2):70-7. Epub 2012/02/22.

[42] Chen C, Lennox BR, Jacob R, Calder A, Lupson V, Bisbrown-Chippendale R, et al. Explicit and implicit facial affect recognition in manic and depressed states of bipolar disorder: A functional magnetic resonance imaging study. Biological Psychiatry. 2006;59(1):31 - 9.

[43] Lumen N, Fonteyne V, De Meerleert G, Ost P, Villeirs G, Mottrie A, et al. Population screening for prostate cancer: an overview of available studies and meta-analysis. International journal of urology : official journal of the Japanese Urological Association. 2012;19(2):100-8. Epub 2011/11/23.

[44] Teasdale JD, Howard RJ, Cox SG, Ha Y, Brammer MJ, Williams SC, et al. Functional MRI study of the cognitive generation of affect. Am J Psychiatry. 1999;156(2):209-15. Epub 1999/02/16.

[45] Critchley H, Daly E, Phillips M, Brammer M, Bullmore E, Williams S, et al. Explicit and implicit neural mechanisms for processing of social information from facial expressions: a functional magnetic resonance imaging study. Hum Brain Mapp. 2000;9(2):93-105. Epub 2000/02/19.

[46] Lange K, Williams LM, Young AW, Bullmore ET, Brammer MJ, Williams SC, et al. Task instructions modulate neural responses to fearful facial expressions. Biol Psychiatry. 2003;53(3):226-32.

[47] Killgore WD, Gruber SA, Yurgelun-Todd DA. Abnormal corticostriatal activity during fear perception in bipolar disorder. Neuroreport. 2008;19(15):1523-7. Epub 2008/09/18.

[48] Van der Schot A, Kahn R, Ramsey N, Nolen W, Vink M. Trait and state dependent functional impairments in bipolar disorder. Psychiatry Res. 2010;184(3):135-42. Epub 2010/11/06.

[49] Pavuluri MN, O'Connor MM, Harral E, Sweeney JA. Affective neural circuitry during facial emotion processing in pediatric bipolar disorder. Biol Psychiatry. 2007;62(2):158-67.

[50] Malhi GS, Lagopoulos J, Ward PB, Kumari V, Mitchell PB, Parker GB, et al. Cognitive generation of affect in bipolar depression: an fMRI study. Eur J Neurosci. 2004;19(3):741-54.

[51] Bermpohl F, Dalanay U, Kahnt T, Sajonz B, Heimann H, Ricken R, et al. A preliminary study of increased amygdala activation to positive affective stimuli in mania. Bipolar Disord. 2009;11(1):70-5. Epub 2009/01/13.

[52] Blumberg HP, Donegan NH, Sanislow CA, Collins S, Lacadie C, Skudlarski P, et al. Preliminary evidence for medication effects on functional abnormalities in the

amygdala and anterior cingulate in bipolar disorder. Psychopharmacology (Berl). 2005;183(3):308-13.

[53] Dickstein DP, Rich BA, Roberson-Nay R, Berghorst L, Vinton D, Pine DS, et al. Neural activation during encoding of emotional faces in pediatric bipolar disorder. Bipolar Disorders. 2007;9(7):679 - 92.

[54] Altshuler L, Bookheimer S, Proenza M, A, Townsend J, Sabb F, Firestine A, et al. Increased Amygdala Activation during Mania:A functional magnetic resonance imaging study. Journal Psychiatry. 2005;162(6):1211-3.

[55] Foland LC, Altshuler LL, Bookheimer SY, Eisenberger N, Townsend J, Thompson PM. Evidence for deficient modulation of amygdala response by prefrontal cortex in bipolar mania. Psychiatry Res. 2008;162(1):27-37.

[56] Altshuler L, Bookheimer S, Townsend J, Proenza MA, Sabb F, Mintz J, et al. Regional brain changes in bipolar I depression: a functional magnetic resonance imaging study. Bipolar Disord. 2008;10(6):708-17. Epub 2008/10/08.

[57] Robinson JL, Monkul ES, Tordesillas-Gutierrez D, Franklin C, Bearden CE, Fox PT, et al. Fronto-limbic circuitry in euthymic bipolar disorder: evidence for prefrontal hyperactivation. Psychiatry Res. 2008;164(2):106-13. Epub 2008/10/22.

[58] Almeida JR, Versace A, Hassel S, Kupfer DJ, Phillips ML. Elevated amygdala activity to sad facial expressions: a state marker of bipolar but not unipolar depression. Biol Psychiatry. 2010;67(5):414-21. Epub 2009/11/26.

[59] Almeida JR, Versace A, Mechelli A, Hassel S, Quevedo K, Kupfer DJ, et al. Abnormal amygdala-prefrontal effective connectivity to happy faces differentiates bipolar from major depression. Biol Psychiatry. 2009;66(5):451-9.

[60] Lawrence NS, Williams AM, Surguladze S, Giampietro V, Brammer MJ, Andrew C, et al. Subcortical and ventral prefrontal cortical neural responses to facial expressions distinguish patients with bipolar disorder and major depression. Biological Psychiatry. 2004;55(6):578-87.

[61] Jogia J, Haldane M, Cobb A, Kumari V, Frangou S. Pilot investigation of the changes in cortical activation during facial affect recognition with lamotrigine monotherapy in bipolar disorder. Br J Psychiatry. 2008;192(3):197-201. Epub 2008/03/04.

[62] Versace A, Thompson WK, Zhou D, Almeida JR, Hassel S, Klein CR, et al. Abnormal left and right amygdala-orbitofrontal cortical functional connectivity to emotional faces: state versus trait vulnerability markers of depression in bipolar disorder. Biol Psychiatry. 2010;67(5):422-31. Epub 2010/02/18.

[63] Malhi GS, Lagopoulos J, Sachdev PS, Ivanovski B, Shnier R, Ketter T. Is a lack of disgust something to fear? A functional magnetic resonance imaging facial emotion recognition study in euthymic bipolar disorder patients. Bipolar Disord. 2007;9(4):345-57.

[64] Lagopoulos J, Malhi G. Impairments in "top-down" processing in bipolar disorder: a simultaneous fMRI-GSR study. Psychiatry Res. 2011;192(2):100-8. Epub 2011/04/16.

[65] Chen CH, Suckling J, Ooi C, Jacob R, Lupson V, Bullmore ET, et al. A longitudinal fMRI study of the manic and euthymic states of bipolar disorder. Bipolar Disord. 2010;12(3):344-7. Epub 2010/06/23.

[66] Chang K, Adleman NE, Dienes K, Simeonova DI, Menon V, Reiss A. Anomalous prefrontal-subcortical activation in familial pediatric bipolar disorder: a functional magnetic resonance imaging investigation. Archives of General Psychiatry. 2004;61(8):781-92.

[67] Almeida JR, Mechelli A, Hassel S, Versace A, Kupfer DJ, Phillips ML. Abnormally increased effective connectivity between parahippocampal gyrus and ventromedial prefrontal regions during emotion labeling in bipolar disorder. Psychiatry Res. 2009;174(3):195-201.

[68] Gross JJ, Thompson AJ. Emotion Regulation: Conceptual Foundations. In: Gross JJ, editor. Handbook of Emotion Regulation. New York: Guilford Press; 2007. p. 3-24.

[69] Chobtang J, de Boer IJ, Hoogenboom RL, Haasnoot W, Kijlstra A, Meerburg BG. The need and potential of biosensors to detect dioxins and dioxin-like polychlorinated biphenyls along the milk, eggs and meat food chain. Sensors (Basel). 2011;11(12):11692-716. Epub 2012/01/17.

[70] Sakagami M, Pan X. Functional role of the ventrolateral prefrontal cortex in decision making. Curr Opin Neurobiol. 2007;17(2):228-33. Epub 2007/03/14.

[71] Wallis JD, Kennerley SW. Heterogeneous reward signals in prefrontal cortex. Curr Opin Neurobiol. 2010;20(2):191-8. Epub 2010/03/23.

[72] Chen CH, Suckling J, Lennox BR, Ooi C, Bullmore ET. A quantitative meta-analysis of fMRI studies in bipolar disorder. Bipolar Disord. 2011;13(1):1-15. Epub 2011/02/16.

[73] Delvecchio G, Fossati P, Boyer P, Brambilla P, Falkai P, Gruber O, et al. Common and distinct neural correlates of emotional processing in Bipolar Disorder and Major Depressive Disorder: a voxel-based meta-analysis of functional magnetic resonance imaging studies. Eur Neuropsychopharmacol. 2012;22(2):100-13. Epub 2011/08/09.

[74] Houenou J, Frommberger J, Carde S, Glasbrenner M, Diener C, Leboyer M, et al. Neuroimaging-based markers of bipolar disorder: evidence from two meta-analyses. J Affect Disord. 2011;132(3):344-55. Epub 2011/04/08.

[75] Townsend J, Altshuler LL. Emotion processing and regulation in bipolar disorder: a review. Bipolar Disord. 2012;14(4):326-39. Epub 2012/05/29.

[76] Strakowski SM, Adler CM, Almeida J, Altshuler LL, Blumberg HP, Chang KD, et al. The functional neuroanatomy of bipolar disorder: a consensus model. Bipolar Disord. 2012;14(4):313-25. Epub 2012/05/29.

[77] Schneider MR, Delbello MP, McNamara RK, Strakowski SM, Adler CM. Neuroprogression in bipolar disorder. Bipolar Disorders. 2012;14(4):356-74. Epub 2012/05/29.

[78] Strakowski SM, Adler CM, Almeida J, Altshuler LL, Blumberg HP, Chang KD, et al. The functional neuroanatomy of bipolar disorder: a consensus model. Bipolar Disorders. 2012;14(4):313-25. Epub 2012/05/29.

[79] Zimbardo PG. Does psychology make a significant difference in our lives? Am Psychol. 2004;59(5):339-51.

[80] Haber SN, Knutson B. The reward circuit: linking primate anatomy and human imaging. Neuropsychopharmacology. 2010;35(1):4-26. Epub 2009/10/09.

[81] O'Doherty JP. Reward representations and reward-related learning in the human brain: insights from neuroimaging. Curr Opin Neurobiol. 2004;14(6):769-76. Epub 2004/12/08.
[82] Baxter MG, Murray EA. The amygdala and reward. Nat Rev Neurosci. 2002;3(7):563-73. Epub 2002/07/03.
[83] Ullsperger M, von Cramon DY. Error monitoring using external feedback: specific roles of the habenular complex, the reward system, and the cingulate motor area revealed by functional magnetic resonance imaging. J Neurosci. 2003;23(10):4308-14. Epub 2003/05/24.
[84] Depue RA, Iacono WG. Neurobehavioral aspects of affective disorders. Ann Rev Psychol. 1989;40:457-92.
[85] Gray JA. The psychology of fear and stress. Cambridge: Cambridge University Press; 1987.
[86] Urosévic S, Abramson L, Harmon-Jones E, Alloy L. Dysregulation of the behavioral approach system (BAS) in bipolar spectrum disorders: Review of theory and evidence. Clin Psychol Rev. 2008;28(7):1188-205.
[87] American Psychiatric Association. Diagnostic and Statistical Manual of Mental Health Disorders. 4 ed: Text Revision ed. Washington, D.C.: American Psychiatric Press; 2000.
[88] Hasler G, Drevets WC, Gould TD, Gottesman II, Manji HK. Toward constructing an endophenotype strategy for bipolar disorders. Biol Psychiatry. 2006;60(2):93-105.
[89] Pizzagalli DA, Goetz E, Ostacher M, Iosifescu DV, Perlis RH. Euthymic patients with bipolar disorder show decreased reward learning in a probabilistic reward task. Biol Psychiatry. 2008;64(2):162-8.
[90] Gorrindo T, Blair R, Budhani S, Dickstein D, Pine D, Leibenluft E. Deficits on a probabilistic response-reversal task in patients with pediatric bipolar disorder. Am J Psychiatry. 2005;162(10):1975-7.
[91] McClure EB, Treland JE, Snow J, Schmajuk M, Dickstein DP, Towbin KE, et al. Deficits in social cognition and response flexibility in pediatric bipolar disorder. Am J Psychiatry. 2005;162(9):1644-51.
[92] Rich BA, Schmajuk M, Perez-Edgar KE, Pine DS, Fox NA, Leibenluft E. The impact of reward, punishment, and frustration on attention in pediatric bipolar disorder. Biol Psychiatry. 2005;58(7):532-9.
[93] Bolles RC. Reinforcement, expectancy, and learning. Psychol Rev. 1972;79:394-409.
[94] Riggs L, McQuiggan DA, Farb N, Anderson AK, Ryan JD. The role of overt attention in emotion-modulated memory. Emotion. 2011;11(4):776-85. Epub 2011/04/27.
[95] Steidl S, Razik F, Anderson AK. Emotion enhanced retention of cognitive skill learning. Emotion. 2011;11(1):12-9. Epub 2010/11/10.
[96] Abler B, Greenhouse I, Ongur D, Walter H, Heckers S. Abnormal reward system activation in mania. Neuropsychopharmacology. 2008;33:2217-27.
[97] Bermpohl F, Kahnt T, Dalanay U, Hagele C, Sajonz B, Wegner T, et al. Altered representation of expected value in the orbitofrontal cortex in mania. Hum Brain Mapp. 2010;31(7):958-69. Epub 2009/12/02.

[98] Nusslock R, Almeida JR, Forbes EE, Versace A, Frank E, Labarbara EJ, et al. Waiting to win: elevated striatal and orbitofrontal cortical activity during reward anticipation in euthymic bipolar disorder adults. Bipolar Disord. 2012;14(3):249-60. Epub 2012/05/03.
[99] McIntosh AM, Whalley HC, McKirdy J, Hall J, Sussmann JE, Shankar P, et al. Prefrontal function and activation in bipolar disorder and schizophrenia. Am J Psychiatry. 2008;165(3):378-84.
[100] Rubinsztein JS, Fletcher PC, Rogers RD, Ho LW, Aigbirhio FI, Paykel ES, et al. Decision-making in mania: a PET study. Brain. 2001;124(Pt 12):2550-63.
[101] Dickstein DP, Finger EC, Skup M, Pine DS, Blair JR, Leibenluft E. Altered neural function in pediatric bipolar disorder during reversal learning. Bipolar Disord. 2010;12(7):707-19.
[102] Taylor Tavares JV, Clark L, Furey ML, Williams GB, Sahakian BJ, Drevets WC. Neural basis of abnormal response to negative feedback in unmedicated mood disorders. Neuroimage. 2008;42(3):1118-26.
[103] Jogia J, Dima D, Kumari V, Frangou S. Frontopolar cortical inefficiency may underpin reward and working memory dysfunction in bipolar disorder. World J Biol Psychiatry. 2011. Epub 2011/08/05.
[104] Linke J, King AV, Rietschel M, Strohmaier J, Hennerici M, Gass A, et al. Increased medial orbitofrontal and amygdala activation: evidence for a systems-level endophenotype of bipolar I disorder. Am J Psychiatry. 2012;169(3):316-25. Epub 2012/01/24.
[105] Aylward EH, Roberts-Twillie JV, Barta PE, Kumar AJ, Harris GJ, Geer M, et al. Basal ganglia volumes and white matter hyperintensities in patients with bipolar disorder. Am J Psychiatry. 1994;151(5):687-93. Epub 1994/05/01.
[106] Noga JT, Vladar K, Torrey EF. A volumetric magnetic resonance imaging study of monozygotic twins discordant for bipolar disorder. Psychiatry Res. 2001;106(1):25-34. Epub 2001/03/07.
[107] Brambilla P, Harenski K, Nicoletti MA, Mallinger AG, Frank E, Kupfer DJ, et al. Anatomical MRI study of basal ganglia in bipolar disorder patients. Psychiatry Res. 2001;106(2):65-80. Epub 2001/04/18.
[108] Sax KW, Strakowski SM, Zimmerman ME, DelBello MP, Keck PE, Jr., Hawkins JM. Frontosubcortical neuroanatomy and the continuous performance test in mania. Am J Psychiatry. 1999;156(1):139-41.
[109] Dolan RJ, Poynton AM, Bridges PK, Trimble MR. Altered magnetic resonance white-matter T1 values in patients with affective disorder. Br J Psychiatry. 1990;157:107-10. Epub 1990/07/01.
[110] Dupont RM, Jernigan TL, Heindel W, Butters N, Shafer K, Wilson T, et al. Magnetic resonance imaging and mood disorders. Localization of white matter and other subcortical abnormalities. Arch Gen Psychiatry. 1995;52(9):747-55. Epub 1995/09/01.
[111] Strakowski SM, Wilson DR, Tohen M, Woods BT, Douglass AW, Stoll AL. Structural brain abnormalities in first-episode mania. Biol Psychiatry. 1993;33(8-9):602-9. Epub 1993/04/01.

[112] Strakowski SM, DelBello MP, Zimmerman ME, Getz GE, Mills NP, Ret J, et al. Ventricular and periventricular structural volumes in first- versus multiple-episode bipolar disorder. Am J Psychiatry. 2002;159(11):1841-7.

[113] Swayze VW, 2nd, Andreasen NC, Alliger RJ, Yuh WT, Ehrhardt JC. Subcortical and temporal structures in affective disorder and schizophrenia: a magnetic resonance imaging study. Biol Psychiatry. 1992;31(3):221-40. Epub 1992/02/01.

[114] Beyer JL, Kuchibhatla M, Payne M, Moo-Young M, Cassidy F, MacFall J, et al. Caudate volume measurement in older adults with bipolar disorder. Int J Geriatr Psychiatry. 2004;19(2):109-14. Epub 2004/02/06.

[115] DelBello MP, Zimmerman ME, Mills NP, Getz GE, Strakowski SM. Magnetic resonance imaging analysis of amygdala and other subcortical brain regions in adolescents with bipolar disorder. Bipolar Disord. 2004;6(1):43-52. Epub 2004/03/06.

[116] Hallahan B, Newell J, Soares JC, Brambilla P, Strakowski SM, Fleck DE, et al. Structural magnetic resonance imaging in bipolar disorder: an international collaborative mega-analysis of individual adult patient data. Biol Psychiatry. 2011;69(4):326-35. Epub 2010/10/30.

[117] Almeida JR, Akkal D, Hassel S, Travis MJ, Banihashemi L, Kerr N, et al. Reduced gray matter volume in ventral prefrontal cortex but not amygdala in bipolar disorder: significant effects of gender and trait anxiety. Psychiatry Res. 2009;171(1):54-68.

[118] Dickstein D, P , Milham M, P , Nugent A, C , Drevets W, C, Charney D, S , Pine D, S , et al. Frontotemporal alterations in pediatric bipolar disorder: results of a voxel-based morphometry study. Archives of General Psychiatry. 2005;62(7):734-41.

[119] Rimol LM, Hartberg CB, Nesvag R, Fennema-Notestine C, Hagler DJ, Jr., Pung CJ, et al. Cortical thickness and subcortical volumes in schizophrenia and bipolar disorder. Biol Psychiatry. 2010;68(1):41-50. Epub 2010/07/09.

[120] Altshuler LL, Bartzokis G, Grieder T, Curran J, Jimenez T, Leight K, et al. An MRI study of temporal lobe structures in men with bipolar disorder or schizophrenia. Biol Psychiatry. 2000;48(2):147-62. Epub 2000/07/21.

[121] Altshuler LL, Bartzokis G, Grieder T, Curran J, Mintz J. Amygdala enlargement in bipolar disorder and hippocampal reduction in schizophrenia: an MRI study demonstrating neuroanatomic specificity. Arch Gen Psychiatry. 1998;55(7):663-4. Epub 1998/07/22.

[122] Brambilla P, Harenski K, Nicoletti M, Sassi RB, Mallinger AG, Frank E, et al. MRI investigation of temporal lobe structures in bipolar patients. J Psychiatr Res. 2003;37(4):287-95. Epub 2003/05/27.

[123] Strakowski SM, DelBello MP, Sax KW, Zimmerman ME, Shear PK, Hawkins JM, et al. Brain magnetic resonance imaging of structural abnormalities in bipolar disorder. Arch Gen Psychiatry. 1999;56(3):254-60. Epub 1999/03/17.

[124] Velakoulis D, Wood SJ, Wong MT, McGorry PD, Yung A, Phillips L, et al. Hippocampal and amygdala volumes according to psychosis stage and diagnosis: a magnetic resonance imaging study of chronic schizophrenia, first-episode psychosis,

and ultra-high-risk individuals. Arch Gen Psychiatry. 2006;63(2):139-49. Epub 2006/02/08.

[125] Blumberg HP, Kaufman J, Martin A, Whiteman R, Zhang JH, Gore JC, et al. Amygdala and hippocampal volumes in adolescents and adults with bipolar disorder. Arch Gen Psychiatry. 2003;60(12):1201-8.

[126] Pearlson GD, Barta PE, Powers RE, Menon RR, Richards SS, Aylward EH, et al. Ziskind-Somerfeld Research Award 1996. Medial and superior temporal gyral volumes and cerebral asymmetry in schizophrenia versus bipolar disorder. Biol Psychiatry. 1997;41(1):1-14. Epub 1997/01/01.

[127] Rosso IM, Killgore WD, Cintron CM, Gruber SA, Tohen M, Yurgelun-Todd DA. Reduced amygdala volumes in first-episode bipolar disorder and correlation with cerebral white matter. Biol Psychiatry. 2007;61(6):743-9. Epub 2006/11/25.

[128] Chang K, Karchemskiy A, Barnea-Goraly N, Garrett A, Simeonova D, I , Reiss A. Reduced amygdalar gray matter volume in familial pediatric bipolar disorder. Journal American Academy of Child Adolesc Psychiatry. 2005;44(6):565-73.

[129] Pfeifer JC, Welge J, Strakowski SM, Adler CM, DelBello MP. Meta-analysis of amygdala volumes in children and adolescents with bipolar disorder. J Am Acad Child Adolesc Psychiatry. 2008;47(11):1289-98.

[130] de Azevedo-Marques Perico C, Duran FL, Zanetti MV, Santos LC, Murray RM, Scazufca M, et al. A population-based morphometric MRI study in patients with first-episode psychotic bipolar disorder: comparison with geographically matched healthy controls and major depressive disorder subjects. Bipolar Disord. 2011;13(1):28-40. Epub 2011/02/16.

[131] Adler CM, DelBello MP, Jarvis K, Levine A, Adams J, Strakowski SM. Voxel-based study of structural changes in first-episode patients with bipolar disorder. Biol Psychiatry. 2007;61(6):776-81.

[132] Adler CM, Levine AD, DelBello MP, Strakowski SM. Changes in gray matter volume in patients with bipolar disorder. Biol Psychiatry. 2005;58(2):151-7.

[133] Javadapour A, Malhi GS, Ivanovski B, Chen X, Wen W, Sachdev P. Increased anterior cingulate cortex volume in bipolar I disorder. Aust N Z J Psychiatry. 2007;41(11):910-6.

[134] Foland-Ross LC, Thompson PM, Sugar CA, Madsen SK, Shen JK, Penfold C, et al. Investigation of cortical thickness abnormalities in lithium-free adults with bipolar I disorder using cortical pattern matching. Am J Psychiatry. 2011;168(5):530-9. Epub 2011/02/03.

[135] Radenbach K, Flaig V, Schneider-Axmann T, Usher J, Reith W, Falkai P, et al. Thalamic volumes in patients with bipolar disorder. Eur Arch Psychiatry Clin Neurosci. 2010;260(8):601-7. Epub 2010/02/04.

[136] Javadapour A, Malhi GS, Ivanovski B, Chen X, Wen W, Sachdev P. Hippocampal volumes in adults with bipolar disorder. J Neuropsychiatry Clin Neurosci. 2010;22(1):55-62.

[137] Doring TM, Kubo TT, Cruz LC, Jr., Juruena MF, Fainberg J, Domingues RC, et al. Evaluation of hippocampal volume based on MR imaging in patients with bipolar

affective disorder applying manual and automatic segmentation techniques. J Magn Reson Imaging. 2011;33(3):565-72. Epub 2011/05/13.

[138] Tost H, Ruf M, Schmal C, Schulze TG, Knorr C, Vollmert C, et al. Prefrontal-temporal gray matter deficits in bipolar disorder patients with persecutory delusions. J Affect Disord. 2010;120(1-3):54-61. Epub 2009/05/08.

[139] Brooks JO, 3rd, Bonner JC, Rosen AC, Wang PW, Hoblyn JC, Hill SJ, et al. Dorsolateral and dorsomedial prefrontal gray matter density changes associated with bipolar depression. Psychiatry Res. 2009;172(3):200-4. Epub 2009/04/09.

[140] Lopez-Larson MP, DelBello MP, Zimmerman ME, Schwiers ML, Strakowski SM. Regional prefrontal gray and white matter abnormalities in bipolar disorder. Biol Psychiatry. 2002;52(2):93-100.

[141] Savitz JB, Nugent AC, Bogers W, Roiser JP, Bain EE, Neumeister A, et al. Habenula volume in bipolar disorder and major depressive disorder: a high-resolution magnetic resonance imaging study. Biol Psychiatry. 2011;69(4):336-43. Epub 2010/11/26.

[142] Nery FG, Chen HH, Hatch JP, Nicoletti MA, Brambilla P, Sassi RB, et al. Orbitofrontal cortex gray matter volumes in bipolar disorder patients: a region-of-interest MRI study. Bipolar Disord. 2009;11(2):145-53. Epub 2009/03/10.

[143] Cotter D, Hudson L, Landau S. Evidence for orbitofrontal pathology in bipolar disorder and major depression, but not in schizophrenia. Bipolar Disord. 2005;7(4):358-69. Epub 2005/07/20.

[144] Brambilla P, Nicoletti MA, Harenski K, Sassi RB, Mallinger AG, Frank E, et al. Anatomical MRI study of subgenual prefrontal cortex in bipolar and unipolar subjects. Neuropsychopharmacology. 2002;27(5):792-9. Epub 2002/11/15.

[145] Benedetti F, Radaelli D, Poletti S, Locatelli C, Falini A, Colombo C, et al. Opposite effects of suicidality and lithium on gray matter volumes in bipolar depression. J Affect Disord. 2011.

[146] Bora E, Fornito A, Yucel M, Pantelis C. Voxelwise meta-analysis of gray matter abnormalities in bipolar disorder. Biol Psychiatry. 2010;67(11):1097-105. Epub 2010/03/23.

[147] Foland LC, Altshuler LL, Sugar CA, Lee AD, Leow AD, Townsend J, et al. Increased volume of the amygdala and hippocampus in bipolar patients treated with lithium. Neuroreport. 2008;19(2):221-4. Epub 2008/01/11.

[148] Moore GJ, Cortese BM, Glitz DA, Zajac-Benitez C, Quiroz JA, Uhde TW, et al. A longitudinal study of the effects of lithium treatment on prefrontal and subgenual prefrontal gray matter volume in treatment-responsive bipolar disorder patients. J Clin Psychiatry. 2009;70(5):699-705. Epub 2009/04/25.

[149] Savitz J, Nugent AC, Bogers W, Liu A, Sills R, Luckenbaugh DA, et al. Amygdala volume in depressed patients with bipolar disorder assessed using high resolution 3T MRI: the impact of medication. Neuroimage. 2010;49(4):2966-76. Epub 2009/11/26.

[150] Hafeman DM, Chang KD, Garrett AS, Sanders EM, Phillips ML. Effects of medication on neuroimaging findings in bipolar disorder: an updated review. Bipolar Disord. 2012;14(4):375-410. Epub 2012/05/29.

[151] Moorhead TW, McKirdy J, Sussmann JE, Hall J, Lawrie SM, Johnstone EC, et al. Progressive gray matter loss in patients with bipolar disorder. Biol Psychiatry. 2007;62(8):894-900.

[152] Brooks JO, 3rd, Foland-Ross LC, Thompson PM, Altshuler LL. Preliminary evidence of within-subject changes in gray matter density associated with remission of bipolar depression. Psychiatry Res. 2011;193(1):53-5. Epub 2011/05/13.

[153] Ellison-Wright I, Bullmore E. Anatomy of bipolar disorder and schizophrenia: a meta-analysis. Schizophr Res. 2010;117(1):1-12. Epub 2010/01/15.

[154] Basser PJ, Mattiello J, LeBihan D. MR diffusion tensor spectroscopy and imaging. Biophys J. 1994;66(1):259-67.

[155] Heng S, Song A, Sim K. White matter abnormalities in bipolar disorder: insights from diffusion tensor imaging studies. J Neural Transm. 2010;117(5):639-54.

[156] Anderson L, Shimamura AP. Influences of emotion on context memory while viewing film clips. The American journal of psychology. 2005;118(3):323-37. Epub 2005/11/01.

[157] Papez JW. A proposed mechanism of emotion.1937. J Neuropsychiatry Clin Neurosci. 1995;7(1):103-12.

[158] Livingston KE, Escobar A. Anatomical bias of the limbic system concept. Arch Neurol. 1971;24:17-21.

[159] Warner TD, Behnke M, Eyler FD, Padgett K, Leonard C, Hou W, et al. Diffusion tensor imaging of frontal white matter and executive functioning in cocaine-exposed children. Pediatrics. 2006;118:2014-24.

[160] Moeller F, Steinberg J, Lane S, Buzby M, Swann A, Hasan K, et al. Diffusion tensor imaging in MDMA users and controls: association with decision making. Am J Drug Alcohol Abuse. 2007;33(6):777-89.

[161] Lane SD, Steinberg JL, Ma L, Hasan KM, Kramer LA, Zuniga EA, et al. Diffusion Tensor Imaging and Decision Making in Cocaine Dependence. PLoS One. 2010;5(7):e11591.

[162] Adams K, Cimino JE, Arnold RM, Anderson WG. Why should I talk about emotion? Communication patterns associated with physician discussion of patient expressions of negative emotion in hospital admission encounters. Patient education and counseling. 2012. Epub 2012/05/12.

[163] Anderson CJ. The psychology of doing nothing: forms of decision avoidance result from reason and emotion. Psychol Bull. 2003;129(1):139-67. Epub 2003/01/31.

[164] Anderson C, Moyle W, McAllister M. Emotion and cardiac technology: an interpretive study. The Australian journal of advanced nursing : a quarterly publication of the Royal Australian Nursing Federation. 2002;20(2):27-33. Epub 2003/01/23.

[165] Taddei F, Bultrini A, Spinelli D, Di Russo F. Neural correlates of attentional and executive processing in middle-age fencers. Medicine and science in sports and exercise. 2012;44(6):1057-66. Epub 2011/12/14.

[166] Bonanno GA, Keltner D, Noll JG, Putnam FW, Trickett PK, LeJeune J, et al. When the face reveals what words do not: facial expressions of emotion, smiling, and the

willingness to disclose childhood sexual abuse. J Pers Soc Psychol. 2002;83(1):94-110. Epub 2002/06/29.

[167] Barnea-Goraly N, Chang K, D, Karchemskiy A, Howe M, E, Reiss A, L. Limbic and corpus callosum aberrations in adolescents with bipolar disorder: a tract-based spatial statistics analysis. Biological Psychiatry. 2009;66(3):238-44.

[168] Oosterwegel A, Field N, Hart D, Anderson K. The relation of self-esteem variability to emotion variability, mood, personality traits, and depressive tendencies. J Pers. 2001;69(5):689-708. Epub 2001/09/29.

[169] Keefe FJ, Lumley M, Anderson T, Lynch T, Studts JL, Carson KL. Pain and emotion: new research directions. J Clin Psychol. 2001;57(4):587-607. Epub 2001/03/20.

[170] Pavuluri MN, Yang S, Kamineni K, Passarotti AM, Srinivasan G, Harral EM, et al. Diffusion tensor imaging study of white matter fiber tracts in pediatric bipolar disorder and attention-deficit/hyperactivity disorder. Biol Psychiatry. 2009;65(7):586-93. Epub 2008/11/26.

[171] Bruno S, Cercignani M, Ron M, A. White matter abnormalities in bipolar disorder: a voxel-based diffusion tensor imaging study. Bipolar Disorders. 2008;10(4):460 - 8.

[172] Hogarty GE, Anderson CM, Reiss DJ, Kornblith SJ, Greenwald DP, Javna CD, et al. Family psychoeducation, social skills training, and maintenance chemotherapy in the aftercare treatment of schizophrenia. I. One-year effects of a controlled study on relapse and expressed emotion. Arch Gen Psychiatry. 1986;43(7):633-42. Epub 1986/07/01.

[173] Sussmann JE, Lymer GK, McKirdy J, Moorhead TW, Munoz Maniega S, Job D, et al. White matter abnormalities in bipolar disorder and schizophrenia detected using diffusion tensor magnetic resonance imaging. Bipolar Disord. 2009;11(1):11-8. Epub 2009/01/13.

[174] Walterfang M, Malhi GS, Wood AG, Reutens DC, Chen J, Barton S, et al. Corpus callosum size and shape in established bipolar affective disorder. Aust N Z J Psychiatry. 2009;43(9):838-45. Epub 2009/08/12.

[175] Wang F, Kalmar JH, Edmiston E, Chepenik LG, Bhagwagar Z, Spencer L, et al. Abnormal corpus callosum integrity in bipolar disorder: a diffusion tensor imaging study. Biol Psychiatry. 2008;64(8):730-3.

[176] Macritchie KA, Lloyd AJ, Bastin ME, Vasudev K, Gallagher P, Eyre R, et al. White matter microstructural abnormalities in euthymic bipolar disorder. Br J Psychiatry. 2010;196(1):52-8. Epub 2010/01/02.

[177] Benedetti F, Yeh PH, Bellani M, Radaelli D, Nicoletti MA, Poletti S, et al. Disruption of white matter integrity in bipolar depression as a possible structural marker of illness. Biol Psychiatry. 2011;69(4):309-17. Epub 2010/10/12.

[178] Anderson CM, Hogarty G, Bayer T, Needleman R. Expressed emotion and social networks of parents of schizophrenic patients. Br J Psychiatry. 1984;144:247-55. Epub 1984/03/01.

[179] Yurgelun-Tood D, A, Silveri M, M, Gruber S, A, Rohan M, L, Pimentel P, J. White matter abnormalities observed in bipolar disorder: a diffusion tensor imaging study. Bipolar Disorders. 2007;9(5):504 - 12.

[180] Versace A, Almeida J, Hassel S, Walsh N, Novelli M, Klein C, et al. Elevated left and reduced right orbitomedial prefrontal fractional anisotropy in adults with bipolar disorder revealed by tract-based spatial statistics. Arch Gen Psychiatry. 2008;65(9):1041-52.

[181] Sui J, Adali T, Pearlson GD, Calhoun VD. An ICA-based method for the identification of optimal FMRI features and components using combined group-discriminative techniques. Neuroimage. 2009;46(1):73-86.

[182] Lin F, Weng S, Xie B, Wu G, Lei H. Abnormal frontal cortex white matter connections in bipolar disorder: a DTI tractography study. J Affect Disord. 2011;131(1-3):299-306. Epub 2011/01/18.

[183] McIntosh AM, Munoz Maniega S, Lymer GK, McKirdy J, Hall J, Sussmann JE, et al. White matter tractography in bipolar disorder and schizophrenia. Biol Psychiatry. 2008;64(12):1088-92.

[184] Mori S, Wakana S, Nagae-Poetscher LM, van Zijl PCM. MRI atlas of human white matter. Amsterdam: ELSEVIER B.V.; 2005.

[185] McIntosh AM, Job DE, Moorhead TW, Harrison LK, Lawrie SM, Johnstone EC. White matter density in patients with schizophrenia, bipolar disorder and their unaffected relatives. Biol Psychiatry. 2005;58(3):254-7.

[186] Chaddock CA, Barker GJ, Marshall N, Schulze K, Hall MH, Fern A, et al. White matter microstructural impairments and genetic liability to familial bipolar I disorder. Br J Psychiatry. 2009;194(6):527-34.

[187] Petrides M, Pandya DN. Efferent association pathways from the rostral prefrontal cortex in the macaque monkey. J Neurosci. 2007;27(43):11573-86. Epub 2007/10/26.

[188] Sui J, Pearlson G, Caprihan A, Adali T, Kiehl KA, Liu J, et al. Discriminating schizophrenia and bipolar disorder by fusing fMRI and DTI in a multimodal CCA+ joint ICA model. Neuroimage. 2011;57(3):839-55. Epub 2011/06/07.

[189] Versace A, Almeida JR, Quevedo K, Thompson WK, Terwilliger RA, Hassel S, et al. Right orbitofrontal corticolimbic and left corticocortical white matter connectivity differentiate bipolar and unipolar depression. Biol Psychiatry. 2010;68(6):560-7. Epub 2010/07/06.

[190] Houenou J, Wessa M, Douaud G, Leboyer M, Chanraud S, Perrin M, et al. Increased white matter connectivity in euthymic bipolar patients: diffusion tensor tractography between the subgenual cingulate and the amygdalo-hippocampal complex. Mol Psychiatry. 2007;12(11):1001-10.

[191] Beyer J, L, Taylor W, D , MacFall J, R, Kuchibhatla M, Payne M, E, Provenzale J, M , et al. Cortical white matter microstructural abnormalities in bipolar disorder. Neuropsychopharmacology. 2005;30(12):2225 - 9.

[192] Frazier JA, Breeze JL, Papadimitriou G, Kennedy DN, Hodge SM, Moore CM, et al. White matter abnormalities in children with and at risk for bipolar disorder. Bipolar Disord. 2007;9(8):799-809. Epub 2007/12/14.

[193] Bearden CE, van Erp TG, Dutton RA, Boyle C, Madsen S, Luders E, et al. Mapping corpus callosum morphology in twin pairs discordant for bipolar disorder. Cereb Cortex. 2011;21(10):2415-24. Epub 2011/03/09.

[194] Lopez-Larson M, Breeze JL, Kennedy DN, Hodge SM, Tang L, Moore C, et al. Age-related changes in the corpus callosum in early-onset bipolar disorder assessed using volumetric and cross-sectional measurements. Brain Imaging Behav. 2010;4(3-4):220-31. Epub 2010/08/06.

[195] Haller S, Xekardaki A, Delaloye C, Canuto A, Lovblad KO, Gold G, et al. Combined analysis of grey matter voxel-based morphometry and white matter tract-based spatial statistics in late-life bipolar disorder. J Psychiatry Neurosci. 2011;36(6):391-401. Epub 2011/02/03.

[196] Walterfang M, Wood AG, Barton S, Velakoulis D, Chen J, Reutens DC, et al. Corpus callosum size and shape alterations in individuals with bipolar disorder and their first-degree relatives. Prog Neuropsychopharmacol Biol Psychiatry. 2009;33(6):1050-7. Epub 2009/06/09.

[197] Pourtois G, Dan ES, Grandjean D, Sander D, Vuilleumier P. Enhanced extrastriate visual response to bandpass spatial frequency filtered fearful faces: time course and topographic evoked-potentials mapping. Hum Brain Mapp. 2005;26(1):65-79. Epub 2005/06/15.

[198] Besnier N, Richard F, Zendjidjian X, Kaladjian A, Mazzola-Pomietto P, Adida M, et al. Stroop and emotional Stroop interference in unaffected relatives of patients with schizophrenic and bipolar disorders: distinct markers of vulnerability? World J Biol Psychiatry. 2009;10(4 Pt 3):809-18. Epub 2009/08/27.

[199] Kravariti E, Schulze K, Kane F, Kalidindi S, Bramon E, Walshe M, et al. Stroop-test interference in bipolar disorder. Br J Psychiatry. 2009;194(3):285-6.

[200] Pompei F, Dima D, Rubia K, Kumari V, Frangou S. Dissociable functional connectivity changes during the Stroop task relating to risk, resilience and disease expression in bipolar disorder. Neuroimage. 2011;57(2):576-82. Epub 2011/05/17.

[201] Brotman MA, Guyer AE, Lawson ES, Horsey SE, Rich BA, Dickstein DP, et al. Facial emotion labeling deficits in children and adolescents at risk for bipolar disorder. Am J Psychiatry. 2008;165(3):385-9.

[202] Brotman MA, Skup M, Rich BA, Blair KS, Pine DS, Blair JR, et al. Risk for bipolar disorder is associated with face-processing deficits across emotions. J Am Acad Child Adolesc Psychiatry. 2008;47(12):1455-61.

[203] Seidel EM, Habel U, Finkelmeyer A, Hasmann A, Dobmeier M, Derntl B. Risk or resilience? Empathic abilities in patients with bipolar disorders and their first-degree relatives. J Psychiatr Res. 2012;46(3):382-8. Epub 2011/12/03.

[204] Olsavsky AK, Brotman MA, Rutenberg JG, Muhrer EJ, Deveney CM, Fromm SJ, et al. Amygdala hyperactivation during face emotion processing in unaffected youth at risk for bipolar disorder. J Am Acad Child Adolesc Psychiatry. 2012;51(3):294-303. Epub 2012/03/01.

[205] Kruger S, Alda M, Young LT, Goldapple K, Parikh S, Mayberg HS. Risk and resilience markers in bipolar disorder: brain responses to emotional challenge in bipolar patients and their healthy siblings. Am J Psychiatry. 2006;163(2):257-64. Epub 2006/02/02.

[206] Green MJ, Lino BJ, Hwang EJ, Sparks A, James C, Mitchell PB. Cognitive regulation of emotion in bipolar I disorder and unaffected biological relatives. Acta Psychiatr Scand. 2011;124(4):307-16. Epub 2011/06/08.

[207] Schneider MR, Delbello MP, McNamara RK, Strakowski SM, Adler CM. Neuroprogression in bipolar disorder. Bipolar Disord. 2012;14(4):356-74. Epub 2012/05/29.

[208] Wessa M, Linke J, Witt SH, Nieratschker V, Esslinger C, Kirsch P, et al. The CACNA1C risk variant for bipolar disorder influences limbic activity. Mol Psychiatry. 2010;15(12):1126-7. Epub 2010/03/31.

[209] McDonald C, Bullmore ET, Sham PC, Chitnis X, Wickham H, Bramon E, et al. Association of genetic risks for schizophrenia and bipolar disorder with specific and generic brain structural endophenotypes. Archives of General Psychiatry. 2004;61(10):974-84.

[210] Hajek T, Gunde E, Bernier D, Slaney C, Propper L, Grof P, et al. Subgenual cingulate volumes in affected and unaffected offspring of bipolar parents. J Affect Disord. 2008;108(3):263-9. Epub 2007/11/27.

[211] Hajek T, Novak T, Kopecek M, Gunde E, Alda M, Hoschl C. Subgenual cingulate volumes in offspring of bipolar parents and in sporadic bipolar patients. Eur Arch Psychiatry Clin Neurosci. 2010;260(4):297-304. Epub 2009/10/09.

[212] Matsuo K, Kopecek M, Nicoletti MA, Hatch JP, Watanabe Y, Nery FG, et al. New structural brain imaging endophenotype in bipolar disorder. Mol Psychiatry. 2012;17(4):412-20. Epub 2011/02/16.

[213] Frangou S. Brain structural and functional correlates of resilience to Bipolar Disorder. Front Hum Neurosci. 2011;5:184. Epub 2012/03/01.

[214] Kempton MJ, Haldane M, Jogia J, Grasby PM, Collier D, Frangou S. Dissociable brain structural changes associated with predisposition, resilience, and disease expression in bipolar disorder. J Neurosci. 2009;29(35):10863-8. Epub 2009/09/04.

[215] McIntosh AM, Job DE, Moorhead TW, Harrison LK, Forrester K, Lawrie SM, et al. Voxel-based morphometry of patients with schizophrenia or bipolar disorder and their unaffected relatives. Biological Psychiatry. 2004;56(8):544-52.

[216] Hajek T, Gunde E, Slaney C, Propper L, MacQueen G, Duffy A, et al. Striatal volumes in affected and unaffected relatives of bipolar patients--high-risk study. J Psychiatr Res. 2009;43(7):724-9. Epub 2008/12/03.

[217] Hajek T, Gunde E, Slaney C, Propper L, MacQueen G, Duffy A, et al. Amygdala and hippocampal volumes in relatives of patients with bipolar disorder: a high-risk study. Can J Psychiatry. 2009;54(11):726-33. Epub 2009/12/08.

[218] Ladouceur CD, Almeida JR, Birmaher B, Axelson DA, Nau S, Kalas C, et al. Subcortical gray matter volume abnormalities in healthy bipolar offspring: potential

neuroanatomical risk marker for bipolar disorder? J Am Acad Child Adolesc Psychiatry. 2008;47(5):532-9.

[219] Versace A, Ladouceur CD, Romero S, Birmaher B, Axelson DA, Kupfer DJ, et al. Altered development of white matter in youth at high familial risk for bipolar disorder: a diffusion tensor imaging study. J Am Acad Child Adolesc Psychiatry. 2010;49(12):1249-59, 59 e1. Epub 2010/11/26.

[220] Sprooten E, Sussmann JE, Clugston A, Peel A, McKirdy J, William T, et al. White Matter Integrity in Individuals at High Genetic Risk of Bipolar Disorder. Biol Psychiatry. 2011. Epub 2011/03/25.

[221] Guo WB, Liu F, Chen JD, Xu XJ, Wu RR, Ma CQ, et al. Altered white matter integrity of forebrain in treatment-resistant depression: A diffusion tensor imaging study with tract-based spatial statistics. Prog Neuropsychopharmacol Biol Psychiatry. 2012;38(2):201-6. Epub 2012/04/17.

[222] Guo WB, Liu F, Xue ZM, Gao K, Wu RR, Ma CQ, et al. Altered white matter integrity in young adults with first-episode, treatment-naive, and treatment-responsive depression. Neurosci Lett. 2012. Epub 2012/06/23.

[223] Henze R, Brunner R, Thiemann U, Parzer P, Klein J, Resch F, et al. White matter alterations in the corpus callosum of adolescents with first-admission schizophrenia. Neurosci Lett. 2012;513(2):178-82. Epub 2012/03/01.

[224] Knochel C, Oertel-Knochel V, Schonmeyer R, Rotarska-Jagiela A, van de Ven V, Prvulovic D, et al. Interhemispheric hypoconnectivity in schizophrenia: fiber integrity and volume differences of the corpus callosum in patients and unaffected relatives. Neuroimage. 2012;59(2):926-34. Epub 2011/10/04.

[225] Kong X, Ouyang X, Tao H, Liu H, Li L, Zhao J, et al. Complementary diffusion tensor imaging study of the corpus callosum in patients with first-episode and chronic schizophrenia. J Psychiatry Neurosci. 2011;36(2):120-5. Epub 2010/12/09.

[226] Kunimatsu N, Aoki S, Kunimatsu A, Abe O, Yamada H, Masutani Y, et al. Tract-specific analysis of white matter integrity disruption in schizophrenia. Psychiatry Res. 2012;201(2):136-43. Epub 2012/03/09.

[227] Wang Q, Deng W, Huang C, Li M, Ma X, Wang Y, et al. Abnormalities in connectivity of white-matter tracts in patients with familial and non-familial schizophrenia. Psychol Med. 2011;41(8):1691-700. Epub 2011/01/06.

[228] Whitford TJ, Savadjiev P, Kubicki M, O'Donnell LJ, Terry DP, Bouix S, et al. Fiber geometry in the corpus callosum in schizophrenia: evidence for transcallosal misconnection. Schizophr Res. 2011;132(1):69-74. Epub 2011/08/13.

[229] Federspiel A, Begre S, Kiefer C, Schroth G, Strik WK, Dierks T. Alterations of white matter connectivity in first episode schizophrenia. Neurobiol Dis. 2006;22(3):702-9.

[230] Pérez-Iglesias R, Tordesillas-Gutiérres D, Barker GJ, McGuire PK, Roiz-Santianez R, Mata I, et al. White matter defects in first episode psychosis patients: A voxelwise analysis of diffusion tensor imaging. Neuroimage. 2010;49(1):199-204.

[231] Muñoz Maniega S, Lymer GK, Bastian ME, Marjoram D, Job DE, Moorhead TW, et al. A diffusion tenso MRI study of white matter integrity in subjectsat hiegh genetic risk of schizophrenia. Schizophr Res. 2008;106(2-3):132-9.
[232] Zou K, Huang X, Li T, Gong Q, Li Z, Ou-yang L, et al. Alterations of white matter integrity in adults with major depressive disorder: a magnetic resonance imaging study. J Psychiatry Neurosci. 2008;33(6):525-30.
[233] Zhu X, Wang X, Xiao J, Zhong M, Liao J, Yao s. Altered white matter integrity in first-episode, treatment-naive young adults with major depressive disorder: A tract-based spatial statistics study. Brain Res. 2011;1369:223-9.

Chapter 6

CBT in Affective Disorders – New Frontiers

Larissa Wolkenstein and Martin Hautzinger

Additional information is available at the end of the chapter

http://dx.doi.org/10.5772/54236

1. Introduction

The basic idea of Cognitive Behavioral Therapy (CBT) for depression (as well as for other disorders) is the intercorrelation of mood, thinking and behavior [1]. These three modalities are reciprocally correlated. That means that a negative mood can result in a reduced level of activity and a negative and constricted way of thinking but at the same time specific behaviors may lead to a bad mood and a negative way of thinking or one thought (or a bad memory) may narrow the behavior and depress mood.

The first step of a successful CBT is to build up a good therapeutic relationship. In a second step, psychoeducation is followed by concrete therapy goals formulation. Within the next CBT sessions one of the central challenges for the therapist is to deduce the basic rationale of intercorrelation of mood, behavior and cognition from the personal experiences described by the patient and to illustrate how this interrelation may end up in a negative spiral. Thus, a rationale of depression has to be provided and the problems of the patient have to be related to this rationale. The main goal of CBT for depression is to stop the negative spiral and to initiate constructive changes on the behavioral as well as on the cognitive level. Thus, CBT undermines cognitive and behavioral maintenance factors of depression leading to re-evaluations of underlying assumptions and beliefs so as to reduce vulnerability and risk factors [2].

A first step to cause changes on the cognitive level, i.e. to reach cognitive restructuring, is to identify negative automatic thoughts the patient has in his/her everyday life as well as the cognitive biases that underlie these negative automatic thoughts. This may be for example 'all-or-nothing thinking' or 'emotional reasoning'. Within the CBT, cognitions are defined as hypotheses instead of being defined as facts and the patient is inspired to test these hypotheses. For this purpose therapists use the technique of Socratic dialogue. In a Socratic dialogue open questions are used to point out inconsistencies in the conclusions of the patient without devaluating, or showing up the patient. Questions therapists pose are short and concise, refer to proximate statements of the patient and are helpful to develop new insights. If a cognition or thought has proven to be wrong alternative explanations and reattributions are developed together with the patient. Pros and Cons as well as short- and long-term consequences of specific attitudes are considered and weighed up.

Besides these techniques that intend to reach cognitive restructuring, behavioral components are also part of the CBT for depression. These components aim to influence patient's behavior directly, to provide immediate help, quick changes and facilitations, to increase positive experiences, as well as to overcome behavioral deficits. The main goals of the behavioral therapeutic elements are 1. to breach the vicious circle of inactivity, passivity, social withdrawal and depressive symptoms, 2. to structure everyday life and the course of specific actions and behaviors, 3. to interrupt and detract from rumination, 4. to acquire new skills and resources to reduce depressive behaviors and relapses, and 5. to support the cognitive interventions by the use of role plays, the enhancement of positive activities, and behavioral exercises that can be understood as experiments and reality testing [1].

One of the first behavioral therapeutic elements that are used in the therapy of depression is the enhancement of positive activities alongside a reduction of negative activities as this allows for early positive experiences and positive reinforcements in the context of the therapy. Often, weekly activity schedules are used for this purpose, so that patients can record their activities. To vividly illustrate the association between behavior and mood patients are often asked to also record how they feel after the different activities they display. On this background the motivation to include more positive activities into the weekly activity schedule can be build up.

Another behavioral therapeutic component is the improvement of social competences. The number of social contacts of depressed patients is often low and social competences of the patients are impaired. Consequently, social relationships of depressed patients are often not satisfactory. In many cases it does not suffice just to reduce the depressive symptomatology to overcome the reduced social contacts or the deficient social competences of the patients. Therefore, the improvement of social competences, communication skills and problem solving skills is an essential part of a promising CBT. The basic instruments in this context are the role play, behavioral exercises and the inclusion of partners and family members.

Within the last therapy sessions of a CBT it is important to address the issue of relapse and recurrence of depression. After CBT, patients should be enabled to get along with future depressive symptoms, crises and possible relapses. Therefore, patients need to repeat and practice what they have learned thoroughly so as to be able to use all the techniques on their own after the CBT has been finished. Probable crises should be brought up to reflect possibilities to get along self-directed. Therefore, all materials that have been used in the therapy should be handed out to the patient so that he/she can use them as utilities. Furthermore, to prevent relapses it has proven to be helpful to fade out therapeutic contacts slowly by extending the time interval between the therapy sessions. This enables the therapist to be available for at least one year in case of crises or relapses after the main part of the therapy has been finished. Many patients value the offering of the so-called booster-sessions.

2. Effectiveness and efficacy of cognitive behavioral therapy in the treatment of depression

Placebo-controlled studies that compared the efficacy of cognitive behavior therapy (CBT) with that of antidepressant medication (ADM) found out that CBT is as efficacious as ADM in the treatment of patients with mild to severe forms of depression and that both treatments are superior to placebos [3-5]. Spoken numerically, about 40-60% of the patients respond to a CBT treatment [6]. However, early studies concluded that ADM is superior to pill-placebo in the treatment of severe depressions whereas CBT is not [7]. Even though this conclusion was mainly based on one study it had a great impact on the perception of treatment effectiveness and resulted in suggestions from the American Psychiatric Association that ADM should be preferred over CBT for patients with more severe forms of depression [8]. Yet, subsequently conducted studies found out that this conclusion was wrong and that CBT fares as well as ADM with severely depressed patients [4, 9]. Accordingly, ADM should not be considered to be superior to CBT for the acute treatment of severe forms of depression. However, it seems as if the efficacy of CBT in the treatment of severe forms of depression depends on a high level of therapist experience [4, 10].

Going beyond the immediate effects of ADM and CBT it has to be kept in mind that while medication usually has a rapid and robust effect it has been shown to prevent the return of depressive symptoms only for as long as it is taken [8]. Thus, the intake of medication does not seem to alter the risk factors that lead to a subsequent recurrence. For that reason medication does not reduce the risk of relapse once its use is terminated [11]. That is why most patients with chronic or recurrent forms of depression are encouraged to stay on medication for an indefinite period [6]. In contrast, CBT appears to have an enduring effect that reduces risk of relapse not only during the time of therapy but also after treatment termination [11-12]. In a meta-analysis of Gloaguen and colleagues it has for example been shown that the one-year relapse rate for patients previously treated with CBT was approximately 25%, whereas 50% of patients previously treated with ADM relapsed in the same period. Furthermore, it has been shown that the preventative effect of prior CBT is at least as large in magnitude as that effect that is produced by keeping patients on medication [13-14]. A combination of CBT and medication holds the benefits of each and thus may enhance the probability of treatment response over a monotherapy, especially in chronic depressions [11].

Despite lower relapse rates associated with CBT as compared to medication relapse is still a substantial problem in CBT of depression. In contrast to addictive disorders where the focus has already many years ago been laid on relapse prevention research has not paid a lot of attention to relapse-prevention in depressive disorders. Patients who have recovered from recurrent major depressive disorder face an 80% rate of recurrence if they do not get further prophylactic treatment [15]. To handle and reduce that risk physicians prescribe either continuation- or maintenance-phase medication. In contrast, it still doesn't seem to be custom to offer psychotherapeutic relapse-prevention after patients responded to the acute phase of depression-specific psychotherapeutic treatments. One concrete suggestion for improving the long-term outcome of depressive patients after a CBT comes from Jarrett and colleagues who suggest to include a continuation or maintenance phase into the CBT [16]. Over an 8-month period the authors found that a CBT including a continuation phase (C-CT) reduced relapse estimates significantly more than a control condition that was defined as evaluation without CT (10% vs. 31%). Over a 2-year follow-up, also including a CBT-free period, C-CT significantly reduced relapse and recurrence estimates in patients with early-onset depression (16% vs. 67% in control). Furthermore, if patients had unstable remission during the late phase of acute treatment, C-CT also significantly reduced relapse and recurrence estimates to 37% as compared to 62% in the control group. Thus, the authors conclude that risk factors influence the necessity for relapse-prevention. In the 12-month follow-up of another study that has been conducted by DeRubeis and colleagues it has been found that patients who completed the CBT and had up to three optional booster sessions afterwards were significantly less likely to relapse than patients who switched to placebo after the acute phase CBT (31% vs. 76%) [4, 13]. Another promising way to reduce relapse-rates seems to be mindfulness-based cognitive therapy (MBCT) that is designed to train recovered patients with recurrent depression to disengage from depressogenic thinking that may mediate relapse. Teasdale and colleagues reported that recovered patients who received treatment as usual (TAU) and MBCT instead of TAU alone had significantly lower relapse rates – however this was only the case for patients with three or more previous depressive episodes [17].

CBT is not only effective in the treatment of acute depression and in relapse-prevention but also in the treatment of residual depressive symptoms. The largest study to date that addressed this issue included 158 patients with residual symptoms after a recent depressive episode that has been treated with ADM [18-19]. These patients either received clinical management alone or clinical management plus cognitive therapy over twenty weeks with two subsequent booster sessions. Patients received continuation and maintenance medication. CBT reduced relapse rates (29% vs. 47% in the clinical management group) as well as persistent residual symptoms. CBT also increased full remission rates at 20 weeks. Furthermore, the addition of CBT produced improvements in social and psychological functioning.

In contrast to CBT there is only little knowledge concerning the long-term efficacy of other psychosocial treatments in relation to that of CBT. One study that aimed to test the theory of change that underlies CBT undertook a component analysis of CBT [20] and thereby treated patients either exclusively with behavioral activation (BA), a combination of BA and teaching of skills to modify automatic thoughts (AT), or the full CBT treatment also including the components that focus on core schema. Jacobson and colleagues [20] did not find an evidence that the complete CBT was superior to either component treatment – neither at the termination of acute treatment nor at the 6-month follow-up. Moreover, both BA as well as AT also altered negative thinking and dysfunctional attributional styles of the patients – just as did the complete CBT treatment. Another study even demonstrated that an expanded BA model was as effective as was ADM with respect to the reduction of acute distress of depressed patients independently of the level of initial depression severity, and superior to CBT when regarding more severely depressed patients [21]. In a more recent randomized controlled trial of interpersonal psychotherapy (IPT) versus CBT it has been shown that even though patients in a treatment as usual condition improve just as do patients in a CBT or an IPT condition, IPT and CBT seem to be superior to TAU in at least some analyses [22]. Another study that aimed to compare the efficacy of interpersonal psychotherapy (IPT) and CBT demonstrated that both therapies are effective in treating depressive disorders, but that CBT seems to be superior in treating severe depression [23]. In contrast, de Mello and colleagues who conducted a systematic review of research findings on the efficacy of IPT for depressive disorders came to the conclusion that CBT is less efficacious than IPT [24].

When searching for the effect size associated with CBT for depression the picture gets less homogenous compared to the question if CBT has an effect at all. CBT has been reported to have a medium effect size (d = .67) relative to a number of different control conditions as for example non-specific controls or the absence of treatment [25]. As expected the effect size of CBT is larger when it is compared to waiting list controls (d=0.88) than when it is compared to treatment as usual (d=0.38) or non-specific controls (d=0.38) [25]. Moreover, a combination of CBT with ADM seems to be superior to ADM alone as it is associated with a somewhat larger effect size (d=0.27). In an older meta-analysis Cuijpers, van Straten, Andersson and van Oppen [26] included 53 studies in which seven types of psychotherapy have been compared with other psychological treatment to examine the efficacy of psychotherapies for depression in adults. The authors concluded that all forms of psychotherapy were efficacious in treating depression. However, it seemed as if IPT was somewhat more efficacious (d = 0.20) whereas non-directive supportive treatment was somewhat less efficacious (d = -0.13) than the other treatments. Furthermore, it has been reported that the efficacy of group CBT (d= 0.15) does not significantly differ from the efficacy of individual CBT [27]. However, it has to be mentioned that the quality of the studies that have been included in the respective meta-analysis was rather low. In a more recent meta-analysis Cuijpers and collaborators [28] found evidence that the effects of psychotherapy for depression have been overestimated in former meta-analyses and that the quality of the studies examining psychotherapy for depression is associated with the effect sizes that have been found. Accordingly, they reported a standardized mean effect size of d = 0.22 for high quality studies as compared to a mean effect size of d = 0.74 in lower-quality studies, even after controlling for the control condition used. This difference has been significant. That lower study quality seems to be related with larger effect sizes has also been confirmed by a more recent review [29]. Moreover, Cuijpers and collaborators [30] found that in dependence of the kind of instrument used to measure improvement following a psychotherapy the effect sizes of studies examining the effect of psychotherapy for depression differ significantly so as to clinician-ratings are associated with a significantly greater effect size than are self-report measures. This has to be kept in mind when drawing conclusions from efficacy-studies.

Besides the efficacy of CBT in sense of recovery and relapse-prevention that is at least comparable with or even superior to the efficacy of ADM it is important to mention that

CBT is also more cost-effective than ADM in the longer term [31]. And not only the efficacy of individual CBT has been well-documented but there are also hints that group CBT seems to be efficacious. In this context Brown and colleagues [32] compared the clinical effectiveness, costs, treatment preference, attrition and patient satisfaction of group and individual CBT in a naturalistic clinical study. Despite the fact that patients preferred individual CBT at baseline, they found no significant differences between group and individual CBT in depressive and distress symptoms at post-treatment and at 3-month follow-up. Furthermore, there were no differences in attrition and satisfaction between the two groups. However, the cost-effectiveness was higher for group CBT. Thus, if this finding holds true in further studies, it could be considered more frequently to conduct group CBT instead of individual CBT.

3. Mediators and moderators of treatment effects of CBT for depression

During the last years the search for moderators and mediators of the response to cognitive behavioral treatments for depression has been intensified. The reason therefore is that not only the response rate could be increased but also the costs could be decreased if we knew which patients are likely to respond to a CBT treatment and which processes mediate the treatment response. A moderator can be understood as a patient characteristic that is present before the treatment and independent of treatment assignment. Furthermore, it has an interactive effect with the treatment condition on the treatment outcome. Thus, a moderator variable influences the direction or the magnitude of the relationship between the independent (treatment condition) and the dependent (outcome) variable. It is important to distinguish between moderator variables that predict differential response to treatment and prognostic factors that predict the outcome in general and irrespective of treatment assignment [33]. In contrast, a mediator variable is an intervening variable that accounts for the relationship between the independent and the dependent variable. Thus, a mediator variable changes due to the treatment and in turn correlates with treatment outcome [33]. In the following section we would like to highlight the main findings concerning moderator and mediator variables of CBT for depression (without drawing a claim on completeness as there are several studies in this field even though the number is small as compared to studies examining moderators and mediators of ADM).

While during the last years the search for possible moderators of the response to CBT treatment for depression has especially focused on the neurobiological activity pattern of the patients, it has already taken other variables into account long before.

Some patient characteristics with unclear status: Prognostic factors or moderator variables for the response to CBT for depression?

An early study of Sotsky et al. [34] in which 239 patients with a depressive disorder have been included has highlighted that six patient characteristics as well as the severity of the depression patients reported before the beginning of the treatment predict treatment outcome (not only of CBT but also of IPT, ADM with clinical management, and placebo with clinical management). These characteristics comprised social dysfunction, cognitive dysfunction, expectation of improvement, endogenous depression, double depression and the duration of the current episode. Partly, these findings have been confirmed by Carter and colleagues who also found that a treatment response to either CBT or IPT is predicted by the perceived logicalness of the therapy (which conforms to the predictive value of the afore mentioned expectation of improvement), recurrent depression, and childhood reasons for the depression [35]. Furthermore, Fournier and colleagues found that older age and chronic depression predict relatively poor outcome following CBT as well as following ADM [36]. Uncontrolled pre-post-studies revealed that being married and displaying a lower initial symptom severity are prognostic of better response to CBT [37-38], however, it is unclear whether this finding is treatment-specific. Furthermore, patients who are above average intelligent seem to be more suitable for CBT than patients with lower intelligence [36, 39].

In the last decades it has also been paid attention to the role of negative cognitive schemata in moderating the effect of CBT. Thereby, it has been assumed that having particular negative cognitive schemata leads to severe and chronic problems that are not changeable with standard CBT and therefore require specific schema-focused procedures [40]. Halford and colleagues examined if this hypothesis holds true for patients with depression or anxiety disorder and found that contrary to this assumption a greater initial endorsement of maladaptive schemata did not predict poor therapy response [41]. Again, it is unclear to date whether the endorsement of maladaptive schemata would also be associated with good treatment response to other psychosocial interventions. Thus, it remains unclear if this is a prognostic factor rather than a moderator variable.

Another variable that has repeatedly been examined is the tendency to ruminate or to distract in response to depressed mood. In this context Teismann and colleagues found that even after controlling for depression scores pretreatment greater symptom- and self-focused rumination pretreatment predicts more self- and interviewer-rated depression as well as greater general symptom severity and lower therapists' appraisal of success posttreatment [42]. However, in another study the same authors found that ruminative responses to depressed mood are neither predictive of the therapeutic alliance nor of patients' receptivity to therapeutic interventions as perceived by the therapist [43]. Moreover, while the pretreatment tendency to distract was not associated with posttreatment depression after a CBT another study found that it is predictive of the patients' receptivity in therapy and the goodness of the therapeutic alliance [42, 44]. Again, it is not clear whether these findings are specific to CBT or also hold true for any other psychosocial treatment.

As it has been described before, during a CBT patients are taught to interrupt automatic emotional processing (e.g., rumination) with controlled processing (e.g., cognitive reappraisal). Accordingly, what a CBT seems to directly address is the sustained emotional reactivity that has repeatedly been associated with depression [45]. Furthermore, it has been shown that depression is associated with an increased and sustained reactivity in brain regions responsible for emotional processing, particularly the amygdala [46-48]. On this background Siegle, Carter and Thase [49] developed the idea that there might be an association between the neural correlates of sustained emotional processing pretreatment and the posttreatment recovery. To test for this hypothesis, the authors subjected their participants to undergo an fMRI during an emotional information processing task before they received a CBT. The authors highlighted that a stronger recovery following a CBT was associated with a decreased reactivity to negative words in the subgenual cingulate cortex and an increased reactivity in the amygdala – both pretreatment. The authors suppose that the pattern of decreased reactivity in the subgenual cingulate cortex in combination with the sustained amygdala reactivity to emotional stimuli reflects a ruminative coping style. Indeed, the patients' percent change in sustained amygdala activity was correlated with the self-reported tendency of the patients to ruminate, i.e., to think repetitively about their depressive symptoms. Accordingly, the authors suggest that their findings demonstrate that those patients benefit most from CBT who show an increased emotional reactivity pretreatment and who are not able to engage regulatory structures pretreatment. According to Siegle, Carter and Thase the latter has been illustrated by the decreased reactivity in the subgenual cingulated cortex pretreatment which suggests a deficient regulation. So, the authors conclude that the presence of emotion regulation deficits, which are targeted in CBT, may be the key to recovery with this specific intervention.

Findings concerning more "severe and complicated patients"

There are some preliminary indications that especially in the treatment of more severe and complicated patients a greater expertise of therapists is required to reach a successful outcome. In this context it has been shown that among patients with more severe depression, who are functionally impaired and have primary support group problems, both BA as well as ADM seem to be superior to pill-placebo whereas CT does not [21]. Furthermore, in another study the personality disorder status of the patients included led to differential response: In this study CT was superior to ADM for patients without personality disorder whereas the reverse was true for patients with personality disorder. However, despite the poor response of patients with comorbid Axis II disorders to CT, nearly all patients who did respond to CT within this study sustained their response over a one-year follow-up [50]. On the background of these studies Coffman and colleagues [51] concluded that "there might be a subset of patients who see themselves as doing better with sustained attention to behavior change in time-limited treatment". However, as the authors correctly indicate, before drawing firm conclusion, this pattern of self-reported non-response to CT should be replicated. Interestingly, other studies that did only focus on increased comorbid personality disorder symptoms instead of diagnosed Axis II disorders found a reverse pattern: For example Carter and colleagues found that increasing comorbid personality disorder symptoms where associated with decreases in response to IPT but not to CBT [35]. Other studies have shown that CBT seems to be more effective for patients who display an elevated level of avoidant personality disorder symptoms whereas IPT seems to be superior for patients displaying an elevated level of obsessive-compulsive personality disorder symptoms [52]. Facing these rather heterogeneous findings concerning the influence of Axis II symptoms and Axis II disorder status on the response to CBT and other psychosocial treatments it gets clear that future investigations are needed to elucidate if this really can be understood as a moderator variable and if so if it is associated with higher or lower response rates to CBT.

In a more recent, prospective, randomized, observer blinded multicenter study Stangier and colleagues compared the rates of relapse in 180 completely remitted depressed patients with three or more previous episodes who either received TAU plus Maintenance Cognitive Therapy (MCT) or TAU plus Manualized Psychoeducation (MAPE) for eight months [53]. Afterwards the patients were followed up for one year. The authors found that time to relapse of MDE did not differ significantly between the two treatment conditions. However, there was a significant interaction between treatment condition and the number of previous MDE episodes (<5 vs. ≥5), indicating that in patients with 5 or more previous episodes MCT was significantly superior to MAPE, whereas this was not true for patients with less than 5 previous episodes. The authors conclude that CBT has significant effects on relapse prevention only in patients with a high risk of depression recurrence whereas for patients with a lower risk of recurrence, non-specific and structured education may be equally effective.

Some moderating patient characteristics

Some patient characteristics examined in the early Sotsky study [34] have been predictive for differential treatment outcome. For instance, a low social dysfunction predicted superior response to IPT while a low cognitive dysfunction predicted superior response to CBT and to ADM. In addition, high depression severity and impairment of function have been associated with a superior response to ADM and IPT while high work dysfunction predicted superior response only to ADM.

Fournier and colleagues found that marriage, unemployment, and having experienced a greater number of recent life events predict superior response to CBT as compared to ADM [36]. Interestingly, in another study Barber and Muenz found that married patients did better with CBT than they did with IPT whereas unmarried patients did better with IPT than with CBT [52].

Patient's "attachment avoidance" has been shown to be associated with a better response to CBT as compared to IPT [54]. Keeping in mind that CBT does not target close relationships as specifically as does IPT this result seems to be intuitive because one would expect that CBT should be less threatening to individuals with high attachment avoidance as compared to IPT. Furthermore, it has been reported that while avoidant and schizoid symptoms predicted poorer response to IPT this was not true for CBT [55].

Another variable that was assumed to interact with treatment group to differentially affect treatment outcome is the patients' preference concerning the intervention [56]. Kocsis and colleagues found that in a randomized multicenter trial that compared the efficacy of Cognitive Behavioral Analysis System of Psychotherapy (CBASP) with that of nefazodone or the combination of both for chronic depression there was an interactive effect of the treatment preference of the patients (as indicated at study entry) and treatment group on the outcome. Patients who preferred medication at study entry had a higher remission rate and a lower symptom severity at study exit if they received medication than if they received CBT. Similarly, patients who preferred CBASP had a higher remission rate and a lower symptom severity at study exit if they received CBASP than if they received medication.

Thus, it can be concluded that patients' preference is a significant moderator of treatment response for chronically depressed patients. However, Leykin and colleagues, who also compared treatment outcomes of patients who received their preferred treatment via randomization versus those who did not, did not find a significant difference in the magnitude of symptom reduction between these two groups [57]. As did Kocsis and colleagues, Leykin and colleagues compared ADM with CBT – however, they did not specifically focus on chronically depressed patients.

The mediating role of neural mechanisms

Hence, as a primary goal of CBT is the replacement of automatic emotional reactivity with more controlled processing it can be assumed that on the neural level CBT might be accompanied by an increase of inhibitory executive control that helps to dampen automatic reactions that are reflected in an increased limbic activity. Indeed, recent studies have shown that CBT affects clinical recovery by modulating the functioning of specific sites in cortical and limbic regions. For example Goldapple and colleagues [58] conducted a resting state positron emission tomography (PET) study and found that treatment response following a CBT is associated with increases in the metabolic activity of the hippocampus, and the dorsal cingulate cortex alongside decreases in the metabolism of the dorsal, ventral, and medial frontal cortex. This study, regarded on the background of older studies that examined the effects of ADM [59-60], suggests that while ADM effects may be targeted to limbic regions and then forwarded CBT may rather target the prefrontal cortex by downtuning cognitive processes that take place automatically. This is also assumed by DeRubeis, Siegle and Hollon [61] in a comprehensive review of treatment outcomes and neural mechanisms of CT and ADM for depression. Furthermore, in a randomized controlled trial Kennedy and colleagues [62] have shown that a treatment response to CBT as well as a treatment response to ADM (venlafaxine) are associated with decreased glucose metabolism bilaterally in the orbitofrontal cortex and left medial prefrontal cortex alongside an increase in the metabolism of the right occipital-temporal cortex. However, metabolic changes in the anterior and posterior parts of the subgenual cingulate cortex and the caudate differentiated CBT and venlafaxine responders. Thus, the authors conclude that while response to either treatment was associated with a reduced metabolism in several prefrontal regions, only response to CBT seems to be associated with a reciprocal modulation of cortical-limbic connectivity.

Looking at further studies using functional neuroimaging techniques it gets obvious that different mediating brain mechanisms have been suggested and underpinned by single studies. One prospective study that included 16 medication-free patients suffering from an acute major depressive disorder has been conducted by Fu and colleagues [63]. During an fMRI scan pre- and posttreatment subjects performed an affect recognition task with morphed facial stimuli displaying sadness. In between patients received 16 CBT sessions. Pretreatment it has been shown that during the acute phase patients show an elevated amygdala-hippocampal activity as compared to healthy controls. At the end of the treatment the amygdala activity of the CBT responders has decreased to healthy niveau. Furthermore, the clinical response of the patients was significantly correlated with their baseline dorsal anterior cingulate activity. Thus, the authors suggest that anterior cingulate activity may be a predictor of treatment response to CBT. In a more recent study Ritchey and colleagues also used fMRI to assess neural responses to negative, neutral, and positive pictures in healthy controls and unmedicated, depressed patients – the latter pre- and posttreatment [64]. As did the study described before, the authors of this study also found evidence that the neural differences between depressed patients and healthy controls during emotion processing can be successfully addressed by CBT. Prior to the treatment the authors found that depressed patients show a reduced activity in the ventromedial prefrontal cortex, a diminished discrimination between emotional and neutral stimuli in the amygdala, caudate and hippocampus and an increased reactivity to negative versus positive pictures in the left anterior temporal lobe and the right dorsolateral prefrontal cortex. After the CBT patients exhibited activity increases in the ventromedial prefrontal cortex, an enhanced discrimination of emotional and neutral items in the amygdala and the caudate, as well as greater activity in response to positive versus neutral items in the left anterior temporal lobe. In accordance with the afore mentioned assumptions these neural changes may reflect increased engagement of processes that are involved in modulating responses to emotional stimuli. Furthermore, some of the identified pre-treatment differences between the two groups were predictive of the patients' treatment response. These included the hyperactivity in the ventromedial prefrontal cortex as well as the negativity bias in the left anterior temporal lobe and in the right dorsolateral prefrontal cortex.

CBT involves at least **3** broad treatment **goals**:
i. **challenge** patients' current way of **coping** with stressful events and problematic interpersonal relationship, attempts to **enhance problem-solving capacities**. Neuropsychological studies show that working memory, cognitive flexibility and other executive funtioning processes are involved. This brings the dorsolateral prefrontal cortex **(dlPFC)** and the hippocampus (**Hc**) into play and makes them potential targets of CBT. ii. **modify** patients' **perspectives** about themselves and their relationships. Neuroimaging studies suggest that cortical midline structure, such as the ventral (**vACC**) and dorsal (**dACC**) anterior cingulate cortex, the ventralmedial (**vmPFC**) and dorsomedial (**dmPFC**) prefrontal cortex, the posterior cingulate cortex (**pCC**) are involved in self-related information processing. These brain areas are potential targets of CBT. iii. assist patients in **regulating distressing emotional** states. CBT may impact brain functions associated with emotional processing, such as insular cortex (**vIns**), the amygdala (**Am**), the ventral and dorsal anterior cingulate cortex (**vACC, dACC**), the dorsolateral prefrontal cortex (**dlPFC**), the ventro-medial prefrontal cortex (**vmPFC**).

Table 1. Mechanisms of change – mediators of outcome

The mediating role of cognitive changes

The assumption of cognitive theory is that depressive symptoms change while the patients change their beliefs and the way they process information [65]. Indeed, besides neural changes that seem to reflect an enhanced cognitive control over emotions after CBT, it has been shown that the habitual tendency to ruminate decreases over the course of a CBT – a finding that fits well to the results concerning the neural level [66]. However, this was nothing unique to CBT but has also been found to occur during a Mindfulness-Based Cognitive Therapy (MBCT) [66]. Moreover, it has been shown that during CBT as well as during ADM automatic negative thoughts decrease and this reduction in turn has been associated with overall clinical improvement, so as to patients who did not benefit from either intervention showed significantly less change on cognitive measures [67-68]. Further studies have confirmed that reductions in negative cognitions are not only present in CBT but that different CBT treatment components are comparably effective in reducing negative cognitions. For instance, cognitive therapy and behavioral activation produce similar reductions in negative cognitions [20, 69]. According to Simons and colleagues these results suggests that cognitive change can be understood as a part of improvement rather than as the primary cause of improvement [68].To clarify the direction of effects DeRubeis and colleagues obtained depression severity scores as well as different measures of cognition not only in the beginning and in the end of a CBT and an ADM but also repeatedly during treatment admission [70]. The authors found that while cognitive change from pretreatment to midtreatment predicted change in depression from midtreatment to posttreatment in the CBT group, this was not the case in the ADM group. Thus, the authors concluded that cognitive changes indeed play a mediating role in CBT but not in ADM. Further support for the importance of cognitive changes in CBT comes from a more recent study in which it has been shown that among those patients who responded to a CBT both the development of CBT coping skills as well as in-session evidence of the independent use of these skills predicted a lower risk of relapse in the year following treatment [71]. Thus, it can be concluded that the development and use of CBT coping skills play an important role in relapse prevention. Similarly, Zindel Segal and colleagues [72] examined whether mood-linked changes in dysfunctional thinking following a sad mood induction predict relapse in depressed patients in remission. Therefore, patients were first randomly assigned to either ADM or CBT. Afterwards, patients who achieved remission underwent a sad mood induction and were then observed and repeatedly examined in the following 18 months. The authors reported two main findings: First, patients who recovered through ADM showed greater cognitive reactivity in response to a negative mood induction than those who recovered through CBT. Second, the magnitude of cognitive reactivity associated with the negative mood induction significantly predicted relapse over the subsequent 18 months – independently of the type of prior treatment.

Whereas changes in more superficial cognitions (i.e., automatic thoughts) seems to be a result of different interventions, changes in more basic cognitions, for example attributional style or dysfunctional beliefs, seem to be significantly larger and thus more unique to CBT [73]. Furthermore, it has been demonstrated that a change of these more stable information-processing proclivities does mediate the smaller rate of relapse following a CBT [73-74]. Thereby it proved to be important that patients do become less extreme in their information-processing instead of becoming unrealistically positive as the latter is also associated with a greater risk to relapse [74-75].

Another study that examined the mediating role of cognitive changes in the efficacy of CBT highlighted that many patients experience so-called "sudden gains" during a cognitive behavioral intervention [76]. Sudden gains refer to large symptom improvements in a single between-session interval that account for about fifty percent of these patients total improvement. These sudden gains were associated with a lower depression-level posttreatment and at an 18-month follow-up. Tang and DeRubeis [76] found that these sudden gains were preceded by considerable cognitive changes in the therapy session that has taken place immediately before the sudden gains and presume that these changes triggered the sudden gains. Furthermore, an improvement of the therapeutic alliance as well as additional cognitive changes followed in the therapy session immediately after the sudden gains. So, it can be assumed that considerable cognitive changes during one CBT session may lead to sudden gains that can be understood as the beginning of an upward spiral. Interestingly, one variable that also seems to predict later treatment outcome is the early improvement in the course of a CBT [77].

4. New developments in the CBT for depression

Within the last years there have been made some attempts to increase the access to CBT resulting in new types of CBT treatments as for example online- and telephone based treatments. Given the high stigmatization that is associated with psychiatric disorders and the therapeutic interventions for these disorders on the one hand and the increasing use of the internet and online programs on the other hand this development seems nothing but logical. Besides the easy accessibility and the potential to offer an approach in a non-stigmatizing environment there are some further advantages in conducting computerized CBT (cCBT). For instance, cCBT has the capacity to deliver structured input consistently with precision and is associated with comparably low costs [78]. Moreover, it has been shown that discontinuation of treatment is a problem that seems to be associated with face-to-face therapy [79]. According to some estimations about 47% of patients may drop out of psychotherapy [80]. Besides the already mentioned stigmatization limited time and the travel that is required to see a therapist might be barriers to the face-to-face treatment.

Before we summarize the findings concerning the efficacy of cCBT we would like to mention that computers and the internet can not only be used as an alternative to the traditional form of CBT but also as an adjunct to the individual contact with a therapist [78]: For example a computer can be used as a tool for screening or diagnosis and information can be provided either in written or in audio/video formats. Furthermore, structured self-help programs can be provided online whereby situations can be easily simulated and graded exposure in highly controlled conditions is possible. Besides that the patient and the therapist may communicate via emails, chats or forums either for therapeutic or administrative purposes. So, it can be concluded that the use of computers and the internet has the potential to enrich the therapeutic possibilities of the traditional face-to-face communication considerably.

However, what do we know concerning these new developments and especially concerning their efficacy? There are many cCBT programs developed for the treatment of depression named for example 'Colour Your Life' or 'Beating the Blues' and it has been shown that they are effective in the treatment of depression [81]. Foroushani and colleagues conducted a meta-review in which they included twelve systematic reviews covering results concerning the effectiveness of cCBT for mild to moderate depression [78]. This meta-review clarifies that while for single cCBT programs, as for example for 'ODIN', there is not enough data with good quality to conclude that they are really effective other cCBTs for depression, as for example 'MoodGYM', 'Beating the Blues', and 'Colour Your Life', have proven to be effective in reducing symptoms of depression. Looking at effect sizes that are reported for cCBT there are greater differences. Concerning to a review by Griffiths, Farrer and Christensten it ranges over different studies between 0.42 to 0.65 for cCBT interventions that included clinically depressed patients [81]. It has been reported that some cCBT packages seem to be more effective than treatment as usual (TAU), equally or less effective than bibliotherapy and no less effective than therapist-led CBT [78]. Even self-help internet interventions have been shown to reduce symptoms although this effect was smaller for depression than for anxiety disorders [78]. Furthermore, studies have indicated that it doesn't seem to be necessary that cCBT interventions are supported by mental health professionals [81] even though there is evidence that the provision of therapist support or the ongoing contact with users during an intervention seems to increase the effect of cCBT [82-83]. Even though it can be said that these first results seem to be quite promising the evidence indicating the effectiveness of cCBT is still limited so far and further randomized controlled trials are required. Another finding in the context of cCBT is that, as one would expect, cCBT reduces therapist time. However, to date it cannot be concluded that cCBT has superior effectiveness as compared to other forms of CBT because the therapist time of an intervention is only one variable amongst a number of variables that determine the cost-effectiveness.

Besides cCBT CBT offered through the telephone (tCBT) has also been shown to have positive effects on depression [84]. Moreover, in a randomized controlled trial Mohr and colleagues compared a 16-week tCBT program with 16 weeks of a supportive emotion-focused therapy also administered via telephone and found that improvements over treatment were significantly greater for tCBT than for the telephone-administered supportive intervention [85]. Furthermore, the treatment gains were still present during 12-month follow-up even though the differences between the two treatments were no longer evident. This study highlights that there is a specific effect of telephone-administered CBT that goes beyond the nonspecific effects of a supportive telephone-based intervention. In a more recent study it has been examined how tCBT performs as compared to face-to-face CBT with respect to attrition and symptom reduction [86]. Thereby, it has been shown that while both treatments were associated with a significant symptom reduction posttreatment, with CBT not being noteworthy superior to tCBT, more patients completed tCBT as compared to traditional CBT. However, even though all participants remained significantly less depressed at 6-month follow-up as compared to baseline participants receiving traditional CBT were significantly less depressed than participants receiving tCBT. Thus, the authors conclude that even though tCBT improves adherence compared with traditional CBT this might go at the cost of some increased risk of poorer maintenance of gains after the time of treatment. Further findings suggest that a telephone-administered CBT might not only be helpful as stand-alone therapy but also as an adjunct to pharmacotherapy. In a randomized trial with 393 depressed patients Ludman and colleagues evaluated usual care versus tCBT plus care management for primary care patients who were beginning an antidepressant treatment and highlighted that a brief, structured, telephone-administered CBT program can improve clinical outcomes for the majority of patients beginning antidepressant treatment in primary care [87].

So far there is only very little knowledge concerning moderator variables of cCBT. One study that investigated whether factors that are prognostic of depression outcome generally do also predict response to online CBT in a sample of depressed patients has been conducted by Button and colleagues [88]. In this study it has been shown that marital status as well as pretreatment severity predicted treatment response of the patients. Thereby, patients who were separated, widowed, or divorced showed a greater symptom reduction following the online CBT than did married patients. Having in mind earlier studies that repeatedly showed that in face-to-face CBT married patients have a better prognosis than unmarried individuals [37-38] this finding may indicate that online CBT is particularly beneficial for separated, widowed, and divorced patients and thus be a first hint on a moderating variable. However, this finding definitely requires replication as it is based on only one single study so far. Another finding of this study was that patients who were more severely depressed also displayed a superior treatment-derived benefit – a result that has already been reported in an earlier study concerning therapist-delivered internet psychotherapy for depression [89]. Furthermore, the authors found weak evidence that treatment effectiveness diminished with an increasing number of recent adverse life events. In contrast, age, educational level, and history of depression did not predict treatment response. Another variable that was assumed to possibly have the potential to moderate the effect of a cCBT and that has also been examined is the chronicity of depression [90]. However, no significant difference between chronic patients and non-chronic patients has been found in treatment outcome. In another randomized trial three hundred and three depressed patients were randomly assigned to either an unsupported online cCBT, a treatment as usual (TAU), or the combination of cCBT and TAU and demographic, clinical, cognitive, and short-term improvement variables have been assessed as potential moderator variables [91]. It could be shown that patients with higher levels of extreme (positive) responding as assessed by the Dysfunctional Attitude Scale-Form A benefited more from cCBT as compared to TAU, whereas patients who had a parental psychiatric history or the diagnosis of a major depressive disorder showed a better treatment response in cCBT and TAU as compared to TAU alone. Irrespective of treatment type current employment, low pretreatment illness severity as well as short-term improvement on clinical variables predicted a greater treatment-benefit.

Concerning mediating mechanisms of change in cCBT there are even les studies than concerning possible moderator variables. One study that evaluated treatment specificity and potential mediators of two online therapies for depressive symptoms included 263 depressed patients who were randomly assigned to either online CBT, online problem-solving Therapy (PST) or a waiting list control group [92]. Interestingly, no differing mechanisms of change have been found: Dysfunctional attitudes, worrying, a negative problem orientation, and perceived control all played a mediating role in online CBT as well as in online PST. Hence, the authors conclude that irrespective of the theoretical background of the therapy the psychological processes that lead to symptom reduction seem to be comparable.

5. Main components of the cognitive behavioral therapy for bipolar disorders

In contrast to unipolar depressive disorders bipolar disorders have long been regarded as purely biological-psychiatric disorders that can only be treated with medication. Therefore, psychotherapy has only had a supporting role, thought to be only helpful in encouraging medication adherence [93]. Due to the insight in the fundamental role of psychosocial factors in the onset and course of bipolar disorders [94-95] a more biopsychosocial explanatory model has only developed during the last decades and has brought about cognitive behavioral treatment approaches among other psychosocial interventions [96-98].

As in the treatment of other psychiatric disorders the first step of a successful CBT for bipolar disorders is the development of a good and sustainable therapeutic relationship. On the basis of this relationship psychoeducational sessions can be offered and concrete and achievable therapy goals can be formulated with the patient. Within the psychoeducation the therapist and the patient develop knowledge concerning factors that initiate and maintain bipolar symptomatology by building on the individual experiences of the patient. Thus, the role of genetic, biological, psychological and social factors in the development and maintenance of the illness are discussed and a vulnerability-stress-model is developed. Furthermore, the patient and the therapist deduce the intercorrelation of mood, behavior and thinking from the individual experiences of the patient so that a rationale of the bipolar disorder as well as a treatment rationale can be developed. The main goal of the CBT for bipolar disorders is to stop the downward spiral leading to depressive episodes as well as to stop the upward spiral leading to (hypo-)manic episodes. Therefore, within the psychoeducational sessions the symptomatology that is specific for depressive or (hypo-) manic episodes respectively is discussed. Furthermore, therapists focus on the course and prognosis of the illness, the role of risk factors and protective factors, as well as individual warning signs and prodromal symptoms. Moreover, medical and psychotherapeutic treatment opportunities are discussed.

A further essential element of the CBT for bipolar disorders is a detailed analysis of the behavior and the preconditions that might have led to former affective episodes. On the basis of this knowledge potential triggers (that might be either negative or positive), early warning symptoms and prodromal symptoms as well as successful and unsuccessful coping strategies can be identified.

On this background it can be made out which further contents should be focused in the remaining therapy sessions. Thereby it might for example be useful to focus on the structure of the everyday life of the patient: While during depressive episodes many patients tend to withdraw and to reduce their daily activities to a minimum, during (hypo-)manic episodes many patients tend to overload their schedule excessively. It may also be useful to concentrate on problem solving or social competence skills, or on dysfunctional attitudes. Working on dysfunctional attitudes also comprises looking at cognitive errors that are characteristic for either depression (as for example all-or-nothing-thinking, overgeneralization, catastrophizing or mental filters) or (hypo-)mania (as for example positive fortune-telling, overevaluation of immediate satisfaction or the misinterpretation of others' intention) and to comprehend these typical errors by looking at individual experiences of the patient [99]. To overcome these typical cognitive errors associated with depressive or (hypo-)manic mood states strategies can be helpful that are also used in the treatment of depression as for example the Socratic dialogue or behavioral experiments and reality testing in order to reach cognitive restructuring.

A further component of the CBT for bipolar disorders is to keep a mood diary during the therapy. This is a good opportunity to collect information and to develop the ability to differentiate between normal and harmless mood swings or fluctuations in the sleeping pattern and first symptoms that are due to the illness [100]. With the aid of a better ability to differentiate between pathological and normal changes in mood and sleeping pattern the patient is able to recognize potential triggers and first symptoms of new episodes in time and to make use of promising coping strategies [101-102]. Coping strategies for depressive mood states comprise for example behavioral activation whereas the strategies of stimulus control and anti-impulsiveness are useful in (hypo-)manic mood states. It can be summarized that the main goal of CBT for bipolar disorder is to make the patients specialists concerning their own illness and to enable them to behave in a way that prevents the occurrence of prodromal symptoms or to counteract occurring prodromal symptoms in time.

In some cases it is also necessary to involve family members in the therapy of bipolar patients. Family members may for example be helpful to identify early warning symptoms as some patients are not able to identify them all alone. Furthermore, in some cases it needs to be discussed how family members can give feedback and offer help to the patient if they have the impression than the patient is developing a new affective episode. On the other hand it is often necessary to clarify and to illustrate that not all mood changes are necessarily indicators for the beginning of a further affective episode but are normal to a certain extent.

As in the case of unipolar depression it is indispensable to address the issue of probable future crises during the last therapy sessions and to reflect possibilities that may help the patient to get along self-directed. Concrete emergency schedules should be developed for depressive symptoms as well as for (hypo-)manic symptoms. Furthermore, it is helpful to fade out therapeutic contacts slowly – just as in unipolar depression.

6. Effectiveness and efficacy of cognitive behavioral therapy in the treatment of bipolar disorders

During the last twenty years randomized controlled trials have shown that CBT for bipolar disorders is not only helpful to encourage medication adherence [93] but as an adjunct to medication also to reduce symptom severity, to accelerate stabilization, to delay relapses, and to improve the level of functioning [e.g., 103, 104-105]. In a recent systematic review Miklowitz and Scott included all randomized trials of adjunctive therapy for bipolar disorders that have been published between 1980 and 2008 [106]. While many of these studies examined the effectiveness of other psychosocial interventions (e.g., psychoeducation, systematic care management, family focused therapy) more than ten studies that have been included have specifically examined the effectiveness and efficacy of CBT for bipolar disorders. Even though Miklowitz and Scott point out that all these studies differ concerning many methodological issues (e.g., different kinds of CBT interventions, different sample characteristics) a great portion of these studies revealed that CBT is superior to routine care (i.e., mood stabilizers plus outpatient support) with respect to many outcome variables as for example the number of relapses, the improvement of social adjustment and the improvement of coping strategies to manage prodromal symptoms. Furthermore, patients who receive CBT seem to have less psychiatric admissions or days in an affective episode. This seems to be not only the case during the time of treatment but has also been shown for longer follow-up periods (e.g., 30 months). Interestingly, over a 30-month follow-up CBT has not only been superior to TAU concerning the clinical outcome variables but also concerning the costs that have been associated with the respective treatment form.

However, most studies that have been conducted to examine the efficacy of CBT for bipolar disorders have compared the effects of CBT against the effects of a TAU condition. Thereby, in most cases the CBT group received the CBT in addition to what has been referred to as TAU (e.g., medication which is associated with regular visits to the psychiatrist). Hence, the patients allocated to the CBT group received more attention and support than patients who have been allocated to the control group in these studies. To control for the effects of the surplus in attention and support that has been associated with the CBT groups in former studies Meyer and Hautzinger conducted a randomized controlled trial in which they compared CBT to a supportive therapy (ST) [107]. The authors found no differences between the two treatment conditions with respect to relapse rates. Thus, it can be assumed that certain characteristics that are shared by many psychosocial interventions as for example providing information or systematic mood monitoring might explain the effects of different kinds of treatments for bipolar disorders. This finding fits to a meta-analysis conducted by

Lynch and colleagues in which amongst others the effectiveness of CBT for bipolar disorders has been examined by pooling data from published trials of CBT that used controls for non-specific effects of intervention [108]. Furthermore, trials of effectiveness against relapse were also pooled if they compared CBT to TAU. In this analysis CBT proved to be ineffective in reducing relapse in bipolar disorder. The authors conclude that based on the present data CBT does not seem to be an effective treatment strategy for relapse-prevention in bipolar disorder. Based on these findings Meyer and Hautzinger summarize that there is not much evidence for specific effects of CBT for bipolar disorders. Therefore, they suggest that future research should focus on matching patients to treatments, that is on examining possible moderator variables of CBT for bipolar disorders.

7. Mediators and moderators of treatment effects of CBT for bipolar disorder

While there are many studies dealing with moderators and mediators of CBT for depression studies examining the moderators and mediating mechanisms of CBT for bipolar disorders have rarely been conducted. However, there are first hints that patients with specific characteristics seem to benefit less respectively more from CBT than do other patients.

Some patient characteristics with unclear status: Prognostic factors or moderator variables for the response to CBT for bipolar disorders?

Lam et al. randomized over one hundred patients to either CBT or a control group and examined whether patients who score highly on the so-called Sense of Hyper-Positive Self Scale (SHPSS) do respond to CBT as well as other patients do [109]. The SHPSS measures to what extent patients suffering from a bipolar disorder value themselves and assume that they possess personal attributes that are associated with a state of being 'mildly high' (e.g., dynamism, productiveness). As expected the authors found that patients with high scores on the SHPSS had a significantly higher rate of relapse after controlling for other clinical variables that are relevant in this context. Another variable that seems to play a role in the responsiveness to CBT is the level of activation the patients display: In this context it has been revealed that patients who show heightened and more volatile activation scale scores show a worse response to CBT than patients who show a contrary pattern [110]. Furthermore, it seems as if patients with fewer than twelve previous affective episodes benefit more from CBT with regard to relapse that patients with more affective episodes [111].

The mediating role of dysfunctional attitudes and further potential mediators

Ball and colleagues conducted a randomized controlled trial of schema-focused CBT that made, besides the typical CBT techniques, use of emotive therapy techniques as for example imagery or reliving of early experiences [112]. In this study fifty-two bipolar patients have been randomized to either CBT plus mood stabilizers or treatment as usual (TAU) plus mood stabilizers. It has not only been revealed that patients who received CBT had lower depression scores at posttreatment but also that they displayed less dysfunctional attitudes than patients who were allocated to TAU. Furthermore, patients who received CBT seemed to show a greater time to depressive relapse as compared to the TAU patients (however, statistically seen this was only significant on a trend level). In the one-year follow-up CBT patients showed a trend toward lower manic symptoms and improved behavioral self-control. Moreover, the change of the severity of illness status from baseline to 18-months follow-up changed more within the CBT group as compared to the TAU group. Even though some methodological issues can be brought up against this study (for example it remains unclear if schema-focused CBT has any advantages in the treatment of bipolar disorders as compared to 'pure' CBT) this study suggests that one mediating mechanism of CBT for bipolar disorder may lay in the change of dysfunctional attitudes. This suggestion finds support in a study by Zaretsky and colleagues in which seventy-nine patients suffering from bipolar disorder have been randomized to either psychoeducation plus CBT or a short course of psychoeducation (PE) alone [113]. While the groups did not differ concerning hospitalization rates, medication adherence, psychosocial functioning, or mental health use, it has been shown that patients who received CBT in addition to PE experienced 50% fewer days of depressed mood over the course of one year and needed antidepressant increases less frequently than patients allocated to PE. Furthermore, dysfunctional attitudes decreased significantly more in the CBT group than in the PE group, suggesting that this indeed might be a mediating variable. Another variable that has also been shown to change during CBT is the coping with prodromal symptoms [114]. Thus, it could be assumed that this might also be a mediating variable for the effectiveness of CBT. However, this association has never been specifically examined.

In contrast to the field of unipolar depression there are, to our knowledge, no studies concerning neural correlates of treatment response in bipolar disorders. Thus, one can only speculate that prefrontal and subcortical areas and networks that are involved in emotion regulation might play a mediating role in CBT for bipolar disorders.

Due to the lack of studies concerning moderators and mediators of CBT for bipolar disorders Miklowitz and Scott list a number of variables that "could provide viable explanations for the effectiveness of various forms of psychotherapy" [106]. Amongst other variables they list for example acquiring emotional self-regulation skills, improving social skills, enhancing medication adherence, stabilizing sleep/wake cycles and other daily routines, and improving the ability to identify and intervene early with relapses.

8. New developments in the CBT for bipolar disorders

While there is a growing body of research concerning cCBT for depression these new developments have hardly been used in the treatment of bipolar disorders. In 2007 Barnes and colleagues described an internet-based disease management platform that has been developed by Sentiens, a mental health service provider in Perth (Australia), called 'Recovery Road' (RR) [115-116]. This platform enables patients and their treating clinicians to keep contact by the use of asynchronous messaging. Furthermore, patients and clinicians are provided with self-report monitoring tools including different online mental health, medication adherence, and quality-of-life questionnaires so that they receive immediate feedback on progress, medication adherence and risk of relapse. Moreover, users have access to a one-year relapse prevention program for bipolar disorders (or psychosocial treatments for other mental illnesses) including ten sessions of CBT that has been developed by Barnes. As far as we know, the results of the randomized controlled trial that has been conducted by Barnes and colleagues to evaluate this cCBT program for bipolar disorder have not been published so far. Therefore, it has to be awaited if cCBT can also be helpful in the treatment of bipolar disorder.

9. Gaps of knowledge and future directions

As we have seen compared to the field of bipolar disorders there are many studies examining potential moderator and mediator variables of CBT for depression. However, in some cases there are contradictory findings that do not allow drawing definite conclusions. For example it is still not clear whether more severe and complicated patients do better or worse in CBT treatment as compared to patients with a less severe symptomatic. It may be that the heterogeneity of the findings concerning this specific patient characteristic is at least in part due to a different extent of therapists' expertise. Therefore, in future studies concerning the outcome of CBT in depression, we recommend to control for the expertise status of therapists, to elucidate the role of illness severity and comorbid personality disorders. In this context it seems important to mention a study that has been conducted by Strunk and colleagues [117]. In this study the therapists' competence has been rated and the authors found that the adequacy of therapists' delivery of the treatment is predictive for symptom change early in treatment. Furthermore, Strunk et al. investigated whether therapists' competence is more important to patients with specific complicating features and found that competence seems to be more important to patients who were characterized by higher anxiety, an earlier age of onset, and who suffered from a chronic form of depression as compared to patients without these characteristics. However, patients with a comorbid personality disorder did not have a greater benefit in dependence of the therapists' competence as compared to those patients who didn't meet criteria for a personality disorder. This study impressively illustrates that the expertise of the therapists may have a strong influence on the findings concerning potential moderator variables of CBT. Therefore, it needs to be taken into account in future studies.

An even more far-reaching problem in the context of studies searching for potential moderator variables of CBT for depression is that in many cases it is not strictly distinguished between moderator variables on one side and prognostic factors on the other. Thus, many studies only examine whether a variable predicts the treatment response to CBT whereas studies also including other psychosocial interventions in addition to CBT to examine the differential prognostic value of potential moderator variables are rather limited. Therefore, it seems necessary to disentangle the meaning of 'predictors/prognostic factors' versus 'moderator variables' and to clearly carve out whether a variable is one or the other. For example, based on findings that demonstrate that those patients benefit most from CBT who show an increased emotional reactivity pretreatment and who are not able to engage regulatory structures pretreatment, Siegle and colleagues propose that the presence of emotion regulation deficits, which are targeted in CBT, may be the key to recovery with this specific intervention. Even though this assumption seems plausible, up till now it is not clear whether this prediction is specific to CBT. It is also possible that the same pattern could be found for other psychosocial interventions, as for example for IPT. To be able to decide what treatment to select for which patient it is necessary to go beyond the investigation of prognostic factors and to examine moderating variables.

A structurally related argument can be brought up against some studies investigating mediator variables. Strictly speaking, some studies that examine mediating mechanisms do not clearly distinguish variables mediating the response to CBT or variables being part of improvement rather than being a cause of improvement. To disentangle this more clearly, it would be required to assess the mediating as well as the outcome variable not only at study entry and the end of the study but also repeatedly during the therapy to make sure that the change of the mediator variable really precedes the change of the outcome variable and to rule out reverse causality.

While more and especially more carefully designed studies are already required concerning moderating and mediating variables of face-to-face CBT this is even more the case for the relatively new developments of cCBT and tCBT. Future studies should shed light on the question if cCBT and tCBT might be helpful especially for those patients who do not benefit as much from traditional CBT as do other patients. If so, these new developments could be routinely implemented into the health care systems and be provided especially to those patients who are not addressed successfully so far. The examination of the therapeutic usefulness of technical devices such as smart phones, tablet pc and apps will be another area of future research.

Even though there are some promising results concerning the effectiveness and efficacy of CBT for bipolar disorders until now it is not clear whether these findings can be traced back to active factors that are specific to CBT or whether these are due to rather unspecific factors that are associated with any kind of psychosocial treatment and even with supportive interventions. Furthermore, to date there is hardly any knowledge concerning moderator variables of the response to CBT for bipolar disorders and concerning mediating mechanisms. However, knowing moderator variables means to have a basis for choosing the best treatment for a given patient and thus is indispensable to improve our treatment assignments as well as to reduce our health care costs. Therefore, it seems necessary to broaden our knowledge in this context. The same holds true for mediating variables as these provide us with an answer to the question how CBT works and thus not only allow to identify mechanisms of change within the patient but also to identify active therapy ingredients in the treatment process. This in turn can be used to develop even more efficacious forms of therapy.

Author details

Larissa Wolkenstein and Martin Hautzinger
University of Tübingen, Germany

10. References

[1] Hautzinger, M., *Depression*. Fortschritte der Psychotherapie. Manuale für die Praxis, ed. D. Schulte, et al. 1998, Göttingen: Hogrefe.

[2] Beck, A.T., et al., *Cognitive therapy of depression*. 1979, New York: Guilford Press.

[3] Elkin, I., et al., *National Institute of Mental Health Treatment of Depression Collaborative Research Program: general effectiveness of treatments*. Archives of General Psychiatry, 1989. 46: p. 971-982.

[4] DeRubeis, R.J., et al., *Cognitive therapy vs. medications in the treatment of moderate to severe depression*. Archives of General Psychiatry, 2005. 62: p. 409-416.

[5] Casacalenda, N., J.C. Perry, and K. Looper, *Remission in major depressive disorder: a comparison of pharmacotherapy, psychotherapy, and control conditions*. American Journal of Psychiatry, 2002. 159: p. 1354-1360.

[6] Hollon, S.D., M.E. Thase, and J.C. Markowitz, *Treatment and prevention of depression*. Psychological Science in the Public Interest, 2002. 3: p. 1-39.

[7] Elkin, I., et al., *Initial severity and differential treatment outcome in the National Institute of Mental Health Treatment of Depression Collaborative Research Program*. Journal of Consulting and Clinical Psychology, 1995. 63: p. 841-847.

[8] American Psychiatric Association, *Practice guideline for the treatment of patients with major depressive disorder (revision)*. American Journal of Psychiatry, 2000. 157: p. 1-45.

[9] DeRubeis, R.J., et al., *Medications versus cognitive behavior therapy for severely depressed outpatients: mega-analysis of four randomized comparisons*. American Journal of Psychiatry, 1999. 156: p. 1007-1013.

[10] Hollon, S.D., *Cognitive and behavior therapy in the treatment and prevention of depression*. Depression and Anxiety, 2011. 28: p. 263-266.

[11] Hollon, S.D., et al., *Psychotherapy and medication in the treatment of adult and geriatric depression: which monotherapy or combined treatment?* Journal of Clinical Psychiatry, 2005. 66: p. 455-468.

[12] Hollon, S.D., M.O. Stewart, and D. Strunk, *Cognitive behavior therapy has enduring effects in the treatment of depression and anxiety*. Annual Review of Psychology, 2006. 57: p. 285-315.

[13] Hollon, S.D., et al., *Prevention of relapse following cognitive therapy vs medications in moderate to severe depression*. Archives of General Psychiatry, 2005. 62: p. 417-422.

[14] Evans, M.D., et al., *Differential relapse following cognitive therapy and pharmacotherapy for depression*. Archives of General Psychiatry, 1992. 49: p. 802-808.

[15] Frank, E., et al., *Three-year outcomes for maintenance therapies in recurrent depression*. Archives of General Psychiatry, 1990. 47: p. 1093-1099.

[16] Jarrett, R.B., et al., *Preventing Recurrent Depression Using Cognitive Therapy With and Without a Continuation Phase. A Randomized Clinical Trial*. Archives of General Psychiatry, 2001. 58: p. 381-388.

[17] Teasdale, J.D., et al., *Prevention of Relapse/Recurrence in Major Depression by Mindfulness-Based Cognitive Therapy*. Journal of Consulting and Clinical Psychology, 2000. 68: p. 615-623.

[18] Scott, J., et al., *Effects of cognitive therapy on psychosocial symptoms and social functioning in residual depression.* British Journal of Psychiatry, 2000. 177: p. 440-446.

[19] Paykel, E., et al., *Prevention of relapse by cognitive therapy in residual depression: a controlled trial.* Archives of General Psychiatry, 1999. 56: p. 829-835.

[20] Jacobson, N.S., et al., *A component analysis of cognitive-behavioral treatment for depression.* Journal of Consulting and Clinical Psychology, 1996(64): p. 295-304.

[21] Dimidjian, S., et al., *Randomized Trial of Behavioral Activation, Cognitive Therapy, and Antidepressant Medication in the Acute Treatment of Adults With Major Depression.* Journal of Consulting and Clinical Psychology, 2006. 74: p. 658-670.

[22] Power, M.J. and C. Freeman, *A randomized controlled trial of IPT versus CBT in primary care: With some cautionary notes about handling missing values in clinical trials.* Clinical Psychology and Psychotherapy, 2012. 19: p. 159-169.

[23] Luty, S.E., et al., *Randomised controlled trial of interpersonal psychotherapy and cognitive–behavioural therapy for depression.* The British Journal of Psychiatry, 2007. 190(6): p. 496-502.

[24] de Mello, M.F., et al., *A systematic review of research findings on the efficacy of interpersonal therapy for depressive disorders.* European Archives of Psychiatry and Clinical Neuroscience, 2005(255): p. 75-82.

[25] Cuijpers, P., et al., *Depression and dysthymic disorders,* in *Handbook of evidence-based practice in clinical psychology,* M. Hersen and P. Sturmey, Editors. 2012, Wiley.

[26] Cuijpers, P., et al., *Psychotherapy for depression in adults: A meta-analysis of comparative outcome studies.* Journal of Consulting and Clinical Psychology, 2008. 76: p. 909-922.

[27] Cuijpers, P., A. van Straten, and L. Warmerdam, *Are individual and group treatments equally effective in the treatment of depression in adults? A meta-analysis.* European Journal of Psychiatry, 2008. 22: p. 38-51.

[28] Cuijpers, P., et al., *The effects of psychotherapy for adult depression are overestimated: A meta-analysis of study quality and effect size.* Psychological Medicine, 2010. 40: p. 211-223.

[29] Thoma, N.C., et al., *A quality-based review of randomized controlled trials of cognitive-behavioral therapy for depression: An assessment and metaregression.* American Journal of Psychiatry, 2012. 169: p. 22-30.

[30] Cuijpers, P., et al., *Self-reported versus clinician-rated symptoms of depression as outcome measures in psychotherapy research on depression: A meta-analysis.* Clinical Psychology Review, 2010. 30: p. 768-778.

[31] Antonuccio, D.O., M. Thomas, and W.G. Danton, *A cost-effectiveness analysis of cognitive behavior therapy and fluoxetine (Prozac) in the treatment of depression.* Behavior Therapy, 1997. 28: p. 187-210.

[32] Brown, J.S.L., et al., *Outcome, costs and patient engagement for group and individual CBT for depression: A naturalistic clinical study.* Behavioural and Cognitive Psychotherapy, 2011. 39: p. 355-358.

[33] Kraemer, H.C., et al., *Mediators and moderators of treatment effects in ranomized clinical trials.* Archives of General Psychiatry, 2002. 59: p. 877-883.

[34] Sotsky, S.M., et al., *Patient predictors of response to psychotherapy and pharmacotherapy: Findings in the NIMH Treatment of Depression Collaborative Research Program.* American Journal of Psychiatry, 1991. 148: p. 997-1008.

[35] Carter, J.D., et al., *Patient predictors of response to cognitive behaviour therapy and interpersonal psychotherapy in a randomized clinical trial for depression.* Journal of Affective Disorders, 2011. 128: p. 252-261.

[36] Fournier, J.C., et al., *Prediction of response to medication and cognitive therapy in the treatment of moderate to severe depression.* Journal of Consulting and Clinical Psychology, 2009. 77: p. 775-787.

[37] Thase, M.E., et al., *Relapse after cognitive behavior therapy of depression - potential implications for longer courses of treatment.* American Journal of Psychiatry, 1992. 149: p. 1046-1052.

[38] Jarrett, R.B., et al., *Clinical, cognitive, and demographic-predictors of response to cognitive therapy for depression - a preliminary-report.* Psychiatry Research, 1991. 37: p. 245-260.

[39] Safran, J.D., et al., *Assessing patient suitability for short-term cognitive therapy with interpersonal focus.* Cognitive Therapy and Research, 1993. 17: p. 23-38.

[40] Young, J.E., *Cognitive therapy for personality disorders: A schema-focused approach.* 1990, Sarasota, FL: Professional Resource Exchange Inc.

[41] Halford, W.K., S. Nernoth-Doolan, and K. Eadie, *Schemata as moderators of clinical effectiveness of a comprehensive cognitive behavioral program for patients with depression or anxiety disorder.* Behavior Modification, 2002. 26: p. 571-593.

[42] Teismann, T., et al., *Bedeutung von Rumination und Ablenkung für den Therapieerfolg depressiver Patienten.* Verhaltenstherapie, 2008. 18: p. 215-222.

[43] Teismann, T., et al., *Influence of rumination and distraction on the therapeutic process in cognitive-behavioral therapy for depression.* Cognitive Therapy and Research, 2012. 36: p. 15-24.

[44] Arnow, B.A., et al., *Rumination and distraction among chronic depressives in treatment: A structural equation analysis.* Cognitive Therapy and Research, 2004. 28: p. 67-83.

[45] Siegle, G.J., et al., *Do the seconds turn into hours? Relationships between sustained pupil dilation in response to emotional information and self reported rumination.* Cognitive Therapy and Research, 2003. 27: p. 365-383.

[46] Siegle, G.J., et al., *Can't shake that feeling: fMRI assessment of sustained amygdala activity in response to emotional information in depressed individuals.* Biological Psychiatry, 2002. 51: p. 693-707.

[47] Deldin, P.J., A.Y. Shestyuk, and P.H. Chiu, *Event-related brain potential indices of memory biases in major depression,* in *Principles of experimental psychopathology: Essays in honor of Brendan A. Maher,* M.F. Lenzenweger and J.M. Hooley, Editors. 2003, American Psychological Association. p. 195-209.

[48] Sheline, Y.I., et al., *Increased amygdala response to masked emotional faces in depressed subjects resolves with antidepressant treatment: an fMRI study.* Biological Psychiatry, 2001. 50: p. 651-658.

[49] Siegle, G.J., C.S. Carter, and M.E. Thase, *Use of fMRI to predict recovery from unipolar depression with cognitive behavior therapy.* American Journal of Psychiatry, 2006. 163: p. 735-738.

[50] Fournier, J.C., et al., *Antidepressant medications v. cognitive therapy in people with depression with or without personality disorder.* British Journal of Psychiatry, 2008. 192: p. 124-129.

[51] Coffman, S.J., et al., *Extreme nonresponse in cognitive therapy: can behavioral activation succeed where cognitive therapy fails.* Journal of Consulting and Clinical Psychology, 2007. 75: p. 531-541.

[52] Barber, J.P. and L.R. Muenz, *The role of avoidance and obsessiveness in matching patients to cognitive and interpersonal psychotherapy: Empirical findings from the treatment of Depression Collaborative Research Program.* Journal of Consulting and Clinical Psychology, 1996. 64: p. 951-958.

[53] Stangier, U., et al., *Maintenance Cognitive Therapy and Manualized Psychoeducation in the Treatment of Recurrent Depression: A Prospective Randomized Multicenter Controlled Trial.* American Journal of Psychiatry, in press.

[54] McBride, C., et al., *Attachment as moderator of treatment outcome in major depression: A randomized control trial of interpersonal psychotherapy versus cognitive behavior therapy.* Journal of Consulting and Clinical Psychology, 2006. 74: p. 1041-1054.

[55] Joyce, P.R., et al., *Temperament, character and personality disorders as predictors of response to interpersonal psychotherapy and cognitive-behavioral therapy for depression.* British Journal of Psychiatry, 2007. 190: p. 503-508.

[56] Kocsis, J.H., et al., *Journal of Clinical Psychiatry.* Patient preference as a moderator of outcome for chronic forms of major depressive disorder treated with nefazodone, cognitive behavioral analysis system of psychotherapy, or the combination, 2009. 70: p. 354-361.

[57] Leykin, Y., et al., *The relation of patients' treatment preference to outcome in a randomized clinical trial.* Behavioral Therapy, 2007. 38: p. 209-217.

[58] Goldapple, K., et al., *Modulation of cortical-limbic pathways in major depression: treatment-specific effects of cognitive behavior therapy.* Archives of General Psychiatry, 2004. 61: p. 34-41.

[59] Mayberg, H., et al., *Regional metabolic effects of fluoxetine in major depression: Serial changes and relationship to clinical response.* Biological Psychiatry, 2000. 48: p. 830-843.

[60] Fu, C.H.Y., et al., *Attenuation of the neural response to sad faces in major depression by antidepressant treatment: a prospective, event-related functional magnetic resonance imaging study.* Archives of General Psychiatry, 2004. 61: p. 877-889.

[61] DeRubeis, R.J., G.J. Siegle, and S.D. Hollon, *Cognitive therapy vs. medications for depression: Treatment outcomes and neural mechanisms.* Nature Reviews Neuroscience, 2008. 9: p. 788-796.

[62] Kennedy, S.H., et al., *Differences in brain glucose metabolism between responders to CBT and venlafaxine in a 16-week randomized controlled trial.* American Journal of Psychiatry, 2007. 164: p. 778-788.

[63] Fu, C.H.Y., et al., *Neural Responses to Sad Facial Expressions in Major Depression Following Cognitive Behavioral Therapy*. Biological Psychiatry, 2008. 64: p. 505-512.

[64] Ritchey, M., et al., *Neural correlates of emotional processing in depression: Changes with cognitive behavioral therapy and predictors of treatment response.* Journal of Psychiatric Research, 2011. 45: p. 577-587.

[65] Beck, A.T., *Cognitive therapy: A 30-year retrospective.* American Psychologist, 1991. 46: p. 368-375.

[66] Manicavasagar, V., T. Perich, and G. Parker, *Cognitive predictors of change in cognitive behaviour therapy and mindfulness-based cognitive therapy for depression.* Behavioural and Cognitive Psychotherapy, 2012. 40: p. 227-232.

[67] Imber, S.D., et al., *Mode-specific effects among three treatments for depression.* Journal of Consulting and Clinical Psychology, 1990. 5: p. 352-359.

[68] Simons, A.D., S.L. Garfield, and G.E. Murphy, *The process of change in cognitive therapy and pharmacotherapy for depression.* Archives of General Psychiatry, 1984. 41: p. 45-51.

[69] Oei, T.P.S. and M.L. Free, *Do cognitive behaviour therapies validate cognitive models of mood disorder? A review of the empirical evidence.* International Journal of Psychology, 1995. 30: p. 145-179.

[70] DeRubeis, R.J., et al., *How does cognitive therapy work? Cognitive change and symptom change in cognitive therapy and pharmacotherapy for depression.* Journal of Consulting and Clinical Psychology, 1990. 58: p. 862-869.

[71] Strunk, D.R., et al., *Patients' competence in and performance of cognitive therapy skills: relation to the reduction of relapse risk following treatment for depression.* Journal of Consulting and Clinical Psychology, 2007. 75: p. 523-530.

[72] Segal, Z.V., et al., *Cognitive reactivity to sad mood provocation and the prediction of depressive relapse.* Archives of General Psychiatry, 2006. 63: p. 749-755.

[73] Hollon, S.D., M.D. Evans, and R.J. DeRubeis, *Cognitive mediation of relapse prevention following treatment for depression: Implications of differential risk,* in *Psychological Aspects of Depression,* R.E. Ingram, Editor. 1990, Plenum: New York. p. 117-136.

[74] Teasdale, J.D., et al., *How does cognitive therapy prevent relapse in residual depression: evidence from a controlled trial.* Journal of Consulting and Clinical Psychology, 2001. 69: p. 347-357.

[75] Hollon, S.D., et al., *Prevention of relapse following cognitive therapy versus medications in moderate to severe depression.* Archives of General Psychiatry, 2005. 62: p. 417-422.

[76] Tang, T.Z. and R.J. DeRubeis, *Sudden gains and critcal sessions in cognitive-behavioral therapy for depression.* Journal of Consulting and Clinical Psychology, 1999. 67: p. 894-904.

[77] Keller, F. and M. Hautzinger, *Klassifikation von Verlaufskurven in der Depressionsbehandlung.* Zeitschrift für Klinische Psychologie und Psychotherapie, 2007. 36: p. 83-92.

[78] Foroushani, P.S., J. Schneider, and N. Assareh, *Meta-review of the effectiveness of computerised CBT in treating depression.* BMC Psychiatry, 2011. 11: p. 131-136.

[79] Horvitz-Lennon, M., et al., *"Usual care" for major depression in the 1990s: Characteristics and expert-estimated outcomes.* American Journal of Psychiatry, 2003. 160: p. 720-726.
[80] Wierzbicki, M. and G. Pekarik, *A metaanalysis of psychotherapy dropout.* Professional Psychology: Research and Practice, 1993. 24: p. 190-195.
[81] Griffiths, K.M., L. Farrer, and H. Christensen, *The efficacy of internet interventions for depression and anxiety disorders: a review of randomised controlled trials.* 2010. 192: p. 4-11.
[82] Andersson, G. and P. Cuijpers, *Internet-based and other computerized psychological treatments for adult depression: A meta-analysis.* Cognitive Behaviour Therapy, 2009. 38: p. 196-205.
[83] Spek, V., et al., *Internet-based cognitive behaviour therapy for symptoms of depression and anxiety: A meta-analysis.* Psychological Medicine, 2007. 37: p. 319-328.
[84] Lynch, D., M. Tamburrino, and R. Nagel, *Telephone counseling for patients with minor depression: Preliminary findings in a family practice setting.* Journal of Family Practice, 1997. 44: p. 293-298.
[85] Mohr, D.C., et al., *Telephone-administered psychotherapy for depression.* Archives of General Psychiatry, 2005. 65: p. 1007-1014.
[86] Mohr, D.C., et al., *Effect of telephone-administered vs face-to-face cognitive behavioral therapy on adherence to therapy and depression outcomes among primary care patients: a randomized trial.* The Journal of the American Medical Association, 2012. 307: p. 2278-2285.
[87] Ludman, E.J., et al., *A randomized trial of telephone psychotherapy and pharmacotherapy for depression: Continuation and durability effects.* Journal of Consulting and Clinical Psychology, 2007. 75: p. 257-266.
[88] Button, K.S., et al., *Factors associated with differential response to online cognitive behavioural therapy.* Social Psychiatry and Psychiatric Epidemiology, 2012. 47: p. 827-833.
[89] Kessler, D., et al., *Therapist-delivered internet psychotherapy for depression in primary care: a randomized controlled trial.* Lancet, 2009. 374: p. 628-634.
[90] Wiersma, J.E., et al., *Treating chronic symptoms of depression in the virtual clinic: Findings on chronicity of depression in patients treated with internet-based computerized cognitive behaviour therapy for depression.* Psychotherapy and Psychosomatics, 2011. 80: p. 313-315.
[91] de Graaf, L.E., S.D. Hollon, and M.J. Huibers, *Predicting outcome in computerized cognitive behavioral therapy for depression in primary care: A randomized trial.* Journal of Consulting and Clinical Psychology, 2010. 78: p. 184-189.
[92] Warmerdam, L., et al., *Online cognitive behavioral therapy and problem-solving therapy for depressive symptoms: Exploring mechanisms of change.* Journal of Behavior Therapy and Experimental Psychiatry, 2010. 41: p. 64-70.
[93] Cochran, S.D., *Preventing medical noncompliance in the outpatient treatment of bipolar disorders.* Journal of Consulting and Clinical Psychology, 1984. 52: p. 873-878.
[94] Alloy, L.B., et al., *The psychosocial context of bipolar disorder: environmental, cognitive, and developmental risk factors.* Clinical Psychology Review, 2005. 25: p. 1043-1075.
[95] Johnson, S.L., *Mania and dysregulation in goal pursuit: a review.* Clinical Psychology Review, 2005. 25: p. 241-262.

[96] Basco, M.R. and A.J. Rush, *Cognitive-behavioral therapy for bipolar disorder*. 1996, New York: Guilford.

[97] Lam, D., et al., *Cognitive therapy for bipolar disorder. A therapist´s guide to concepts, methods and practice*. Vol. 2. 2010, New York: Wiley.

[98] Meyer, T.D. and M. Hautzinger, *Manisch depressive Störungen - Kognitive Verhaltenstherapie zur Rückfallprophylaxe*. 2004, Weinheim: Beltz.

[99] Hautzinger, M. and T.D. Meyer, *Bipolare affektive Störungen. Fortschritte der Psychotherapie*. 2011, Göttingen: Hogrefe.

[100] Meyer, T.D., *Bipolare Störungen*, in *Lehrbuch der Verhaltenstherapie*, J. Margraf and S. Schneider, Editors. 2008, Springer: Berlin.

[101] Bauer, M., et al., *Using technology to improve longitudinal studies: self-reporting with ChronoRecord in bipolar disorder.* Bipolar Disorders, 2004. 6: p. 67-74.

[102] Lam, D. and G. Wong, *Prodromes, coping strategies and psychological interventions in bipolar disorders.* Clinical Psychology Review, 2005. 25.

[103] Miklowitz, D.J., *Adjunctive psychotherapy for bipolar disorder: state of evidence.* American Journal of Psychiatry, 2008. 165: p. 1408-1419.

[104] Scott, J., *Psychotherapy for bipolar disorders - efficacy and effectiveness.* Journal of Psychopharmacology, 2006. 20: p. 46-50.

[105] Lam, D.H., et al., *Cognitive therapy for bipolar illness: pilot study of relapse prevention.* Cognitive Therapy and Research, 2000. 24: p. 503-520.

[106] Miklowitz, D.J. and J. Scott, *Psychosocial treatments for bipolar disorder: cost-effectiveness, mediating mechanisms, and future directions.* Bipolar Disorders, 2009. 11: p. 110-122.

[107] Meyer, T.D. and M. Hautzinger, *Cognitive behaviour therapy and supportive therapy for bipolar disorders: relapse rates for treatment period and 2-year follow-up.* Psychological Medicine, 2012. 42: p. 1429-1439.

[108] Lynch, D., K.R. Laws, and P.J. McKenna, *Cognitive behavioural therapy for major psychiatric disorder: does it really work? A meta-analytical review of well-controlled trials.* Psychological Medicine, 2010. 40: p. 9-24.

[109] Lam, D., K. Wright, and P. Sham, *Sense of hyper-positive self and response to cognitive therapy in bipolar disorder.* Psychological Medicine, 2005. 35: p. 69-77.

[110] Scott, J., A. Garland, and S. Moorhead, *A pilot study of cognitive therapy in bipolar disorders.* Psychological Medicine, 2001. 31: p. 459-467.

[111] Scott, J., et al., *Cognitiv behaviour therapy for severe and recurrent bipolar disorders: a randomised controlled trial.* British Journal of Psychiatry, 2006. 188: p. 313-320.

[112] Ball, J.R., et al., *A randomized controlled trial of cognitive therapy for bipolar disorder: focus on long-term change.* Journal of Clinical Psychiatry, 2006. 67: p. 277-286.

[113] Zaretsky, A., et al., *Is cognitive-behavioural therapy more effective than psychoeducation in bipolar disorder?* Canadian Journal of Psychiatry, 2008. 53: p. 441-448.

[114] Lam, D.H., et al., *A randomized controlled study of cognitive therapy for relapse prevention for bipolar affective disorder: outcome of the first year.* Archives of General Psychiatry, 2003. 60: p. 145-152.

[115] Tannenbaum, D. and C. Barnes, *Infrapsych bipolar affective disorder recovery road program.* Bipolar Disorders, 2004. 6: p. 24.

[116] Barnes, C., et al., *Evaluation of an Online Relapse Prevention Program for Bipolar Disorder. An Overview of the Aims and Methodology of a Randomized Controlled Trial.* Disease Management and Health Outcomes, 2007. 15: p. 215-224.

[117] Strunk, D.R., et al., *Therapist Competence in Cognitive Therapy for Depression: Predicting Subsequent Symptom Change.* Journal of Consulting and Clinical Psychology, 2010: p. 429-437.

Section 3

Novel Psychotherapeutic Developments

CBASP with Intensified Significant Other History Exercise for Chronic Major Depression with Antecedent Dysthymic Disorder in Outpatient Treatment: Rationale, Assessment and Effects on the Hypothesized Core Content of the Patient's in-Session Interpersonal Fear in Relation to Symptom Reduction

Dieter Schoepf

Additional information is available at the end of the chapter

http://dx.doi.org/10.5772/51638

1. Introduction

Mayor depressive disorder (MDD) with antecedent dysthymic disorder is characterized by the simultaneous occurrence of two unipolar depressions with distinctive symptom severity and course patterns that have different age of onset profiles. The dysthymic disorder usually begins with an insidious onset before the age of 21 with depressive symptoms that are present more days than not over a period of two years or more, sometimes referred to as either "a recurrent veil of sadness and hopelessness" or "a loss of self confidence and self-efficacy". A more severe course of the disorder is reached when worsening of depressive symptoms leads to the onset of either a long lasting single MD-episode or recurrent MD-episodes with or without interepisode recovery, accounting for up to 75% of all cases of chronic MDD (Klein et al, 1996). The overall prevalence of detected dysthymic disorder with and without superimposed MDD is estimated to be approximately 3%, the lifetime prevalence 6% (DSM-IV-TR, 2000). Because many patients do not come to professional psychiatric attention, this likely is an underestimate of the number of cases who have fallen ill. In addition, even after the onset of a MD-episode, many affected patients delay or avoid getting treatment. The multiple negative effects on quality of life and physical health in combination with an increased risk of suicide, as well as the burden that patients are unlikely to remit over time compared to pure (episodic) MDD, make it important for clinicians (1) to identify the disorder as early as possible, (2) to encourage affected patients to take advantage of treatment as early as possible, and (3) to become familiar with effective pharmacological and disorder specific psychosocial interventions (Schoepf & Neudeck, 2011).

The pathogenesis of chronic MDD with antecedent dysthymic disorder results, to a large degree, from bi-directional interaction between disturbed stress regulation on the one hand and a developmental history that implicates a dysfunctional home life during childhood and the intervening adolescence epoch on the other hand. As a rule, a diagnosis of chronic MDD with antecedent dysthymic disorder is accompanied by a dysfunctional learning environment with- or without early-life adversities, ranging from childhood maltreatment (sexual abuse, physical abuse or emotional abuse) to experiencing neglect to witnessing domestic violence or to having a life-threatening injury (Schoepf et al., 2007; Schoepf & McCullough, 2009; McCullough et al., 2010; Schoepf & Penberthy, 2010; Schoepf & Neudeck, 2011; McCullough, 2012a; Neudeck et al., 2012). From a learning theory perspective a dysfunctional learning environment - in which the child's emotional capacities are recurrently exceeded without providing a (behavioral) solution to stop the condition - may involve survival circuits that detect key conditioned stimuli as a behavioural phenomenon for life. Such classical conditioned stimuli particularly trigger emotional and behavioral species-specific defence reactions, as well as stress associated changes in the inner workings of the body's organs and glands. Increasing evidence suggests that such exposed children may endure long-lasting neural consequences that place them at increased risk for the development of an interpersonal stile that is characterized by either moving away from or moving against the other person, and respectively the self (Schoepf et al., 2007; Schoepf & Penberthy, 2010; McCullough et al., 2011; Schoepf & Neudeck, 2011; Neudeck et al., 2012). Anatomically, predefined pathways that connect the limbic system with the neocortex are considerably stronger than those from the neocortex to the limbic system. The asymmetry of these connections as well as mechanisms of sensitization within survival-circuits (escape and avoidance learning) that involve high reactivity of the anterior insular and the amygdale may be the two most important biologically based reasons, why the developmental influences of the disorder remain prevalent in the form of a refractory cognitive-emotional dilemma over time (Schoepf et al., 2007; Schoepf et al, 2008; Schoepf & Neudeck, 2011). In other words, whenever an interpersonal event induces an arousal in the domain in which the origin of the interpersonal fear is established, the individual has no adaptive pro-active behaviour at hand to turn it off at will. In full agreement with these learning-theory and neurobiological based considerations, recent imaging studies demonstrated how chronic environmental stress in child victims of family violence – physical abuse, physical neglect and verbal abuse – primes the brain of the on-growing child for future mental illness by setting it's stress system in a permanent state of high alert as well as lead to corticostriatal-limbic gray matter reduction in the intervening adolescent epoch (McCrory et al, 2011). Furthermore, hippocampal and striatal alterations in adults are associated with reported emotional neglect during childhood, suggesting that such neglect may have long-lasting effects on corticostriatal-limbic regions subserving emotion regulation (Edmiston et al., 2011).

Effective treatment of chronic MDD with antecedent dysthymia that aims to achieve complete syndromal remission and, ultimately, long-term, successful outcomes of social functioning is an unsolved problem and remains an outstanding need in psychiatry (McCullough et al., 1996; Kessler et al., 2003; Schoepf et al., 2007; Nelson et al., 2008; Schoepf & Neudeck, 2011). With respect to psychosocial interventions, Cognitive Behavioral Analysis System of Psychotherapy (CBASP) - the only model of psychotherapy specifically developed for chronic MDD - showed divergent short-term effectiveness in the two worldwide most important (NIHM funded) chronic depression studies (Keller et al., 2000; Kocsis et al., 2009). It is important to note that in the earlier Nefazadone/CBASP study – that reported in a cross-over design a short-term overall response rate of 73% for the combined treatment in it's Intention-To-Treat (ITT) population (with up to 20 sessions of psychotherapy offered that were demanded with a rate of 80% by the patients) - for the sub-population of patients with a history of self-reported childhood trauma, CBASP proved to be significantly more effective in the reduction of depressive symptoms than medication alone (Nemeroff et al., 2003). In contrast, the later Research Evaluating the Value of Augmenting Medication with Psychotherapy (REVAMP) study was not able to confirm the results of the earlier study in a different study design (Kocsis et al., 2009). In non- and partial responders of 12-week antidepressant medication CBASP add-on augmentation (again up to 20 sessions of therapy offered but significantly less demanded by the ITT population in comparison to the earlier study) with introducing the technique of "Situational Analysis" (SA) in the third session of therapy was found not to be more effective in the reduction of depressive symptoms in it's ITT population than pharmacological augmentation or augmentation with Brief Supportive Psychotherapy (BSP), a type of "non-directive psychotherapy". However, pharmacotherapy with CBASP was associated with greater improvement in problem solving in the population of completers than pharmacotherapy plus BSP, or medication alone (Klein et al., 2011). Further differences between both studies with respect to the patient and the technique variable are:

- The preference for drug treatment was higher in the REVAMP population compared to the CBASP/Nefazadone population. The rate of patients that were prior to study inclusion adequately treated with antidepressant medication was 32% in the REVAMP population. In contrast, 60% of the included patients in the Nefazadone/CBASP population were adequately treated with antidepressant medication.
- The inclusion criterion for the co-occurrence of alcohol abuse varied in both studies. Unlike the CBASP/Nefazadone population, in the REVAMP population alcohol abuse was permitted if an affected patient was embedded in a group of anonymous alcoholics or if a patient was actively treated pharmacologically.
- The number of unemployed patients varied in both studies. Unemployment was higher in the REVAMP population than in the Nefazadone/CBASP population (32 versus 15%).
- The prevalence of chronic MDD with antecedent dysthymic disorder was lower in the REVAMP population than in the Nefazadone/CBASP population (33.1 versus 42.3%).

In the context of these two NIHM funded studies small "dismantling" and "f-MRI system mapping" studies recently begun to look for different mediating mechanisms (McCullough et al., 2010). Another research line started to focus on the moderator variables that deal with the patient's pre-treatment status and co-morbidity issues, such as alcoholism (Penberthy, 2010). From a CBASP technique variable perspective it is not clear if the early introduction of the technique of SA in the third session of therapy in the REVAMP trial has a positive or a negative effect on in-session acquisition learning and outcome-measures (Schoepf et al., 2011; Schoepf & Neudeck, 2011). A formal public description of the Significant Other History (SOH) procedure with a scheduled time period of one therapy session that was applied in the NIHM studies was recently presented by McCullough and colleagues (McCullough et al., 2011). In Bonn academic CBASP out-patient studies, the technique of SA is usually introduced after the fourth+x session of therapy in the case of chronic MDD with antecedent dysthymic disorder. A prolonged pre-SA phase of treatment in comparison to the NIHM studies implies a prolonged reconstruction process of the emotional learning history in antecedent- consequent way by conducting the SOH procedure as an intensified - more than one session – exposure-based procedure, called I-SOH procedure. The adapted protocol draws a clear distinction between a "pre-SA phase of treatment" that essentially includes the application of the I-SOH procedure, and the following "SA/ IDE phase of treatment", in which circular (two-way) formal-operational functioning is achieved.

1.1. Aim of chapter

This chapter-article provides a comprehensive overview of using CBASP`s original one-session scheduled SOH technique in an adapted, intensified and prolonged form for improving treatment in chronic MDD out-patients with antecedent dysthymia.

The first part starts with a recapitulation of key learning theory considerations about the origin of the disorder that follows our previous work published elsewhere (Schoepf & Neudeck; 2011). This starting point provides the foundation for a better comprehension of the rationale to use the techniques of disciplined personal involvement (DPI) early in therapy to shape a sensitive patient-therapist relationship. In the next section I turn to the technique description of the I-SOH procedure, i.e. the I-SOH procedure is described in detail and the underlying learning mechanisms are elucidated. Then the key frontiers in the administration of the I-SOH procedure are outlined. These frontiers include the prerequisites prior to out-patient CBASP psychotherapy (patient variable) as well as the "therapist" variable (Schoepf et al., 2007; Schoepf and Neudeck, 2011, Schoepf et al., 2011, and Neudeck et al., 2012). With respect to CBASP`s interpersonal focus, and particularly it's emphasis using the patient-therapist relationship as a therapeutic tool, in the following section the focus is laid on how the hypothesized core content of the patient`s interpersonal fear is specifically counter-conditioned in the SA/IDE phase of treatment. In the last section, the assessment for the I-SOH procedure is described in the form of an example and the relevant reference is given, in which the evaluation of the safety-signal impact on the hypothesized core content of the patient's in-session interpersonal fear is described.

In the second part typical CBASP-treatment trajectories of my self treated patients are provided without further systematic statistical evaluation as the studies are still running. The trajectories clearly show - without any further necessary explanation - the effect of the I-SOH procedure on the hypothesized core content of the patient`s in-session interpersonal fear in relation to symptom reduction. Feasibility and the implications of the I-SOH procedure on the syndromal short term effects as well as the effects over time are summarized and the scientific-related challenges are outlined.

2. First part

2.1. The origin of the disorder - key learning theory considerations

CBASP is a highly disorder-oriented psychotherapy method from the "third generation" of behaviour therapy models that is based on modern learning theory considerations (McCullough et al., 2011; Schoepf & Neudeck, 2011; Neudeck et al., 2012). From a modern learning theory perspective, the origin of chronic MDD with antecedent dysthymic disorder is due to classical conditioned interpersonal fear that often goes hand in hand with traumatically processed experiences of learned helplessness during childhood and the adolescent epoch. The (Pavlovian) fear is perpetuated by several forms of (Skinnerian) avoidance, thus accounting for an uncoupling of the person-environment connection as a contributing cause of depressive symptomatology. Functional brain changes may include that (1) the signal-reinforcer-relationship in relation to the implicit regulation of attentional control is biased towards stimuli that predict uncontrollability and unpredictability, and that (2) the behaviour-reinforcer-relation with respect to the implicit regulation of situational outcome is biased towards an independent of response expectation of some sort of punishment (Schoepf et al., 2007; Schoepf & Neudeck; 2011).

2.2. Disciplined personal involvement and the patient-therapist relationship

In CBASP, the patient-therapist relationship represents a central agent of behaviour change. A unique type of therapist intervention, called disciplined personal involvement (DPI), advocates a non-neutral role for the therapist. The techniques of DPI are based on early concepts of objective counter transference and interpersonal reactions that provide the authorization for using "self disclosures" to shape a sensitive patient-therapist relationship particularly in the early phase of treatment (Schoepf & McCullough, 2009; Schoepf & Neudeck, 2011). The most important precondition for the effective use of the techniques of DPI is that the overt and covert emotional, cognitive, and behavioral responses the patient evokes in the therapist (the patient`s stimulus vale) are validly measured by using the Kiesler's Impact Message Inventory after the first session of therapy (Kiesler, 1983). The results of the IMI (Schmidt et al., 1999) provide the necessary information about how the therapist feels like behaving towards the patient that will guide his clinical choices and his plan of treatment. This holds particularly for the use of personal meta-communicative feedback techniques and the way the I-SOH procedure is applied – the latter described in section 2.5. The technique of "Contingent Personal Responsivity" (CPR) is used in instances where the therapist consequates the behaviour of the patient by disclosing personal responses and feelings produced in the therapist by the behaviour of the patient (McCullough, 2006; Schoepf & McCullough 2009). The positive form of the CPR technique compares the moment-to-moment differences between before and after in case of pro-active in-session behaviour (Schoepf & Neudeck, 2011). As a therapeutic effect, intrapersonal positive reinforcement is induced which allows the patient to experience a new in-session interpersonal reality that increasingly becomes meaningful during the early phase of treatment. For example, in a preceding event a patient denied visual and verbal contact towards the therapist, then in the subsequent event he approached to the therapist and disclosed a fact that he had attributed as a "personal failure". The patient`s behaviour to consequate is "telling the therapist to have forgotten the homework ". The patient expects that his behaviour of "disclosing the failure" will be met with an interpersonal reaction of "some sort of punishment". The fact that the therapist reacts with "non-punishment" and that instead the patient is made aware of the positive effects his approaching behaviours have on the therapist by pointing to the contrast between how the therapist felt before (when the patient reacted in a hostile way) and after (when the patient approached) leads to an absence of the negative consequence expected by the patient, and thus to stress reduction. Consequently, it becomes more probable that, in a future situation, the patient talks to the therapist about a failure he has done (Schoepf & Neudeck, 2011). It is important to note that in the original CBASP protocol the imposed IMI data are not shared with the patient (McCullough & McCullough, 2009); the same is valid for the modified I–SOH procedure protocol (Schoepf & McCullough, 2009).

2.3. Restructuring helplessness memories in antecedent-consequent way

Theorists of exposure and cognitive approaches widely agree that effective psychotherapeutic treatment must in some way access or activate past traumatically processed memories, thoughts, and feelings, while providing corrective information that serves to modify the person's unrealistic expectations of harm and danger as well as to reduce excessive negative affectivity (Ehlers & Clark, 2000; Foa et al., 2007). In full agreement with this knowledge the (adapted) I-SOH procedure is primarily designed as an exposure-based technique that first activates the patient's helplessness memories and then restructures these early memories in antecedent-consequent way. The relation between the patient`s individual developmental history of interactional adversities and his interpersonal functioning in the presence is made explicit by helping the patient to respectively translate the formative influences of his SOs into Causal Theory Conclusions (CTCs). A CTC is a transference prediction that is defined as the interpersonal expectation which is transferred to the interacting partner. From the perspective of the therapist he gains self-reported access to the patient's interpersonal-emotional history with SOs and therefore is able to identify the individual origins of the patient`s core content of his interpersonal fear as well as how the patient behaved in painful encounters with malevolent SOs. The therapist therefore gains access to the necessary information for formulating the specific Therapy Hypotheses (TH), which will be worked out in the following SA/Interpersonal Discrimination Exercise (IDE) phase of treatment to assist the patient in achieving two-person circular functioning. The TH represents the hypothesized core content of the patient's interpersonal fear in the form of a predictive-hypothesis that informs the therapist about how the patient is likely to behave interpersonally in "hot spot" in-session events as well as what the patient is likely to expect interpersonally from the therapist. The TH also informs the CBASP therapist how he has to behave in order to address, train and thereby "repair" developmental trauma arising from experiences of felt helplessness with SOs in the SA/IDE phase of treatment (McCullough et al., 2010; Neudeck et al., 2012). It is important to note, that after the I-SOH procedure is finished an in-session zone of felt-safety has usually come into being, but the patient has yet not developed the ability to perceptually discriminate the behaviour of the therapist from the behaviour of his SO`s in "hot spot" situations. The zone of felt safety is made explicit in the later SA/IDE phase of treatment through IDE-work, i.e. the patient's behaviour in "hot spot" situations is specifically counter-conditioned with dyadic reciprocity (McCullough et al., 2011). A "hot spot" situation is some behavior/event involving the patient and the therapist that occurs during the therapy session that implicates the TH signaling that an IDE should be administered before the session ends (McCullough & McCullough, 2009). Due to IDE work the therapist demonstrates how the therapist's behaviour in "hot spot" interpersonal situations stands in contrast to the behaviour of SOs, similar to the patients' experiences earlier in his life. Thereby, the deeply personal nature of the therapist–patient relationship "is put into the foreground of therapeutic efficacy". Here we have both: A "moderator variable of in-session acquisition learning" as well as a therapist who creates a situational context where the patient is exposed to avoided emotions and thoughts (Schoepf & McCullough, 2009; Schoepf et al., 2011; Schoepf & Neudeck, 2011; Neudeck et al., 2012).

2.4. Major therapeutic goals of the pre-SA-phase of treatment (early phase)

The major therapeutic goals of the pre-SA phase of treatment are:

1. To teach the patient in the first session to self-monitor the intensity of his depression by using the BDI-II and the IDS-SR and to work through the results together at the beginning of every session from a behavioral perspective.
2. To reconstruct the course of the depression from a behavioral perspective in the second session of therapy.
3. To clarify the origins of the patient's interpersonal fear by using the I-SOH procedure (Schoepf et al.,2011; Schoepf & Neudeck, 2011), i.e. an intensified and prolonged form of the original one-session SOH technique described by McCullough and colleagues (McCullough et al., 2011) that is applied in the modified protocol as an exposure-based intervention.
4. To teach the patient to recapture the ability to re-experience repressed emotions by recalling key memories about what it was like being around a SO.
5. To teach the patient to think in an antecedent-consequent way in the interpersonal domain in which the origin of his interpersonal fear was established by supporting him to formulate a core conclusion for every SO about the formative influence the SO

exerted on him, i.e. the interpersonal influence of the SO that is effective in the presence (CTC).

6. To modify dysfunctional and attacking in-session behaviour as well as to induce positive intrapersonal reinforcement of approaching behaviour by using the various forms of the CPR technique.
7. To build-up a sensitive patient-therapist relationship with an attachment bond as well as creating an in-session zone of felt safety.

2.5. Technique description of the I-SOH procedure

This section will give the reader an insight into the I-SOH outpatient protocol. In Bonn university, the I-SOH procedure is usually applied in the treatment of chronic MDD patients with antecedent dysthymic disorder, i.e. in the cross-over study "differential responses of CBASP Vs Escitalopram" (clinical trial) and the effectiveness study "CBASP Vs SYSP" (Schramm et al., 2011). A formal technique description of the I-SOH procedure and an elucidation of the underlying learning mechanisms are not presented or discussed in public so far.

Overall view: At a glance, the I-SOH procedure is administered in a highly structured sequence on the flip-chart. The use of the flip-chart helps the therapist to control the risk of inducing excessive and overwhelming negative affectivity (fear, guilt, shame, anger) and it sets the stage for the patient to draw causal connections between the past and the presence. Under a condition of focused attention four tasks are consecutively carried out in order to reveal how SOs affected the patient to behave in his everyday relationships. In the first task the patient is prepared for the I-SOH procedure by the submission of detailed information about the content and the objectives of the procedure. In the second task the patient is focused on the procedure and the flip-chart is introduced. The third task and the fourth task are intended as causal reasoning exercises that build-up on each other. Both exercises emphasize more the processing and the active restructuring of the patient's thinking in the domain in which the origins of past helplessness memories were established than the thinking process itself. However, the I-SOH procedure can also be seen as an exposure-based intervention. The remembered early memories are usually painful for patients to acknowledge, and the sustained attention to these memories are associated with an increase of negative affect and agitation. Therefore, it is imperative for the therapist to help the patient to reduce his aversive reactions by teaching him effective top-down strategies. The challenge for the therapist is to ensure that each task is always within the patient's realm of possibility and comprehension.

2.5.1. Task one: Preparing

After the reconstruction process of the course of the depression is finished (before the end of the session) the I-SOH procedure is introduced to the patient. The entering wedge is to request the patient to bring into the next session of therapy a list of up to six SOs who shaped the patient to be who he is at present (McCullough & McCullough, 2009;

McCullough et al., 2011). It is explained that a SO is defined as a person, who played a major informing role in the patient's development history and that a SO can be attributed either positive or negative. It is recommended to highlight the following five topics:

1. SOs are not "just friends" or "acquaintances". Instead a SO is defined as a significant person in the life of the patient, with whom the patient grew up, or with whom the patient currently interacts and who exerted either a positive or negative formative influence on the way the patient lives, thinks and feels (parents, siblings, uncles, aunts, grandparents, teachers, etc.).
2. Most patients will list 3-6 SOs who exerted a relevant impact that influenced the direction their life took.
3. In the following sessions the origins of the patient's interpersonal problems are clarified by applying the I-SOH procedure.
4. The results of the I-SOH procedure are a "conditio sine qua non" for the therapist to develop the specific TH. The specific TH represents the hypothesized core content of the patient's interpersonal fear in the form of a predictive-hypothesis that informs the therapist about how the patient is likely to behave interpersonally in "hot spot" situations as well as what the patient is likely to expect interpersonally from the therapist.
5. The detection of the specific TH is necessary for the therapist in order to be prepared for perceiving "hot spot" situations in the subsequent SA/IDE phase of treatment. It is recommended to inform the patient that such "hot spots" are high probability occurring interpersonal events in therapy (McCullough & McCullough, 2009; Schoepf & McCullough, 2009).

At the beginning of the next session it is recommended to address consecutively the following three topics to set the stage for the exposure aspects of the procedure:

1. The I-SOH procedure is of utmost relevance for the therapy, because the therapist has to come to know in detail the origins of the patient's chronic state of depression in order to determine the dominant interpersonal theme domain that describes the negative consequences the patient received from his SOs while interacting with them in that domain (McCullough, 2008).
2. Aversive feelings like fear, pain and sadness as well as shame and guilt may be evoked in the case of a negative SO. The therapist is blind for "hot spot" situations at this time of therapy, such that he can not apply CBASP`s specific DPI techniques like the IDE. Instead, the therapist will help the patient to control the evoked arousal by teaching him top-down interventions that will simultaneously prepare the patient for SA work in later therapy (Schoepf & McCullough, 2009; Schoepf et al., 2011; Schoepf & Neudeck, 2011).
3. In the original US-protocol the time instruction for the SOH procedure is one therapy session (second session). It is recommended to explain that this time instruction was taken back by the author of the CBASP in the planning phase of Bonn CBASP-studies, and that according to the modified protocol the emotional reconstruction process of one SO in an antecedent-consequent format usually takes one single up-to one double session of therapy, especially when a positive history of family violence or childhood trauma exists (Schoepf & McCullough 2009; Schoepf et al., 2011; Schoepf & Neudeck, 2011).

After clarifying the content of each topic in its meaning, the therapist goes to the second task.

2.5.1.1. *What is learned?*

Early-onset chronically depressed patients with a history of low-to high grade childhood trauma have not enough precedent emotional experiences like the capability to trust another human being or what it is like to be loved and cared for (McCullough, 2012). From a communication perspective, the submission of detailed information about the content and the objectives of the up-coming tasks stands in contrast to the patient`s expectation that "one person does not care for the other person". The patient learns that the therapist behaves in a way that stands opposite to the behaviour of his malevolent SOs. Specifically, the therapist establishes a learning environment that is characterized by foreseeable events, openness, trust and care. The door is opened for the development of a sensitive patient-therapist relationship that includes a powerful potential for enhancing and accelerating the up-coming tasks through increased attention and readiness to cooperate. This will shape the patient and produce a relevant impact, or paradigm shift, that also will affect the patient's subsequent interpersonal experiences as well as affect the patient's self-actualization process. From a learning theory perspective, learning of stimuli and behaviour can only occur if there is a discrepancy between the stimulus that is expected (typical behaviour of malevolent SOs) and the one that actually occurs (the therapist's preparing behaviour, Bouton, 2007).

2.5.2. *Task two: Focusing*

In the second task the names of the SOs are written on the flip-chart in the order the patient had listed them. Then the list is reviewed together. After the reviewing process is finished, the patient is informed that in the third task both the therapist and the patient go together through the list in the order it was defined by the patient.

2.5.2.1. *What is learned?*

In early-onset chronically depressed patients all roads usually lead to the self (McCullough, 2006). By the use of the flip-chart the patient's attention is drawn to the outside. Forgetting is prevented that may occur because of interference as well as because of retrieval failure. In addition, the review process gives the patient time to habituate to a sometimes distinctive evoked arousal. Finally, the patient learns that the procedure slows down the speed of the task.

2.5.3. *Task three: Restructuring of closed perceptual systems in antecedent-consequent way*

In the third task the patient's relevant relationships that exerted a formative influence on his life are restructured in antecedent-consequent way. It is recommended that the therapist remains continuously in a friendly and curious position to give birth to causal learning processes and insights the patient experiences during the exercise, but not to do the work for him.

First sub-step: Creation of awareness for key past encounters. The patient is first prompted to describe in storytelling form what it was like growing or being around with his SO. The therapist must be aware, that this prompt is directly addressed to open the patient`s perceptual systems that are closely related to his refractory affectivity (fear, anxiety, and psychological pain), i.e. the early-onset chronically depressed patient is confronted with all aspects of his avoided reactions. In particular, earlier memories that are associated with traumatically processed events evoke significant emotional arousal that often seems to be overwhelming from the patient's subjective point of view. The therapist's responsivity is to immediately interrupting the patient's narrative form of reproduction and to teach him to control the induced arousal by (re-)describing a typical encounter from a purely observational descriptive modus (sterns in the example 2.11). Observational-descriptive modus is defined as a report of the key behavioral interactions with extinction of intrusive and destructive behavioral response patterns until the therapist comes to know what happened first, then second, etc. The beginning and the end point of the encounter have to be clearly addressed, not unlike watching an excerpt of a silent movie. As a rule, the therapist writes the reported interactions word by word on the flipchart and clarifies their meaning in behavioural terms. Then the therapist repeats the event. After the intensity of negative emotions is decreased the patient returns to the storytelling form. It is important to note that the therapist should instruct the patient to stay in the alteration between the storytelling form and the observational descriptive form of key encounters to avoid an escalation of negative affect and agitation or in the worst case retraumatization.

Second sub-step: Elicitation of self-referential interpretations and identification of causal relations between the past and the presence. After the first-sub step is finished the patient is prompted to causally think about how the SO`s interactional behaviours influenced the course of his life in a way that is still present today or how the SO`s interactional behaviours influenced the patient to be the kind of person he is at present. A two-step strategy is applied. First, the patient's self-referential interpretations of his key encounters are elicited; for instance "I felt hurt when my father insulted me", or "I thought I am stupid when I was blamed". Then, the patient is prompted to draw causal relations between his interpretations and his typical interactional responses (behavioral, emotional, cognitive, and physiological) in his everyday relationships, i.e. in antecedent-consequent way. It is recommended to facilitate this causal reasoning task by writing a preparation theorem on the flip-chart, i.e.: "The influence of this SO on me/my everyday relationships is that ...". Now the patient is prompted to add the impacts/effects. The therapist's responsivity is to clarify every reported word in its meaning and to help the patient to restructure his thoughts by organizing the influences according to the patient's personal relevance, as the patient usually thinks in global ways without considering the time and the causality relation.

The exercise ends with a learning summary of the step.

2.5.3.1. What is learned?

In this task the patient is exposed at past helplessness memories that contribute to his dysfunctional outcome expectations. When a SO had exerted a negative formative influence on the patient`s life painful reactions (avoided thoughts, avoided emotions, and physiological responses) are evoked. When a SO had exerted a positive formative influence on the patient`s life "often forgotten" feelings of affection are evoked. Counter-conditioning according to the principle of reciprocal inhibition takes place by the benevolent reactions of the therapist, who helps the patient to identify and (re-) describe key encounters with his SO from a behavioral observational descriptive focus. Counter-conditioning means that a stimulus–response connection that was established through classical conditioning is unlearned or reconditioned through conditioning with novel stimuli (Schoepf et al., 2007; Schoepf & Neudeck, 2011; Neudeck et al. 2012). According to our clinical experience, an implicit learning process is started at this point during which the therapist becomes safety signal character at the end of the pre-SA phase. The term "safety signal character" implicates that the patient`s behaviour has the capacity to terminate the overwhelming character of the aversive feeling that is present. The initiated safety signal learning process is strengthened through associative learning of behavioral effects. The patient`s behaviour chain - first report a past stressful event from an observational-descriptive focus, then elicit the cognitive-emotional attributions and finally draw causal relations in antecedent consequent way - is enhanced in the presence of the therapist because it removes or prevents an aversive event (negative reinforcement). Negative enforcement is defined as a specific event in which behaviour is strengthened because it prevents an aversive effect that is a negative reinforcer. In other words, that the therapist reacts with "non-punishment" leads to an absence of the negative consequences expected by the patient, and thus to a further stress reduction. Automatically, there results a felt increase of the potency of the therapist to reduce interpersonal distress during the in-session encounter and a new interpersonal reality of a sensitive therapist-patient relationship comes into being meaningful to the patient.

2.5.4. Task four: Translation of tacit knowledge into explicit causal knowledge

In the fourth task the patient has to identify and to translate the most relevant causal relation between the SO`s behaviour in the past and his transference prediction in the presence that contributes to maintain the disorder. The "so called" Causal Theory Conclusion (CTC) can be formulated either in the form of an (ego-based) transference prediction that becomes prevalent in the patient`s everyday relationships or as a conditional rule in the form of an (ego-based) "if then" statement that predicts the patient`s prototypical interactional emotional response in relation to the expected up-coming event, i.e. some sort of punishment if a SO had exerted a negative informing influence.

First sub-step: Identification of the compensatory rule that underlies the CTC. The following four questions have to be answered successively by the patient.

1. What was the SO`s interactional behaviour that stands in relation to your typical behaviour in everyday encounters?
2. Identify your most relevant emotional interpretation by going through the key encounters with the corresponding interpretations.

3. What is the underlying compensatory rule in behavioral terms that protects you from the effects the SO`s interactional behaviour had on you? Example 2.11: Avoiding closeness to my father protected me not to get hurt.
4. Proof the rule by going through all key events written on the flipchart from a prosecutor perspective.

Second sub-step: Creation of awareness for the up-coming event when acting against the compensatory rule. Again the patient has to answer successively four questions.

1. Judge from a prosecutor perspective to what up-coming event (behavioral consequence of the SO) your most relevant interactional emotional response was related in the past?
2. Proof the up-coming event (behavioral consequence of the SO) by your drawn causal relations in the second sub-step of the last task and test alternative events you may have forgotten to mention.
3. Explain what the up-coming event (behavioral consequence of your SO) was when acting against the compensatory rule? Example 2.11: Overt punishment, i.e. being critized, being yelled at.
4. Proof the identified up-coming event (behavioral consequence of the SO) and your emotional response by going through all key events written on the flipchart from a juror perspective.

Third sub-step: Development of the CTC. Three questions have to be answered successively.

1. What do you feel is the most relevant emotional impact that the SO exerted on you that is most relevant in your everyday relationships?
2. Formulate the corresponding CTC with the help of the underlying compensatory rule and the identified up-coming event when acting against the compensatory rule. The CTC should built-up on the legacy you feel the SO has left on you. It can be formulated either in the form of an (ego-based) transference prediction that makes-up how you emotionally experience the world or as a conditional rule in the form of a "if then" statement that predicts your prototypical emotional response in relation to the expected up-coming event (behavioral consequence). Example 2.11: I am afraid of authoritarian dominant men (CTC as a conditional prediction), or if I come closer to an authoritarian man then I freeze (CTC as a "if then" statement). To note, from a learning theory perspective the "if then" statement is a conditioned response with predictive strength that is self reinforcing.
3. Proof the CTC by going through all key events written on the flipchart.

The exercise ends with a learning summary of the step.

2.5.4.1. What is learned?

The fourth task can be described as a top-down guided re-evaluation process of the results of the previous task. The therapist helps the patient to translate the most relevant formative influence of his SO into a transference prediction that was established while living together with the SO, i.e. a CTC. With respect to exposure aspects, the patient becomes exposed at tacit knowledge about what behaviour predicts at what time a negative reinforcer or the absence of a positive reinforcer when a SO had exerted a negative formative influence on the patient's life, as well as what behaviour predicts at what time a positive reinforcer or the absence of a negative reinforcer when a SO had exerted a positive formative influence on the patient's life. Concerning associative learning of behavioral effects the early-onset chronically depressed patient - sometimes for the first time of his life - becomes aware (feels) that the key encounters with his SO are taken seriously by the therapist. In addition, the therapist does not attack the patient`s difficulties in causal reasoning. Instead, the therapist cooperatively helps the patient to work-out the most meaningful relation between his previous learning experiences and his interpersonal transference prediction. The therapist thus contributes to meaningfully inform the patient. A second fact is important to note: The behaviour of the patient to explore and verbally designate a CTC respectively terminates the overwhelming character of the aversive feelings that usually increase and decrease several times during the fourth task. The termination of the uncomfortable emotional state respectively represents a different (or opposite) outcome compared to the patient`s independent of response expectation of being punished in some way. The patient therefore experiences in the presence of the therapist that cooperating in logically thinking is an effective strategy of affect regulation that has the capacity to stop the induced aversive cognitions and feelings as well as to become less afraid of or threatened by traumatic processed helplessness memories and reminders of failure events themselves, helping the patient to integrate trauma memories and reminders into his self-image. This new element of reaction amplifies the conditional relationship between positive efficacy beliefs and positive outcome expectations. Furthermore, the patient`s perceptive and interpretative performance is sensitized by means of attention-focused interventions under aspects of awareness. In sum, the patient`s door is opened to bring into the subsequent SA/IDE treatment phase stressful everyday encounters all of which play in the interpersonal domain in which the origin of the interpersonal fear was established.

2.6. Key frontiers in the administration of the I-SOH procedure

2.6.1. Patient variable

CBASP psychotherapy includes much exposure aspects in its cutting edge techniques of behaviour change (Schoepf et al, 2011; Schoepf & Neudeck, 2011; Neudeck et al., 2012). According to our clinical experience, the following six prerequisites should be fulfilled prior to out-patient CBASP therapy in the sub-group of patients who suffer of chronic MDD with antecedent dysthymic disorder:

1. The patient should be sufficiently self-motivated to learn to effectively interact with his environment. A good indirect clinical clue is when a patient comes in a reliable way to the preceding diagnostic dates.
2. Simple relationships between behaviour and its effect with respect to adaptive behaviour should be understood by the patient. A good clinical clue is how a patient responds to contingent personal responsivity in case of a proactive behaviour - like asking the clinician clarifying questions during the diagnostic phase.

3. The patient should be able to respond to contingent personal responsivity in case of pro-active behaviour with affects that can be clearly defined and specified in simple discrimination exercises.
4. If necessary, the patient should be adjusted to a stable antidepressant medication before CBASP psychotherapy starts.
5. Both somatic and mental co-morbidity should be sufficiently treated before CBASP psychotherapy starts. Do not start CBASP if a different mental disorder is leading or a somatic disorder is untreated.
6. Criteria for termination of outpatient treatment in case of a severe increase of world-weariness/or acute suicidal behaviour as well as a severe "breaking-through" MD-episode that needs antidepressant medication should be defined and clarified.

If the prerequisites are not fulfilled a multi-step psychotherapy approach that integrates McCullough's model, has proven to be successful in a small regular ward at Bonn University equipped with a specialized outpatient department (Schoepf & Neudeck, 2011).

2.6.2. Therapist variable

According to Winnicott "objective" counter transference is the constricted feelings, attitudes, and reactions of a therapist induced by a patient (Winnicott, 1949). Within CBASP, Winnicott's concept constitutes the most important basic assumption, establishing how, with the help of DPI, the patient's resistance that is caused by reactions of negative transference is dealt with and the integration of traumatic learning experiences into his or her self-image is achieved. This implies according to McCullough that the CBASP therapist:

1. Applies objective counter-transference as a vehicle of in-session change.
2. Is able to be oneself with the patient in the therapy, i.e. that the patient encounters an authentic therapist who is neither afraid to be himself nor to walk with the patient as a "comrade" (McCullough, 2012) .
3. Salubriously uses personal responsivity.
4. Arranges contingencies so that the patient can learn.
5. Makes moment-to moment decisions with respect to CBASP treatment goals.
6. Self-monitors the patient's moment-to-moment verbal- and nonverbal messages.
7. Is focused in supervision on his non-reflected verbal- and nonverbal messages that interfere with CBASP treatment goals.

As a rule (and as described in 2.2), optimal use of DPI techniques requires that the therapist has learned to alternate between the dominant and submissive octants of the Kiesler circle as the in-session occasion requires. The therapist has also to remain on the friendly side of the interpersonal circle so as to avoid reinforcing the negative interpersonal transference expectancies early-onset patients often act out during treatment (McCullough & McCullough, 2009).

2.7. Identification of the dominant interpersonal-emotional theme domain and formulation of the TH

After the I-SOH procedure is finished the CBASP patient`s manual for patients is distributed and the patient is prepared for the SA/IDE phase of treatment that starts in the subsequent session. In the period until the beginning of the first therapy session of the SA/IDE phase of treatment the TH is formulated in the absence of the patient, especially in early-onset chronically depressed patients with a history of family violence or childhood trauma (McCullough, 2006: page 130; McCullough, 2012b). For this purpose, the dominant interpersonal-emotional theme domain is defined by the therapist. The interpersonal-emotional theme reflects the early learning history of the patient and is derived from the CTCs. CBASP assumes four transference areas of interaction in early-onset chronically depressed patients that, from the perspective of developmental psychology, play an important role in the patient's relationship with significant others. His theoretical considerations concerning the transference hypothesis refer to the concept of "tacit knowledge"(Polanyi, 1966) and the idea of "reasoning based on implicit causal theories" (Nisbett and Wilson, 1977). Specifically, McCullough (2006) describes working with the construct of transference as an exercise in "focused attention." The TH differs from Freud's concept of transference since it can be actively acted out in session with the therapist and then processed within the IDE. From a learning theory perspective the transference hypothesis includes the hypothesized core content of the patient`s in-session interpersonal fear that most likely reflects the patient's expectancy of the therapist's reactions toward the individual (McCullough et al., 2010). The four transference areas of interpersonal dysfunction in that "hot spots" occur are:

1. In-session moments of intimacy (either felt by the patient or the therapist) that evoke in the patient (Pavlovian) fear of being physically or emotionally abused (intimacy area).
2. In-session events in which the patient discloses emotional needs toward the therapist that evoke in the patient (Pavlovian) fear of being ridiculed or censored (disclosure of need area).
3. In-session events during which the patient makes mistakes towards the therapist (i.e. not doing his or her homework or being unable to solve problems presented during therapy sessions) that evoke in the patient (Pavlovian) fear of severe physical or emotional punishment (mistake and failure area).
4. In-session events in which the patient expresses negative affects towards the therapist that evoke in the patient (Pavlovian) fear of punishment (expression of negative affect area).

The TH then becomes central in the IDE because it defines the starting point of IDE or interpersonal "hot spot". Through the controlled use of the IDE in "hot spot" situations it becomes possible for the patient during the course of the treatment, to clearly distinguish the therapeutic relationship from the relationships the patient experienced with his SOs (Schoepf & Neudeck, 2011).

2.8. Therapeutic goals of the SA/IDE phase of treatment

The SA/IDE phase of treatment starts with introducing the SA. The major therapeutic goals of this phase are:

1. To focus the patient on the situational consequences of behaviour and to demonstrate him continuously that what he does matters through SA work.
2. To strengthen functional interpersonal behaviour contingently.
3. To counter-condition fear reactions those occur during the practising of realistic and goal-oriented behaviour in the elicitation phase of SA work.
4. To shape action-related interpretations and missing behavioral aspects in the remediation phase of SA work.
5. To help the patient to process how the present patient-therapist relationship differs from his past relationships with his SOs due to the various forms of the IDE - that are employed in relation to the progress of therapy (Schoepf & McCullough, 2009; Schoepf & Neudeck, 2011; Neudeck et al., 2012).

2.9. Achieving in-session two-way circular functioning in the SA/IDE phase of treatment

The core content of the patient's interpersonal fear is counter-conditioned in the SA/IDE phase of treatment due to IDE work. The technique of IDE was formerly described by our group as a bottom-up technique that is assumed to be the major CBASP technique of (explicit) in-session acquisition learning (Schoepf et al. 2007; Schoepf & McCullough, 2009; Schoepf et al., 2011; Schoepf & Neudeck, 2011). In general, bottom-up techniques like the IDE are designed to lead the patient from the concrete therapeutic situation to interpersonal situations which resemble the therapeutic situation (Neudeck et al., 2012).

Table 1 represents the learning context and the different phases of the IDE (adapted from Schoepf et al., 2011; Schoepf & Neudeck, 2011).

The starting point of an IDE is defined by the presence of an in-session "hot-spot" event/moment. The core content of the patient's interpersonal fear is activated any time the dyad encounters an in-session relationship issue signaling that a relational "hot spot" is encountered (McCullough et al., 2010). Three different forms of the IDE are applied in Bonn out-patients:

1. In the cognitive form of the IDE the principle of counter-conditioning cognitive evoked (Pavlovian) fear is limited to the negative phase. The mechanism of sensitization is started in the positive phase and is increased in the healing phase (adapted from Neudeck et al., 2010; Schoepf & Neudeck, 2011; Neudeck et al., 2012).
2. In the emotional form of the IDE the principle of counter conditioning of re-experienced (Pavlovian) fear predominates within all IDE phases (Schoepf et al., 2011; Schoepf & Neudeck, 2011). A strong feeling of "safety" within the therapy dyad results that usually elevates the probability of generalizing outside of therapy to the patient's other relationships (adapted from Schoepf & Neudeck, 2011).

Learning context
The therapist directs the focus of attention to the just happened "hot spot"in-session event/moment and writes the patient's „hot spot" behaviour on the flip-chart. Then the three phases of the IDE are consecutively carried out.
Negative phase
The patient is gently asked to recall a typical past social interaction with one or two of his maltreating "Significant Other's" in a similar situation. In the cognitive form the patient has to describe the behavioral consequences on himself caused by the behaviour of his significant other. In particular bad thoughts are evoked through tacit knowledge. In the emotional form the patient is additionally gently asked to re-experience the associated hurtful (refractory) emotions in the presence of the therapist. In particular negative feelings like fear, pain and sadness are evoked. Counter-conditioning according to the principle of reciprocal inhibition takes place by the benevolent therapist's reaction (Schoepf et al., 2007; Schoepf et al., 2011; Schoepf & Neudeck, 2011).
Positive phase
After the intensity of negative thoughts and emotions is decreased the patient is gently asked to describe his perception of the therapist's reactions. Furthermore, he has to characterize the feelings that have been evoked by the current incident with the therapist. He is then asked to compare the therapist's behaviour to the recalled behaviour (and the corresponding emotion in the emotional form of IDE) of his significant others in a similar situation. The felt distress of the patient usually decreases at this moment of the exercise.
Healing phase
Sensitive to the timing and the magnitude of the felt decrease of distress in the healing phase of the IDE, the patient is encouraged by the therapist to identify the contrast between the therapist's behaviour and the significant other's' behaviour. "Automatically" there results a felt increase of the potency of the therapist to specifically reduce interpersonal distress during the experienced "hot spot" situation and a new interpersonal reality of the therapist-patient relationship comes into being meaningful to the patient.

Table 1. Learning context, negative phase, positive phase and healing phase of the IDE (adapted from Schoepf & Neudeck, 2011).

3. In the double counter conditioning form of the IDE interpersonal fear is first counter-conditioned with the goal of modifying strikingly maladaptive behavioral patterns. Then the cognitive or the emotional form of the IDE is coupled contrasting the reactive behaviour of the therapist against the maladaptive behaviour of one or two SOs (adapted from Schoepf et al., 2011; Schoepf & Neudeck, 2011).

2.9.1. The three options to use the various forms of the IDE

The IDE is used in it various forms to address, train, and thereby "repair" developmental trauma memories and associated symptoms arising from negative experiences with abusive

SOs. It is recommended to use the three various forms of the IDE in relation to the progress of therapy throughout the SA/IDE phase of treatment, table 2 (Schoepf et al., 2011; Schoepf & Neudeck, 2011; table 2).

First option – when a patient shows early benefit in SA work
When patients show sufficient symptom reduction in the pre-SA phase of treatment and fast benefit of SA-work during the SA/IDE phase of treatment the cognitive form of IDE has approved itself to specifically reduce interpersonal distress by helping the patient to cognitively discriminate the therapist's interactional behaviour in "hot spot" in-session events from the interactional behaviour of hurtful SOs in similar past encounters (McCullough et al., 2011).
Second option – when a patient shows delayed benefit in SA work
When patients show sufficient symptom reduction in the pre-SA phase of treatment and delayed benefit of SA work during the SA/IDE phase of treatment the emotional form of IDE has approved itself to modify closed perceptual trauma domains that perpetuate the cognitive-emotional dilemma of the patient (Schoepf et al., 2011; Schoepf & Neudeck, 2011).
Third option – when a patient does not show benefit in SA work
When patients show little symptom reduction in the pre-SA phase of treatment and do not benefit from SA work during the SA/IDE phase of treatment a modified form of the IDE (double-counter conditioning) to modify strikingly maladaptive in-session behavior has approved itself to be successful (Schoepf et al., 2011). An example of the modified form of IDE is published elsewhere (Schoepf et al. 2011; Schoepf & Neudeck 2011).

Table 2. Early benefit, delayed benefit and no benefit in CBASP psychotherapy as orientation for the use of the three various forms of the IDE in the SA/IDE phase of treatment.

2.10. Evaluation of the safety-signal impact

The goal of measuring if interpersonal safety is achieved in the domain in which the origin of the patient's interpersonal fear is established is accomplished with the use of the Personal Questionnaire (PQ). The PQ represents a patient-self-report methodology comprised of paired comparisons using three cards that are each compared to one another (McCullough, 2006). The three cards contain the same content of the TH used in the various forms of IDE work, but formulated with (1) a baseline illness-level indicating no perceived change observed between the therapist and malevolent SOs, (2) an improvement-level indicating some perceived change observed between the therapist and malevolent SOs, and a (3) recovery level indicating clear perceived change observed between the therapist and malevolent SOs. The scoring of specific increases in expected in-session emotional safety with respect to CBASP`s TH construct are done by the patient himself and blind to the therapist before the beginning of every session and in the absence of the therapist. The patient is instructed not to tell the therapist the scoring results. The therapist obtains after 32-35 therapy sessions a feedback about the scoring of the results. The safety signal impact of the therapist on the hypothesized core content of the patient's in-session interpersonal fear is highest at a scoring of 1 and lowest at a scoring of 4. The procedure is clearly outlined by McCullough (McCullough, 2006, pp 163-167). The self-report questionnaire represents a cost-effective option to systematically, reliably, and validly evaluate the safety signal impact of the therapist on the patient because it is inexpensive in terms of professional time needed for administration, and does not require special training for administration.

2.11. Assessment of the I-SOH procedure up-to the TH

TASK 1: Preparing, see text
TASK 2: Focussing, see text (flip-chart)
List of SOs reported by the P: Father, mother, first girl friend, later girl friend, and his travelling companion.
TASK 3: Reconstruction of closed perceptual systems in antecedent-consequent way (flip-chart). To note, the third and the fourth tasks are carried out successively for all SO`s.
Example of first listed SO Father (exerted a negative formative influence with high impact)
First sub-step: Creation of awareness for key past encounters ***: T teaches P to respectively describe one typical key interpersonal encounter in behavioral terms (using the flip-chart)**
Report of the patient. My father was frequently absent. His manner was quick-tempered, i.e. he often yelled and demanded obedience without notice[1*]. He punished verbally if someone did not follow his rules[2*]. In addition he always reacted angrily if someone disclosed an emotional need. He himself had great difficulties in showing any of his feelings. He reacted extremely angry if I had a different opinion [3*]. On the other hand he helped his friends and he was proud of his son. Confidence on each other is his highest inner worth until today. Another attitude of him is, that you have to work harder then the rest to be respected. He sent me to an off-shore oil platform after school [4*].
Second sub-step: Elicitation of self-referential interpretations and identification of key causal relations between the past and the presence **Eliciting self-referential interpretations (flip-chart)**
I (always) felt defeated when he yelled at me ([1*].) I (always) thought that I am a looser ([2*]). I (always) froze when I saw the anger in his face before he yelled at me ([3*]). I (always) felt so lonely ([4*]).

Identification of key causal relations between the past and the presence (flip-chart) **Preparation theorem: The impact of my father on me/my everyday relationships is that....**
I do not disclose what I feel (1*). I do not express my own opinion (2*). I am convinced that something bad will happen if I do not follow the rules of authorities (3). I avoid conflicts by running away (3*) I submit myself authorities (4*).
TASK 4: Translation of tacit knowledge into explicit causal knowledge (flip-chart)
First sub-step (underlying compensatory rule): Avoiding closeness to my father protected me to get hurt. Second sub-step (up-coming event when acting against the rule): Overt punishment. Third sub-step (CTC): I am afraid of authoritarian dominant men - if I come closer to a authoritarian man then I freeze -
CTCs of other listed SOs, i.e. after the patient has formulated one CTC for each SO
Mother (exerted a negative formative influence with high impact) I am afraid of dominant-hostile women, i.e. if I come closer to women then I will be punished irrationally. First girlfriend (exerted a negative formative influence with traumatically processed impact) I am afraid of attractive hysterical women, i.e. if I come closer to attractive women I will become existentially hurt. Second girl-friend (exerted a positive formative influence with low impact) If I keep distance then I can trust a woman in some way. Travelling companion (exerted a positive formative influence with low impact) If I interact with a calm and composed non-authoritarian man who has no prejudice against my background I feel happy.
Determination of the dominant interpersonal theme domain - ascertained in the absence of the patient
The patient does not know how to relate emotionally with humans. He can not trust in relations (intimacy area)
Transference hypothesis, i.e. the associated in-session transference prediction related to the therapist for IDE work
If I (patient) come emotionally close to Dr. Schoepf, I am sure that he will point on my deficits and something hurtful will happen that is lying out of my control and that will make me feel lonely (here formulated as a baseline illness sentence).

Table 3.

3. Third part

3.1. Treatment trajectories of early-onset chronically depressed outpatients

Typical treatment trajectories over 32 sessions in 48 weeks (figures 1-5) of 5 younger to middle age adult chronic MDD outpatients with antecedent dysthymic disorder that were treated according to the modified protocol are represented without further systematic statistical evaluation as the studies are still running.

The SCID I and II were used for diagnosis. Early life trauma and live events were assessed by using the Childhood Trauma Questionnaire and the Early Trauma Inventory. The external ratings (HAMD or MADRAS as primary-outcome measures) were done blind to the therapy method; the PQ ratings were done blind to the therapist. All therapy sessions were videotaped. Concerning feasibility, all patients completed the treatment. The adapted I-SOH procedure protocol proved to be feasible and there were no major difficulties with side effects of potential symptom aggravations, affective overflow or potential retraumatization.

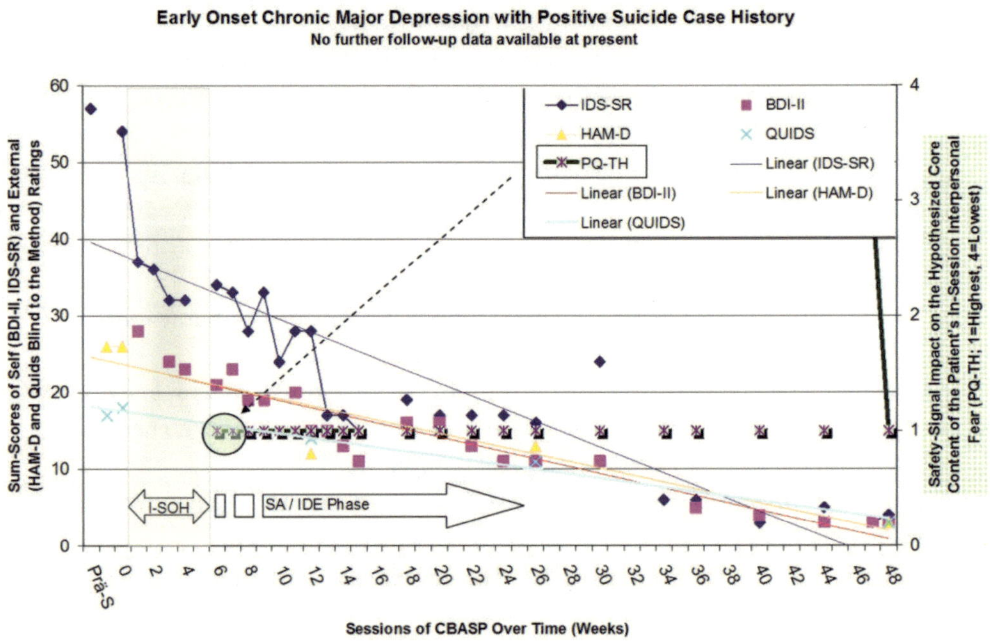

Figure 1. Female patient under 30 years. X-axis: Prä-S = pre-screening. 0 = just before start of treatment. 1st Y axis (left): Full syndromal remission according to self-ratings at week 36 (BDI-II </= 10). 2nd Y axis (right): The highest possible safety-signal impact of the therapist on the hypothesized core content of the patient's in-session interpersonal fear at the start of the SA/IDE phase of treatment (week 6, arrow) maintained until the end of treatment.

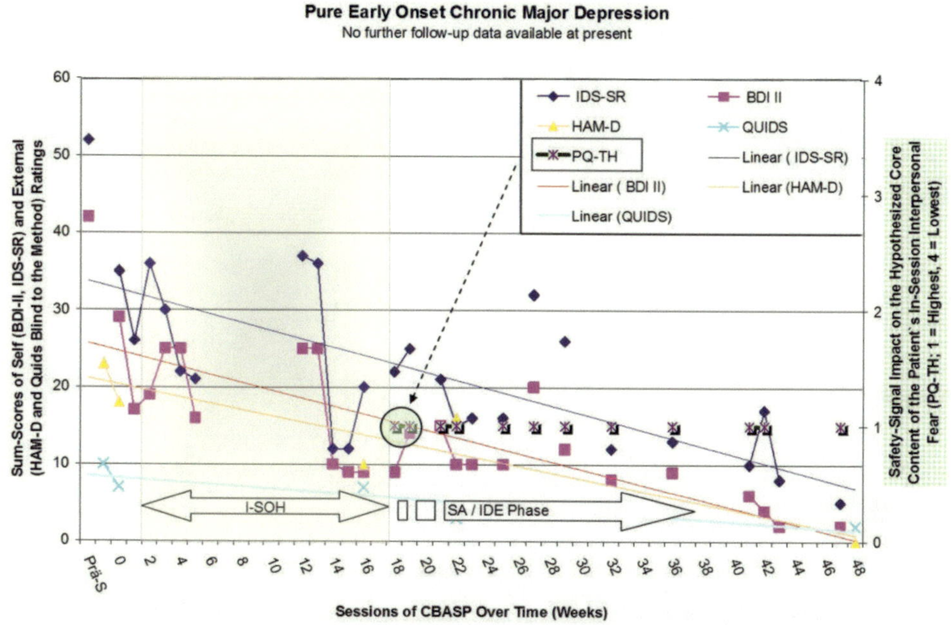

Figure 2. Female patient in middle age under 50 years. The pre-SA phase of treatment was interrupted with no ones fault between the fifth until the 12th week. Full syndromal remission is reached at week 13 (BDI-II</= 10). The highest possible safety-signal impact of the therapist is reached at the start of the SA/IDE phase of treatment (week 17, arrow) and maintained until the end of treatment. Axis labels as in figure 1.

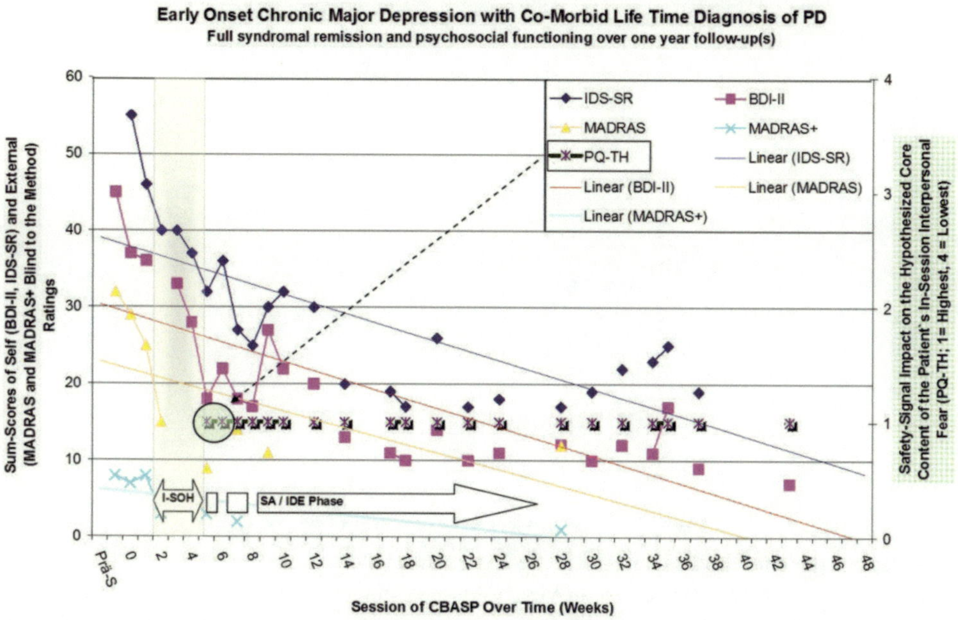

Figure 3. Female patient under 40 years. The highest possible safety-signal impact of the therapist is reached at week 6 (arrow) and maintained until the end of treatment. Full syndromal remission at week 17 (BDI-II </= 10). PD = Panic Disorder..

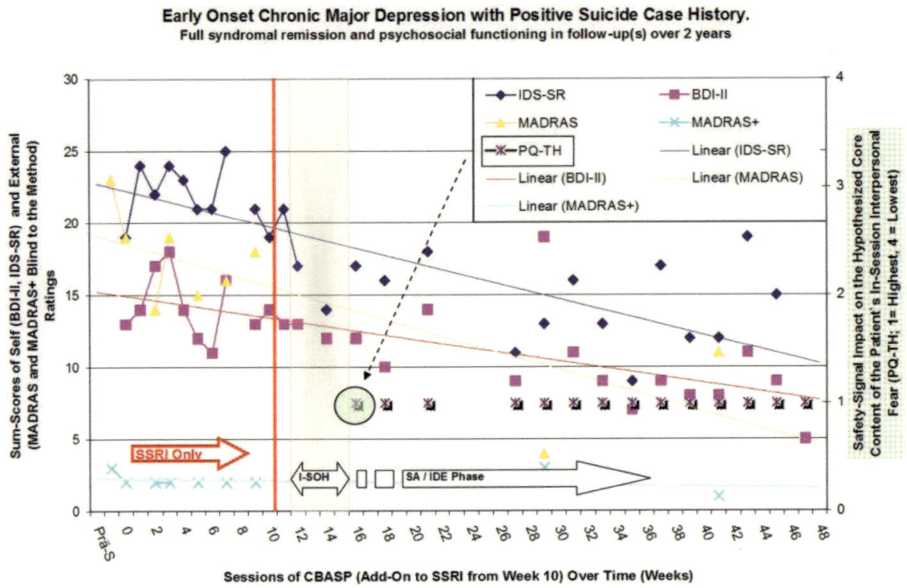

Figure 4. Male patient with age under 50 years. Start with SSRI treatment alone. CBASP added after week 8 because of non-response (Reduction MADRAS sum score < 20%). Red vertical line signifies the start of CBASP. The highest safety-signal impact of the therapist is reached at week 16 (arrow) and maintained until the end of treatment. Full syndromal remission at week 18 (BDI-II </=10).

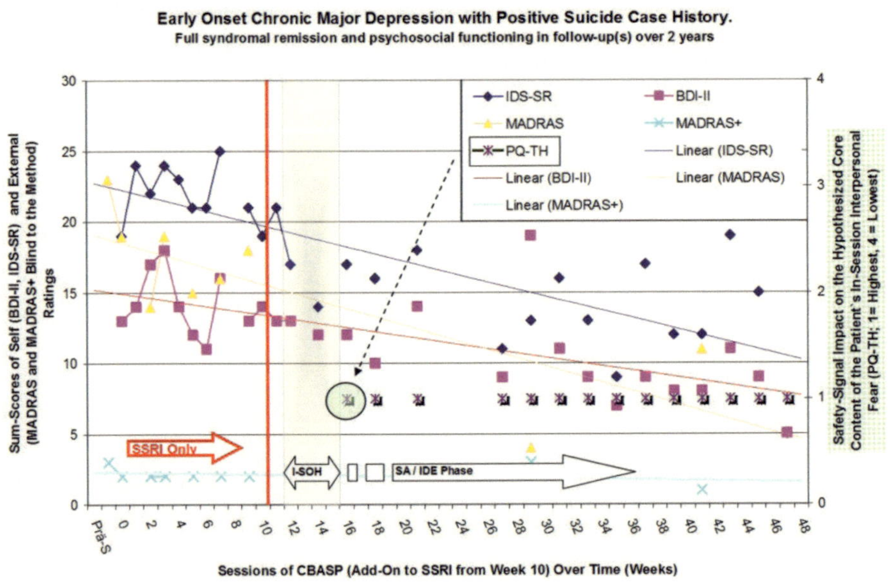

Figure 5. Female patient with age under 40 years. Start with SSRI treatment alone. CBASP added after week 8 because of non-response (Reduction MADRAS sum score < 20%). Red vertical line signifies the start of CBASP. The time period of the I-SOH procedure is short. Correspondingly, the safety-signal impact of the therapist is low (arrow) at the beginning of the SA/IDE phase. The highest safety-signal impact of the therapist is reached at week 35 on a stable niveau. Full syndromal remission is achieved at week 14 (BDI-II </=10).

The treatment trajectories clearly show - without any further necessary explanation – a positive short-term effect of the I-SOH procedure on the hypothesized core content of the patient's in-session interpersonal fear in relation to symptom reduction. In addition, over the period of the treatment a state of full syndromal remission was achieved in all patients. In addition, the treatment trajectories demonstrate that under out-patient study conditions the adapted study protocol works best with a dosage of up-to 35 sessions. The first three figures represent treatment trajectories of CBASP only treated patients which were highly motivated for the method. Figures four and five represent trajectories of CBASP add-on treatment to non-response to previous 8-week SSRI treatment. The SSRI medication was further prescribed and controlled during the course of therapy. Both patients had no preference for one of the two methods but were highly motivated to be included into the study.

3.2. Challenges and future directions

Around 3.7 million children are assessed for childhood maltreatment each year alone in the United States. Converging data support adverse effects of early life stress on morphologic development of corticostriatal-limbic structures (Edmiston EE, et al., 2011). Clinically, there is ample evidence that a persisting state of depressed emotion and interpersonal anxiety in chronic MDD with antecedent dysthymic disorder cannot be shacked easily by any kind of antidepressant medication or biophysical intervention; neither in a dozen of disorder specific therapy sessions that are embedded in a conceptually framework that has just started to point in public to the exposure aspects of its major techniques of change (Neudeck et al., 2012) nor by simply changing the situational thoughts and/or problem solving capabilities (Schoepf et al., 2007; Kocsis et al., 2009; Schoepf & Neudeck, 2011; Schoepf et al.; 2011; McCullough, 2012).

Animals and human beings view the world causally; exactly the same early-onset chronically depressed patients. However, the patient's bottoms-up and top-down driven processes largely operate in the absence of cognitive awareness as stimulus learning of stressful encounters with their SO`s in the past dominates over social adaptive outcome-effect learning in the presence. Based on my clinical experiences and the treatment effects of my self treated patients that are represented in this chapter article in the form of simple treatment trajectories without further statistical evaluation, I assume that the successful mastering of the I-SOH procedure in the presented exposure based form - that primarily focuses on activating and restructuring past helplessness memories with SOs in the early phase of treatment - represents a key stepping stone in CBASP out-patient treatment that turns the page from the patient's idiosyncratic functioning at the beginning of therapy to circular formal-operational functioning and long term success in the later therapy process. McCullough would say: The I-SOH procedure in the presented form thrusts the therapist into the core perceptual-emotional arena involving the patient and his SOs. I have to add, that at the end of the pre-SA phase of treatment, the technique loosens these emotional connections, replacing them with a salubrious new connection to the therapist. Additionally, every SA a patient brought to therapy in the second treatment phase played in the dominant interpersonal theme domain, in which recurrent experiences of helplessness were earlier made. This is motivation to change and approaching behaviour from the patient's side and challenges the therapist.

Behaviour therapists often express that working with exposure is quite rewarding, as fear inhibitory learning allows the therapist and the patient a more flexible adjustment of fear related associations in changing environments, exposure is intellectually and behaviourally stimulating, and exposure has the potential to facilitate lasting change in the patient. However, in the treatment of chronic MDD with antecedent dysthymic disorder potential challenges may come about severe side effects of potential symptom aggravations, potential retraumatization and affective overflow that may be caused by techniques like the I-SOH procedure that confront the patients with their helplessness memories that are sometimes traumatically processed. Indeed, helplessness memories and associated core-beliefs are often quite painful for patients to acknowledge, and sustained attention to closed perceptual systems in session is usually associated with an increase of negative affect and agitation. Not only then, it is important for the therapist to be able to be oneself with the patient in the therapy, i.e. that the patient encounters an authentic therapist who is neither afraid to be himself nor to walk with the patient as a "comrade" (McCullough, 2012). It is also imperative, that the patient learns from the beginning of therapy to effectively use specific interventions of CBASP`s functionality teaching and skills teaching dimension to deal with these inevitable and for the progress of therapy necessary symptom aggravations. Because fear inhibitory learning is not attained fully after one session, the patient may experience a temporary increase in symptoms in between sessions. Therapists should anticipate this and should meet special agreements in the form of additional short sessions.

Although CBASP, as a "difficult to learn" treatment package that can only be acquired through intensive training, showed significant effects for treating refractory outpatients with chronic MDD in one of the two large NIHM funded studies, especially in its combination with medication (Keller et al., 2000) and developmental trauma (Nemeroff et al., 2003), rarely research is conducted concerning the role exposure aspects play in patient change. Thus, a much-needed direction for future research is to dismantle specific CBASP interventions and to evaluate their efficacy in reducing depressive symptoms, improving functioning, and improving quality of life. Such process research has to involve a time-series analysis of standardized assessments completed at the beginning and the end of each therapy session, and across the course of multiple sessions. In addition, by the research on the neural mechanisms of chronic depression and the impact of CBASP on behavioural and neural functioning (Schnell et al., 2010), more is learned about the fundamental processes of learning and memory that take place during administering CBASP intervention strategies (Walter et al., 2009).

3.3. General conclusion

In this chapter, I have given an overview of an important excerpt of my clinical work under study conditions that I have carried out in the last six years. The I-SOH procedure and the modified protocol have been discussed with Jim McCullough, Kim Penberthy and Henrik Walter since 2006 and later Knut Schnell. The fifth colleague of this core working group is Peter Neudeck who joined the Bonn CBASP Centre of Competence 2009. Peter is an excellent exposure therapist whom I supervise in CBASP until today as I have been supervised by Jim McCullough once (2007-2008). All of us strongly emphasize the aspects of modern learning theory in CBASP as CBASP therapists and all of us feel the need to further dismantle CBASP`s interventions for better treatment. Hopefully, this chapter has persuasively articulated a constructive use of the modified out-patient protocol for chronic MDD patients with antecedent dysthymic disorder. It is again my concern to bring into consciousness that disciplined personal involvement CBASP techniques that are both reliable and valid can only be learned through intensive training. This is the reason why, to this day, even McCullough himself conducts training for selected learning therapists, using video-supervised case studies. As CBASP-providers, CBASP-supervisors and CBASP-therapists, these therapists are responsible for the distribution and quality control of CBASP in their respective countries (Schoepf & Neudeck, 2011). Further information is available at www.cbasp.org. Like the last year, when I wrote the 2011 CBASP overview chapter, I found myself again fueled by hope that this articulation can be of assistance to other psychiatrists and psychotherapists, as well to other mental health practioners who are interested in working with chronically depressed patients in a constructive way to help their patients to get out of their prison of negative thoughts and outcome expectations, as well as to change their destructive interpersonal behaviors.

Author details

Dieter Schoepf
Bonn University, Department of Psychiatry and Psychotherapy,
CBASP-Centre of Competence, Germany

Acknowledgement

I am grateful for the collaboration of James P McCullough JR, Commonwealth University of Virginia; Jennifer Kim Penberthy, University of Virginia Health System; Wolfgang Maier, Department of Psychiatry, University of Bonn; Henrik Walter, now Department of Psychiatry, University of Berlin; Knut Schnell, now Department of Psychiatry, University of Heidelberg; and Elisabeth Schramm, Department of Psychiatry, University of Freiburg. I also thank CBASP-network and the whole Bonn CBASP-1 and CBASP-2 study team for their pro-active work, as well as the whole team of my inpatient department.

4. References

American Psychiatric Association: Diagnostic and statistical manual of mental disorders, 4th edition, text revision (2000). Washington DC, American Psychiatric Association.

Bandura A (1969). Principles of behaviour modification. New York; Holt, Rineheart & Winston.

Bouton ME (2007). Learning and behaviour: A contemporary synthesis. Sunderland; Mass: Sinauer Associates, Inc.

McCrory EJ, et al. (2011). Heightened neural reactivity to threat in child victims of family violence. Current Biology; 21 (33): doi: 10.1016.

Edmiston EE, et al. (2011). Corticostriatal-limbic gray matter morphology in adolescents with self-reported exposure to childhood maltreatment. Arch Pediatr Adolesc Med; 165(12):1069-1077.

Ehlers, A & Clark, DM (2000). A cognitive model of persistent Posttraumatic Stress Disorder. Behaviour Research and Therapy, 38, 319-345.

Foa EB, et al., (2007). Prolonged exposure therapy for PTSD: Emotional processing of traumatic experiences. New York: Oxford University Press.

Keller MB, McCullough JP, et al. (2000) A comparison of nefazadone, the cognitive behavioural analysis system of psychotherapy, and their combination for treatment of chronic depression. New England Journal of Medicine; 342: 1462-1470.

Klein DN et al. (2011). Social problem solving and depressive symptoms over time: a randomized clinical trial of Cognitive-Behavioral Analysis System of Psychotherapy, Brief Supportive Psychotherapy, and Pharmacotherapy. Journal of Consulting and Clinical Psychology; 79 (3): 342-352.

Klein DN, Kocsis JH, et al. (1996). Symptomatology in dysthymic and major depressive disorder. Psychiatr Clin North Am; 19 (1): 41-53.

Kocsis JH, Gelenberg AJ, et al. (2009). REVAMP Investigators: Cognitive behavioural analysis system of psychotherapy and brief supportive psychotherapy for augmentation of antidepressant nonresponse in chronic depression: the REVAMP Trial. Arch Gen Psychiatry; 66:1178-1188.

McCullough JP (2012a). The way early-onset chronically depressed patients are treated today makes me sad. Open Journal of Psychiatry; 2: 9-11.

McCullough JP (2012b). Answer of McCullough to official request of E. Schramm after supervisor meeting in CBASP Vs SYSP. Freiburg, Germany.

McCullough JP et al. (2011). The significant other history: An interpersonal-emotional history procedure used with the early-onset chronically depressed patient. Am J Psychotherapy; 65(3):225-48. .

McCullough JP et al. (2010). A method for conducting intensive psychological studies with early-onset chronically depressed patients. American Journal of Psychotherapy; 64: 317-337.

McCullough JP, McCullough RF (2009). CBASP intensive training workbook. A 2-day-CBASP-professional workshop. The author of the CBASP present at the second day. University Bonn, CBASP Centre of Competence, September 19th and 20th.

McCullough JP (2008). Personal discussion between workshop leader (McCullough) and co-leaders (Penberthy and Schoepf) during one work intensive training week. Richmond, USA.

McCullough JP (2007). What are we trying to teach our early-onset chronically depressed patients? Contemporary learning therapy and CBASP psychotherapy for chronic depression (book in preparation). Los Angeles; Psychiatry Grand Rounds, June 26.

McCullough JP (2006). Treating chronic depression with disciplined personal involvement: CBASP. New York; Springer.

Nemeroff CB, Heim CM, et al. (2003). Differential responses to psychotherapy versus pharmacotherapy in patients with chronic forms of major depression and childhood trauma. Proc Natl Acad Sci USA; 100(24):14293-6. Erratum in Proc Natl Acad Sci U S A. 2005 Nov 8; 102(45):16530.

Neudeck P, Walter H, Schoepf D (2012). Exposure aspects of the interpersonal discrimination exercise (IDE) and the situational analysis (SA) in Cognitive Behavioral Analysis System of Psychotherapy (CBASP). In: Exposure Therapy - Rethinking the Model - Refining the Method (ed. by Peter Neudeck & Hans-Ulrich Wittchen). Springer International (pp. 153-166). 233 Spring Street, New York, NY 10013, U.S.A.

Nisbett, Richard, & Wilson, Timothy (1997). Telling more than we can know: verbal reports on mental processes. Psychological Review, 84: 231-259.

Penberthy JK (2010). CBASP and the chronically depressed alcoholic. WCBCT, Boston, June 3; Symposium 33: KCB 101.

Polany Mi (1966). The tacit dimension. Doubleday; Garden City, NY.

Schmidt, JA et al., (1999). Psychometric and circumplex properties of the Octant Scale Impact Message Inventory (IMI-C): A structural evaluation. Journal of Counselling Psychology, 46, 325–334.

Schnell K, Schoepf D, et al. (2010). Insights into the „Helpless Brain"– an fMRI-Model of perceived functionality in chronic depression. WCBCT, Boston, June 3; Symposium 33: KCB 101.

Schoepf D, Neudeck P (2011). Cognitive Behavioral Analysis System of Psychotherapy (CBASP): a disorder-oriented, theory-driven psychotherapy method from the "third generation" of behaviour therapy models, designed for the treatment of chronic depression. In: Uehara T (Ed.) Psychiatric Disorders - Worldwide Advances (pp. 87-120). ISBN: 978-953-307-833-5.

Schoepf D, Neudeck P, Walter H (2011). Learning theory aspects of the Interpersonal Discrimination Exercise (IDE) and Clinical Applications. International CBASP-Network Conference, Lübeck, August 25 - 27.

Schoepf D, Penberthy JK (2010). Cognitive Behavioural Analysis System of Psychotherapy (CBASP): new applications and neurobiological mechanisms. WCBCT, Boston, June 3; Symposium 33: KCB 101.

Schoepf D, McCullough JR (2009). CBASP`s cutting edges to change the behaviour of the chronically depressed patient. Paper presented at the professional 2-day workshop with the author of the CBASP present at the second day, University Bonn, September 19th and 20th.

Schoepf D, Schnell K, Walter H (2008). Das Cognitive Behavioral Analysis System of Psychotherapy (CBASP): Theoretische Basis und Therapiestrategien. DGPPN Kongress, P-012-: Depression, II, Track: Depression/Affektive Erkrankungen

Schoepf D, Konradt B, Walter H (2007). Specific psychotherapy of chronic depression with the Cognitive Behavioral Analysis System of Psychotherapy. Nervenheilkunde 26: 790-802.

Schramm et al. (2011). Comparative efficacy of the Cognitive Behavioral Analysis System of Psychotherapy versus Supportive Psychotherapy for early onset chronic depression: design and rationale of a multisite randomized controlled trial. BMC Psychiatry, 11:134.

Walter H, Berger M, Schnell K (2009) Neuropsychotherapy. Conceptual, Empirical and Neuroethical Issues. European Archives of Psychiatry and Clinical Neuroscience 259, Suppl. 2, 173-182.

Winnicott DW (1949). Hate in the counter transference. International Journal of Psychoanalysis; 30: 69-75.

Chapter 8

Adaptation of Cognitive Behavioral Analysis System of Psychotherapy in a 29 Year Old Female Patient with Chronic Major Depression and Antecedent Dysthymic Disorder Who Switched Under Combined SSRI/CBASP Outpatient Treatment into Bipolarity: A Case Report

Viola Oertel-Knöchel and Dieter Schoepf

Additional information is available at the end of the chapter

http://dx.doi.org/10.5772/51963

1. Introduction

Affective disorders are among the main psychiatric illnesses reaching from **ma**jor **d**epressive **d**isorder (MDD) and **b**ipolar **d**isorder (BD) to schizoaffective disorder.

Under a historical perceptive, the beginning of the conceptualisation of affective disorders was done in 1854, when Jean-Pierre Falret named recurrent episodes of mania and depression as *folie circulaire* (Sedler & Falret, 1983). This was followed by Emil Kraepelin's definition as *manic-depressive psychosis*, which include the observation by Kraepelin that symptom-free intervals and acute illness episodes alternates in these patients (Kraepelin, 1921). A categorical distinction between two spectra with different diseases and different clinical courses, i.e. the *unipolar* spectrum and the *bipolar* spectrum, was first introduced by Karl Leonhard in 1957 (Beckmann, 1999).

With respect to the unipolar spectrum, MDD is among the most debilitating diseases worldwide with high disability compared with all human diseases (Falagas, Vardakas, & Vergidis, 2007). Lifetime prevalence of MDD is up to 20% once a life (Williams et al., 2007). In one third of the cases, the course of the illness is chronic, with often "difficult to treat" patients suffering from high social disturbances, resulting in a higher rate of mortality compared to pure MDD, higher economic costs and bad long-term prognoses compared to pure MDD (Schoepf et al., 2007). Chronicity is defined as unipolar depressive disorder lasting two or more years with less than a two-month period during which the individual reports no symptoms. The rating is contingent upon the density of symptoms at the time of assessment, every day in chronic MDD and more days than not in dysthymia. Manic, mixed or hypomanic episodes are listed as exclusion criteria (Schoepf & Neudeck, 2011). Studies assessing the course of unipolar depression (15 years range) indicate that approximately 15%-46% of the patients initially diagnosed with non-psychotic MDD or chronic MDD develop their symptoms into BD (Walden & Grunze, 2006). It is important to note, that 80% of initially unipolar diagnosed patients who suffer of a psychotic MD-episode develop their symptoms into the classic phenotype of manic-depressive illness within 5 years. This phenomenon is called *switch*. In general, the most obvious characteristic of BD are mood fluctuations and mental excitement those usually cause a marked change in the patient's baseline level of daily functioning (AACAP 1995). In paediatric BD, instability of mood in the early course of the disorder often interfere with the child's capacity to develop or maintain stable representations of self and others and results more often than not in difficulties to develop or maintain self-esteem. Bipolar children show co-morbidity rates of 13% with conduct disorder, 88% with oppositional defiant disorder, 98% with attention deficit hyperactivity disorder, and 11% with pervasive developmental disorders. In "older adolescent-onset" BD (aged 14-19 years) the symptom presentation, natural course of illness, phenomenology, and mental co-morbidity appear more similar to the classical symptoms described for adults in DSM-IV. In adult patients with manic depressive illness the life-time prevalence of concomitant occurrence of BD and other psychiatric disorders is 100% for one co-morbid axis-I disorder and 96% for > two co-morbid axis-I disorders with the highest co-morbidity rates for substance use disorders (alcoholism 30% -50%) and anxiety disorders (45%). Life-time prevalence rates of BD range from 5 % to 10% in the general population for all types and subtypes within the bipolar spectrum (Angst 1998). Further important public health issues are that BD (1) is a lifelong cyclical illness, (2) that the peak onset of BD is between 15–30 years, (3) that suicide is highest within 10 years of the onset of BD, (4) that frequent and repeated hospitalizations occur more often than not, (5) that the rate of promiscuity is increased compared to the general population, (6) that financial disasters, repeated job changes and/or losses are often associated with acute illness states, (7) that the coexistence of BD with other psychiatric disorders results in higher recurrence rates, higher suicide rates and a greater extent of psychosocial impairment, (8) that non-adherence to medication is common, and (9) that BD is associated with an increased risk of cardiovascular mortality on the long run of the illness. Commonly, a BD disorder needs approximately eight years to be correctly diagnosed (Wagner & Bräunig, 2000). One reason of the delay in correct diagnosis is that the disorder frequently starts with MD-episodes (60-80 % of all cases; (Wagner & Bräunig, 2000), so that primarily a MDD is diagnosed (Walden & Grunze, 2006). Further more, - clinical pathological - hypomanic or manic symptomatic states are often, mainly at the beginning of an episode, without psychological strain for the involved person (M. Hautzinger & Meyer, 2002). To be finished, the currently existing diagnostic instruments to validate manic or depressive symptoms might be impaired by self-evaluation (M. Hautzinger & Meyer, 2002).

With respect to disease classification within the bipolar spectrum, the current prominent psychiatric classification systems, which are used in clinical and research settings, are the *Diagnostic and Statistic Manual of Mental Disorders* (DSM-IV; American Psychiatric Association, 1994), and the *International Classification of Disease* (ICD-10; World Health Organization, 1992). In general, both don't differ in the descriptions of the symptomatology of BD, but there are differences regarding the definition of the subcategories: In the DSM-IV, the occurrence of depressed and hypomanic episodes during the course of the illness is subsumed under the diagnosis BD-II, whereas the occurrence of MD-episodes and manic or mixed episodes are classified as BD-I. In the longitudinal course of BD-I, mayor mood episodes are demarcated by either partial or full remission for at least 2 month or a switch to an episode of opposite polarity. The categorical approach of DSM-IV (Text Revision 2000) conceptualises four heterogeneous phenotypes of BD and works out two subtypes of BD-I and BD-II according to episode frequency:

1. BD-I, the classic "phenotype" of manic-depressive illness, that is diagnosed when a patient experiences at least one full manic episode severe enough to require psychiatric hospitalisation or is accompanied by DSM-IV psychotic features of psychotic misperceptions of environmental stimuli. DSM-IV manic features can include elation, irritability, and increased energy with hyperactivity, racing thoughts, pressured rapid speech, a decreased need for sleep, and an increased involvement of pleasured activities. BD-I has a life-time prevalence of approximately 1% of the world's population.
2. The "softer" BD–II phenotype, defined as one or more MD-episodes and hypomania over lifetime. BD-II is more common in females, young patients and early-onset patients with a strong association to depressive mixed states, atypical features of depression, and rapid-cycling features.
3. Cyclothymic disorder, defined as a period of 1 year or more in which there are depressive and hypomanic symptoms that do not meet full criteria for either a MD-episode or a manic episode, but that do interfere with daily functioning.
4. BD **n**ot **o**therwise **s**pecified (BD-NOS): Patients, who have very brief (shorter than a week), although sometimes severe, episodes that do not fall within the DSM-IV definition of rapid-cycling but are classified as having BD not otherwise specified.
5. Rapid cycling (RC): The phenomena of rapid cycling (first introduced by Dunner 1974) in the long-term course of BD is defined as the occurrence of at least four episodes (MD, manic-, mixed-, or hypomanic episode) within a given year.
6. Ultra-RC and Ultradian-RC: Cycle lengths as short as 48 hours or even 24 hours are sometimes referred to as Ultra-RC (episodes occurring within the course of days to week) and Ultradian RC (moods shifts within a day), respectively (Kramlinger 1996).

At present, it is unclear whether RC, ultra-RC and ultradian-RC are distinct subtypes of BDs or just a clinical phenomenon toward one extreme on a continuum of episode frequencies (Bauer, 1996). Rapid cycling has been associated with female gender, BD-II, a longer duration of illness, a positive family history of mood disorders, the presence of clinical or subclinical hypothyroidism, non-response to prophylactic lithium treatment, and the use of antidepressants (Shelton, 2000). In general, rapid-cycling is associated with increased resistance to standard pharmacological treatments and a poorer prognosis than classic BD (Calabrese, 2001). Some of the subcategories are not present in the ICD-10, but can be relevant for diagnostic and pharmacological considerations. Other subtypes which were conceptualized by clinical researchers include the BD-III1/2 (multiple substance abuse caused hypomanic- and manic episodes) and BD-IV (individuals who develop depression later in life from a lifelong background of hyperthymic temperament) concept. This concept was first introduced by Gerald Klerman in 1981 (Young & Klerman, 1992). Akiskal (Akistal, 1995), enlarged the concept by Gerald Klerman and defined six different types of bipolar disorders based on clinical features. However, in the current classification systems, these subtypes are not included. Nevertheless, current researchers dispute the use and the clinical relevance of these concepts. With respect to the classification of schizoaffective disorder as a mood disorder there is a worldwide controversy and a poor agreement rate, i.e. schizophrenia, schizoaffective disorder and BD with psychotic symptoms overlap in many dimensions as they involve as well psychotic as affective symptoms.

Current pathophysiological models of affective disorders imply that a large number of pathophysiological mechanisms which have been implicated in MDD and BD as well. Beside genetic and environmental risk factors, abnormal molecular factors, aberrant neuronal mechanisms and dysfunction of neuronal networks are known to have important implications for the disease progression, see Figure 1 (Schneider et al., 2011).

Common treatment models of BDs combine individual pharmacological and psychotherapeutic strategies (Grunze & Walden, 2003). The treatment of acute hypomanic or manic episodes is normally implemented during inpatient therapy. In exceptional cases, like if there is a good psychosocial network, a good compliance and only slight symptoms, it might be possible to treat acute hypomanic / manic symptoms with an outpatient form of therapy. Many recent studies have demonstrated benefits from the addition of psychotherapy to pharmacotherapy, especially when an individual is still in an acute episode (Frank et al. 2005). From a perspective of disorder-specific psychotherapy, several research groups have adapted revised behaviour theory approaches like cognitive therapy of Beck, interpersonal theory approaches like Klerman's interpersonal therapy and family-focused psycho educational treatment of BD. The most promising and best evaluated adaptation seems the **I**nterpersonal and **S**ocial **R**hythm **T**herapy (IPSRT) by Ellen Frank, a therapy which built on a model of aetiology that is widely accepted in the field. IPSRT strongly focuses on modulating both biological and psychosocial factors to mitigate the patient's circadian and sleep-wake cycle vulnerabilities, to improve overall functioning, and better manage the potential chaos of bipolar symptomatology (Frank et al. 2000).

1.1. Overview of chapter

In this chapter-article, we describe the adaptation of **C**ognitive **B**ehavioral **A**nalysis **S**ystem of **P**sychotherapy (CBASP), the only model of psychotherapy that is specifically developed for chronic MDD, to a female early-onset chronically depressed outpatient who switched

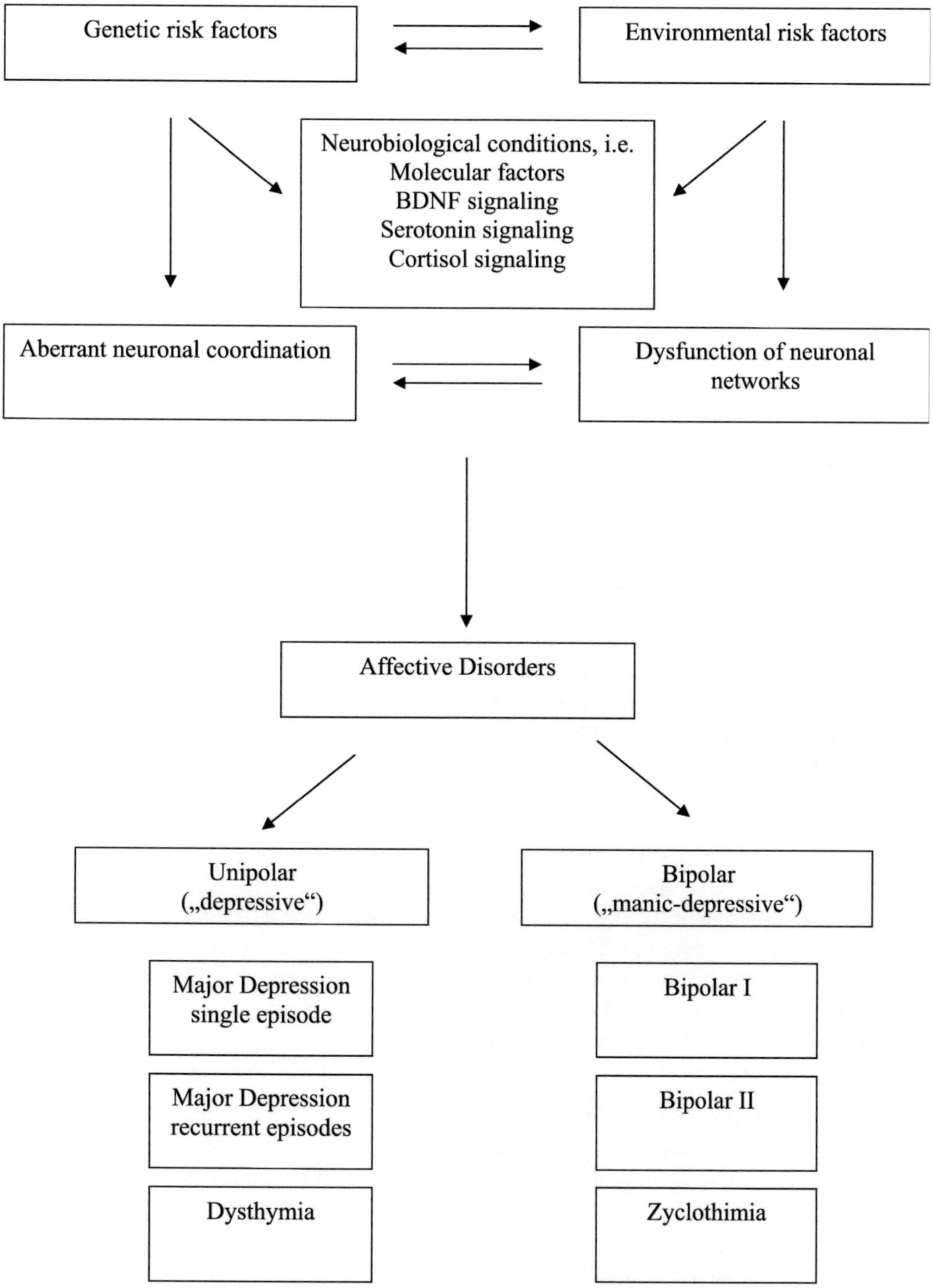

Figure 1. Pathophysiological mechanisms of affective disorders and dimensional classification of affective disorders spectrum.

into a first hypomanic episode during the outpatient treatment course. The reported case is a 29-years aged female patient, who was initially diagnosed as chronic MDD with antecedent dysthymic disorder during inpatient treatment in University Frankfurt, at that time suffering from a moderate(-to severe) MD-episode. There was no direct or indirect evidence for an earlier manic, mixed or hypomanic episode. After 27 sessions of CBASP – that included a prolonged SOH procedure according to a modified protocol - she reached a stable state of full syndromal remission and achieved in-session two-way circular functioning. She switched under combined SSRI/CBASP outpatient treatment for 6 months, without any obvious forewarning or stressful encounter, into a first hypomanic episode (Type II) (ICD-10 F 31 [WHO, 1992]). The hypomanic episode was followed by a prolonged phase of mood instability before another hypomanic episode occurred one year later. The applied psychotherapy from session 28-50 faithfully followed the conception of CBASP in an adapted way. We attempt to illustrate which part of the CBASP concepts might be useful in acute hypomanic/manic episodes of BDs. We suggest that the presented strategies here might be implemented in an advanced form of BD treatment strategies.

2. CBASP

CBASP was originally developed by James McCullough for the specific treatment of chronic depression as an outpatient protocol that is not yet evaluated for the treatment of BD (McCullough, 2000, 2006). CBASP`s interventions include elements from both classical and cognitive behaviour therapies as important elements of "third generation" psychotherapy methods that deal with models of self-regulation with respect to motivational and perceptual factors in meta-cognitive processing. In contrast to any other psychotherapy model the therapist is viewed as the primary choreographer of behaviour change using a disciplined personal involvement role that stands in contrast to the relationships the early-onset chronic depressed patient has experienced with his **S**ignificant **O**ther's (SOs) during childhood (Schoepf & Neudeck, 2011). CBASP demonstrated significant therapeutic effects for treatment patients with chronic MDD with antecedent dysthymic disorder as well as chronic MDD without antecedent dysthymic disorder. Especially, CBASP has demonstrated greater efficacy than antidepressant medication for patients with histories of childhood trauma ranging from childhood maltreatment (sexual abuse, physical abuse or emotional abuse) to experiencing neglect to witnessing domestic violence or to having a life-threatening injury (Schoepf et al., 2007; Schoepf & McCullough, 2009; McCullough et al., 2010; Schoepf & Penberthy, 2010; Schoepf & Neudeck, 2011; McCullough, 2012; Schoepf, in this book).

Treatment resistance or chronic MDD is quickly becoming a clinical reality, with up to 15% of patients not responding to intensified pharmacological and psychotherapeutic approaches. McCullough suggests that chronically depressed individuals have a primitive cognitive functioning that is unaffected by the logical reasoning and reality-based views of others. In addition, these patients most often perceive that the causal influences in their life are beyond their personal control. They have a poor ability to use a problem-focused coping style and problems are described in a global way, resulting in feelings of hopelessness and helplessness. This results in a pervasive degree of social isolation, which worsens the depressive mood. CBASP specifically focuses on central mechanisms of affective and motivational regulation via an interpersonal contemporary learning acquisition model, utilizing disciplined personal involvement to aid acquisition of perceived functionality in the patient. For example, a basic CBASP technique is to enable the patient to recognize his own impact on the therapist's behaviour (adapted and modified from the 2010 proposal written by K.Penberthy: "CBASP: New applications and Neurocognitive mechanisms").

3. Main treatment concepts of bipolar disorders

There are the following recommended practices for a positive prognosis of the long-term course of BD: Good responses to the pharmacological treatment, avoidance of misuse of drugs and alcohol, early detection of acute episodes, social capabilities and a good relationship to attachment figures. Current BD treatment models combine individual pharmacological and psychotherapeutic strategies (Grunze & Walden, 2003). The pharmacological treatment includes mood stabilizer, antidepressant, benzodiazepine and neuroleptic medication (Wagner & Bräunig, 2000) in dependence of the respective illness state. Psychotherapy has to be seen as supplementary to the pharmacological treatment, not instead of. The psychotherapeutic measures are divided into different stages, acute (manic / depressive) treatment, maintenance (inter-episodic) treatment and prophylaxis. But it is important to see the whole spectrum of illness states, not only single stages. The best suitable starting time to begin an outpatient psychotherapy is after the retreat of acute symptoms (M. Hautzinger & Meyer, 2011). There are a number of classical psychotherapeutic methods used in the treatment of BD.

In general, the psychotherapeutic concepts set the focus on improvement of compliance for medication, psycho education, relapse prevention, prophylaxis and social rhythms strategies (Meyer & Hautzinger, 2000). Examples of approaches focusing on those subjects are the *cognitive-behavioral therapy* (CBT; (Basco & Rush, 2005), the IPSRT, (Frank, 2005)), the *family-focused treatment approach* (FFT; (Miklowitz & Goldstein, 1997)) and the *psychoeducation-based group therapy (PEG)*(Schaub, Bernhard, & Gauck, 2004).

The FFT is a cognitive-behavioral-based method that focuses on the integration of attachment figures into the therapy. The goal is to modify dysfunctional thoughts of the attachment figures, to modify social skills and to identify early symptoms.

The IPSRT (Frank, 2005) consists of three modules, including compliance for medication, social rhythms and reduction of interpersonal difficulties. Interpersonal psychotherapy (IPT) including maintenance IPT, brief IPT, and interpersonal and social rhythm therapy for the treatment of BD have recently adapted for both group and individual treatment of both BD and unipolar disorders. In addition, Frank recently completed a study with Italian researchers (University Pisa) that aims to achieve a better understanding of the clinical importance of sub-syndromal mood and anxiety conditions and their impact on the outcome of interpersonal psychotherapy and SSRI for depression.

In Germany, the most established cognitive-behavioral program for the therapy of BD is the CBT approach of Meyer and Hautzinger (2004), which contains four modules, including psycho education, prophylaxis, and relapse prevention, modification of dysfunctional cognitive beliefs and formatting of additional interpersonal and social skills. The module psycho- education has the aim of training the patient about the cause of the illness and treatment possibilities. During prophylaxis, patients are trained to identify and modify early symptoms through the keeping of a daily diary. Also, they are taught to improve social rhythms. During acute hypomanic / manic episodes, the program tries to reduce acute symptoms, e.g., sleep disturbances, blowing money, agitation and distractibility. To reduce such symptoms, the manual shows strategies to reduce the activity level, to reduce social contacts and to introduce breaks and calm activities.

4. Case history

In the following sections, we describe the psychotherapeutic treatment of a 29-years-aged female patient, who was initially diagnosed with "difficult to treat" chronic MDD with antecedent dysthymic disorder during inpatient treatment in the University Frankfurt, at that time suffering from a moderate (-to severe) non-psychotic MD-episode. The inpatient treatment lasted 6 weeks, followed by an outpatient treatment, lasting 25 months, using an adaptation of the CBASP. This was the first in- and outpatient psychiatric and psychotherapeutic treatment for the affected patient. After six months of combined SSRI/CBASP outpatient treatment, the patient switched from a state of syndromal remission, without any obvious forewarning or stressful encounter, into a hypomanic episode (Type II) (ICD-10 F 31 (WHO, 1992)). This was followed by a prolonged phase of mood instability before another hypomanic episode occurred one year later.

4.1. Psychiatric and medical history

Clinically, the patient suffered from "double depression", made obvious by social withdrawal, loss of energy and drive since the age of 17 years with superimposed MD-episodes. Eight weeks in advance of the inpatient treatment, worsening of depressive symptoms had led to the onset of a new MD-episode: Mood changed for the worse, she cried a lot. In addition, there was also a loss of concentration and a loss of social, domestic and job-related capacities. This was followed by sleep disorders, undifferentiated anxiety and uneasiness. Just before she wanted to start outpatient treatment, she felt like wishing to commit suicide and told this to her sister. The operationalized diagnosis of a recurrent depressive disorder, moderately (-to severe) episode (ICD-10 (WHO, 1992), F 33.1) together with an antecedent dysthymic disorder (F 34.1) ("double depression") was ensured using the Structured Clinical Interview for DSM-IV (SKID-I and SKID-II, (Wittchen, Zhao, Abelson, Abelson, & Kessler, 1996). There was neither any direct or indirect sign for a prior hypomanic episode nor of hypomanic features (irritability, mood swings, crowded thoughts, sexual arousal, psychomotor acceleration, increased talkativeness) during the current MD-episode. There was no significant somatic history. The patient stated to smoke 20 cigarettes / daily; no other drugs were consumed.

4.2. Autobiographical history

The female patient was born and raised in a family with father, mother and a younger sister (- 2 years). The father worked as a teacher, the mother was a housewife. There was no family history of psychiatric disorders according to DSM-IV criteria (American Psychiatric Association, 1994). She reported a close relationship to the other family members, but, the patient noted that, beside this close relationship, there was a lot of pressure to perform. During her childhood, the patient was a successful athlete of track and fields athletics. This was very important for her relationship to her father, because he joined every training and competition session and assisted her a lot. At the age of 17 years, her performance decreased due to a lack of body height. She called this event as a personal "trauma", because this was a break in the close relationship to her father. Since then, she refused to do any sports. The patient finished school at the age of 19 years, and then she began a formation in the field of advertising. She broke off the education after one year due to conflicts with her boss. After a few months of unemployment, she began to work in shifts work as an employee in a company. Further, she married in the age of 30 years and is living together with her husband, without a child.

5. Progress of therapy

During the six-week combined pharmacologic and psychotherapeutic inpatient treatment, the course of the symptoms was measured weekly using the Beck Depression Inventar (BDI-II, (M. Hautzinger, Keller, & Kühner, 2006)). The BDI-II is a 21 item multiple-choice self-report questionnaire. It is one of the most widely used instruments for measuring the severity of depression. The applied psychotherapy during this phase mainly included basic psychotherapeutic strategies with an emphasis on supportive elements in order to relieve the patient from symptom pressure. This was followed by 50 outpatient psychotherapeutic sessions (each lasting 45 minutes), during a time span of 25 months. An adaptation of CBASP was used after the switch into bipolarity. The frequency of the sessions differed between weekly during acute episodes and monthly during symptom-free episodes. The psychotherapy was complemented by pharmacological treatment prescribed from a psychiatrist.

5.1. Progress of medical treatment

During the inpatient stay, a pharmacological treatment with Citalopram (40 mg / d) to reduce the acute depressive symptoms was initiated. This resulted in a reduced score of the BDI-II: Week 1: 41 points, week 6: 35 points; view Figure 1). The following progress of medical treatment reflects the clinical perspective of the responsible psychiatrist, showing a changed symptomatology including hypomanic symptoms according to the operationalized criteria. The antidepressant therapy was reduced during the first hypomanic episode six months after the start of the outpatient therapy (Citalopram 30 mg/d), and a neuroleptic treatment (Aripiprazol) was initiated. Under this medical treatment, the patient gained 10 kg of weight during a time span of 3 months most likely due to unrestrained eating behaviour. This was the reason to change the pharmacological therapy to the mood stabilizer Lithium. The following combined antidepressant and mood-stabilizing therapy was continuously kept up until the patient stopped it rapidly without consultation. This was followed by a second hypomanic episode. The treatment was then changed to Valproat going on through the whole following therapy time span without any further problems. The progress of medical treatment after the switch reflects the diagnostic dilemma in a switch situation. Although - according to the operationalized criteria - definitely a switch into BD-II is described, it has to be indirectly assumed that the responsible psychiatrist has done his clinical decisions from a clinical perspective of a transition from early-onset chronic MDD to BD-I.

5.2. Outpatient CBASP therapy before switch into bipolarity

At the beginning of outpatient therapy the symptom-severity was reduced to a slight characteristic (BDI-II sum score: 25 points). The patient mainly reported social withdrawal, undifferentiated anxiety and bad social skills as core symptoms at this state. Interestingly, during the whole time span of therapy, the outside appearance of the patient was eye-catching, with multi-coloured clothes and hair. The psychotherapy faithfully followed the conception of CBASP in an adapted way including two treatment phases.

5.2.1. Sessions 1-10: First out-patient treatment phase (pre-SA phase)

The major therapeutic goals of the early treatment phase (pre-SA phase) are summarized in the Schoepf chapter in this book. Here, the major treatment goals were:

1. That she learned to self-monitor the intensity of her depression and to work through the results of the BDI II from a behavioral perspective together with the therapist.
2. To shape a sensitive patient-therapist relationship in the early treatment phase. The patient's stimulus value was initially hostile-submissive, i.e. the patient had always a jacket and a cap on at the beginning of out-patient therapy, evoking *hostile-dominant* responses in the therapist. For enhancing and accelerating the up-coming tasks, the therapist always responded to the patient in a non-dominant and friendly way. In addition, the SOs (parents, husband, sister) of the patient were asked by the patient to fill out the ***I****mpact* ***M****essage* ***I****nventory* (IMI-R; (Kiesler, 1987). The feedback was positive (friendly, adorable, interesting person) so that the patient was very impressed. The resulting changes in her hostile-submissive interpersonal messages, as perceived by the therapist and the supervisor, were associated with decreased anxiety and approaching behaviour. After six therapeutic sessions, the patient appeared, for the first time, without her cap. Additional elements comprised fundamental and additional CBASP specific therapeutic interventions that are described elsewhere (Schoepf & Neudeck, 2011).
3. The reconstruction of the patient`s *emotional learning history* in antecedent consequent way. This was achieved by applying the SOH procedure over a prolonged time interval of up-to 8 sessions of therapy with eliciting the *causal theory conclusions* of the patient,

continued by setting up the *therapy hypothesis* (TH). Key past encounters with her SOs were characterized by a lot of pressure for performance, strong devaluation, ignoring the feelings of the patient and a lot of dominant behaviours. As described in 4.2, there was a meaningful personal trauma at the age of 17 years, when she was refused to do any further track and fields athletics. Beyond this age, the father did no longer support her and he stopped to give her any heed. The father was one of her SOs who had exerted a negative formative influence with high impact on her life. Additionally, shortly after the end of the track and fields athletics, her mother asked the patient to leave her parents' home. The patient remembered that "the mother's motivation was the wish for her daughter to be autonomous". However, in the view of the patient, this was a meaningful refusal by one of her SOs. The reconstruction of the emotional learning history resulted in the identification of the dominant interpersonal-emotional theme domain that she had to "perform well all the time" as she "always under-achieved the expectations of others". According to CBASP`s TH construct, in this patient in-session events during which she makes mistakes towards the therapist (i.e. not doing her homework or coming late) evoke in her (Pavlovian) fear of punishment (mistake and failure area). The TH includes the hypothesized core content of the patient`s in-session interpersonal fear that most likely reflects the patient's expectancy of the therapist's reactions toward the individual (McCullough et al., 2010). The TH *was*: "If I make a mistake during the session, Ms. Oertel will punish me in some way".

Altogether, the first treatment phase lasted 10 therapeutic sessions. This was uncommonly long compared to McCullough's original outpatient protocol due to the generalization of the heavy personal trauma (sports) into all other social and performance situations.

5.2.2. Sessions 11-27: Second out-patient treatment phase (SA/IDE phase)

The SA/IDE phase of treatment started with introducing the technique of *Situational Analysis* (SA) with the major treatment goal to help her to start thinking and acting more according to formal operational criteria (Schoepf *et al.*, 2007).

At a glance, SA has the aim to train the patient in a highly structured sequence to perform in a goal-orientated way. However, SA can also be seen as a top-down intervention that strengthens the executive functions by: (1) reinforcing and sensitizing the perceptive and interpretative performance by means of attention-focused interventions under aspects of awareness; (2) building-up the ability to control and perform with competence in a given situation, by means of contrasting past behaviour with the desired goal behaviour; and (3) shaping mental functions to think and act according to formal operational criteria. In this patient, SA work predominantly focussed on the counter-conditioning of fear reactions those occurred during the practising of realistic and goal-oriented behaviour in the elicitation phase of SA work.

Second, the core content of the patient's interpersonal fear was counter-conditioned due to *Interpersonal Discrimination Exercise* (IDE) work. IDE work helped this patient to perceive how the patient-therapist relationship differed from her past relationships with her SOs due to the various forms of the IDE - that were employed in relation to the progress of therapy (Schoepf, this book). The technique of IDE was formerly described by us as a bottom-up technique that is assumed to be the major CBASP technique of (explicit) in-session acquisition learning (Schoepf et al. 2007; Schoepf & McCullough, 2009; Schoepf et al., 2011; Schoepf & Neudeck, 2011). For a further description of the use of the various forms of the IDE see the I-SOH chapter in this book (Schoepf).

Learning context: The patient usually brings into therapy a completed SA worksheet of either a distressing or pleasant daily living encounter that happened during the last week. The review of the worksheet is usually carried out in two consecutively phases on the flip-chart (some therapists additionally distinguish a learning and transfer phase for didactic reasons).
Elicitation phase: In the first step the interactional (social) event has to be described by the patient from an observational-describing focus. The beginning and the end point have to be clearly addressed. During the second step the patient's cognitive-emotional attribution is elicited. Relevant and accurate forms represent self-referential emotional or self-referential cognitive interpretations, as well as describing (interactional) interpretations and action interpretations. In the following three steps the verbal and nonverbal interactional responses, the actual outcome (AO) in behavioural terms, and the way the patient wanted to behave in the situation – his desired outcome (DO) - are elicited. In the case of a distressing event a clear discrepancy appears between the patient's AO and DO. At this point a condition of negative-reinforcement is created by the therapist. The induced cognitive dissonance is later reduced by the finding of more adaptive strategies. The last two steps are important for the patient in order to become aware of the discrepancy between his AO and DO. The patient has first to decide if he got what he wanted by comparing his AO with his DO. Then he is gently asked to explain why he did not behave in the way he wanted to behave.
Remediation phase: In this phase, the therapist and patient work together on solutions for the patient, to behave in a way that is efficient with respect to his DO. Shaping of functional interpretations (first step) as well as shaping of missing behavioural aspects of the DO (second step), learning summary (third step), transfer to a future situation and skill training (fourth step) amplifies both the new element of reaction and experience as the conditional relationship between positive efficacy beliefs and positive outcome expectancies. Transfer is maximized because the target situations come out of the daily living experiences of the patient.

Table 1. SA: Description of learning context, elicitation phase and remediation phase (adapted from Schoepf & Neudeck, 2011).

In the course of this phase, the patient initially showed an increase in interpersonal anxiety, e.g. through short-term cancellation of the sessions. The patient needed exercising several SA exercises and IDE`s with positive feedback in a friendly manner by the therapist to perceive that the relationship to the therapist did not depend on her performance during the tasks. This was visible in the following obvious signs: After 13 therapeutic sessions she appeared without her jacket. Also, during the 13th session, the patient asked the therapist, for the first time, a personal question (about clothes). This was interpreted as reduced interpersonal distance. The IDE showed that the patient felt to be closer to the therapist than before. Simultaneously, the BDI-II sum score was reduced to 9 points. From then on, the patient always participated without the cap and the jacket. To receive positive feedback of a social interaction partner was a new and unexpected experience of the patient with respect to her interpersonal history. The positive feedback together with the IDE by the therapist helped the patient to reduce interpersonal anxiety and was therefore useful in this case although this is not common in early-onset chronically depressed patients. In the following sessions, a marked reduction of interpersonal anxiety developed, which the patient was able to keep up outside the therapy. With respect to CBASP`s skills teaching dimension the patient started to keep a diary of the relationship between behaviour and consequences ("effective diary"). For example, the patient was asked to test the consequences of doing any kind of sports (which she had been refused to do for years, see above). Through this exercise, she learned that physical training improves mood. Since that moment, the patient reintegrated sports into her leisure time. At the end of the SA/IDE phase she reached a stable state of full syndromal remission, i.e. here defined as a BDI-II sum score <=10. As described in the I-SOH chapter by Schoepf, the course of treatment in this young female patient demonstrates that under out-patient conditions an adapted CBASP protocol with a prolonged SOH procedure works best with a dosage of up-to 35 sessions in patients with chronic MDD and antecedent dysthymic disorder.

5.3. Sessions 28-50: Adapted CBASP out-patient therapy after switch into bipolarity (adapted phase)

5.3.1. First hypomanic episode

Starting at session 28, the patient switched, without any obvious forewarning or stressful encounter, into a hypomanic episode (Type II) (ICD-10 F 31 (WHO, 1992)). She had less need for sleep, elevated mood and energy level, extravagant style, expanded self-esteem, increased consumption of nicotine and alcohol, she talked more often and had higher mood. The pharmacological treatment was changed as described in 5.1. The hypomanic state lasted 14 days.

Behaviour-related strategies were adopted to reduce acute symptoms, i.e. calm activities, more breaks between activities, quiet environment. Another weekly inventory (beside the BDI-II), the *Bech Rafaelsen Mania Scale* (BRMAS)(Bech, Rafaelsen, Kramp, & Bolwig, 1978), asking for hypomanic / manic behaviour, was introduced into the therapeutic sessions. The scores of the BRMAS increased between the 28th and the 30th session (up to 41 points), but decreased in the following weeks. In addition, the technique of ***C**ontingent **P**ersonal **R**esponsivity* (CPR) was applied more frequently than before in a "here to now" way to consequate "difficult to treat" inpatient behaviour by disclosing personal responses and feelings produced by the "chaotic" behaviour of the patient in order to help her constructive solutions to emerging interpersonal and social dilemmas. For a further description of the CPR exercise the interested reader may refer to the Schoepf I-SOH chapter in this book.

5.3.2. Inter-episode

The acute hypomanic episode was followed by a prolonged phase of mood instability (beginning at the 34th session, end at the 44th session), lasting approximately one year. In the inter-episodic phase, we added psycho educative elements that included the concept of "time disturbers" to reduce disease risk and fall-back and to increase the compliance of the patient. Other important motivational elements of this therapy phase included abbreviated forms of SAs to improve goal-orientated (action-outcome) behaviour in order to improve (1) self-efficacy, (2) to adapt action-outcome expectancies, (3) and to help the patient to better perceive that a specific situational behaviour (desired outcome) leads to a positive emotional state. To improve the social rhythms, the patient filled in weekly the "so-called" effective diary. Topics of this diary were to improve shift work, to continue the physical trainings and to improve social rhythms. Every session began with the request of potential hypomanic / manic or depressive symptoms, using the BDI-II and the BRMAS inventories. During the inter-episodic phase, the BDI-II scores ranged between 8 and 12 points, the BRMAS scores ranged between 18- 22 points. The frequency of the therapeutic sessions was changed to monthly sessions.

5.3.3. Second hypomanic episode

After one year of inter-episodic phase, another hypomanic episode (ICD-10 F 31 (WHO, 1992)) came up. The patient reported that she had reduced the psychiatric medication four weeks ago without any consultation. The symptoms were similar to that one year before, starting with less need for sleep, elevated mood and energy level, extravagant style, expanded self-esteem and increased consumption of nicotine and alcohol. The hypomanic state of this episode lasted 18 days. The most important therapeutic step was to prove the pharmacological treatment as described in 5.1. This was followed by behavioural strategies, e.g. reduced social contacts, reduced activities and introducing of breaks and calm behaviour. Interestingly, IDEs were helpful to increase the compliance of the patient: the patient reported that, based on her close relationship, she wanted to follow the track of the therapist, independently of her opinion that she did not need any therapeutic elements at that moment of subjective "well-being".

6. Discussion

In this chapter-article, we described the successful outpatient treatment of a 29-years aged female patient who was initially diagnosed with chronic MDD and antecedent dysthymic disorder, who switched during combined pharmacologic and CBASP out-patient therapy after six months into a hypomanic episode. After a prolonged phase of mood instability, another hypomanic episode came up one year later.

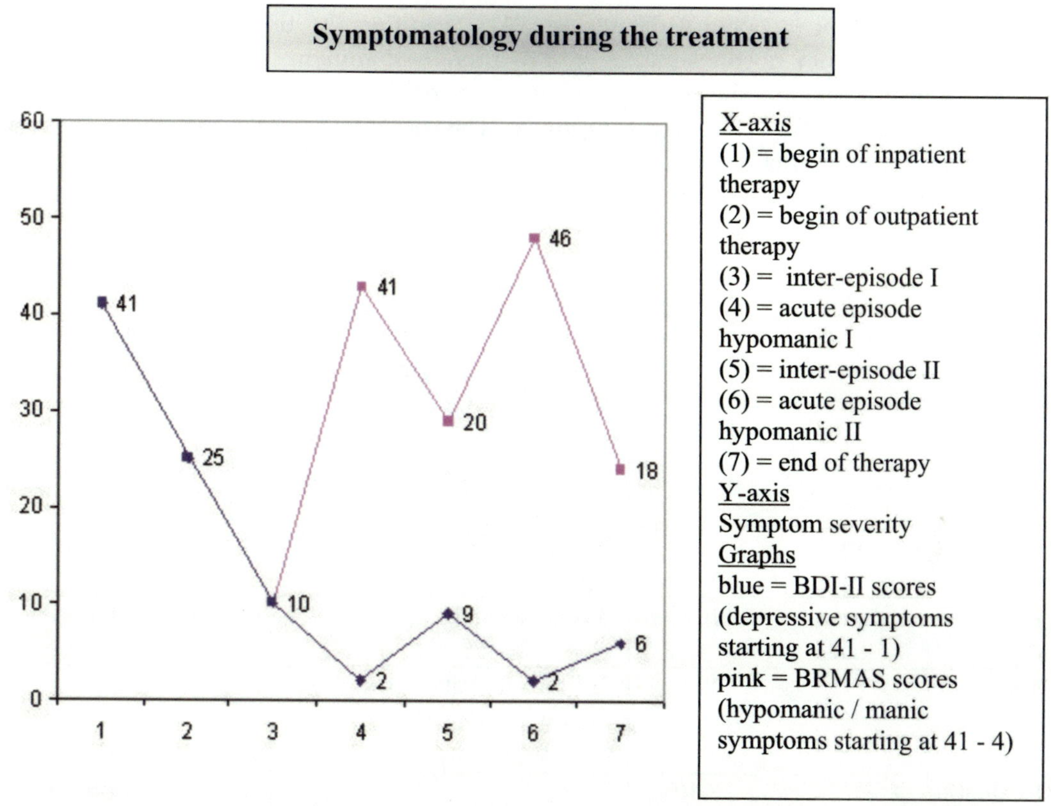

Figure 2. Course of the scores of the scale for depressive (BDI II) and hypomanic / manic (BRMAS) symptoms across the different episodic stages.

6.1. Resume of specific CBASP therapeutic strategies

The psychotherapeutic treatment followed an adaptation of CBASP. Therapeutic elements of this case report included a number of treatment steps, including diagnostic stage, the evaluation of emotional cognitive and behavioural attitudes, the reconstruction of the emotional learning history in antecedent-consequent way, setting up the TH, SAs and cognitive-behavioural strategies, IDE`s using the person's individual *Hot-spot*, and CPR (see Table 2).

The outpatient treatment of the chronically depressed state included three treatment phases based on CBASP elements. During the first phase of treatment, the emotional learning history was determined over a prolonged time interval with eliciting the causal theory conclusions of the patient, continued by setting up the TH. The TH was set up in absence of the patient. Further elements comprised fundamental and additional CBASP specific therapeutic interventions that are described elsewhere (Schoepf & Neudeck, 2011). During the SA/IDE phase of treatment, we started to conduct SA with the goal to help the patient to start thinking and acting more according to formal operational criteria (Schoepf et al, 2007), as well as IDEs to integrate painful experiences with her Significant Other's early in her life into her self-concept (Schoepf & Neudeck, 2011). Additionally, the personal style of the patient changed from hostile-submissive into friendly-dominant. From a perspective of psychosocial functioning, she was upgraded in her position (job) and the relationship to Significant Others (father, sister) was improved. The cognitive type has the aim to contrast different attitudes. In this case, the cognitive type leads to an increase in the compliance and motivation of the patient. Also, the patient renewed healthy behaviour, like doing sports.

Element	**Session Nr.**	**Notes**	**Stage of Treatment**
Emotional history	1-10	High level of pressure, lot of pressure to perform, strong devaluation, ignoring the feelings of the patient and a lot of dominant characters in the family	1st treatment phase
Core causal theory conclusions	10	Example: „ I cannot fulfil the expectations of others".	1st treatment phase
Interpersonal theme domain	10	Making Mistakes	In between phases
TH	10	„If I do a mistake during the session, Ms Oertel will punish me in some way"	In between phases
Evaluation of Significant Others	3-10		1st treatment phase
Interpersonal discrimination exercises (IDEs)	11-50		2nd treatment phase And after switch
Controlled personal involvement	11-50		2nd treatment phase and after switch
Situational Analysis	11-27		2nd treatment phase
Learning of specific interpersonal behaviours	11-27		2nd treatment phase
Effective diary	11-27		SA
Reduction of activites,	28-30		Acute hypomanic state treatment
Psychoeducation	31-34		Acute hypomanic state treatment
- relapse prevention - behavior effect training - Training of learned strategies	34-44		Inter-episode treatment
Compliance for medication	44		Acute hypomanic state treatment

Element	Session Nr.	Notes	Stage of Treatment
Reduction of activities, keeping a diary, reduction of social contacts, behavior rules, IDE (cognitive type)	44-46		Acute hypomanic state treatment
Repition of relevant topics of the psychotherapy End of therapy	47-50		End of the outpatient treatment

Table 2. Therapeutic elements of the outpatient treatment.

After the switch into bipolarity, especially during the treatment of the two acute hypomanic episodes, the technique of CPR predominated in a "here to now" way to consequate "difficult to treat" in-session behaviour by disclosing personal responses and feelings produced by the "chaotic" behaviour of the patient in order to help her constructive solutions to emerging interpersonal and social dilemmas. In the inter-episodic phase we added psycho-educative elements that included the concept of "time disturbers" to reduce disease risk and fall-back and to increase the compliance of the patient.

Situation	Session Nr.	Topic	Notes
Strip of the cap	6	Closeness	Remarkable reduction of BDI II score (9 points)
Open the jacket	10 - 13	Reduction of interpersonal anxiety	
Strip of the jacket	13	Reduction of interpersonal anxiety	
Short-term cancellation of sessions	13-16	Increase in interpersonal anxiety, anxiety to fail	
To give an opinion	11 -27	Reduction of interpersonal anxiety	To bring forward outside the therapeutic sessions
Improvement of Compliance, cognitive type of IDÜ	28-31 44-47	- interpersonal relationship - closeness	Acute hypomanic state

Table 3. Changes of the interpersonal behavior of the patient during the course of the outpatient treatment.

However, in contrast to classical cognitive-behavioural therapy, CBASP works predominantly goal-directed and interpersonal. Specific CBASP elements were used to improve behaviour-related and interpersonal-related attitudes. There was no need for assessing and restructuring dysfunctional cognitions or related cognitive interventions in addition to the SA remediation phase work, because of the aim to lay the focus of the therapy on behavioural induced changes. The success of the presented case report is visible through the fact that the patient did not need any inpatient treatment during a time-span of 25 months, which is – in our opinion - very impressive for that kind of serious mental illness. Despite the two acute hypomanic episodes during the treatment, the psychotherapeutic and pharmacological treatment was able to successfully reduce the acute symptoms both in the depressive and the hypomanic pole. The patient also improved directly important aspects: She renewed her sports activity during the chronically depressed state, she was upgraded in her working position at the end of the second treatment phase, and she improved her social skills and her interpersonal behaviour which resulted in better relationships to Significant Others. A critical point, which could not yet change, was the shift work which is inappropriate for patients with BD disorders. This might be important for the long-term prognosis of the patient. The positive course of the treatment over the long run leads to the assumption that the implementation of specific CBASP interventions in BD patients might be successful in the adaptation of emotional and motivational processes, and might help to develop a new treatment option for BD patients.

6.2. Conclusions

The represented case report demonstrates that interpersonal and behaviour-related CBASP strategies that include the disciplined personal involvement of the therapist were successful in reducing acute symptoms and maladjusted interpersonal behaviour, increasing over the long run the compliance and reducing disease risk and fall-back into maladapted depressive behaviour in this patient who switched into Bipolarity during the course of out-patient treatment. The main change in the core belief system of the patient was, in our opinion, connected to her belief of SOs. The restructuring of helplessness memories in antecedent-consequent way during the early treatment phase on the one hand, and the addressing, training, and thereby repairing of developmental trauma memories through IDE work in the SA/IDE treatment phase on the other hand, resulted in a high safety impact of the therapist on the hypothesized core content of the patient`s in-sessions fear that later generalized outside the therapy room. The resulting change in maladjusted interpersonal behaviour was clearly marked in (1) a change of the personal style from hostile-submissive into friendly-dominant, (2) and a positive adaptation of beliefs and predictions concerning self-efficacy and action-outcome learning. In addition, (3) the carefully timed self-disclosures during CPR interventions inhibited maladjusted rule-guided behaviour and counteracted the patient's maladaptive interpersonal assumptions in both hypomanic episodes and the inter-episodic phase, which was characterized by on-going symptom fluctuations in both the depressive and the hypomanic pole.

Author details

Viola Oertel-Knöchel*

Department of Psychotherapy, Psychosomatic Medicine and Psychotherapy, Johann Wolfgang Goethe-University, Frankfurt / Main, Germany

* Corresponding Author

Dieter Schoepf
Bonn University, Department of Psychiatry and Psychotherapy,
CBASP Centre of Competence, Germany

7. References

Akistal, H. S. (1995). The Prevalent Clinical Spectrum of Bipolar Disorders: Beyond DSM-IV. *J Clin Psychopharmacology, 16*(2).

American Psychiatric Association. (1994). *Diagnostic and statistical manual of mental disorders (4th edition)*. Wahington, D.C.: American Psychiatric Association.

Basco, M. R., & Rush, A. J. (2005). *Cognitive-behavioral Therapy For Bipolar Disorder*: Guilford Press.

Bauer, M.S., Whybrow, P. (1996). Validity of rapid cycling as a modifier for bipolar disorder in DSM-IV. In: DSM-IV Task Force of the American Psychiatric Association. DSM-IV Source Book. Washington, DC: American Psychiatric Press.

Bech, P., Rafaelsen, O. J., Kramp, P., & Bolwig, T. G. (1978). The mania rating scale: Scale construction and inter-observer agreement. *Neuropharmacology, 17*.

Beckmann, H. (1999). *Classification of Endogenous Psychoses and their Differentiated Etiology* (2th ed.). New York/Wien: Springer-Verlag.

Calabrese JR, Shelton MD (2001). Current research on rapid cycling bipolar disorder and its treatment. J Affect Disord; 67: 241 – 255.

Falagas, M. E., Vardakas, K. Z., & Vergidis, P. I. (2007). Under-diagnosis of common chronic diseases: prevalence and impact on human health. *Int J Clin Pract 61*, 1569-1579.

Frank, E. (2005). *Treating Bipolar Disorder: A Clinician's Guide to Interpersonal and Social Rhythm Therapy*. New York: Guilford Publication.

Grunze, H., & Walden, J. (2003). *Die bipolaren Störungen, manisch-depressive Erkrankungen: Ratgeber für Betroffene und ihre Angehörigen*. Stuttgart: Thieme.

Hautzinger, M., Keller, F., & Kühner, C. (2006). *Das Beck Depressionsinventar II. Deutsche Bearbeitung und Handbuch zum BDI II*. Frankfurt: Harcourt Test Services.

Hautzinger, M., & Meyer, T. D. (2002). *Diagnostik affektiver Störungen*. Göttingen: Hogrefe.

Hautzinger, M., & Meyer, T. D. (2011). *Bipolar affektive Störungen. Reihe: Fortschritte der Psychotherapie - Band 43* Hogrefe.

Kiesler, D. J. (1987). *Research Manual for The Impact Message Inventory*. Palo Alto, CA: Consulting Psychologists Press.

Kraepelin, E. (1921). Manic-depressive Insanity and Paranoia.

McCullough JP (2000). Treatment for chronic depression: Cognitive Behavioral Analysis System of Psychotherapy (CBASP). Guilford Pubn.

McCullough, J. (2006). *Treating Chronic Depression With Disciplined Personal Involvement: CBASP*.

McCullough, J. P. (2010). CBASP, the third wave and the treatment of chronic depression. *European Psychotherapy, 9*(1), 169-190.

McCullough JP (2012). The way early-onset chronically depressed patients are treated today makes me sad. Open Journal of Psychiatry; 2: 9-11.

Meyer, T. D., & Hautzinger, M. (2000). *Bipolare affektive Störungen. In: Hautzinger, M. Kognitive Verhaltenstherapie bei psychischen Störungen*. Weinheim: Psychologie Verlags Union.

Meyer, T. D., & Hautzinger, M. (2004). *Manisch depressive Störungen - Kognitive Verhaltenstherapie zur Rückfallprophylaxe*. Weinheim: Beltz.

Miklowitz, D. J., & Goldstein, M. J. (1997). *Bipolar disorder. A family-focused treatment approach.* New York: Guildford Press.

Neudeck P, Walter H, Schoepf D (2012). Exposure aspects of the interpersonal discrimination exercise (IDE) and the situational analysis (SA) in Cognitive Behavioral Analysis System of Psychotherapy (CBASP). In: Exposure Therapy - Rethinking the Model - Refining the Method (ed. by Peter Neudeck & Hans-Ulrich Wittchen). Springer International. 233 Spring Street, New York, NY 10013, U.S.A.

Schaub, A., Bernhard, B., & Gauck, L. (2004). *Kognitiv-psychoedukative Gruppentherapie für Patienten mit bipolaren Erkrankungen*. Göttingen: Hogrefe.

Schneider, B., Prvulovic, D., Oertel-Knochel, V., Knochel, C., Reinke, B., Grexa, M., et al. (2011). Biomarkers for major depression and its delineation from neurodegenerative disorders. *Prog Neurobiol, 95*(4), 703-717.

Schoepf, D., & Neudeck, P. (2011). Cognitive Behavioral Analysis System of Psychotherapy (CBASP): a disorder-oriented, theory-driven psychotherapy method from the "third generation" of behaviour therapy models, designed for the treatment of chronic depression. In T. Uehara (Ed.), *Psychiatric Disorders - Worldwide Advances* (pp. 87-120) InTech. ISBN: 978-953-307-833-5.

Schoepf D, Neudeck P, Walter H (2011). Learning theory aspects of the Interpersonal Discrimination Exercise (IDE) and Clinical Applications. International CBASP-Network Conference, Lübeck, August 25 - 27.

Schoepf D, McCullough JR (2009). CBASP`s cutting edges to change the behaviour of the chronically depressed patient. Bonn University, September 19th and 20th.

Schoepf, D., Konradt, B., & Walter, H. (2007). Spezifische Psychotherapie der chronischen Depression mit dem Cognitive Behavioral Analysis System of Psychotherapy

Sedler, M. J., & Falret, J. P. (1983). Falret's discovery: the origin of the concept of bipolar affective illness. In M. J. S. a. E. C. Dessain" (Ed.), *American Journal of Psychiatry* (Vol. 140, pp. 1127-1133).

Shelton, M.D., Calabrese, J.R- (2000). Current concepts in rapid cycling bipolar disorder and its treatment. Curr Psychiatry Rep; 2: 310 – 315.

Wagner, P., & Bräunig, P. (2000). *Psychoedukation bei bipolaren Störungen. Ein Therapiemanual für Gruppen*. Stuttgart: Schattauer.

Walden, J., & Grunze, H. (2006). *Bipolare affektive Störungen. Ursachen und Behandlung*. Stuttgart: Thieme.

WHO. (1992). *The ICD-10 Classification of Mental and Behavioural Disorders*. Geneva: World Health Organisation.

Williams, D. R., Gonzalez, H. M., Neighbors, H., Nesse, R., Abelson, J. M., Sweetman, J., et al. (2007). Prevalence and distribution of major depressive disorder in African Americans, Caribbean blacks, and non-Hispanic whites: results from the National Survey of American Life. *Arch Gen Psychiatry, 64*, 305-315.

Wittchen, H., Zhao, S., Abelson, J. M., Abelson, J. L., & Kessler, R. C. (1996). Reliability and procedural validity of UM-CIDI DSM-III-R phobic disorders. *Psychological medicine, 26*, 1169-1177.

Young, R. C., & Klerman, C. L. (1992). Mania in late life: focus on age at onset. *Am J Psychiatry, 149*, 867-876.

Chapter 9

Group Cognitive Behavioral Analysis System of Psychotherapy (Group-CBASP): Adaptation to a Group Modality for the Treatment of Chronic Depression

Liliane Sayegh and Gustavo Turecki

Additional information is available at the end of the chapter

http://dx.doi.org/10.5772/51339

1. Introduction

Cognitive Behavioral Analysis System of Psychotherapy (CBASP) is a treatment model designed specifically, by McCullough (2000; 2006), to help individuals suffering from chronic depression. This model was developed initially as an individual treatment modality and will be discussed in this chapter solely in its adaptation to a group modality for the treatment of chronic depression with psychiatric outpatients.

The CBASP model is based on contemporary learning theory with its primary goal being: (1) to connect the patient perceptually to others (the environment) so that others can begin to inform / influence the behaviour of the patient in positive ways – CBASP is based on a Person X Environment Causal Determinant Model of Behavior; (2) to acquire stimulus learning (through the therapeutic and other more adaptive relationships) and response learning (acquire more adaptive coping behaviours to reduce interpersonal avoidance and increase positive reinforcements) (McCullough Jr, 2008). CBASP is a highly structured, skills-oriented and interpersonal approach, which teaches concrete skills to help patients overcome their interpersonal problems and is also a focused approach aimed at achieving tangible and attainable goals (Klein in McCullough, 2006). Keller et al., (2000) mounted a long-term, multi-site clinical trial showing the best-yet response rates for chronic depression when CBASP and pharmacotherapy are combined.

As stated by McCullough (2003), the success of CBASP is contingent upon the demonstration to patients that their behavior has consequences on others which in turn empowers the patient to overcome the despair over feelings of loss of control in one's life.

This person X environment causal determinant model of behavior is founded primarily on the reciprocal and bidirectional nature of human interaction, as elaborated by Bandura's Social Cognitive Theory (1999). In Social Cognitive Theory, the cognitive, affective and biological variables of each individual are thought to interact with their behavioral patterns, and with environmental events to influence one another within social systems (Albert Bandura, 1999). McCullough would agree with Bandura's statement that to better understand human behavior, it is best to conceive of an integrated causal system in which individuals create, organize and regulate social structures in order to manage their affairs according to some preset rules and sanctions which are also influenced by psychological mechanisms (Albert Bandura, 1999).

However, Bandura's bi-directional model of human interaction cannot be used when treating the chronically depressed patient, according to McCullough (2006), since the pre-operational structural functioning of the depressed patient precludes this "normal" social bi-directionality. CBASP therapists conduct treatment from a unidirectional perspective using strategies to inform patients of the consequences of their interpersonal behavior, in an attempt to help them move into a bi-directional involvement with the therapist and others. McCullough adds that this process involves the acquisition of formal operational functioning on the patient's part. Patients also learn alternative ways of behaving and responding with the therapist and learn to transfer these relational skills to their daily interactions with others and also learn to take increasing responsibility for the changes they are realizing in their lives.

McCullough (2000; 2006) describes a perceptual disconnection between the depressed patient and his or her interpersonal environment, such that the person's behavior with others results in consequences that have no informing influence on what the person subsequently does or does not do. McCullough has named this construct *perceived functionality* (J. P. McCullough, 2000; 2006; J. P. McCullough, Jr. & Penberthy, 2011) which he defines as being able to identify the consequences of one's interpersonal behavior (James P. McCullough, Lord, Conley, & Martin, 2010). The refractory or recurrent nature of this chronic illness is characterized by inflexible cognitive patterns and rigid interpersonal behavior which McCullough portrays as the "egocentric circular functioning" of these patients. The outcome of the depressed patient's inability to receive feedback from others, is an interminable circle of "sameness" and a "perceptual disengagement" when facing the therapist or even significant others, according to McCullough (2000).

There is increasing evidence of significant deficits in the mentalizing functions of depressed individuals. A concept used to understand the impaired social functioning of depressed patients is the "Theory of Mind" (ToM) (Baron-Cohen, 1989). Both ToM and mentalization are terms that denote the mental capability of a person to infer another's beliefs, affective states, or intentions (James P. McCullough, et al., 2010). Gotlib and Lee (1989) found that depressed patients report more social functioning difficulties, even after symptom remission, than non-depressed patients or non-psychiatric subjects in the community. Inoue et al. (2004) reported deficits in areas of the brain associated with social functioning and in

ToM abilities, even after symptom recovery from unipolar depression. In addition, depressed patients with ToM deficits have higher rates of relapse and a poorer social adjustment, after remission (Inoue, Yamada, & Kanba, 2006).

These findings are corroborated by further evidence that patients with major depression have impairments in affective and cognitive components of humour processing and have reduced mentalizing capabilities (Uekermann et al., 2008). Uekermann et al, 2008 postulate that these deficits may be a result of the working memory load involved in humour processing. Wolkenstein et al. (2011) did not find depressed patients to have impaired decoding abilities, contrary to other findings (Lee, Harkness, Sabbagh, & Jacobson, 2005; Wang, Wang, Chen, Zhu, & Wang, 2008) and suggest that only severely depressed patients appear to have a decoding impairment in theory of mind. They did however find these depressed patients to have a deficit in their reasoning ability. There appears to be some support for the hypothesis that chronically depressed patients with early onset depression, with characteristics described by McCullough (1990), may be among those who have more impairment in ToM abilities. These patients often report early experiences of trauma, physical or psychological abuse. Wolkenstein et al. (2011) found that depressed patients, in their study, show a higher accuracy rate in decoding negative mental states than healthy controls, while there is no difference between the two groups in their decoding accuracy of neutral and positive mental states. To explain these findings, Wolkenstein et al (2011) suggest that depressed patients may show a hypervigilance to negative emotional stimuli, although they add that it is not clear if this hypervigilance to negative social cues may be a risk factor for depression in these individuals. The authors conclude from their findings that depression may be associated with impairment in depressed patients' ability to draw valid conclusions about the mental states of others, reflecting, more specifically, difficulties in their capacities to integrate contextual information about another person (Wolkenstein, et al., 2011, pp.110). This may be understood as indicating deficits in higher order functions, as explained by ToM according to these authors.

2. Group-CBASP: Theoretical model

In light of the detailed descriptions provided by McCullough (2000, 2003; 2006) of the primitive thought structure, language patterns and the behavioral patterns of the chronically depressed adult patients, it becomes easy to understand how a group modality can provide an environment that is more enabling and empowering and that succeeds from the start at breaking the cycle of isolation and despair which these patients report on a continual basis at the start of therapy. In addition, the group setting helps to counter the individual therapist's temptation to want to rescue the depressed patient (J. P. McCullough, 2000) with group members instead making specific recommendations to each other on how to resolve certain difficulties. A group modality places individuals in an interactive mode in which they are repeatedly confronted with communication between group members from the start. The group is a social network in which members can influence each other intentionally, therefore exercising personal agency and enhancing self-efficacy (A. Bandura, 2012). Group members' beliefs in their capabilities develop through their experience of mastery by working together on Situational Analyses that are challenging social problem-solving exercises. Through social modeling (A. Bandura, 2012), group members learn to persevere and observe how others in the group with similar depressive symptoms succeed at reaching their interpersonal goals. Finally, learning occurs through the effects of social persuasion (A. Bandura, 2012) with group members influencing and encouraging each other. The group also provides a naturally rewarding environment resembling the one patients left behind, being on disability from work or having withdrawn from family and friends. The group is a form of simulation or "social laboratory" replicating to some extent reality-based, expected levels of functioning for each individual. For example, group members are expected to attend each and every group session or to notify of their absence in case of an emergency. Group members are also asked to respect a limited set of rules covering issues of confidentiality and acceptance to work on individual objectives.

For this reason, depressed patients are often reluctant initially to participate in group therapy, which they perceive as an exposure experience to the much feared stimuli that they have successfully managed to avoid, which is interactions with others. Indeed, interactions between group members are very few and far between, at the start of group therapy. Their interpersonal behaviors are characterized by what is described in pre-operational children as "parallel play". Group members listen to others but rarely engage one another in a discussion on a particular topic and often avoid eye contact with others in the group, especially at the beginning of group therapy. Nevertheless, the presence of other group members whom patients see as having very similar difficulties as themselves including social avoidance comes as a great relief to them who quickly begin to feel inadequate and ashamed of their own interpersonal difficulties.

Depressed patients in a group openly acknowledge their difficulties identifying personal life regarding goals that govern their interpersonal interactions. They often report dissatisfaction and frustration about feeling misunderstood by others, which in turn appear to reinforce social avoidance and the vicious cycle of defeatist thinking and hopelessness that McCullough (2000) has clearly articulated in his description of the dynamics of chronic depression. In the group setting, members work together and in parallel to understand each other's interpersonal motives or lack thereof, which is framed in terms of a "Desired Outcome" obtained at the end of a specific interpersonal "slice of time", as is explained to them. They learn to solve "one problem at a time", as taught be McCullough (2000), to succeed at overcoming a chronic depression.

The Situational Analysis (SA) is the main skill acquisition exercise taught to depressed patients in Group-CBASP. The SA requires that patients attend to the various steps involved in the analysis of an interpersonal situation and calls on the very mentalizing executive functions that these patients are lacking and that CBASP aims to help them recover. They learn to attend to reality-based elements of an interpersonal situation such as characteristics of their non-verbal behavior within the situation outlined, the Actual *observable* Outcome of the situation and finally their Desired Outcome which needs to be under their control, realistic and attainable in order for them to reach it. Participants are also made aware of their thoughts during the interpersonal situation described. In the revision of the SA, patients need executive cognitive functions to determine if their thoughts or "read" of the situation was relevant or not to the actual verbal exchange that took place and learn to identify an "Active Interpretation" which will lead them more directly to the "Desired Outcome", being their interpersonal goal they previously identified. They also learn how intense emotions impede their ability to "read" an interpersonal situation accurately.

In Group-CBASP depressed patients learn early in therapy that their interpersonal motives or goals are anything but unambiguous. These patients acknowledge, early on in the group, their use of avoidance strategies in the face of interpersonal conflict. They find themselves however in a situation of cognitive dissonance within the group, being drawn into the cohesion that develops between group members on one hand and their withdrawing behaviors in the face of this social situation on the other. Group members appear to respond to this dissonance by being very reticent to contribute to their learning by bringing difficult interpersonal situations to be discussed in the group using the SA exercise, as they are instructed to do. Their feeling is that the group is already an exposure situation that is, in many cases, more intense than what they will have experienced in a long while considering their degree of social isolation and withdrawal. Even significant others in their community appear to have accommodated to these patients' passive and helpless stance.

For the reasons previously described, the goals of Group-CBASP parallel those described by McCullough (2010) for individual therapy. The group therapist "choreographs and directs the interpersonal learning processes" (James P. McCullough, et al., 2010, p.321) in order to achieve two essential learning goals: (1) The group setting helps to counter-condition the patient's pervasive interpersonal fear, replacing it with *felt interpersonal safety*. This goal is achieved when patients can perceptually discriminate group members from maltreating Significant Others (Sos) and come to feel safe with each other. (2) The second learning goal of Group CBASP is realized when patients' interpersonal avoidance strategies are replaced with approach behaviors. Group members begin to assert themselves in the group and communicate with each other about what they want or don't want and begin to think about how they will attain these interpersonal goals. The development of *perceived functionality*, previously described, becomes more perceptible with group members expressing their understanding of each other's SAs.

3. The interpersonal circumplex as a psycho-educational tool

A useful approach to integrate in a Group-CBASP model is the use of the interpersonal circumplex as a psycho-educational tool to help depressed patients understand and improve their interpersonal functioning. The interpersonal circumplex (IPC) model conveys a more interpersonal explanation of psychopathology and places normality and abnormality on a continuum using the same dimensions and constructs of motivation, self-efficacy and behavior, to delineate them (Pincus & Wright, 2011). This model complements CBASP and helps to reposition the maladaptive functioning and possible personality psychopathology of chronically depressed patients within their present interpersonal environment and to observe their manifestations in the group setting. This interpersonal approach helps to circumvent the avoidance behaviors of participants in the group by normalizing the process by which their maladaptive functioning is explored and addressed.

The interpersonal circumplex reflects the relationship between two categories of interpersonal behaviors, traits or motives. On the horizontal axis the dimension of *affiliation* represents the need for closeness with others and a sense of communion with others. On the vertical axis the dimension of *agency* portrays the sense of having control, dominance or power over one's life. These two dimensions represent the two challenges which we are faced with since childhood; that is the need to get along with others and the need to move forward in life with independence and autonomy (Bakan, 1966; Horowitz et al., 2006).

Group-CBASP helps participants gain a better understanding of their interpersonal difficulties and behaviors by focusing on their interpersonal goals. They are encouraged to see that some form of intention or goal motivates most of our interpersonal interactions, whether it is conscious or not (Horowitz, 2004; Horowitz, et al., 2006). The Revised Interpersonal Circumplex Model described by Horowitz et al. (2006) is presented to participants to help conceptualize their interpersonal relations and interpersonal conflicts with some distance from the negative emotions which these have come to evoke in them. We discuss the central role of one's intentions or goals within each interpersonal "slice of time", as described in the CBASP model, and we focus on how their ambiguity from one person to another and from one situation to another may in turn lead to miscommunication and to a frustrating or unsatisfying interpersonal outcome (Horowitz, 2004; Horowitz, et al., 2006).

The concept of interpersonal complementarity, according to Horowitz's revised model of the interpersonal circumplex, is introduced to group members to emphasize the importance of a bi-directional communication between two parties and to explain that "an interpersonal action *invites*, rather than elicits, the partner to react in a particular way, but an invitation does not guarantee the desired reaction" (Horowitz, 2004, p.68). As such, the complement of one particular interpersonal behavior would therefore be the reaction from person B that would satisfy person A's motive (Horowitz, et al., 2006). Person B may in turn choose not to respond according to A's desired motive or may also misunderstand this motive. Group members are shown how an unambiguous interpersonal behavior can have as its complement from the other a response that is similar with respect to the horizontal axis (connection invites connection, detachment invites detachment) and reciprocal with respect to the vertical axis (influence invites deference and deference invites influence) (Horowitz, et al., 2006). Therefore, a response which might frustrate A's motive may then be considered to be non-complementary. Interpersonal theory and empirical evidence suggest that complementary interactions that tend towards the fulfillment of motives within a dyad are more rewarding than non-complementary interactions resulting from miscommunication or the frustration of motives (Horowitz, 2004).

Horowitz et al. (2006) outlined the application of his revised model in the context of personality disorders by proposing that most personality disorders contain a single salient interpersonal motive that organizes the other features. Similarly, the Desired Outcome, within a Situational Analysis, can be presented as the interpersonal motive that reframes and organizes the depressed person's personal conflict in a person X environment context of the interpersonal circumplex. This allows us to transpose a personal or intrapsychic conflict into one that is more easily externalized and discussed in an interpersonal space that is more visual and that situates the Desired Outcome relative to the two higher order motives of agency and affiliation. Patients become more attentive and attuned to the consequences of theirs and others' behaviors and consequently develop the mentalizing skills needed to improve their social skills.

Through the use of Situational Analyses the group discusses the interface between their interpersonal motives (Desired Outcomes), their perceived interpersonal self-efficacy in being able to reach these goals, their behavioral strategies used to reach a Desired Outcome, and their coping strategy or emotional reaction when these efforts fail. This adaptation of Horowitz et al.'s (2006) model to Group-CBASP facilitates a group discussion that remains interactive and that involves all members in the discussion of one particular Situational Analysis. Group members gain a better understanding of why they often feel frustrated in their interpersonal relations when they become more sensitized to their miscommunications that result from an ambiguous or unattainable Desired Outcome.

To personalize the presentation of the interpersonal circumplex, group members receive the results of self-report questionnaires completed at the start of the group, which indicate their profile along the two dimensions of Agency and Affiliation with regards to their interpersonal values (Locke, 2000), their interpersonal self-efficacy (Locke & Sadler, 2007) and their self-reported interpersonal problems (Horowitz, Alden, Wiggins, & Pincus, 2000). Locke (2000) developed the Circumplex Scale of Interpersonal Values (CSIV), which measures the value or preferences that individuals place on certain interpersonal outcomes or modes of conduct associated with each octant of the Interpersonal Circumplex. Respondents rate (on a scale from 1 to 4) the importance of various interpersonal outcomes or modes of conduct that they anticipate to have in the group setting. The scale demonstrates very good internal consistency for the eight scales of the circumplex, with a Cronbach's alpha ranging from .76 to .86. Also, the intercorrelations of the eight CSIV scales reveal the expected positive correlations between adjacent octants and high negative correlations between polar opposite octants on the interpersonal circumplex. Overall, the pattern of correlations showed a circular ordering with no reversals. The CSIV shows good convergence with a measure of adaptive interpersonal traits, the Bem Sex Role Inventory (Ben, 1974), and with a measure of maladaptive interpersonal traits, the Inventory of Interpersonal Problems-Circumplex (IIP-C; Alden, Wiggins, & Pincus, 1990); as well as with a measure of implicit interpersonal motives, the Thematic Apperception Test (TAT; Atkinson, 1958) and explicit interpersonal motives, the Interpersonal Goals Inventory (IGI; Dryer & Horowitz, 1997).

The Circumplex Scales of Interpersonal Efficacy (CSIE), also developed by Locke and Sadler (2007), is also a self-report measure of individuals' confidence in their ability to perform interpersonal behaviours successfully associated with each of the 8 octants of the Interpersonal Circumplex (such as giving orders or following orders). Respondents rate (on a scale from 0 to 10) how confident or sure they are that they can do certain specific behaviors within the group setting. Higher scores indicate greater self-efficacy. The scales of the CSIE have been shown to have internal consistency (Cronbach alphas ranging from .66 to .83 for each of the 8 scales), they conform to a circumplex structure and show good convergent validity with the scales of the IIP and CSIV.

There is evidence supporting the findings that both self-efficacy and values, as described above, have shared variance regarding the prediction of interpersonal behaviour, although self-efficacy alone explains unique variance in interpersonal behaviour that is not explained by values (Locke & Sadler, 2007). Locke and Sadler (2007) explain that this follows Bandura's (1997) hypothesis that "people will not attempt a behaviour if they do not believe that they can complete it successfully".

The Inventory of Interpersonal Problems (IIP; Horowitz, et al., 2000) is a 64-item self-report instrument that identifies a person's most salient interpersonal difficulties. A brief version containing 32 items (IIP-32) is used instead as it preserves the scale structure of the 64-item version and retains the four items of each scale with the highest item-total correlations. The internal consistency for the IIP-32 scale is high with reliability coefficients ranging from .68 to .93. Good test-retest reliabilities which compare to the ones obtained for the longer 64-item scale. Correlations between the scale scores of the IIP-64 and IIP-32 range from .88 to .98 and are all significant, suggesting that the IIP-32 scales, particularly the total score, are a good estimate of the IIP-64 scores.

The Group-CBASP model set within the interpersonal circumplex framework lends itself well to the study of the interpersonal pathoplasticity of depression. Some recent studies are revealing very useful information regarding the relationship between the course and outcome of major depressive disorder (MDD), which can vary widely, and the interpersonal style of the individuals. Cain et al. (2012) were the first to use the IPC and a Latent Profile Analysis to examine interpersonal pathoplasticity in the course of MDD and identified six distinct, homogeneous interpersonal groups of depressed individuals that did not differ on baseline symptom severity. In addition, they found individuals endorsing a submissive interpersonal style reporting a more chronic depressive course and poorer functioning over the course of a ten-year follow-up period, having controlled for the effects of a personality diagnosis.

In a pilot study (Sayegh et al., 2012) of Group-CBASP with chronically depressed outpatients, conducted by the present authors, twelve sessions of group therapy showed significant decreases in self-reported symptoms of depression and in the use of Emotion-Oriented Coping (Endler & Parker, 1999), as well as increases in overall social adjustment (Weissman, 1999) and Interpersonal Self-Efficacy (Locke & Sadler, 2007) when compared to their pre-treatment levels. Moreover, the beneficial effects on overall depression and social adjustment were quite strong. Group-CBASP appeared to facilitate the acquisition of interpersonal skills as seen in patients' improved Interpersonal Self-Efficacy in the area of agentic behaviors that include assertive, self-confident, and independent behaviors. The authors recommend extending the duration of Group-CBASP to 20 sessions in order for improvements to reach levels of remission for both depression and adaptive social functioning.

The ongoing research at the Depressive Disorders Program of the Douglas Mental Health University Institute also confirms previous findings (McCullough et al., 1994) that chronically depressed individuals tend to have interpersonal profiles on the Interpersonal Circumplex that are within the submissive/avoidant and submissive/dependent quadrants and more so with regards to their perceived Interpersonal Self-Efficacy (Locke & Sadler, 2007) at the start of group-CBASP. The group setting offers an opportunity for depressed patients to learn interpersonal skills that help them improve their self-efficacy and begin to reintegrate a more functional and active life-style. Further research is being carried out at the Douglas Institute to show how Group-CBASP differs from a Behavioral Activation group treatment in the acquisition of interpersonal self-efficacy and social functioning, while both groups may experience similar remission from depressive symptoms.

4. Group-CBASP methodology and procedure

The Group-CBASP manual was developed at the Depressive Disorders Program of the Douglas Mental Health University Institute, Montreal, Quebec and follows the basic learning paradigm of the model developed by McCullough (2000). The group manual, which was approved by Dr. McCullough, contains two modules: the first is a Behavioral Activation module addressing the life style of the depressed person and the compliance to medication and the second is the CBASP-proper module which adapts the CBASP approach to a group setting and includes the Interpersonal Circumplex as an educational tool.

4.1. Selection criteria and pre-group preparation

Patients with major depressive disorder are referred to Group-CBASP by the treating psychiatrist who will have begun pharmacological treatment. Each patient is met individually by one of two group therapists, prior to the beginning of the group, for at least two sessions. In these sessions current symptoms are reviewed and the usefulness of Group-CBASP as a possible therapeutic modality is discussed with each patient, provided there are no contra-indications.

4.1.1. Contra-indications to Group-CBASP

1. Group-CBASP is not recommended for patients who are at high risk for suicide, as these patients need individualized, crisis intervention tailored to their particular difficulties.

2. Group-CBASP is not recommended for patients who are so regressed that they do not make any eye contact with the therapist during the entire initial individual sessions. These patients often speak with few words and appear openly anxious. The group experience is premature for such individuals who also often have very little insight into their non-verbal behaviors. More individual sessions are needed to help build a therapeutic alliance and consequate these individuals' withdrawn and submissive behaviors in order to bring them to accept to work with an interpersonal approach such as CBASP.
3. Group-CBASP is not recommended for patients who become angry with the therapist during the initial individual clinical interviews while the Significant Other History exercise is carried out, as preparation for the group. These patients often present with a personality disorder, as demonstrated by the rapid development of a negative transference reaction within the first or second session. The presence of a personality disorder does not preclude the possibility of participating in Group-CBASP, it is rather the patient's capacity to contain anxiety and to control acting-out behaviors which determine his/her ability to tolerate the tension of being in a group setting and the need to share attention with others.
4. Group-CBASP is not recommended for patients actively abusing substances. These patients will need to initiate participation in a substance-abuse program concurrently as they attend Group-CBASP, in the least, and be abstinent during group sessions.
5. Although patients with psychotic symptoms may find the group setting very anxiety provoking, Group-CBASP may be adapted to help certain patients with a psychotic depression learn to ground themselves in the behavioral and reality-based anchors of an interpersonal situation. A discussion of how to accurately describe the Actual Outcome according to observable and behavioral indicators, for example, can help such a patient discriminate between ideas of reference or delusional thinking and the reality-based outcome of the interpersonal slice of time.

If there are no contra-indications for Group-CBASP and the patient accepts to work within a group setting, the patient and therapist carry out the Significant Other History exercise, which has been very well described elsewhere (J. P. McCullough, 2000; J. P. McCullough, Jr. & Penberthy, 2011). The purpose of this exercise is to establish a Transference Hypothesis identifying an interpersonal domain that represents a "core content of each patient's interpersonal fear" (James P. McCullough, et al., 2010, p. 324). The Transference Hypothesis is formulated in an "if this…, then the group members will respond that…." manner. The transference Hypothesis, comprising the interpersonal domain of difficulty (see below, CBASP interpersonal Domains) for each group member, will be integrated within the group work and serves as a measure of acquisition learning of felt-safety with others. This learning is the basis upon which participants begin to discriminate between the safety experienced within the group and the malevolent Significant Others who have hurt them or with whom there has been a deficit in early attachment (Shaver & Mikulincer, 2011). Each participant is made aware of his/her Transference Hypothesis as this is frequently referred to at intervals during Group-CBASP in the form of a *Personal Questionnaire* that uses a paired comparison-rating task (J. P. McCullough, 2006). This is discussed below in the section on "Measuring acquisition learning in Group-CBASP".

Following the individual sessions, participants are given self-report questionnaires to complete, some of which are used to provide information during sessions about each group member's interpersonal values, self-efficacy and interpersonal problems, previously described. Patients are given some basic information regarding the structure of the group, such as: (1) each group accepts a maximum of six patients, (2) group sessions are two-hours long, and (3) the group meets for 20 consecutive weeks. Participants undergo a semi-structured interview with another team member who administers the Hamilton Rating Scales for depression (HAM-D-21; Hamilton, 1967) and anxiety (HAM-A; Hamilton, 1959), the Inventory of Depressive Symptoms (IDS-C; Rush, Carmody, & Reimitz, 2000; Rush, Gullion, Basco, Jarrett, & Trivedi, 1996a) and the Life-RIFT (Leon et al., 1999), which is a brief semi-structured interview designed to assess functional impairment. The Life-RIFT is derived from the Longitudinal Interval Follow-up Evaluation (LIFE; Keller et al., 1987).

4.2. Group-CBASP sessions outlined

1. **Group session 1 -** During the very first group session, group members begin with brief personal introductions followed by a presentation by the group therapist of the outline of all group sessions. Some basic group rules are agreed upon and questions about procedures are answered. Then, everyone receives their completed Inventory of Depressive Symptoms- self-report questionnaire regarding symptoms of depression experienced in the last month. This helps the new and often uncomfortable members talk about their depressive symptoms while maintaining some degree of privacy regarding other personal issues that they would rather not reveal at the present time. A discussion follows on the particular manifestation of depressive symptoms for each member.

   Following this first group discussion, the group therapist reviews the diagnostic criteria for major depressive disorder and discusses how this differs from dysthymia and from chronic depression. With the help of some graphs, some definitions of what are a relapse and a recurrence and the importance of compliance and maintenance of long-term pharmacotherapy for recurrent depression are reviewed. Another group discussion is held around the particular course, early or late-onset, of each member's depressive illness. All members having received a diagnosis of the more severe or chronic form of major depression, hearing other members share their experiences often helps them feel reassured that they are not alone experiencing these symptoms. A discussion regarding their experiences with medication ensues.

   This first group session ends with a suggestion to members that they chart their mood over the course of the next month using a distributed mood chart. Then a homework assignment is given asking the members to chart on an activity schedule their typical activities in the next week including times at which they wake-up and go to sleep, times at which they take their meals, go out for a walk and even carry out their personal hygiene. They are also instructed to include any social interactions they may have during the week even if these are telephone calls with a friend or acquaintance.

2. **Group session 2 -** In the second group session, the activity charts are reviewed and a discussion is held on the current life style of each group member in their present state of health. We identify aspects of their daily routine that may be problematic particularly with regards to the frequently mentioned isolation which results from their avoidance of contacts with just about anyone. The therapists then present a behavioral activation module on healthy living which includes the importance of a balanced diet, physical activity, good sleeping habits, attention to personal hygiene, ways to stimulate one's cognitive functioning and attention to one's environment. The idea of reintroducing positive reinforcements and pleasure experiences, which have been dramatically reduced since the onset of the depression, is discussed.

   Members are encouraged to choose one area of their personal life style that they need to make changes in and to choose one social activity that would represent a challenge for them but that is also a preferred activity. These activities may be in the area of physical exercise, eating or sleeping habits, or in improving personal hygiene. The concept of graded task assignments is explained and positive reinforcement from discussing these challenges with peers in the group who understand them is very supportive for patients. The members are asked to identify a time in the week when they will begin to put into practice these selected activities which come to represent their "challenge" for the week. Every week until the end of group therapy, members discuss at the beginning of each session how they were able to carry out the challenge of the past week and then identify a new level for this challenge for the following week or perhaps identify a new challenge. This summarizes the behavioral activation module that is integrated into a Group-CBASP model.
3. **Group sessions 3 & 4 -** At the beginning of the third and at every other group session, activity charts are reviewed first and every member indicates the degree to which he/she was able to reach the behavioral goal they will have given themselves for the past week. Each member also sets a new level for this goal or decides on another goal to reach for the following week. This discussion often entails readjustments of members' expectations that are too high or too low and the possibility to validate this with other group members instead of having only the therapist's view, as is the case in individual therapy.

   Following this discussion on behavioral activation, the third group session introduces the CBASP model with a discussion of the cycle of hopelessness and global thinking that generates helplessness and defeatism, which in turn result in feeling misunderstood by others and in avoidance of others. The long-standing social isolation brings about the perception described very well by McCullough (2000), on the part of chronically depressed individuals, that they have no effect on others in their environment and that others' feedback has little if any impact on them nor informs their own behavior. This results in the inability of these individuals to identify interpersonal motives for their behaviors that are intrinsic and self-determined. They do not understand nor identify the consequences of their own behaviors on others or vice versa. The interaction between the person and the environment is severed, as described by McCullough, as these individuals begin to feel that they have lost control over their lives. Following a presentation by the group therapist on this vicious cycle, group members take a few moments to write down their own personal cycle of global thinking that leads to hopelessness and withdrawal from others. A discussion follows with each participant sharing his/her experience that has led to such a feeling of loss of control over his or her life.

5. The situational analysis within a group setting

The therapists introduce the exercise of the Situational Analysis (SA) in the third or fourth group session, presenting it as a strategy that helps break the vicious cycle of chronic depression and hopelessness. This exercise is described in great detail by McCullough (2000) who provides the rationale for each step of the exercise, explaining the do's and don'ts and the objectives to reach. The SA will only be described here in its adaptation to a group modality maintaining the same rationale and objectives described by McCullough, although the empowering effects of group learning and sharing enhance the experience. Participants are encouraged to learn to regain control over their lives by solving one interpersonal problem at a time (J. P. McCullough, 2000). An example of an interpersonal interaction that may have been stressful or frustrating is requested from any group member to demonstrate the exercise of the SA in this group session.

The group therapist first teaches members how to listen to an interpersonal interaction and to extract from it a specific "slice of time" with a clear beginning and an end marked each by a distinguishable behavior and then to describe the content of what was said within this slice of time. An example is given of a telephone call, which begins and ends with a specific marking point. We may at times go over several social interactions within the group before someone mentions a conflictual interpersonal issue. This SA exercise is difficult for group members to learn as it engages the mentalizing and executive functions that are found to be lacking or diminished in patients with chronic depression. For this reason two to three sessions are taken-up explaining the SA using an example provided by each group member in turn. The tendency is for group members to deny having interpersonal problems as they report feeling safe having withdrawn from almost all social interactions.

In order for all group members to participate in the exercise together, each member is asked to complete the five steps of the exercise on their own SA form while the whole group discusses the particular example of one individual's SA. Doing the exercise together contributes to the group's cohesion and helps each member learn to formulate a succinct sentence to explain what they mean, which in turn enhances their mentalizing functions. The five steps of the SA are carried out within the group in the following format:

5.1. Elicitation phase of the SA

- **The first step of the SA** involves a description of an interpersonal situation recounted by one of the group members (the protagonist) who is first instructed then asked to indicate the beginning and end of the "slice of time". The group therapist writes out on a board the member's exact words while recounting the event with specific instructions given to "tell us who said what" without any editorializing.

- **In the second step of the SA**, the group therapist asks each group member to imagine himself or herself in a similar situation as the member recounting the event (the protagonist) and to think about how they would "interpret" or "read" this situation if they had been involved. The protagonist also performs this step reflecting on his/her own experience. This step elicits the thoughts or interpretations of the protagonist from the beginning to the end of the "slice of time" described, asking group members: "how did you read what happened?" A few minutes are spent writing out this second step and a discussion follows beginning with the protagonist describing his/her interpretations/thoughts about the event, as the group therapist writes this out on the board. The other group members take turns sharing their interpretations/thoughts, imagining that they had been in such a situation.
- **In the third step of the SA**, the group therapist asks the protagonist to describe his/her non-verbal behavior within the "slice of time" recounted in step one, including the tone of voice, eye contact, gesturing or any other adjective describing observable appearance only. Other group members, who witness how the protagonist recounted the event with non-verbal indicators that are often similar to the original situation, often corroborate this description. The group therapist writes this on the board and members complete their form in their own words.
- **In the fourth step of the SA**, all group members are asked to take a moment to think and to write down the "Actual Outcome" of the "slice of time" recounted by the protagonist. Group members are instructed to describe how the situation ended for the protagonist with a focus on the "observable" behaviors only and not on theirs or the protagonist's feelings about it. Participants often have difficulty understanding how to recount an Actual Outcome in behavioral terms and more time is spent early on in Group-CBASP to explain the need to "stick to the facts" and recount only "what happened". Later on as participants learn to do SAs, group therapists suggest that steps four and five are reflected upon together and that participants write them both down before discussing and sharing their responses within the group. This will give them more time to think of their own personal experience with a similar situation. When step four is discussed, the group therapist first asks the protagonist to describe how the situation ended for him/her ("Actual Outcome"), writes it on the board, and then each of the other members' answer is heard. The group therapist observes how difficult it is for members to provide an "Actual Outcome" that is observable and that uses behavioral indicators and this difficulty is discussed in the group. Some group members continue to have this difficulty for at least two months into Group-CBASP until they finally come to understand near the end of group treatment.
- **In the fifth step of the SA**, the group therapist asks the protagonist how he/she would have liked the situation to end; that is his/her "Desired Outcome". Instructions are given to all group members to specify a Desired Outcome that is given in behavioral terms, that is "realistic and attainable" by the protagonist within the "slice of time" that was previously described and that is within his/her control to reach. The other group

members are instructed to think of how they would have wanted such a situation to end, for themselves, if they had been in this or in a similar interpersonal situation in place of the protagonist; that is their own "Desired Outcome" for themselves. Many members misunderstand these instructions and instead suggest how they think the protagonist ought to have behaved or ended the situation, revealing their focus on the other and increased ability to help others but not themselves.

The fifth step of the SA is the most difficult for depressed patients as this is the step that raises the issue of their inability to identify an interpersonal motive or goal. Initially, the group therapist does not insist on giving too many instructions in order to avoid turning the session into a classroom where members become preoccupied with performance. A discussion ensues instead on the negative emotional arousal that such a frustrating interpersonal interaction, recounted in the "slice of time", triggered in the protagonist and in others who identified with the situation. Group members often describe a Desired Outcome that is not under their control but that depends on the other person in the interaction to whom the protagonist was speaking. Members learn to use the method of Socratic questioning to ask themselves and each other whether it is possible to attain a Desired Outcome that is not under their control. An example of such a Desired Outcome is: "I want to make him understand what I am trying to say…" Often the protagonist will not be able to identify a Desired Outcome at all for the remaining of the group session. This is certainly accepted and normalized and the attention can be turned to how others in the group would have wanted to end such an interpersonal interaction recounted in the "slice of time". The group therapist guides a discussion around the problematic interpersonal conflict and the feeling of powerlessness about not knowing what one wants. The group therapist can then return to the protagonist to ask if this discussion helps him/her identify a Desired Outcome.

Group members are very supportive of each other throughout this process. Nevertheless the protagonist may begin to experience an uncomfortable cognitive dissonance between experiencing on one hand a pull to avoidant others in the group and on the other the positive reinforcement from group members who similarly feel confused or discouraged about having ambiguous or ambivalent interpersonal motives. These discussions gradually move the group members towards a better understanding of what it means to formulate a Desired Outcome in behavioral terms that is under the control of the protagonist and that is attainable. The role of the group therapist is very critical at this step of group learning and needs to remain focused on highlighting the tense emotional experience of learned helplessness while beginning to consequate the. members' interpersonal behaviors during group discussions. The group therapist choreographs the group process to assure that the focus remains on learning goals of CBASP. As such, McCullough (2000) clearly outlines the need to follow the sequence of the 5-step SA exercise, indicating the rational for each one. This procedure alone assures that the therapist does not "take over" the process and provide the answers that will inevitably undermine the group members' efforts and struggles to find their own individual solutions.

- **Step six of the SA** is a question posed to the protagonist once the Desired Outcome has been formulated correctly. The group therapist asks the protagonist: "Did you reach your Desired Outcome?" McCullough (2000) explains and stresses the importance of this step as being one which allows the negative emotional reaction of the protagonist to rise and be expressed with regards to his/her lack of readiness to behave in the way he or she would have wanted, as outlined in their Desired Outcome. If the protagonist answers "no" to the question raised, the group therapist asks why and the protagonist usually describes the usual maladaptive pattern of behavior that results in the same unsatisfactory outcome he/she feels is not under his/her control. The protagonist only answers "yes" to the question if the Desired Outcome is the same as the Actual Outcome. This only occurs when the group is discussing an interpersonal event that was satisfying to the protagonist and did not engender any distress. Such an example may be useful in teaching the SA exercise or in cases where there is a great resistance or fear in the group to discuss any interpersonal conflict. At other times, the group therapist may observe that the protagonist answers "yes" to the question although he/she appears dissatisfied with the Desired Outcome. It is important to point out the non-verbal behavior that may be contrary to the verbal content of the Desired Outcome. The group therapist asks the protagonist if he/she is satisfied with this Desired Outcome given and the answer often changes to a "no". The protagonist explains that he/she feels powerless to do anything else and this generates more discussion in the group about this inner conflict.

5.2. Remediation phase of the SA

Following these six steps of the "Elicitation Phase" of the SA in Group-CBASP, the group therapist introduces the "Remediation Phase" of the SA involving the following steps:

a. Once the Desired Outcome is identified, described in behavioral terms and appears to be under the protagonists' control, the discussion moves to the Remediation Phase following the answer given to question six above. Having expressed distress over maladaptive patterns of behavior that prevent the protagonist from reaching his/her Desired Outcome, the group therapist suggests that the protagonist and others in the group turn their attention to the interpretations in step two of the SA to see if these help the protagonist reach his/her Desired Outcome or not. McCullough (2000) describes the resolution of the Remediation Phase as being a negative reinforcement experience in the sense that the protagonist will feel relief from distress in the face of his/her maladaptive interpersonal behavior, if these steps are carried out properly. The group therapist asks the protagonist and others in the group, to review each interpretation and consider whether each one is *relevant* to the situation described in step one and whether it is *accurate or true.* Group members explore and discuss these questions and ask themselves if the interpretations provided by the protagonist, or by themselves,, are grounded in the event in that each interpretation ought to "reflect what actually happened in the slice of time". If this is the case, then the interpretation is said to be *relevant*. "A *relevant* interpretation plants your feet solidly in the event", according to McCullough (2000). Also, the interpretation is accurate if it describes what actually happened between the protagonist and others within the given slice of time, rather than reflecting only the feelings, thoughts or perceptions of the protagonist.

- If the interpretation is *relevant* and *accurate* then the group therapist will suggest keeping it and asks how this interpretation helps the protagonist reach his/her Desired Outcome. If the interpretation doesn't help reach the Desired Outcome, it is not retained although it may have been relevant and accurate.
- The Desired Outcome may be revised at this step if the protagonist acknowledges that it is not attainable or realistic. Otherwise, the same exercise is done to revise each of the remaining interpretations.

b. The second step in the revision of the SA is to construct an *Active Interpretation* that prepares the protagonist to move towards the Desired Outcome. The group therapist asks the protagonist: "What do you need to say to yourself about what you need to do to reach your Desired Outcome, your goal?" Other group members may help the Protagonist find a self-statement that will help him/her reach the desired interpersonal goal.

c. The group therapist then asks the protagonist "If you had used this Active Interpretation, how would your behavior have changed (in that slice of time)?" The protagonist needs to answer this question and will always reveal an insightful statement, if he/she will have been able to do the SA from beginning to end. The group therapist then asks, "If you had behaved this way, would you have gotten what you wanted, that is, your desired outcome?" Finally, the group therapist asks the protagonist and other group members, "What did you learn doing this exercise?" McCullough (2000) underlines the importance of allowing the protagonist to think and identify the learning that took place and most of all the behavior that needs to change in order for a person to reach his/her interpersonal goals. It may take time for group members to name what they learned and more practice with the SA may help, however hearing other group members' learning experience is also very helpful. Often group members will point out an important aspect of the SA that the protagonist didn't give himself/herself credit for.

d. Once the Situational Analysis is completed, the group may practice social skills training and learn interpersonal skills through role-plays and in-vivo exposure with other group members, practicing the new behaviors they have identified in the previous step.

Once all these steps of the Elicitation and Remediation Phases of the SA have been discussed in the group setting, participants will have all had a first-hand experience with this problem-solving strategy to help them deal with interpersonal conflict. The group therapist collects at the end of each group session the members' SA forms that have been completed, having asked them not to change their first responses to each step of the SA. These forms will be used to monitor learning over the course of Group-CBASP and contribute to a clinical profile for each group member.

4. **Group sessions 5 to 8:** Sessions five to eight are spent practicing the SAs using participants' interpersonal experiences that are discussed during the first hour of the group or using examples of interpersonal interactions that have been conflictual for them in the recent past. Throughout group therapy, members are asked to bring each week a completed SA form describing an interpersonal interaction they had difficulty with. They are encouraged to do the exercise whether the five steps have been completed or not.

6. The interpersonal circumplex in Group-CBASP

The Situational Analysis is a challenging exercise that engages both cognitive and interpersonal skills of group participants. This is particularly demanding for chronically depressed patients who have developed an avoidant style of relating to their environment. Group therapists often find themselves facing a passive group of participants who have not done their homework and who maintain their levels of interpersonal conflicts or frustrations to a minimum. It becomes difficult to ask them to explore their "stressful interpersonal situations", as suggested by the Situational Analysis, in a group setting. Therefore, by introducing the Interpersonal Circumplex to participants and providing them with their own personal profiles on this circumplex, they soon come to realize that many of them share a common interpersonal style that situates them in the non-agentic and often non-affiliative quadrant of the interpersonal circle. The model is introduced in the following way:

6.1. Group sessions 9-10

The group therapist draws the Interpersonal Circumplex on the board and distributes to all participants their own results on the circumplex for each of the three assessment measures (discussed above), which they will have completed before the beginning of the group. The following discussion, initiated by the group therapist regarding the use of the interpersonal circle in Group-CBASP, has been adapted from Horowitz et al.'s (2006) Revised Interpersonal Circumplex Model explaining the following:

- The group therapist suggests to group members that we can conceive our interpersonal relations as consisting of exchanges between others and ourselves because we have a reason to interact. We may speak to another in an attempt to get closer to that person or in an attempt to distance ourselves from him or her. Similarly, some individuals may interact in an attempt to influence or control others, while other individuals may seek, on the contrary, to be led or helped by another. Therefore, if you do not know the motive behind a person's desire to interact with you, it can be difficult to understand what the person wants from you and to evaluate or anticipate the impact this may have on you.
- Generally, interpersonal behaviors are motivated and oriented towards a goal: each person usually wants something from another when he/she interacts. By speaking to you this way, my motive is to influence you in a positive way. I will feel satisfied about having fulfilled this motive if I receive from you what I expect, that is your

attention. I may also not be aware of my motives and these may also vary in importance for me. We all have different motives to which we attribute different degrees of importance. You can see this in your own Circumplex profile of interpersonal values.

- According to this model of the Interpersonal Circumplex, there are two large categories of motives that are at the top of the hierarchy of motives: that is motives concerning our *communion* with others and motives concerning our feeling that we are active *agents* in our lives. The Circumplex reflects the relationship between two these two categories that drive our interpersonal interactions. *Communion* is on the horizontal axis and represents our need to get close to others, to feel loved, to belong, to establish friendships with others around us and other such affiliative behaviors. *Agency* is on the vertical axis and represents influence, dominance, competitiveness, or power over others and other such assertive behaviors. These two dimensions are in fact the two biggest challenges that we face from early childhood on; that is the need to get along with others and the need to move ahead and realize ourselves as autonomous individuals. These dimensions go from one extreme to another, such that at one end of the horizontal axis you may feel that you are too close in your relationships with others and that you tend to lose your boundaries, while at the other end you may want to distance yourself from others completely. At one end of the vertical axis, you may want to exercise ultimate control over others, while at the other end you may be too submissive to others and feel too dependent.
- Your own profiles will show whether you are at one or more extremes in terms of how confident you feel about being able to interact with others (on the efficacy scale) and about the importance you attribute to various interpersonal values that are in fact preferences for certain outcomes in interactions with others (on the values scale). You will also find a profile for the interpersonal problems that you reported in your responses to another questionnaire (on the Inventory of Interpersonal Problems – IIP). This last profile provides an indication of where on the circle you feel that you are experiencing distress in your interactions with others.
- Some of your behaviors may be driven by two motives that go together or that are in conflict. For example, you may want to influence a person and get close to this person as well. This may go over well or it may become a problem in certain situations. We may therefore place just about all your interpersonal behaviors on this Circumplex and define them along these two dimensions. We can then assume that when one person approaches another, his/her behavior is motivated, although the person may not necessarily be aware of their motive or objective at the time or of its importance to themselves. Also, the importance of interpersonal motives varies from one person to another and from one stage of life to another within the same person. Generally speaking, satisfying an important motive is associated with positive feelings, while frustrated motives are associated with negative feelings (Lazarus, 1991). We may also have conflicting motives that we are not aware of. This may generate such distress that in turn has a negative effect on mood and can place a person at risk for depression or an anxiety disorder.

- In summary, the meaning of our interpersonal behaviors largely depends upon the underlying motives that drive them. When these motives are not clear, behaviors can become ambiguous and lead to misunderstandings and even conflicts.

6.2. Interpersonal complementarity and the circumplex

Our interpersonal behaviors seek to evoke, invite or elicit a response or a reaction from another person. The response of this other person is called the "complement" of the behavior that we initiated.

According to Horowitz (2006), the complement of a behavior, is the response of the other that will **satisfy** your motive for your behavior. We generally feel satisfied when the person we are addressing responds to us in the way that we expect. These complements are usually found to be:

1. Similar with respect to the horizontal axis: Affiliative behaviors invite the same affiliative responses, while distancing behaviors invite another to also distance themselves.
2. Reciprocal with respect to the vertical axis: Control/influence invites another to yield or cooperate and vice versa a call for help invites another person to take control.

- Serious interpersonal problems may arise when others regularly frustrate motives that are important to you. You might come to feel that you want to withdraw from others as a result and this often occurs with chronic depression. You might also learn to develop motives that protect you from feeling vulnerable or weak and these may be related to interpersonal patterns of behaviors or schemas (Young, Klosko, & Weishaar, 2003).
- Having had some important motives frustrated for many years of your life, you may have developed **strategies** to use in order to avoid further rejection or negative judgments or to camouflage your true motives (Horowitz, et al., 2006). Many depressed individuals have come to avoid others and most of all avoid conflicts with others. Other individuals have learned to please others instead, as a way of avoiding criticism or rejection. Still others may have learned to be on the offensive or to be very guarded to avoid being victimized. Many depressed individuals with unrelenting standards for themselves and perfectionistic traits may hide their need for support and help from others by taking charge in all their interpersonal interactions. Some of these strategies may become too extreme and maladaptive causing stress and strain in your relationships with others particularly if they fail to obtain the desired response. This may lead in turn to increased destructive behaviors such as excessive drinking, hoarding, binge eating or purging, or sleep disturbances or to physical violence.

The Group-CBASP therapist uses the Interpersonal Circumplex to portray the importance of the Desired Outcome in Situational Analyses. The Desired Outcome can now be seen as the motive that clarifies and gives meaning to the interpersonal interaction described within the chosen slice of time. Group members can now visualize the Desired Outcome on the Circumplex and decide how to orient their behavior to agree with a most valued interpersonal outcome.

Group members can also better understand how ambiguous or unclear motives can lead to interpersonal conflicts. Each Situational Analysis that is done in the group can now bring forth the responsibility of the protagonist to determine a Desired Outcome that is under their own control if they want to increase their chances of obtaining a "complementary" response from the other person that will satisfy them and fulfill their Desired Outcome. Group members begin to visualize their behaviors on the Interpersonal Circumplex and begin to think about the impact that their behaviors have on others with whom they interact. They can take more responsibility for their own behaviors and develop more curiosity about how the other will respond, accepting that each member of a dyad has control over their own behavior. As an example, one group member who understood the principle of complementarity with regards to the horizontal axis of affiliation realized that if he began to smile to people he crossed in his neighborhood during his daily walks, they would smile back and say hello. This group member shared his experience with others in the group and felt empowered to find that he could have that effect on people around him that he wanted, as he described himself as being a friendly person who had been a leader in a dominant role both at work and at home prior to his major depressive episode. He shared with others in the group his desire to move out of the distant/yielding lower quadrant and move into the friendly/dominant quadrant.

Similarly, the Interpersonal Domain can also be used to bring forth the particular interpersonal theme that is problematic for each group member and reframe it as being the most salient motive that can be situated within one of the quadrants of the Interpersonal Circumplex. This is explained in the following section.

7. Interpersonal domains in Group-CBASP

Group sessions 11 & 12: We may now return to the interpersonal domain that was identified with each group member during the two individual sessions prior to the beginning of Group-CBASP (described earlier). These four "transference domains of interaction" (J. P. McCullough, 2000, p. 90) that are assessed at specific intervals during group therapy include the following:

1. Moments in which *interpersonal intimacy* are felt/verbalized by either the group member or by the therapist.
2. Situations in which the group member *discloses/expresses emotional needs* to others in the group either directly or indirectly.
3. Situations in which a group member *fails at something* or *makes an obvious mistake* during a group session (such as learning the SA).
4. Situations in which *negative affect* (fear, frustration, anger, etc.) is obviously felt or expressed, either directly or indirectly, by a group member towards others in the group.

McCullough (2000; 2006) explains that these themes were chosen to reflect the "maltreatment themes" that chronically depressed patients typically report, such as getting close to a significant other, experiencing emotional needs with a significant other, failing or making mistakes around a significant other and having negative feelings toward a significant other. Each group member enters Group-CBASP having discussed the function of his/her interpersonal domain as being the central motive or objective that will be addressed within the group. Each group member has a Transference Hypothesis formulated in an *if (one of the 4 domains is manifested in the group)….then (group members may respond in an anticipated negative way)*. Some group members will have been able to identify, at the initial individual interview, the interpersonal domain as being the one they want to work on and improve during group therapy. These individuals are more aware of having learned maladaptive coping behaviors and strategies but do not yet see the impact of these on others nor do they assume the consequences of these behaviors. Other individuals who are less clear on what they want or need to change with regards to interpersonal motives or who have little insight, may learn from others during group therapy and gain a better understanding of how their interpersonal domain manifests itself within the group. Varying levels of awareness and insight within the group can stimulate learning and contribute to group cohesion.

It is often very difficult, however, for group members to discuss at the beginning of group therapy the way that these domains are problematic in their lives as these are at the heart of their avoidance behaviors. The outcomes, as formulated in the Transference Hypothesis, being negative, chronically depressed individuals have come to develop strategies to protect themselves from this negative outcome. For example, an individual avoids disclosing needs and feelings to others because he/she expects the hurtful humiliation experienced from malevolent significant others. Instead, this person may have learned to please others to avoid a reprimand or in the hope of gaining the long-awaited love and recognition. In time, this strategy, comes to replace the need for self-disclosure, albeit unconsciously, but it becomes so demanding that the individual may choose to avoid others altogether in order to minimize the increasing burden of trying to please everyone. Although an individual may agree that the Interpersonal Domain of disclosing needs or feelings to others is problematic for him/her, it may not be obvious to this person that he/she developed the strategy of pleasing others to protect the self from a perceived negative outcome associated with self-disclosure. The link between the Interpersonal Domain, which is the salient motive that individuals want to work through in therapy, and the maladaptive strategies developed to cope and attempt to arrive eventually at this most salient motive, can be made in group therapy. The group therapist points out the more adaptive function of the Desired Outcome in the Situational Analysis in helping group members reach their interpersonal motive within a particular social domain.

This is why most group members may not understand at the beginning of group therapy how their Interpersonal Domains will be worked through in the group in front of strangers as they are unaware of the strategies they have built to avoid disclosure, intimacy, expressing a negative emotion or admitting to a mistake. During group therapy members begin to see their strategies operate defensively even though they increasingly feel safe and engaged within the group. Gradually through discussions and the use of the Interpersonal Discrimination Exercise (described below), the therapist consequates the maladaptive behaviors used in these defensive strategies, placing the group member in a mismatching experience with in vivo consequences of their behaviors on others in the group. This requires that the group member use a more formal operations perspective and mentalizing capacities to focus on the consequences of his/her behaviors on others and often chooses to change these maladaptive behaviors. Gradually, these maladaptive strategies are replaced with more risk-taking behaviors within the group involving the Interpersonal Domain that each had identified as the central motive important to work on in group therapy. The Interpersonal Discrimination Exercise (described below) can be used to help group members see the impact of their behavior on others in the group when they attempt, consciously or not, to manifest a behavior related to their Interpersonal Domain. More interactive exchanges take place in the group as the group therapist keeps the focus on working with Situational Analyses. Group members can now see the value of a Desired Outcome, in an interpersonal "slice of time", as helping them gain control over the impact that they can have and want to have on others, just as they have learned of the impact that they have on members within the group. The concept of "solving one problem at a time" becomes clearer as group members see the gains they make with each new Situational Analysis.

8. The interpersonal discrimination exercise (IDE) in Group-CBASP

Group sessions 13-18: The IDE is a technique used in CBASP to help group members discriminate between their emotional responses and behaviors experienced within the group and the emotional responses and behaviors they developed using maladaptive strategies with malevolent significant others. The IDE provides an opportunity to use an operant conditioning paradigm (Neudeck, Schoepf, & Penberthy, 2010) to show group members how they can change their attitudes and behaviors following the negative reinforcement experienced from positive responses of others in the group, which are contrary to the expected responses of past malevolent Significant Others. Group members learn to improve their level of empathy with this exercise by feeling how others respond to them in ways that satisfy their motives and desired outcomes. Their risk-taking behavior is rewarded and its consequences are felt. This helps repair the person X environment rift that had been growing and alienating everyone including the depressed person herself or himself.

- **Example of an IDE** - A group member, usually agreeable and pleasing, comes in group one day and reports in a frustrated tone that she did not interact with anyone all week and did not do anything towards reaching her behavioral challenge for the week. Everyone in the group is silent awaiting the response of the group therapist who also decides to wait silently. Another member steps in and adds that he did not reach his goal either and expresses his understanding to the first member or perhaps directs this comment to the group therapist. The therapist nods in support, validates that this is difficult and asks the first member how she feels. This generates a discussion around the table about how others feel about her challenge and theirs and about the possibility that the member may have aimed too high or been too critical of a smaller step that was taken but was minimized. This often leads to a reformulation of the behavioral challenge by the member herself towards a goal that she feels is more attainable.

- Following this discussion, the group therapist returns to this member and identifies the Interpersonal Domain that she manifested, in this case *expressing negative emotions*. The therapist is aware of the importance of each Interpersonal Domain for each group member and decides to use this interpersonal experience (referred to by McCullough, (2000; 2006) as being a "hot spot") to carry out the Interpersonal Discrimination Exercise (IDE) with her. The group therapist brings the member's attention to the fact that she expressed a negative emotion to the group. The therapist then asks this member how a maltreating Significant Other would have responded to her if she had expressed herself this way. This group member may not recall this information with others watching and listening however the focus is kept on the current difficulty she has expressing negative emotions and what is at stake in doing so, in this case risking being rejected. This reminder raises the person's level of tension as she recalls her behavior and its implications for her. She reflects on what she did and may feel uncomfortable. The group therapist brings the person's attention away from herself and her discomfort and asks her how others in the group responded to her when she expressed these negative emotions. It is often difficult for depressed individuals to put themselves in the other's shoes, as it would counter the preferred avoidant position. This "mismatching" interpersonal situation provides an opportunity for this group member to take notice of the support and acceptance of others in her time of need, thus enlisting her empathic skills and mentalizing functions. She and others engage in a spontaneous discussion of the importance of the supportive feedback of group members for them and this discussion contributes to building a strong sense of cohesion and belonging within the group. The group member, in this example, is astonished to realize that she has indeed expressed negative emotions quite openly without negative consequences. She gradually comes to understand that her strategy was to always try to appear perfect, wanting to be the "best patient" to please the therapist and impress others, out of fear of being rejected and unwanted if she expressed negative emotions.

The remaining group sessions are spent reviewing Situational Analyses that can now be seen as useful problem-solving tools that help group members regain control over their lives. The group therapist successfully choreographs the interactions between group members, as described above, to assure that a return is always made back to the Situational Analysis as the primary focus of learning in group therapy.

Group sessions 19 & 20: These last two sessions are used to review the group members' group therapy experience and to discuss ways in which they handle losses, separations and farewells. The group therapist introduces these themes around session 18 to suggest that group members think about their group therapy experience and identify goals that they feel they've reached as well as goals that they have not reached or new ones they can now identify. These are discussed during group sessions 18 or 19. In addition, follow-up group sessions once per month are introduced as an opportunity to receive some feedback and share their experiences generalizing the skills learned in group therapy. Patients will also be meeting with their treating team, at the end of Group-CBASP, to go over the improvements made and determine the individual follow-up for each patient. The theme of farewells and

"Adieus" are kept for the last session or can be discussed earlier, depending on each group's process and dynamics. Each group member has an opportunity to express themselves to specific individuals in the group or to the group as a whole.

9. Contingent personal responsivity in Group-CBASP

McCullough (2006) introduced CBASP as an interactive therapeutic modality in which the therapist uses his own personal responsivity during sessions to consequate the patient's in-session maladaptive behaviors and help him/her change them. The therapist responds in a *disciplined manner* (J.P. McCullough, 2006) to help the patient with early or late-onset depression to connect perceptually with his/her environment, in this case group members. The interpersonal environment of the chronically depressed patient comes to have no "informing influence" on the individual's behavior, which only serves to reinforce social isolation. McCullough (2006) provides numerous examples in which the patient's maladaptive behaviors interfere with progress in therapy and demonstrates how the therapist consequates this behavior by showing the patient in a *disciplined manner* the effect he/she has on the therapist.

Similarly in Group-CBASP, the group therapist assumes a position that models this *disciplined involvement* for all group members. The group therapist choreographs, as described by McCullough, contingencies in each group session to keep the group members focused on the steps of the SA and brings forth the learning acquired. This focus also places emphasis on the discomfort and distress experienced when group members determine that they are not reaching their desired outcomes, followed by relief when this dilemma is resolved in remediation of the SA. The group therapist asks each member what he or she learned in each SA and points out behavior changes that are discussed. Each group member also consequates each other's behaviors during group sessions following such behavior modeled by the group therapist. The best examples of this occur when group members give feedback to a protagonist during a Situational Analysis. By speaking from the point of view of their own experience in a similar interpersonal situation, group members say how they would have responded at each step of the SA (as described above). The protagonist learns to observe his/her own maladaptive behaviors and thinks about the impact these may have on others.

The Group-CBASP therapist has the difficult task of keeping the group members focused on the task at hand. He/she counters the pull to allow the group to avoid discussing interpersonal conflict while on the other hand not becoming too directive and rescuing the members during a difficult SA. The group therapist also reframes interpersonal avoidance as being a hostile reaction, whether apparent in missed group sessions (not due to an emergency as indicated by the group rules at the start of Group-CBASP), or whether manifested during group sessions by withdrawal and detached interpersonal behaviors. The group therapist again calls attention to the effect of this behavior on others in the group and focuses on the maladaptive nature of this strategy in being able to achieve a Desired Outcome.

10. Measuring skill-acquisition in Group-CBASP

McCullough (2010) outlines a new empirical method for measuring the change that occurs in CBASP for chronically depressed patients and suggests some new directions for future research into the active ingredients that contribute to the success of CBASP. In addition to the application of these same guidelines to Group-CBASP, the current authors have added further instruments that will also be discussed relative to their contribution to recovery from chronic depression.

In its adaptation to a group modality, the role of all group members as well as of the group therapist become instrumental in Group-CBASP, being essentially an interpersonal model of psychotherapy. Following McCullough's guidelines (2010), treatment is implemented in the therapist to group member interactions as well as in the group member to group member interactions. The vehicle of change is therefore shared among all participants in the group, however the group therapist retains the same responsibility, described in greater detail by McCullough (2000; 2006; 2010), of choreographing and directing the interpersonal learning processes by consequating group members' behaviors with each other. As such, the group therapist strives to achieve two essential learning goals specified by McCullough and adapted to Group-CBASP:

1. The group therapist counter-conditions the group members' pervasive interpersonal fear of being together in a group, replacing the fear with *felt interpersonal safety*. This first goal is achieved when the group members can perceptually discriminate the group members, including the therapist, from maltreating or malevolent Significant Others (Sos). The group members will come to experience safety and a sense of "belonging" within the group such that they take more ownership for the group process by the end of group therapy. Also, they come to perceive the group therapist as an equal member who will consequate their behaviors just as they have learned to expect from others in the community.
2. The second learning goal of Group-CBASP is realized when each group member's interpersonal avoidance is replaced with approach behaviors. Group members begin to assert themselves and communicate spontaneously together on the topic of what they want or don't want and on their current level of interpersonal difficulty, without the therapist's interventions or assistance. There is no doubt that in order for Group-CBASP to help depressed patients solve interpersonal problems and achieve *perceived functionality* (previously described), they will need to have learned to identify the consequences of their interpersonal behaviors.

10.1. Measuring goal one: Achieving *felt interpersonal safety*

The goal of measuring whether group members achieve interpersonal safety together is accomplished with the use of the Interpersonal Discrimination Exercise (IDE) (McCullough, 2006). McCullough (2009; 2010) operationalized the IDE exercise into a four-step-performance task that each group member can learn to self-administer. Using the Form for

Scoring the Self-Administered Interpersonal Discrimination Exercise (SAd-IDE; J. P. McCullough, 2009), the two co-therapists can rate the group members' performance using the SAd-IDE form which each scores independently to obtain a measure of inter-rater reliability. This measure is described in greater detail by McCullough (2010) for individual therapy and has been adapted by the current authors for Group-CBASP. In short, the IDE is administered with each group member whenever one of them encounters a "hot spot" (i.e., statements made by a group member that includes material specific to his/her Transference Hypothesis) in an interaction with others in the group. Criterion performance is defined as being able to self-administer the IDE without corrective assistance from the therapist and obtaining 4 performance "hits" for the IDE exercise in two successive trials. The group co-therapists can then independently rate the SAd-IDE scoring form at the end of the group therapy session.

In addition to this measure, the Personal Questionnaire is also given at regular intervals (approximately every third group session) throughout Group-CBASP to assess the group members' perceptual capacity to discriminate the group members (including therapists) from maltreating or malevolent Significant Others. The Personal Questionnaire is a *patient self-report methodology* comprised of paired comparisons using three cards that are each compared to one another by each group member separately (J. P. McCullough, 2000; 2006). These cards contain the same content of the Transference Hypothesis used for the IDE exercise but formulated with a (1) baseline illness-level indicating no perceptual difference observed between group members and malevolent Significant Others (e.g., *More often than not* I feel that if I disclose my needs and feelings to others in the group, *then they will* humiliate and reject me.); an (2) improvement-level indicating some perceptual change observed between group members and malevolent Significant Others (e.g., *Sometimes* I feel that if I disclose my needs and feelings to others in the group, *then they may not* humiliate or reject me.); and a (3) recovery-level indicating a clear perceptual change observed between group members and malevolent Significant Others (e.g., *More often than not* I feel that if I disclose me needs and feelings to others in the group, *then they will not* humiliate or reject me.). This exercise can be administered at the beginning of the group session by distributing to each group member a set of three cards containing the graded formulation of their own Transference Hypothesis and recording their responses to each of three comparisons. The scoring procedure is clearly outlined by McCullough (2006, pp. 163-167).

10.2. Measuring goal two: Achieving *perceived functionality*

Whether administered individually or in group therapy, Situational Analysis (SA) is the active ingredient of CBASP (J. P. McCullough, 2000) that is administered at almost every session of Group-CBASP and is the predominant focus of learning. Acquiring the ability to self-administer SA is directly related to the individual's awareness of the consequences of their behaviors and is therefore the technique used to measure the attainment of this second learning goal. SA is a "mismatching" exercise carefully choreographed by the group therapist within a group setting, following guidelines provided by McCullough, without digressing into other areas of the patient's intrapsychic functioning. The group therapist keeps the focus instead on the problematic interpersonal behaviors that maintain feelings of helplessness and loss of control reported by depressed individuals. It is the correct application of the SA by the group therapist that successfully demonstrates to group members "that the interpersonal consequences they report are, for the most part, self-produced" (James P. McCullough, et al., 2010, p.326). Measuring this learning acquisition will then enable the clinician to monitor the patient's ability to generalize these skills to situations outside group therapy. As previously described (see The Situational Analysis within a group setting), the group therapist collects the SAs from each group member at the end of every group session for the SA that was done that day as a group and may collect SAs that group members have done on their own during the previous week. These SAs are dated and rated by independent raters using the operationalized steps outlined by McCullough (2000, p.201). Group members will need to show they can self-administer the SA to criterion level performance along the five-step SA exercise procedure described by McCullough (2000; 2010) twice in succession without assistance from the clinician. In addition, these two trials will need to receive a score of "5-step-hits" for this learning goal to be achieved.

10.3. Measuring the learning content of Group-CBASP and its impact on treatment-outcome

A patient profile can be constructed comprising the acquisition-learning data collected above in the achievement of the two essential learning goals of CBASP, plotted over the 20 Group-CBASP sessions. In addition, a 20-item questionnaire has been constructed by the current authors comprising items measuring change in Behavioral Activation, in Interpersonal Self-Efficacy (Locke & Sadler, 2007) and in symptoms of depression (IDS-SR; Rush, Gullion, Basco, Jarrett, & Trivedi, 1996b). Group members complete these items at the beginning of each group session. Together, these measures provide an evolving picture of each group member's personal learning and contribute to the compilation of group data that can be used towards more empirically-driven research questions that may seek to compare Group-CBASP to other group treatment models. Changes in behavioural activation and in depressive symptoms reduction are important indicators of the generalization of learning to other areas of the patient's functioning. Furthermore, acquired Interpersonal Self-Efficacy, particularly along the dimension of Agency as demonstrated in a pilot study (Sayegh, et al., 2012), may be a good indicator of the empowering experience of Group-CBASP in helping depressed individuals regain control over their lives. The current authors, in a randomized-control study comparing Group-CBASP with a group Behavioral Activation program, will verify this hypothesis empirically in the ongoing development of Group-CBASP research. As recommended by McCullough (2010) and similarly for Group-CBASP, further research is also needed to identify the "essential mechanism of change" (pp. 334) in this effective treatment modality.

11. Group-CBASP maintenance and follow-up

The reality of chronic depression is that follow-up in the form of continuation and maintenance sessions of Group-CBASP is as important as long-term pharmacotherapy. Group-CBASP helps chronically depressed patients resume interpersonal interactions and a more active life in more fulfilling ways, however their newly acquired learning will take time and practice to reach levels that are rewarding and that reinforce adaptive behavior. It is recommended that monthly Group-CBASP sessions be provided to group members who have completed the 20-week program. This monthly session provides an opportunity to review Situational Analyses and the generalization of adaptive behaviors to interpersonal situations outside of therapy. In the authors' experience, it has not been necessary to provide individual follow-up concurrently with Group-CBASP. It is useful however for the treatment team to meet with each patient a short time following the end of Group-CBASP to discuss maintenance and continuation and to continue assessing change with a follow-up evaluation. This provides an opportunity to set new goals and to evaluate the effectiveness of the psychotherapeutic treatment plan.

Author details

Liliane Sayegh*
Department of Psychology, McGill University, Depressive Disorders Program, Douglas Mental Health University Institute, Montréal, Qc, Canada

Gustavo Turecki
Department of Psychiatry, McGill University, Chief, Depressive Disorders Program, Douglas Mental Health University Institute, Montréal, Qc, Canada

12. References

Alden, L. E., Wiggins, J. S., & Pincus, A. L. (1990). Construction of circumplex scales for the Inventory of Interpersonal Problems. *Journal of Personality Assessment, 55*, 521-536.

Atkinson, J. W. (1958). *Motives in fantasy, action and society*. Princeton, NJ: Van Nostrand.

Bakan, D. (1966). *The duality of human existence: Isolation and communion in Western man.* Boston: Beacon.

Bandura, A. (1997). *Self-efficacy: The exercise of control*. New York: Freeman.

Bandura, A. (1999). Social Cognitive Theory: An agentic perspective. *Asian Journal of Social Psychology, 2*, 21-41.

Bandura, A. (2012). On the functional properties of perceived self-efficacy revisited. *Journal of Management, 38*(1), 9-44.

Baron-Cohen, S. (1989). The autistic child's theory of mind: A case of specific developmental delay. *J of child psychol psychiatry, 30*, 285-297.

* Corresponding Author

Ben, S. L. (1974). The measurement of psychological androgyny. *Journal of Counselling and Clinical Psychology, 42*, 155-162.

Cain, N. M., Ansell, E. B., Wright, A. G. C., Hopwood, C. J., Thomas, K. M., Pinto, A., . . . Grilo, C. M. (2012). Interpersonal Pathoplasticity in the Course of Major Depression. *Journal of Consulting and Clinical Psychology, 80*, 78-86.

Dryer, D. C., & Horowitz, L. M. (1997). When do opposites attract? Interpersonal complementarity versus similarity. *Journal of Personality and Social Psychology, 72*, 592-603.

Endler, N. S., & Parker, J. D. A. (1999). *Coping Inventory for Stressful Situations (CISS)*. Toronto: Multi-Health Systems Inc.

Gotlib, I. H., & Lee, C. M. (1989). The social functioning of depressed patients: A longitudinal assessment. *Journal of Social and Clinical Psychology, 8*(3), 223-237.

Hamilton, M. (1959). The assessment of anxiety states by rating. *British Journal of Medical Psychology, 32*, 50-55.

Hamilton, M. (1967). Development of a rating scale for primary depressive illness. *Br J Soc Clin Psychol, 6*(4), 278-296.

Horowitz, L. M. (2004). *Interpersonal Foundations of Psychopathology*. Washington DC: American Psychological Association.

Horowitz, L. M., Alden, L. E., Wiggins, J. S., & Pincus, A. L. (2000). *Inventory of Interpersonal Problems (IIP) - Manual*: The Psychological Corporation a Harcourt Assessment Company.

Horowitz, L. M., Wilson, K. R., Turan, B., Zolotsev, P., Constantino, M. J., & Henderson, L. (2006). How interpersonal motives clarify the meaning of interpersonal behavior: A Revised Circumplex Model. *Personality and Social Psychology Review, 10*(1), 67-86.

Inoue, Y., Tonooka, Y., Yamada, K., & Kanba, S. (2004). Deficiency of theory of mind in patients with remitted mood disorder. *Journal of affective disorders, 82*, 403-409.

Inoue, Y., Yamada, K., & Kanba, S. (2006). Deficit in theory of mind is a risk for relapse of major depression. *Journal of affective disorders, 95*(125-127).

Keller, M. B., Lavori, P. W., Friedman, B., Nielsen, E., Endicott, J., McDonald-Scott, P., & Andreasen, N. C. (1987). The Longitudinal Interval Follow-up Evaluation. A comprehensive method for assessing outcome in prospective longitudinal studies. *Arch Gen Psychiatry, 44*(6), 540-548.

Keller, M. B., McCullough, J. P., Klein, D. N., Arnow, B., Dunner, D. L., Gelenberg, A. J., . . . Zajecka, J. (2000). A comparison of nefazodone, the cognitive behavioral-analysis system of psychotherapy, and their combination for the treatment of chronic depression. *N Engl J Med, 342*(20), 1462-1470.

Lazarus, R. S. (1991). *Emotion and Adaptation*. New York: Oxford University Press.

Lee, L., Harkness, K. L., Sabbagh, M. A., & Jacobson, J. A. (2005). Mental state decoding abilities in clinical depression. *Journal of affective disorders, 86*, 247-258.

Leon, A. C., Solomon, D. A., Mueller, T. I., Turvey, C. L., Endicott, J., & Keller, M. B. (1999). The Range of Impaired Functioning Tool (LIFE-RIFT): a brief measure of functional impairment. *Psychol Med, 29*(4), 869-878.

Locke, K. D. (2000). Circumplex scales of interpersonal values: reliability, and applicability to interpersonal problems and personality disorders. *Journal of Personality Assessment, 75*((2)), 249-267.

Locke, K. D., & Sadler, P. (2007). Self-efficacy, values, and complementarity in dyadic interactions: Integrating interpersonal and social-cognitive theory. *Personality and Social Psychology Bulletin, 33*(1), 94-109.

McCullough, J. P. (2000). *Treatment for chronic depression : cognitive behavioral analysis system of psychotherapy (CBASP).* New York: Guilford Press.

McCullough, J. P. (2003). Treatment of Chronic Depression: Cognitive Behavioral Analysis System of Psychotherapy (CBASP). *Journal of Psychotherapy Integration, 13*(3-4), 241-263.

McCullough, J. P. (2006). Treating chronic depression with disciplined personal involvement cognitive behavioral analysis system of psychotherapy (CBASP)

McCullough, J. P. (2006). *Treating Chronic Depression with Disciplined Personal Involvement: CBASP*. New York: Springer.

McCullough, J. P. (2009). *Form for scoring the Self-Administered interpersonal discrimination exercise (SAd-IDE).* Virginia Commonwealth University, Richmond, VA.

McCullough, J. P., Braith, J. A., Chapman, R. C., Kasnetz, M. D., Carr, K. F., Cones, J. H., . . . Roberts, W. C. (1990). Comparison of early and late onset dysthymia. *Journal of Nervous and Mental Disease, 178*, 577-581.

McCullough, J. P., Jr., & Penberthy, J. K. (2011). Cognitive behavioral analysis system of psychotherapy for chronic depression *Treatment of depression in adolescents and adults* (pp. 183-220). Hoboken, NJ: John Wiley & Sons Inc; US.

McCullough, J. P., Lord, B. D., Conley, K. A., & Martin, A. M. (2010). A method for conducting intensive psychological studies with early-onset chronically depressed patients. [Peer Reviewed]. *American Journal of Psychotherapy, .64*(4), 317-337.

McCullough Jr, J. P. (2008). The Cognitive Behavioral Analysis System of Psychotherapy: A value-added strategy for chronic depression. *Psychiatric Times, 25*(10).

Neudeck, P., Schoepf, D., & Penberthy, J. K. (2010). Learning theory aspects of the Interpersonal Discrimination Exercise (IDE) in CBASP *The Behavior Therapist, 33* (3), 58-63.

Pincus, A. L., & Wright, A. G. C. (2011). Interpersonal diagnosis of psychopathology. In L. M. Horowitz & S. Strack (Eds.), *Handbook of Interpersonal Psychology: Theory, research, assessment and therapeutic interventions* (pp. 359-381). New Jersey: John Wiley & Sons, Inc.

Rush, A. J., Carmody, T., & Reimitz, P. E. (2000). The Inventory of Depressive Symptomatology (IDS): Clinician (IDS-C) and Self-Report (IDS-SR) ratings of depressive symptoms. *International Journal of Methods in Psychiatric Research, 9*(2), 45-59.

Rush, A. J., Gullion, C. M., Basco, M. R., Jarrett, R. B., & Trivedi, M. H. (1996a). The Inventory of Depressive Symptomatology (IDS): psychometric properties. *Psychological Medicine, 26*, 477-486.

Rush, A. J., Gullion, C. M., Basco, M. R., Jarrett, R. B., & Trivedi, M. H. (1996b). The Inventory of Depressive Symptomatology (IDS): psychometric properties. *Psychol Med, 26*(3), 477-486.

Sayegh, L., Locke, K. D., Daniele Pistilli, D., Penberthy, J. K., Chachamovich, E., McCullough, J. P., & Gustavo Turecki, G. (2012). Cognitive Behavioural Analysis System of Psychotherapy for Treatment-Resistant Depression: Adaptation to a Group Modality. *Behavior Change, 29*(2), 97-108.

Shaver, P. R., & Mikulincer, M. (2011). An attachment-theory framework for conceptualizing interpersonal behavior. In L. M. Horowitz & S. Strack (Eds.), *Handbook of Interpersonal Psychology: Theory, research, assessment and therapeutic interventions* (pp. 17-35). New Jersey: John Wiley & Sons, Inc.

Uekermann, J., Channon, S., Lehmkämper, C., Abdel-Hamid, M., Vollmoeller, W., & Daum, I. (2008). Executive function, mentalizing and humor in major depression. *Journal of the International Neuropsychological society, 14*, 55-62.

Wang, Y., Wang, Y., Chen, S., Zhu, C., & Wang, K. (2008). Theory of mind disability in major depression with or without psychotic symptoms: a componential view. *Psychiatry research, 161*, 153-161.

Weissman, M. M. (1999). *Social Adjustment Scale- Self-report (SAS-SR) - technical manual.* Toronto: Multi-Health Systems Inc.

Wolkenstein, L., Schönenberg, M., Schirm, E., & Hautzinger, M. (2011). I can see what you feel, but I can't deal with it: Impaired theory of mind in depression. *Journal of affective disorders, 132*, 104-111.

Young, J. E., Klosko, J. S., & Weishaar, M. E. (2003). *Schema Therapy: A Practitioner's Guide.* New York: The Guilford Press.

Section 4

Co-Morbidity Frontiers

Co-Occurring Chronic Depression and Alcohol Dependence: A Novel Treatment Approach

J. Kim Penberthy, Christopher J. Gioia, Andrea Konig,
Aaron M. Martin and Stephanie A. Cockrell

Additional information is available at the end of the chapter

http://dx.doi.org/10.5772/51196

1. Introduction

Major depression and alcohol dependence are two of the most prevalent psychiatric disorders affecting the general population, resulting in significant consequences to society at large, including lost productivity, health care demands, psychosocial disruption, and even increased mortality rates [1]. Recent research suggests that excessive alcohol use and depression account for an estimated $223.5 billion and $83.1 billion, respectively, in economic costs to the United States alone [2,3]. In addition, prevalence rates of co-morbidity between alcohol dependence and depression are rising; 12-month prevalence rates of alcohol dependence among individuals with a 12-month *Diagnostic and Statistical Manual of Mental Disorders, Fourth Edition, Text Revision* [4] diagnosis of major depression and dysthymia were 11.03% and 9.62%, respectively [5]. As a result of the deleterious psychological impact on the individual and the economic burden on society, there is a growing interest in increasing understanding of the co-occurrence of alcohol dependence and major depression, and development and implementation of effective treatments for these significant and prevalent disorders.

Multiple empirically supported behavioral treatments exist to treat chronic depression and alcohol dependence separately, but there is less research examining concomitant or integrated treatment for co-occurring chronic depression and alcohol dependence. Although there has been a modicum of research regarding the etiology, relationships, and treatment of chronic depression and alcoholism, the specific common mechanisms and effective treatments have been elusive. Of note, the majority of so-called "third wave" cognitive behavioral therapies have not yet been rigorously studied for this specific population of chronically depressed alcohol dependent individuals. Specifically, Cognitive Behavioral Analysis System of Psychotherapy (CBASP) has demonstrated effectiveness in treating chronic depression [6,7], but has not yet been studied in a large trial with persons with co-occurring alcohol dependence and chronic depression. Therefore, the purpose of this chapter is to discuss the therapeutic model of CBASP and the rationale for its proposed use in treating chronic depression and alcohol dependence concurrently. The paper begins with a description of the characteristics of persons who suffer from chronic depression and alcohol dependence and how these characteristics contribute to a challenging therapeutic scenario. Theories behind the co-morbid development of the two disorders are then presented, followed by a brief review of the literature regarding treatment for co-occurring depression and substance use. The therapeutic model of CBASP and its adaptation for treating co-occurring disorders is then discussed. Finally, the paper concludes with the introduction of an ongoing research study using CBASP to treat chronic depression and alcohol dependence simultaneously.

2. Characteristics of Chronically Depressed Alcohol Dependent (CDAD) individuals and treatment challenges

Chronically depressed alcohol dependent (CDAD) individuals possess unique characteristics, especially when compared to depressed-only individuals, and these characteristics present unique challenges for the therapist and for therapy. CDAD patients are often younger at their first psychiatric hospitalization, have experienced a greater number of major depressive episodes and suicide attempts, and have poorer physical and psychiatric outcomes [8,9]. Untreated alcoholism can exaggerate depressive states and enhance the chances of self-destructive behaviors, suicide attempts, and even suicide [10]. Thus, there is a greater possibility of early death in CDAD individuals. Individuals who suffer from co-occurring alcohol dependence and major depression are also more likely to relapse and prematurely dropout of treatment [8]. Individuals with CDAD typically report a high rate of adverse early home environments, a lifelong history of intrapersonal and interpersonal failure, and an earlier onset of disorders. They have higher rates of comorbidities, a more severe course of illness, and they demonstrate a predominant interpersonal style of avoidance and detachment [9,11,12]. Early abuse or trauma history impairs development of adequate interpersonal coping skills, resulting in depression, social isolation, or withdrawal for many in this population [13]. In addition, real-world and prolonged environmental stressors usually accompany CDAD individuals' presenting complaints. They are often skeptical or ambivalent about change, and the processes of change are often slow, irregular, and inconsistent. In fact, a pattern of success followed by a setback is common and periodic plateaus in progress occur.

Research suggests that poor treatment outcomes for CDAD individuals occur, in part, due to these complex characteristics which these individuals possess that make their treatment more challenging [9,10,14,15]. Chances of poor outcomes increase among individuals who (a) are diagnosed with both depression and alcohol dependence, compared to those diagnosed with a single disorder [10,14]; and (b) suffer from major depression during and/or after treatment of alcohol dependence. This second aspect is important because depressed mood has been found to be an important trigger for alcohol relapse [5,14] Importantly, there is some evidence [16] that early intervention for alcohol dependence may improve not only problems with alcohol but also mood.

Challenges to treatment are numerous and the CBASP therapist must possess specific skills to be successful in administering therapy to this population. The CDAD patient may be ambivalent about changing either or both of the symptoms of alcoholism and/or depression and motivation for change is typically low for these patients, as is hope for the future. As stated, the processes of change are slow and irregular. The patient is typically interpersonally avoidant, and may lack effective interpersonal communication skills as well as problem-solving and coping skills. They may use alcohol as a maladaptive coping strategy, placing themselves at risk for alcohol-related injuries and negative consequences.

Thus the therapist must possess skills to help clarify the patient's ambivalence and increase motivation to change. These are the same skills a therapist may use in motivational enhancement therapies or motivational interviewing. In addition, the therapist must be patient and empathic, with an ability to be genuine and respond in a way that is judicious and self-disciplined. It is helpful if the therapist is aware of his or her own transference hypotheses and appreciative of his/her own interpersonal impact on others. Acquisition of such knowledge is formalized and is typically part of the required training for CBASP therapists. Such training and knowledge is conceptualized as crucial in helping CBASP therapists gain insight into their own interpersonal pulls and pitfalls that could inadvertently sabotage the therapeutic process and/or promote burnout in the therapist.

3. Theoretical explanations for co-morbid major depression and alcohol dependence

The co-morbidity of chronic depression and alcohol dependence is prevalent and debilitating and warrants significant investigation regarding what predisposes the co-occurrence of these disorders. Research has found CDAD individuals to have several predisposing factors that increase the likelihood of experiencing co-morbid major depression and alcohol dependence. Research on twin studies suggests a shared genetic risk factor for depression and alcoholism, and recent findings suggest an association between the CLOCK gene and the co-morbid condition of alcohol misuse and depressive disorders. [17,18]. Data also supply evidence of overlapping neuroanatomical correlates for both disorders. For example, regions of the brain such as the ventromedial prefrontal cortex which are important for homeostasis, emotional regulation, and decision making, show dysfunction in both depression and alcohol dependence [19,20]. Other areas of the brain, such as the dorsolateral prefrontal cortex, the amygdala, and the insula have been reported to be important in both depression and alcohol dependence [21].

There are also psychological and behavioral correlates similar in both disorders. Brewer et al. [21] review the role of rumination and stress, which are both commonly seen in these two disorders. They conclude that depression and substance use disorders including alcoholism, share several phenotypes such as stress vulnerability and rumination, which suggests possible mutual underlying neurobiological dysfunction. There is also evidence to support the claim that early childhood trauma plays an important role in comorbidity between the two disorders. Common scenarios reported by CDAD individuals include an early victimization or trauma (e.g., death of a loved one, parental divorce or separation, physical or sexual abuse) that leads to major depression and subsequent alcohol abuse, or experiencing negative consequences from abusing alcohol that leads to major depression [22]. Both scenarios are related to a third predisposing factor – that is, CDAD individuals have ineffective internal mechanisms to cope with negative psychological symptoms, such as depressive symptoms. As a result, CDAD individuals learn to use alcohol to alleviate depressive affect (e.g., via modeling or operant conditioning), a theory known as self-medication. In effect, individuals who suffer from major depression are at an increased risk for alcohol dependence and relapse [23].

Finally, Merrill and Read [24] have assessed multiple pathways leading to alcohol drinking. They found a difference between individuals who drink to cope and specific problem domains. In their study, individuals who used alcohol as a way to cope with negative affect also had a direct association with academic/occupational difficulties and risky behaviors, as well as poor self-care. Nelson, Little, Heath, and Kessler [25] noticed that when role impairment and poor self-care in individuals who consume alcohol is present, it predicts future progression to more severe symptoms such as dependence. Thus, those individuals who drink and display negative affect and depressive symptoms may be at additional risk for an increased severity of disease.

4. Treatment of co-occurring depression and substance related problems: A comparison of approaches

The shared characteristics and etiological underpinnings of two of the more prevalent forms of psychopathology have resulted in an increased interest in the co-occurrence of these disorders. Despite the recognition of a need for an integrated treatment approach for mood disorders and substance abuse – and chronic depression and alcohol dependence more specifically – empirical examination of such interventions is limited. Data from The National Survey on Drug Use and Health indicate that of adults experiencing co-occurring significant psychological distress and a substance use disorder, a majority did not receive treatment for either disorder [26]. Only approximately 12% were treated for both disorders. This shortfall is likely the result of a lack of availability of empirically supported integrated treatments for comorbidities of this type.

While there are currently multiple empirically supported behavioral treatments for depression and alcoholism as individual disorders, knowledge about effective integrated treatment options is far from complete. Carroll [8] and others [27,28] acknowledge that there have been few well-specified behavioral therapies with an integrated approach (versus parallel) to treating symptoms of both disorders. Integrated treatment models are those in which treatment for both the mood disorder and the substance use disorder is delivered at the same time, in the same program, by the same staff. This is in contrast to sequential treatment where the addiction is treated prior to the depression, or parallel treatment, in which patients are treated for mental illness in one system and for the substance use disorder in another [29].

Carroll [8] reviewed the most common evaluated types of behavioral therapies for co-occurring disorders and included cognitive behavioral therapy (CBT), motivational interviewing (MI), and contingency management (CM). Cognitive behavioral therapy (CBT) and coping skills strategies have been shown to be effective across a wide range of substance use and psychiatric disorders, including alcohol dependence and depression [30-32], but controlled trials for co-occurring alcoholism and depression are limited, both in supply and design. In a qualitative review, Hides and colleagues [33] concluded that while CBT is more efficacious than no treatment control conditions, there is limited evidence to suggest that CBT is better suited for treating co-occurring depression and substance use compared to other psychotherapeutic interventions. In part, they site poor heterogeneity between existing studies as a key reason why the evidence is inconclusive.

Conversely, a more recent quantitative review of the literature highlights the effectiveness of CBT to reduce depressive symptoms and alcohol use [34]. In one study a moderate effect on alcohol use and/or depressive symptoms with Cognitive Behavior Therapy- Depression (CBT-D) was demonstrated, but included only patients with elevated depression (Beck Depression Inventory ≥ 10), not diagnosed depressive disorders [14]. Another study found that adding CBT-D for alcoholics with significant depressive symptoms was more effective on mood and alcohol use measures than standard treatment alone within an individual, but not a group treatment modality [35]. However, it is possible that treatment effects were due to the added therapist contact in the individual condition.

More systematic investigations have also been conducted in recent years. One randomized clinical trial compared the effectiveness of computer versus therapist delivered CBT with MI components [36]. All patients had comorbid depression with substance misuse, a substantial portion of which was alcohol misuse, and each received a single session of integrated CBT/MI before being randomized to a no treatment control condition, or nine sessions of CBT/MI delivered by a psychotherapist or a computer. As hypothesized, treatment conditions were associated with significant reductions in alcohol use and symptoms of depression, with long-term intervention having a greater impact. A similar RCT performed by Baker and colleagues [37] sought to determine the effectiveness of CBT/MI that is single-focused or integrated. Results found integrated treatment to be associated with greater improvement in alcohol use as well as depressive symptoms when compared to single-focus interventions. Similar support has been found in adolescent samples, which highlight treatment gains even at two years post-treatment [38].

Although there is good empirical support for the effectiveness of MI in substance use disorders and related behavioral domains [39-41], well-controlled evaluations of MI as a stand-alone treatment or MI adapted for co-occurring disorders are rare, and demonstrate improvements in treatment engagement/retention, motivation, and satisfaction, but not improvements in mood or decreased substance use [42-44]. In one small sample study (N = 5), MI was integrated with CBT for bipolar patients with comorbid substance use [45]. Modest reductions in both mood symptoms and substance use were observed.

Contingency Management (CM) has demonstrated more robust findings when used in depressed cocaine addicted populations [46,47]. In a pilot study which employed an integrated CM approach, opioid dependent patients experienced decreases in depressive symptoms, but decreases in usage were not significant. However, it has not been implemented with CDAD individuals and CM is not always logistically or financially feasible.

In addition to those interventions highlighted by Carroll [8], mindfulness training (MT) and behavioral activation have seen more limited attention in the treatment of co-occurring disorders. Brewer and colleagues [21] reviewed the evidence for a shared mechanism in depression and substance abuse that might allow MT to reduce substance use and improve psychiatric symptoms. Another treatment study focused on inner-city substance users with mild to moderate depression and found that a modified version of behavioral activation was successful at reducing depressive symptoms of patients during residential substance abuse treatment [48]. Interpersonal psychotherapy has also seen moderate support in the reduction of depressive symptoms, but less so for days abstinent from alcohol with the converse being the case for brief supportive therapy [49]. Another study comparing integrated CBT with twelve-step facilitation (TSF) found both to be effective, with TSF producing slightly better improvements in depression and abstinence [50]. The aforementioned findings appear to support the hypothesis that an integrated therapy possessing components of motivational enhancement, cognitive and behavioral therapy, as well as management of reinforcements, would be most ideal when targeting co-occurring depression and alcoholism.

5. CBASP for chronically depressed alcohol dependent individuals

Despite the aforementioned similarities found among individuals dealing with chronic depression and alcohol dependence, investigation of more synthesized treatment approaches has occurred in a limited fashion. "Third wave" cognitive behavioral therapies represent one underexplored subset of treatment approaches. Specifically, the Cognitive Behavioral Analysis System of Psychotherapy (CBASP) [51, 52] has demonstrated effectiveness in treating chronic depression, demonstrating effects equal to antidepressant medications as well as enhancing the effects of pharmacotherapy [6,7]. CBASP has yet to be studied in a large trial with persons with co-occurring alcohol dependence and chronic depression. However, in a case report from clinical practice, CBASP has been effective in reducing symptoms of chronic depression and significantly reducing alcohol intake to healthy drinking levels in CDAD individuals [53]. CBASP is particularly proficient for use with the early onset variety of unipolar mood disorders. Its etiological premise is that chronic depression arises as a result of a developmental history characterized by significant interpersonal trauma (e.g., physical/sexual abuse) or low grade, but continuous stream of psychological insults (e.g., punishment/rejection of some form); both lead to a preoperational form of thinking about one's social world. This derailment is particularly characterized by a lack of causal awareness and egocentrism in the depressive patient. This often results in a presentation of poor functioning and/or low motivation for change [51].

Additionally, a lack of awareness for their interpersonal impact and poor interpersonal problem-solving skills is prevalent [51,52,54,55]. CBASP takes a person-by-environment perspective in modifying depressive symptoms by raising a patient's awareness about their interpersonal impact on others [51,56,57]. This is done by highlighting the interpersonal interaction as it occurs in the therapeutic setting. Recognizing one's own stimulus value in the interpersonal context allows the chronic depressive to amend how he or she presents and copes with stressful interpersonal situations. CBASP holds that the interpersonal fear that drives avoidance, the central theme in many interpersonal failures, must be counter-conditioned. This is done by aiding the patient in discriminating their experience with the therapist, from those experiences with harmful significant others to create a sense of felt interpersonal safety that can then be generalized outside of the therapy setting [57].

Another major component of CBASP is Situational Analysis (SA). SA is an interpersonal problem-solving tool that is used in-session to help a patient actively re-experience an interpersonal encounter [51,56,57]. The goal of SA is to elicit the original cognitions and emotions during the target situation. This involves having the client first isolate an event, describe it in exclusively behavioral terms, and identify the situational outcome. The goal of this exercise is to help the client identify alternative ways of behaving and thinking that would lead to more desirable consequences. New ways of behaving interpersonally are often met with obtaining desirable outcomes, reinforcing effective problem-solving skills, and allowing the patient to perceive his or her contingent relationship with the environment. Through these means the patient may acquire "perceived functionality" – that is, the patient's ability to recognize and begin to change the interpersonal consequences of their behavior.

CBASP has demonstrated effectiveness in treating chronic depression, and is more effective than antidepressant monotherapy in individuals with early trauma or adversity [7,58-60]. Moreover, both the therapeutic relationship and the ability of the patient to learn SA effectively have been shown to independently contribute to a reduction in depressive symptoms [61]. Additionally, there is some evidence to support the notion that CBASP may be efficacious for individuals who do not respond to a trial of antidepressant medications initially [62]. CBASP has also been shown to outperform interpersonal psychotherapy in treating chronic depression [63], suggesting it may offer more when treating co-occurring chronic depression and alcoholism. Strong support for CBASP has been tempered by recent results [64], which found that neither CBASP nor Supportive psychotherapy was more effective than medication alone for chronically depressed treatment resistant patients. The lack of positive findings in that study were hypothesized to be related to the small number of CBASP sessions (mean = 12.5 sessions) and the effect of an aspect of the study design which focused on pharmacological switching and augmentation that may have had a negative impact on patients' interests in and expectations of, psychotherapy [65]. CBASP has been used to treat chronically depressed pregnant smokers and was found to be more effective than standard treatment at increasing abstinence and decreasing depressive symptoms six months post treatment. CBASP was more effective in women with higher levels of baseline depressive symptoms [66]. CBASP has also proven useful in a small sample study demonstrating that increases in positive affect and a decrease in depressive symptoms are associated with greater likelihood of prolonged abstinence from cigarette smoking [67].

6. Rationale for and adaptations of CBASP for CDAD individuals

Those entering substance abuse treatment programs with co-occurring disorders report using multiple drugs, having more recent admissions to psychiatric and medical facilities, and experiencing more severe medical, social, and family problems compared to those diagnosed solely with a substance use disorder [23]. These characteristics are unique in nature, suggesting the need for specialized treatment addressing depression and alcoholism simultaneously. The Substance Abuse and Mental Health Services Administration (SAMSA) in the USA [26] has come to similar conclusions in their recommendations for Center for Substance Abuse Treatment (CSAT) treatment improvement protocols with co-occurring disorders, suggesting individualized, integrated dual primary diagnosis-specific treatment interventions matched to diagnoses, phase of recovery, stage of change, and severity. Interestingly, no studies have evaluated the use of a behavioral treatment approach that can address these specific mood and addiction symptoms that characterize the CDAD individual.

CBASP is a behavioral treatment that addresses the unique characteristics of chronically depressed individuals, most of which are highly relevant for alcohol dependent individuals as well. CBASP is designed for persons who may (a) be less functional and less motivated to change; (b) have traumatic or impoverished developmental or reinforcement histories; and (c) lack awareness of their interpersonal impact or have poor interpersonal problem-solving skills. Thus, CBASP appears to be a plausible behavioral approach for use with CDAD individuals who may report traumatic developmental histories, manifest impoverished interpersonal relations, interactions and coping skills, and demonstrate additional chronic under-functioning [59,61,67]. Because of its structured but individualized and collaborative design, emphasis on teaching effective coping strategies, and employment of motivational, cognitive, behavioral, and interpersonal techniques, CBASP is uniquely suited for use in treating alcoholism in the context of chronic depression [7,67].

The major goals of CBASP are (a) to enable patients to feel increased emotional safety, thus allowing them to more fully approach and engage in treatment and reduce avoidance behavior, including drinking; and (b) to allow patients to recognize how they contribute to their own interpersonal psychopathology (perceived functionality) and begin to learn how to negotiate interpersonal situations successfully and without the use of alcohol.

Importantly, CBASP provides an empirical method to facilitate and measure exactly what and how much is being learned during the course of therapy [57]. Both felt emotional safety in the therapeutic dyad and learned acquisition of perceived functionality are hypothesized to be related to the outcome of treatment and, over time, to the maintenance of the therapeutic gains. These skills can be measured in multiple correlated ways, including evaluation of learning in session via achievement of therapeutic interpersonal tasks, performance on psychological tests of prediction of interpersonal response, and fMRI assessment of the neurobiological correlates of perceived functionality that have been identified in chronic depressives [68].

In sum, treatment for CDAD individuals must be targeted or personalized for the underlying interpersonal issues and skill deficits of the individual in order to be most effective. CBASP is a behavioral treatment which can be adapted to comprehensively address these issues and deficits to successfully treat both alcohol dependence and chronic depression simultaneously.

7. Current research with CBASP to treat co-occurring chronic depression and alcohol dependence

We have developed an enhanced integrative CBASP for use in reducing both depressive symptoms and alcohol intake in CDAD patients. The augmented CBASP includes all the aspects of traditional CBASP and adds coping skills training for reducing alcohol intake. One of the most important components of successfully conducting CBASP with this population is helping the patient discover the causal connections between their mood symptoms and drinking behavior and ultimately change the functional linkages between their depression and drinking. The drinking behavior is conceptualized as a maladaptive coping strategy that is often an outcome of interpersonal situations for this patient population. Drinking behavior is also conceived of as avoidance behavior, which interferes with learning and practicing effective interpersonal problem solving and coping. Further augmentations include additional assessment and monitoring of stage of change and motivation levels for both depressive symptoms and alcohol use. During the middle phase of treatment and in session after the Coping Survey Questionnaire (Situational Analysis) has been remediated, alcohol reduction coping skills are identified and taught in the same manner that traditional CBT is conducted. Significant adaptations for use with this population involve setting and assessing alcohol consumption goals in addition to depressive symptoms and quality of life/level of functioning goals for treatment. A harm reduction approach, similar to that utilized in CBT for alcohol dependence, is used to address alcohol consumption. Thus, patients do not need to be abstinent when in treatment and do not necessarily have to set abstinence as their goal, although it is preferred. The overall approach to symptom change is compatible with the CBASP essence of treatment, which allows the patient to establish how the therapy session will proceed and enables the patient to do the work of change.

A twenty-session pilot study examining the use of our augmented CBASP for persons with co-occurring chronic depression and alcohol dependence is currently underway at the

University of Virginia School of Medicine in the Department of Psychiatry and Neurobehavioral Sciences in Charlottesville, Virginia. Sessions were individually administered weekly for one hour by two trained Ph.D. level clinical psychologists with extensive experience in addictions treatment and depression. Sessions were audio taped to be rated for adherence, and follow up data regarding alcohol intake and depressive symptoms collected at one month and three months post termination. Preliminary results from this small study indicate that this patient population exists and is willing to seek and participate in such extensive and intensive treatment. Below are brief descriptions of the course of treatment for two participants in our current study.

Participant 01, "Denise" is a 54-year-old, Caucasian female who is divorced and lives alone. She works full-time as a nurse. At intake, she was diagnosed with Dysthymia, early onset, Major Depressive Disorder, recurrent, in partial remission, and Alcohol Dependence. She reported that she had been on vacation for three weeks prior to intake and that her symptoms of depression and alcohol use had reduced as a result. Denise noted that interpersonal stress at work and with family members was a primary trigger for her depression. She recognized that she drank to avoid her negative emotions and interpersonal problems. At intake, stage of change data indicated that Denise had already begun to reduce her alcohol intake and that she was ready to reduce her symptoms of depression. Her stated goals for treatment were to learn how to manage her mood so that she no longer used alcohol to cope with depression, and to drink at a reduced level because she enjoys the taste of alcohol. As shown in Figure 1, at session 1, she was drinking 28 drinks per week and her score on the Hamilton Depression Rating Scale was 14. In her final session, she was drinking 17 drinks per week and her score on the Hamilton Depression Rating Scale was 3. In session 10, Denise began effectively using Situational Analysis to solve interpersonal problems. As can be seen in Figure 1, she continued to practice Situational Analysis using the coping survey questionnaire on a weekly basis. By session 16, she reported that she no longer needed to drink to manage her mood. She noted, "For the first time in my life, I am finally taking control of situations and facing my demons." Much of her ability to take control of situations in her life involved learning through Situational Analysis to set boundaries with others. Setting boundaries with others was difficult for her due to fear of interpersonal rejection. Her difficulty setting boundaries often caused her to feel taken advantage of by others which led to depression and subsequent drinking behavior. Her fear of interpersonal rejection was also related to fear of making mistakes. Denise's transference hypothesis was "If I make a mistake with my therapist, I will disappoint her and she will think I am not good enough." This fear of interpersonal rejection was addressed in treatment using the Interpersonal Discrimination Exercise, and by session 7 the participant was able to discriminate between the feedback from the therapist and feedback from significant others when she made a mistake. As such, she reported an increased sense of safety and she demonstrated an increased ability to assert herself with the therapist. Across the final weeks of treatment Denise's learning generalized and she was regularly setting appropriate boundaries with significant others in her life. At termination, the participant stated that she no longer felt fear or guilt about expressing her limits to others and setting boundaries.

Participant 02, "Paul" is a 45-year-old, Caucasian male who is divorced and lives alone. He works part-time as a food vendor and also receives monthly social security disability benefits. At intake, he was diagnosed with Major Depressive Disorder, Recurrent and Alcohol Dependence. Paul reported an extensive drug and alcohol use history, further noting how his substance use helped him to avoid negative emotions and interpersonal problems. At intake, stage of change data indicated that he was planning to reduce both his alcohol intake and symptoms of depression. His stated goals for treatment were to learn how to better manage his mood so that he no longer used alcohol to cope with depression (he reported no drug use for the past five years), and to drink at a reduced level because he enjoys drinking alcohol. As shown in Figure 1, at session 1, he was drinking 48 drinks per week and his score on the Hamilton Depression Rating Scale was 16. In his final session, Paul was drinking 15 drinks per week and his score on the Hamilton Depression Rating Scale was 3. As can be seen in Figure 1, he continued to practice Situational Analysis using the Coping Survey Questionnaire on a weekly basis and began to gain an understanding of the importance of communicating to others to achieve socially desirable outcomes. This was especially true with regard to expressing negative affect to others. Paul's transference hypothesis was "If I express negative affect, emotions, or feelings to my therapist, then he will be angry or upset with me, and reject me." This fear of interpersonal rejection was addressed in treatment using the Interpersonal Discrimination Exercise. Despite the participant's difficulty discriminating between feedback from the therapist and feedback from significant others when he expressed negative affect, he reported an increased sense of self-confidence to assert himself with the therapist and others. In addition, Paul stated that whereas he was more concerned with others' reactions to his assertiveness in the past, across the final weeks of treatment he was more concerned with obtaining socially desirable outcomes than with what others' reactions were to him.

CBASP has been successfully augmented and implemented with a new and challenging patient population in much need of effective treatment options. Although neither patient set abstinence as their drinking goal, instead opting to cut back or reduce their alcohol intake to a less risky level, they made progress on these goals and remained engaged in treatment. Both patients reduced their depressive symptoms dramatically over the course of twenty weeks. More importantly, both patients were able to gain insight into the negative impact of their transference hypotheses and avoidance behaviors upon their mood and drinking behavior, and begin to implement causal thinking to approach and solve interpersonal problems. Indeed, preliminary investigations of this pilot study data suggest that treatment is most effective when tailored or personalized to the underlying interpersonal issues and skill deficits of the patient as presented in the Transference Hypothesis.

Preliminary results from the research examining CBASP for CDAD outpatients in individual therapy are presented in Figures 1, 2, and 3 below, but should be interpreted with caution due to the very small sample size (N = 2). However, the results are promising, as both participants showed reductions in their drinking measured via the Timeline Followback Calendar [69] and depressive symptoms measured via the Hamilton Rating Scale for Depression [70], as the number of completed Coping Survey Questionnaires increased.

Additional completed study participants are necessary to confirm these preliminary findings and additional data collection is underway.

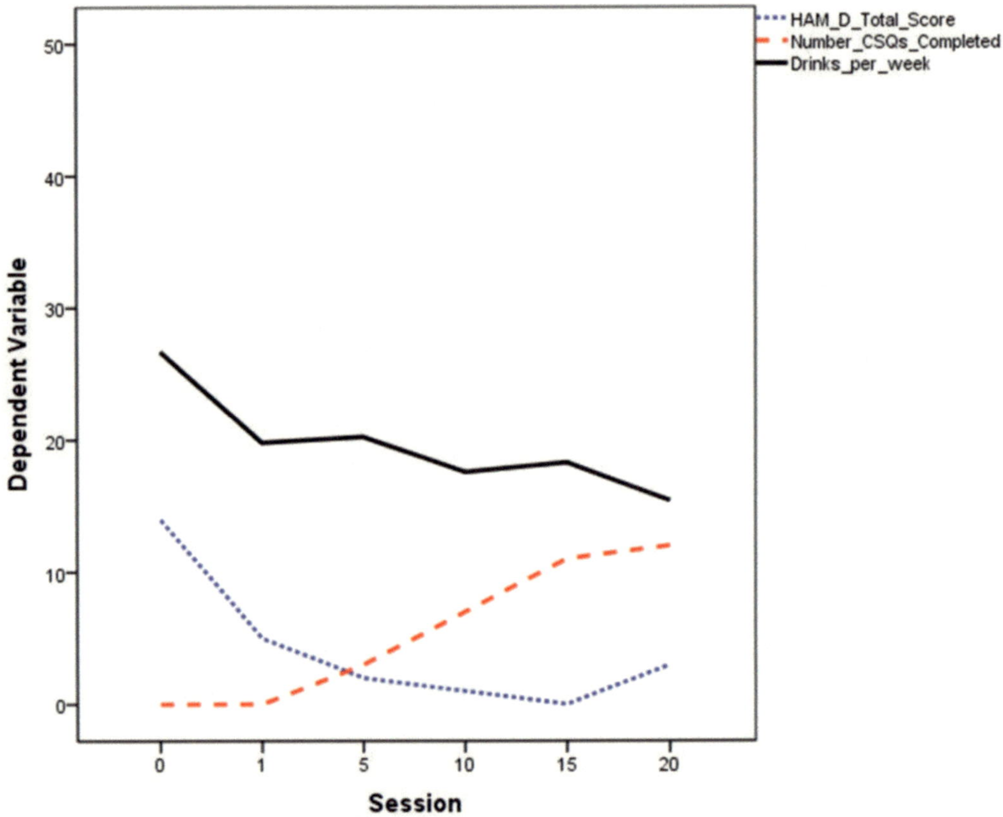

Figure 1. Number of Coping Survey Questionnaires completed, Hamilton Rating Scale for Depression scores, and drinks per week by session for Participant 01. Session 0 refers to the participant's scores at baseline.

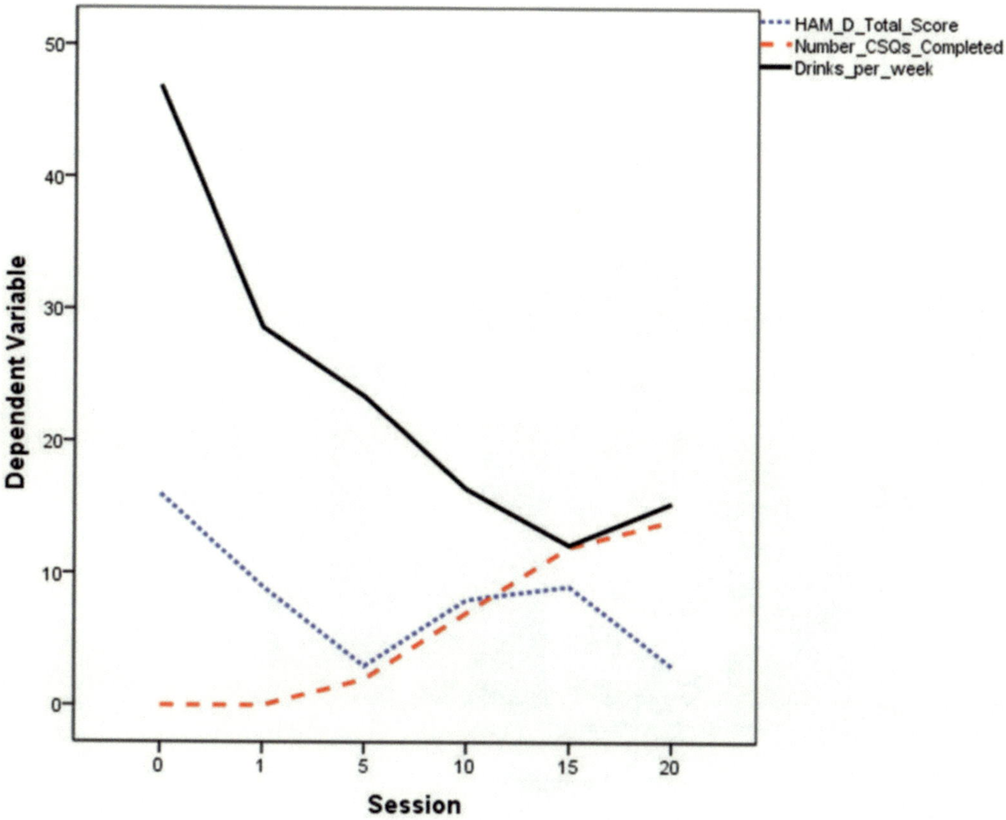

Figure 2. Number of Coping Survey Questionnaires completed, Hamilton Rating Scale for Depression scores, and drinks per week by session for Participant 02. Session 0 refers to the participant's scores at baseline.

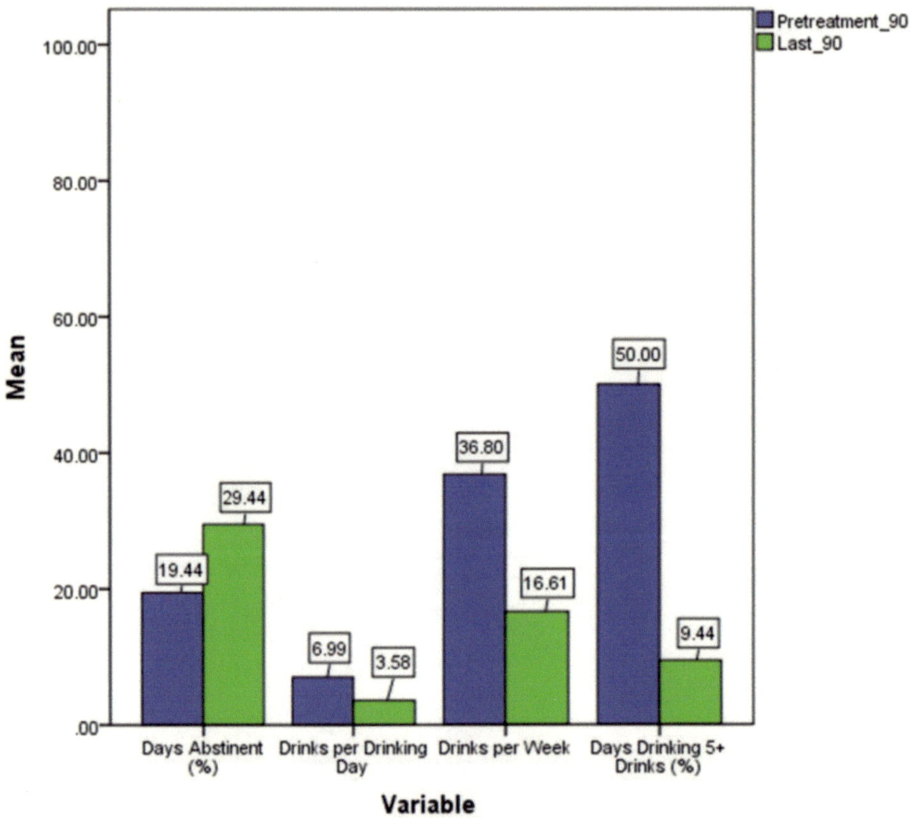

Figure 3. Differences between 90 days pretreatment (blue) and last 90 days in treatment (green) on four drinking variables for the study participants.

Author details

J. Kim Penberthy, Christopher J. Gioia, Andrea Konig and Stephanie A. Cockrell
Department of Psychiatry & Neurobehavioral Sciences, University of Virginia School of Medicine, Charlottesville, Virginia, United States

Aaron M. Martin
Department of Psychology, Virginia Commonwealth University, Richmond, Virginia, United States

Acknowledgement

We would like to thank Dr. James P. McCullough, Jr., the developer of CBASP and Dr. Penberthy's primary mentor, for his guidance and advice on this project. He has been a tireless advocate for those suffering from chronic depression and we are pleased to expand the application of CBASP to the chronically depressed alcohol dependent population.

8. References

[1] Goetzel RZ, Hawkins K, Ozminkowski RW, Wang S. The Health and Productivity Cost Burden of the "Top 10" Physical and Mental Health Conditions Affecting Six Large U.S. Employers in 1999. Journal of Occupational and Environmental Medicine 2003;45(1) 5-14.

[2] Bouchery EE, Harwood HJ, Sacks JJ, Simon CJ, Brewer RD. Economic Costs of Excessive Alcohol Consumption in the United States, 2006. American Journal of Preventive Medicine 2011;41(5) 516-524.

[3] Greenberg PE, Kessler RC, Birnbaum HG, Leong SA, Lowe SW, Berglund, PA, et al. The Economic Burden of Depression in the United States: How Did it Change Between 1990 and 2000? Journal of Clinical Psychiatry 2003;64(12)1465-1475.

[4] Spitzer RL., editor. Diagnostic and Statistical Manual of Mental Disorders (4th ed., text revision). Washington, DC: American Psychological Association; 2000.

[5] Grant BF, Stinson FS, Dawson DA, Chou P, Dufour MC, Compton W, et al. Prevalence and Co-Occurrence of Substance Use Disorders and Independent Mood and Anxiety Disorders. Archives of General Psychiatry 2004;61(8) 807-816.

[6] McCullough JP. Treatment For Chronic Depression Using Cognitive Behavioral Analysis System of Psychotherapy (CBASP). Journal of Clinical Psychology 2003;59(8) 833-846.

[7] Keller MB, McCullough JP, Klein DN, Arnow B, Dunner DL, Gelenberg AJ, et al. A Comparison of Nefazodone, Cognitive Behavioral Analysis System of Psychotherapy, and Their Combination for the Treatment of Chronic Depression. New England Journal of Medicine 2000;342(20) 1462-1470.

[8] Carroll KM. Behavioral Therapies for Co-Occurring Substance Use and Mood Disorders. Biological Psychiatry 2004;56(10) 778-784.

[9] Sher L, Stanley BH, Harkavy-Friedman JM, Carballo JJ, Arendt M, Brent DA, et al. Depressed Patients with Co-Occurring Alcohol Use Disorders: A Unique Patient Population. Journal of Clinical Psychiatry 2008;69(6) 907-915.

[10] Thase ME, Salloum IM, Cornelius JD. Comorbid Alcoholism and Depression Treatment Issues. Journal of Clinical Psychiatry 2001;62(20) 32-41.
[11] Riso LP, Miyatake RK, Thase ME. The Search for Determinants of Chronic Depression: A Review of Six Factors. Journal of Affective Disorders 2002;70(2) 103-115.
[12] Sartor CE, Lynskey MT, Heath AC, Jacob T, True W. The Role of Childhood Risk Factors in Initiation of Alcohol Use and Progression to Alcohol Dependence. Addiction 2007;102(2) 216-25.
[13] Hayden EP, Klein DN. Outcome of Dysthymic Disorder at 5-year Follow-Up: The Effect of Familial Psychopathology, Early Adversity, Personality, Comorbidity, and Chronic Stress. American Journal of Psychiatry 2001;158(11) 1864-1870.
[14] Brown RA, Evans DM, Miller IW, Burgess ES, Mueller TI. Cognitive-Behavioral Treatment for Depression in Alcoholism. Journal of Consulting and Clinical Psychology 1997;65(5) 715-726.
[15] Sullivan LE, Fiellin DA, O'Connor PG. The Prevalence and Impact of Alcohol Problems in Major Depression: A Systematic Review. American Journal of Medicine 2005;118(4) 330-341.
[16] Petrakis IL, Gonzalez G, Rosenheck R, Krystal JH. Comorbidity of Alcoholism and Psychiatric Disorders. Alcohol Research & Health 2002;26(2) 81–89.
[17] Davis L, Uezato A, Newell J, Frazier E. Major Depression and Comorbid Substance Use Disorders. Current Opinion in Psychiatry 2008;21(1) 14-18.
[18] Nurnberger JI, Foround T, Flury L, Su J, Meyer ET, Hu K, et al. Evidence for a Locux on Chormosome 1 that Influences Vulnerability to Alcoholism and Affective Disorder. American Journal of Psychiatry 2001;158( ) 718-724.
[19] Drevets WC, Price JL, Furey ML. Brain Structural and Functional Abnormalities in Mood Disorders: Implications for Neurocircuitry Models of Depression. Brain Structure and Function 2008;213(1-2) 93-118.
[20] Everitt BJ, Robbins TW. Neural Systems of Reinforcement for Drug Addiction: From Actions to Habits to Compulsion. Nature Neuroscience 2005;8(11) 1481-1489.
[21] Brewer JA, Bowen S, Smith JT, Marlatt GA, Potenza MN. Mindfulness-Based Treatments for Co-Occurring Depression and Substance Use Disorders: What Can We Learn From the Brain? Addiction 2010;105(10) 1698-1706.
[22] Nikulina V, Widom CS, Brzustowicz LM. Child Abuse and Neglect, MAOA, and Mental Health Outcomes: A Prospective Examination. Biological Psychiatry 2012;71(4) 350-357.
[23] Gil-Rivas V, Grella C, Prause J. Substance Use After Residential Treatment Among Individuals with Co-Occurring Disorders: The Role of Anxiety/Depressive Symptoms and Trauma Exposure. Psychology of Addictive Behaviors 2009;23(2) 303-314.
[24] Merrill JE, Read JP. Motivational Pathways to Unique Types of Alcohol Consequences. Psychology of Addictive Behaviors 2010;24(4) 705-711.
[25] Nelson CB, Little RJ, Heath AC, Kessler RC. Patterns of DSM-III-R Alcohol Dependence Symptom Progression in a General Population Survey. Psychological Medicine 1996;26(3) 449-460.

[26] Substance Abuse and Mental Health Services Administration. SAMHSA: Adults with Co-Occurring Serious Mental Illness and a Substance Use Disorder. http://www.oas.samhsa.gov/2k4/coOccurring/cooccurring.pdf (accessed 1 February 2012).

[27] Moak DH, Anton RF, Latham PK, Voronin KE, Waid RL, Durazo-Arvisu R. Sertraline and Cognitive Behavioral Therapy for Depressed Alcoholics: Results of a Placebo-Controlled Trial. Journal of Clinical Psychopharmacology 2003;23(6) 553-562.

[28] Myrick H, Brady KT. Current Review of the Comorbidity of Affective, Anxiety, and Substance Use Disorders. Current Opinion in Psychiatry 2003;16(3) 261-270.

[29] Pettinati HM, Dundon WD. Comorbid Depression and Alcohol Dependence: New Approaches to Dual Therapy Challenges and Progress. Psychiatric Times 2011;28(6) 1-8.

[30] Morgenstern J, Longabaugh R. Cognitive-Behavioral Treatment for Alcohol Dependence: A Review of the Evidence for its Hypothesized Mechanisms of Action. Addiction 2000;95(10) 1475-1490.

[31] Rupke SJ, Blecke D, Renfrow M. Cognitive Therapy for Depression. American Family Physician 2008;73(1) 83-86.

[32] Wampold BE, Minami T, Baskin TW, Callen-Tierney S. A Mete-(re)Analysis of the Effects of Cognitive Therapy Versus "Other Therapies" for Depression. Journal of Affective Disorders 2002;68(2-3) 159-165.

[33] Hides L, Samet S, Lubman D I. Cognitive Behaviour Therapy (CBT) for the Treatment of Co-Occurring Depression and Substance Use: Current Evidence and Directions for Future Research. Drug and Alcohol Review 2010;29(5) 508-517.

[34] Baker AL, Thornton LK, Hiles S, Hides L, Lubman DI. Psychological Interventions for Alcohol Misuse Among People with Co-Occurring Depression or Anxiety Disorders: A Systematic Review. Journal of Affective Disorders 2011;Doi:10.1016/j.jad.2011.08.004.

[35] Turner RW, Wehl CK. Treatment of Unipolar Depression in Problem Drinkers. Advances in Behavior Research & Therapy 1984;6(2) 115-125.

[36] Kay-Lambkin FJ, Baker AL, Lewin TJ, Carr VJ. Computer-Based Psychological Treatment for Comorbid Depression and Problematic Alcohol and/or Cannabis Use: A Randomized Controlled Trial of Clinical Efficacy. Addiction 2009;104(3) 378-388.

[37] Baker AL, Kavanagh DJ, Kay-Lambkin FJ, Hunt SA, Lewin TJ, Carr VJ, et al. Randomized Controlled Trial of Cognitive Behavioural Therapy for Coexisting Depression and Alcohol Problems: Short-Term Outcome. Addiction 2010;105(1) 87-99.

[38] Cornelius JR, Douaihy A, Bukstein OG, Daley DC, Wood SD, Kelly TM, et al. Evaluation of Cognitive Behavioral Therapy/Motivational Enhancement Therapy (CBT/MET) in a Treatment Trial of Comorbid MDD/AUD Adolescents. Addictive Behaviors 2011;36(8) 843-848.

[39] Burke BL, Arkowiz H, Menchola M. The Efficacy of Motivational Interviewing: A Meta-Analysis of Controlled Clinical Trials. Journal of Consulting and Clinical Psychology 2003;71(5) 843-861.

[40] Dunn C, Deroo I, Rivara FP. The Use of Brief Interventions Adapted from Motivational Interviewing Across Behavioral Domains: A Systematic Review. Addiction 2001;96(12) 1725-1742.

[41] Miller WR, Wilbourne PL. Mesa Grande: A Methodological Analysis of Clinical Trials of Treatments for Alcohol Use Disorders. Addiction 2002;97(3) 265-277.

[42] Barrowclough C, Haddock G, Tarrier N, Lewis SW, Moring J, O'Brien R. Randomized Controlled Trial of Motivational Interviewing, Cognitive Behavioral Therapy and Family Intervention for Patients with Comorbid Schizophrenia and Substance Use Disorders. American Journal of Psychiatry 2001;158(10) 1706-1713.

[43] Carey KB. Substance Use Reduction in the Context of Outpatient Psychiatric Treatment: A Collaborative, Motivational, Harm Reduction Approach. Community Mental Health Journal 1996;32(3) 291-306.

[44] Grothues JM, Bischof G, Reinhardt S, Meyer C, John U, Rumpf H.-J. Differences in Help Seeking Rates After Brief Intervention for Alcohol Use Disorders in General Practice Patients With and Without Comorbid Anxiety or Depressive Disorders. International Journal of Methods in Psychiatric Research 2008;17(1) S74-S77.

[45] Jones SH, Barrowclough C, Allott R, Day C, Earnshaw P, Wilson I. Integrated Motivational Interviewing and Cognitive–Behavioural Therapy for Bipolar Disorder with Comorbid Substance Use. Clinical Psychology & Psychotherapy 2011;18(5) 426-437.

[46] Drake RE, Mercer-McFadden C, Mueser KT, McHugo GJ, Bond GH. Review of Integrated Mental Health and Substance Abuse Treatment for Patients with Dual Disorders. Schizophrenia Bulletin 1998;24(4) 589-608.

[47] Gonzalez G, Feingold A, Oliveto A, Gonsai K, Kosten TR. Comorbid Major Depressive Disorder as a Prognostic Factor in Cocaine-Abusing Buprenorphine-Maintained Patients Treated with Desipramine and Contingency Management. The American Journal of Drug and Alcohol Abuse 2003;29(3) 497-514.

[48] Daughters SB, Braun AR, Sargeant MN, Reynolds EK, Hopko DR, Blanco C, et al. Effectiveness of a Brief Behavioral Treatment for Inner-City Illicit Drug Users with Elevated Depressive Symptoms: The Life Enhancement Treatment for Substance Use (LETS Act!). Journal of Clinical Psychiatry 2008;69(1) 122-129.

[49] Markowitz JC, Kocsis JH, Christos P, Bleiberg K, Carlin A. Pilot Study of Interpersonal Psychotherapy Versus Supportive Psychotherapy for Dysthymic Patients with Secondary Alcohol Abuse or Dependence. Journal of Nervous and Mental Disease 2008;196(6) 468-474.

[50] Glasner-Edwards S, Tate SR, McQuaid JR, Cummins K, Granholm E, Brown SA. Mechanisms of Action in Integrated Cognitive-Behavioral Treatment Versus Twelve-Step Facilitation for Substance-Dependent Adults with Comorbid Major Depression. Journal of Studies on Alcohol and Drugs 2007;68(5) 663-672.

[51] McCullough JP. Treatment for Chronic Depression - Cognitive Behavioral Analysis System of Psychotherapy (CBASP). New York: Guilford Press; 2000.

[52] McCullough JP. Skills Training Manual for Diagnosing and Treating Chronic Depression - Cognitive Behavioral Analysis System of Psychotherapy (CBASP). New York: Guilford Press; 2001.

[53] Penberthy JK. CBASP for Co-Occurring Chronic Depression and Alcohol Dependence. In: Belz, Caspar, Schramm (Eds). CBASP in Practice - Basic Concepts and New Developments. New Jersey: John Wiley & Sons; 2012

[54] McCullough JP. Patient's Manual for CBASP. New York: Guilford Press; 2003.

[55] McCullough JP. Treatment for Chronic Depression: Cognitive Behavioral Analysis System of Psychotherapy (CBASP). Journal of Psychotherapy Integration 2003;13 241-263.

[56] McCullough JP. Treating Chronic Depression with Disciplined Personal Involvement. New York: Springer Science + Business Media; 2006.

[57] McCullough JP, Lord BD, Conley KA, Martin AM. A Method for Conducting Intensive Psychological Studies with Early-Onset Chronically Depressed Patients. American Journal of Psychotherapy 2010;64(4) 317-337.

[58] Hirschfeld RMA, Dunner DL, Keitner G, Klein DN, Koran LM, Kornstein SG, et al. Does Psychosocial Functioning Improve Independent of Depressive Symptoms? A Comparison of Nefazodone, Psychotherapy, and their Combination. Biological Psychiatry 2002;51(2) 123-133.

[59] Manbe R, Arnow BA, Blasey C, Vivian D, McCullough JP, Blalock JA, et al. Patient's Therapeutic Skill Acquisition and Response to Psychotherapy, Alone, and in Combination with Medications. Journal of Psychological Medicine 2003;33(4) 693-702.

[60] Nemeroff CB, Heim CM, Thase ME, Klein DN, Rush AJ, Schatzberg AF, et al. Differential Responses to Psychotherapy Versus Pharmacotherapy in the Treatment of Patients with Chronic Forms of Major Depression and Childhood Trauma. Proceedings of the National Academy of Sciences 2003;100(24) 14293-14296.

[61] Santiago NJ, Klein DN, Vivian D, Arnow BA, Blalock JA, Koscis JH, et al. The Therapeutic Alliance and CBASP-Specific Skill Acquisition in the Treatment of Chronic Depression. Cognitive Therapy & Research 2006;29(6) 803-817.

[62] Schatzberg AF, Rush AJ, Arnow BA, Banks PLC, Blalock JA, Borian FE, et al. Chronic Depression: Medication (Nefazodone) or Psychotherapy (CBASP) is Effective When the Other is Not. Archives of General Psychiatry 2005;62(5) 513-520.

[63] Schramm E, Zobel I, Dykierek P, Kech S, Brakemeier E-L, Külz A, et al. Cognitive Behavioral Analysis System of Psychotherapy Versus Interpersonal Psychotherapy for Early-Onset Chronic Depression: A Randomized Pilot Study. Journal of Affective Disorders 2011;129(1-3) 109-116.

[64] Kocsis JH, Gelenberg AJ, Rothbaum BO, Klein DN, Trivedi MH, Manber M, et al. Cognitive Behavioral Analysis System of Psychotherapy and Brief Supportive Psychotherapy for Augmentation of Antidepressant Nonresponse in Chronic Depression: The REVAMP Trial. Archives of General Psychiatry 2009;66(11) 1178-1188.

[65] Schramm E, Reynolds CF. Where Do We Go From Here? Response to REVAMP. Electronic letter, Archives of General Psychiatry 2010.

[66] Cinciripini PM, Blalock JA, Minnix JA, Robinson JD, Brown VL, Lam C, et al. Effects of an Intensive Depression-Focused Intervention for Smoking Cessation in Pregnancy. Journal of Consulting & Clinical Psychology 2010;78(1) 44-54.

[67] Blalock JA, Fouladi RT, Cinciripini PM, Markowitz JC, Klein DN, Rothbaum BO, et al. Cognitive and Behavioral Mediators of Combined Pharmacotherapy and Psychotherapy of Chronic Depression. Cognitive Therapy & Research 2008;32(2) 197-211.

[68] Walter H, Berger M, Schnell K. Neuropsychotherapy: Conceptual, Empirical, and Neuroethical Issues. European Archives of Psychiatry & Clinical Neuroscience 2009;259 S173-S182.

[69] Sobell LC., Sobell MB. Timeline Follow-Back: A Technique for Assessing Self-Reported Alcohol Consumption. In Litten R, Allen J. (Eds.) Measuring Alcohol Consumption - Psychosocial and Biochemical Methods. Totowa, NJ: The Humana Press; 1992. p41-72.

[70] Hamilton M. A Rating Scale for Depression. Journal of Neurology, Neurosurgery, & Psychiatry 1960;23 56-62.

Chapter 11

Psychosocial Intervention for Co-Existing MDD and PTSD

Todd K. Favorite and Todd Vance

Additional information is available at the end of the chapter

http://dx.doi.org/10.5772/51297

1. Introduction

This chapter will focus on the relationship between chronic depression and posttraumatic stress disorder (PTSD). This relationship has become increasingly critical to our understanding of the etiology of early onset chronic depression. For the patient presenting with early onset chronic depression we typically find a developmental profile of maltreatment in the form of emotional abuse or neglect, physical abuse or neglect, and sexual abuse [1]. In addition, interpersonal maltreatment is not the only childhood experience occurring within the context of family and caregiver relationships. Children are also subject to a range of losses, sociopolitical stressors, and environmental disasters that can have a dramatic negative impact on their view of self, other and their world [2].

It is generally accepted that early onset depression has a traumatic substrate that is rooted in a child's developmental history [3, 4, 5]. The derailment of a secure attachment and requisite cognitive-affective development produces negative self-other attributions and an enhanced fear response toward unfamiliar or threatening environmental stimuli. Behaviorally, this is manifested in a predominantly avoidant coping strategy, which, in turn, increases the strength of the fear structure [6]. Chronic depressive trajectories stemming from late onset or adult trauma have received less attention in the literature and yet present with frequency among veterans. For instance, a large proportion of veterans diagnosed with PTSD also carry a diagnosis of depression [7,8]. This population has a high treatment refractory rate for both antidepressant medication and psychosocial interventions [9].

2. Problem statement

Rates of co-morbidity

PTSD and Major Depressive Disorder co-occur at high rates. Gerrity et al [10] found that 86% of depressed VA patients (N=398) reported a history of trauma and severity of PTSD symptoms was strongly associated with severity of depressive symptoms. Rates of reported Co-Morbid PTSD and Major Depression vary, but are generally quite high. For example, in a multi-site study (N=677), Campbell et al [11] reported 36% of patients met criteria for PTSD and Major Depression. In a large epidemiological study (N=5877), Kessler et al [12] found that 48% of those studied reported co-occurring PTSD and Major Depression.

According to DSM-IV-TR criteria, specific symptom overlap exists in Major Depression and PTSD [13]. In the DSM-IV-TR, anhedonia, sleep problems, and difficulty concentrating are specific symptoms that are included as criteria for both PTSD and a Major Depressive Episode. Depressed mood, a criterion for Major Depression, in some patients can present as restricted range of affect, a diagnostic criterion for PTSD. Irritability and anger, criteria for PTSD, also co-occur in depressed mood, specifically for children and adolescents. However, clinical experience indicates that anger is frequently present in chronically depressed patients, and this may be especially true in depressed men [14, 15].

PTSD is a chronic often disabling disorder that affects approximately 6.8% of the U.S. population with a lifetime prevalence of 3.6% for males, and 9.7% for females [12]. There is a complex interaction among neurobiological and psychosocial factors that involve the overactivation of the Hypothalamic-Pituitary-Adrenal (H-P-A) axis [16]. The Veterans Health Study [17] showed that 31% of the over 2,000 veterans sampled had experienced significant depressive symptoms with 54% of these depressed veterans evidencing one or more psychiatric co-morbidity, predominantly PTSD. Additionally, 88% had medical co-morbidities such as hypertension, heart disease, diabetes, and degenerative joint disease. The lifetime prevalence of Major Depressive Disorder in patient populations such as combat veterans who have a diagnosis of PTSD has been reported to be as high as 68% [18]. A community co-morbidity sample demonstrated that individuals who have PTSD are 3-5 times more likely to develop Major Depressive Disorder over their lifetime [19].

While the empirical literature has begun to outline the interaction of these two disorders, most of the treatment literature focuses on effective interventions with MDD or PTSD alone. This presents a gap in our understanding about how to clinically address the patients with co-morbid MDD/PTSD. Patients suffering from co-occurring Major Depression and PTSD also experience overlap in subjective symptoms. For example, problems with relationships, lack of intimacy, poor emotion regulation, social isolation, feelings of worthlessness, low self-esteem, helplessness and hopelessness, and cognitive and behavioral rigidity characterize both chronic depression and PTSD.

3. Clinical presentation of co-morbid MDD/PTSD

The distinction that we are treating co-occurring and interactive disorders rather than two separate or sequential disorders makes a significant difference in our approach to treatment. On the one hand the clinician is faced with a singular treatment goal of working through a patient's trauma symptoms when their motivation is poor, and avoidant behavioral patterns make trauma focused treatment problematical. On the other hand, treatment directed only at depressive symptoms may by derailed by the expression of trauma symptoms that serve to undermine the patient's sense of safety and trust within the therapeutic relationship, and negatively impact treatment adherence. What is clinically evident is that when these disorders co-occur, patients report greater symptom distress, and treatment interventions are often highly problematic or refractory [11]. Although first line psychosocial treatments such as, Prolonged Exposure Therapy (PE) and Cognitive Processing Therapy (CPT) for trauma disorders describe a remission of depressive symptoms when PTSD symptoms are actively addressed, it is argued that some chronically depressed patients find it difficult to engage in exposure therapies that directly activate trauma memories and require adherence to between session imaginal and in vivo exposures. This problem is represented in a 40% drop-out rate for veterans with PTSD who receive only trauma-based treatment, It many of whom had co-occurring disorders, including MDD [18].

4. Etiology of complex PTSD and chronic depression

Various authors [19,20,21] have conceptualized "complex PTSD" in which the affected person is exposed to repeated traumas over a number of years. In persons with complex PTSD other problems often develop, including substance use disorders, Major Depression, and Axis II diagnoses. However, in persons with complex PTSD, these co-occurring disorders may present in different ways compared to a patient who presents with any of these disorders alone [20].

A history of Major Depression may predispose one to developing PTSD. As Brady et al noted [22], Major Depression can result from exposure to a trauma and previous Major Depression is a risk factor for developing PTSD. Some researchers have found that early, toxic environmental milieus are correlated with the development of chronic depression [1,3], such as emotional maltreatment (active or passive); physical abuse or neglect; and sexual abuse.

An early, abusive environment may lead to the phenomenon of learned helplessness, which primes the person to develop Major Depression [26]. If that same person is then thrust into an environment in which a discreet traumatic event occurs, the person's learned helplessness may then be reinforced by this trauma event.

5. Application area

Implications for assessment and treatment

The clinician should consider both PTSD and Major Depressive Disorder during the initial. In fact, Kessler et al [12] advised considering all traumas, not only the most serious trauma during assessment. When assessing for co-occurring recurrent Major Depression and PTSD, the clinician must assess the patient's history in a way that allows developmental insults to be revealed. Often the patient's early environment was characterized by unpredictability, physical or emotional harm, or being thrust into a care-giving role. Chronic depression is correlated with these various types of trauma in the early, developmental environmental [1, 3]. The Significant Other History is used in CBASP to assess the nature and extent of early psychological insults [3].

Becoming a source of perceived safety is one of the first tasks of the clinician treating a patient with PTSD and chronic Major Depression. The principle of "safety first" has long been recognized for its importance in the treatment of PTSD [20]. What may be less widely recognized is that the same principle is operative with the chronically depressed patient. In order for learning to take place, the therapist must first become an inhibitor or "safety signal" for the patient [23]. Becoming a source of safety and helping the patient differentiate between the therapist and toxic others, and between past toxic environments and the therapeutic environment is critical in successful treatment of depressed persons who have experienced early trauma.

Regarding treatment of co-occurring chronic depression and PTSD, the question arises as to which disorder to treat first. Foa and Rothbaum [6] stated that in cases of severe depression, depression should be treated first, as severe depression is likely to limit a patient's ability to benefit from cognitive-behavioral therapy for PTSD. Others have argued that addressing the relational aspect of trauma is a key element of successful treatment for PTSD [20].

6. Theoretical considerations

Learning theory posits that learning theory, the early abusive environment that often characterizes the developmental history of the chronically depressed patient establishes both Pavlovian and Skinnerian learning. Typically, the patient who has a history of abuse associates that abuse with specific persons and then generalizes his or her fear response to other persons, so that all or nearly all people elicit a Pavlovian fear response. Additionally, the patient with a history of early trauma demonstrates Skinnerian learning by avoiding people in order to decrease the fear response (negative reinforcement). While this strategy of interpersonal avoidance decreases anxiety, social isolation serves to maintain chronic depression [23].

For persons who have a history of trauma in the early environment, other traumatic events (e.g., combat, rape) reinforce previous learning. Specifically, subsequent traumas can heighten the fear response and further generalize interpersonal avoidance. Therefore, traumas from which distinct PTSD symptoms develop reinforce what was previously learned in the toxic early environment.

In addition, McCullough [3] also references Piaget's theory of cognitive development in his formulation of the chronic depressive patient as having a predominant reliance on preoperational or concrete thought processes, which are characterized by precasual, prelogical thinking that precludes the use of abstractions and interpersonal empathy. As such the chronic depressive patient is stuck in a pattern of avoidant behaviors that limit alternative perspective taking and cognitive flexibility. Within this preoperational cognitive frame the individual fails to make perceptual connection between their behavior and the outcome of interpersonal events. Therefore they find it difficult to learn the consequences of particular behaviors that lead to negative outcomes. This lack of *perceived functionality* is hypothesized by McCullough [23] to be a precursor of learned helplessness and hopelessness that is characteristically exhibited by the chronically depressed patients.

7. Cognitive behavioral analysis system for psychotherapy

McCullough's Cognitive-Behavioral Analysis System of Psychotherapy (CBASP) is the only empirically supported treatment developed specifically for chronic depression [3]. CBASP offers a type of therapy that addresses the relational aspect of chronic depression and PTSD. The therapist using CBASP becomes a safety signal to the patient, allowing the patient to feel safe and then to move toward extinguishing the previously learned response of interpersonal avoidance [23]. Because interpersonal avoidance characterizes the chronically depressed patient as well as the patient with chronic PTSD, treatment with CBASP may pave the way for the patient to feel safe enough to remain in therapy and address the traumas that are related to the unique symptoms of PTSD, such as re-experiencing symptoms.

CBASP, as an integrative methodology, is fundamentally attuned to traumatic experiences in early development. Systematic exploration of interpersonal situations occurring in the patient's current interactions typically reveal patterns of interpretations and behaviors that reflect aspects of the individual's developmental experiences of maltreatment from caregivers, as well as significant traumatic events that have shaped their self-other perspectives. To the extent that interpretation of interpersonal situations and coping behaviors are maladaptive and rely primarily on avoidant coping strategies, it can be expected that these patterns will resurface in the therapeutic dyad. An initial task for the CBASP therapist is to collaboratively define the significant relationships in the patient's history and develop a casual conclusions stemming from these relationships that have had an adverse impact on the self-other, and world view. This process assists the therapist and the patient to arrive at a pivotal "*Transference Hypothesis*" that becomes the cornerstone for new interpersonal learning by means of the therapist's judicious use of CBASP techniques, such as "*Interpersonal Discrimination*" and "*Disciplined Personal Involvement,*" which are only mentioned here, but can be best understood by referencing McCullough [3,23].

Based on our work with depressed patients who have co-existing PTSD, the use of the *Significant Other History* (SOH) to also record salient traumatic experiences, has provided therapeutic utility for assessment and intervention. Obtaining a record of the significant people in the patient's formative history as well as the linkage to specific traumatic experiences allows the therapist to respond directly to expression of trauma symptoms as they surface in treatment.

8. Significant traumatic events

Significant traumatic events (STE) are frequently parallel the patient's recounting of their experiences leading to the casual analysis stemming from their Significant Other History. In conducting the STE the therapist collaboratively explores the primary thematic domain within the following areas: *Safety, Trust, Control, Closeness, and Self-esteem*. These thematic domains come from research conducted by Resick, et al. [30] that demonstrated that these overlapping interpersonal themes account for the predominant sources of psychological distress for traumatized patients. These connect to both intrapsychic and interpersonal changes for patients with PTSD. This adaptation to the SOH can assist therapists in understanding the impact of the patient's trauma on their cognitive-affective attributions and relational environment. In other words, what does the patient do on a cognitive, emotional, and interpersonal level when this traumatic theme is re-experienced. This is often expressed during sessions in the form of trauma related symptoms, but may also reflect an interpersonal "pull" with the therapist that is maladaptive due to distorted interpretations of the interpersonal environment.

During the treatment process, the therapist working with the co-morbid patient needs to attend to both interpersonal *hotspots* as well as trauma *hotspots*, which are typically addressed at the conclusion of the Situational Analysis. These modifications parallel and interact with the standard CBASP methods and require the therapist's mapping of trauma events along the depression timeline provided by the patient, and the addition of the Significant Trauma Event description and causal conclusion in reference to the Significant Other History. Additionally, these adaptations are reflected in the Interpersonal Discrimination Exercise (IDE) in which the patient is taught to differentiate internal arousal signals from environmental stimuli. These adaptations are reflected schematically in Figure 1.

9. Research course

Methods

In a sample of 12 male veterans, aged 48-65, diagnosed with chronic depression and PTSD, CBASP was delivered as an individual psychotherapy over the course of 24 sessions. All sessions were conducted by three clinical psychologists trained in CBASP as well as the added interventions for PTSD symptoms. In each of the cases the veterans were on psychotropic medications and had dropped out of trauma focused psychotherapy at least once prior to engaging in CBASP. Veterans with psychosis, bipolar disorder and/or current substance abuse were excluded from the sample. The adaptations, outlined above were implemented to address co-existing PTSD symptoms and each of the therapist were trained in the application of these methods.

Pretreatment measures were administered to establish baseline scores on BDI-II and PCL-C. At the end of 24 sessions of CBASP the BDI-II and PCL-C were administered again and the scores were analyzed by a t-test to determine the level of change for each measure.

Participant's narrative responses on weekly Coping Questionnaires were analyzed using the Standard Cognitive Developmental Classification System (SCDCS) that was developed by Ivey [26] to score patient narratives across cognitive domains, and was used to ascertain shifts in participants' predominant cognitive orientation.

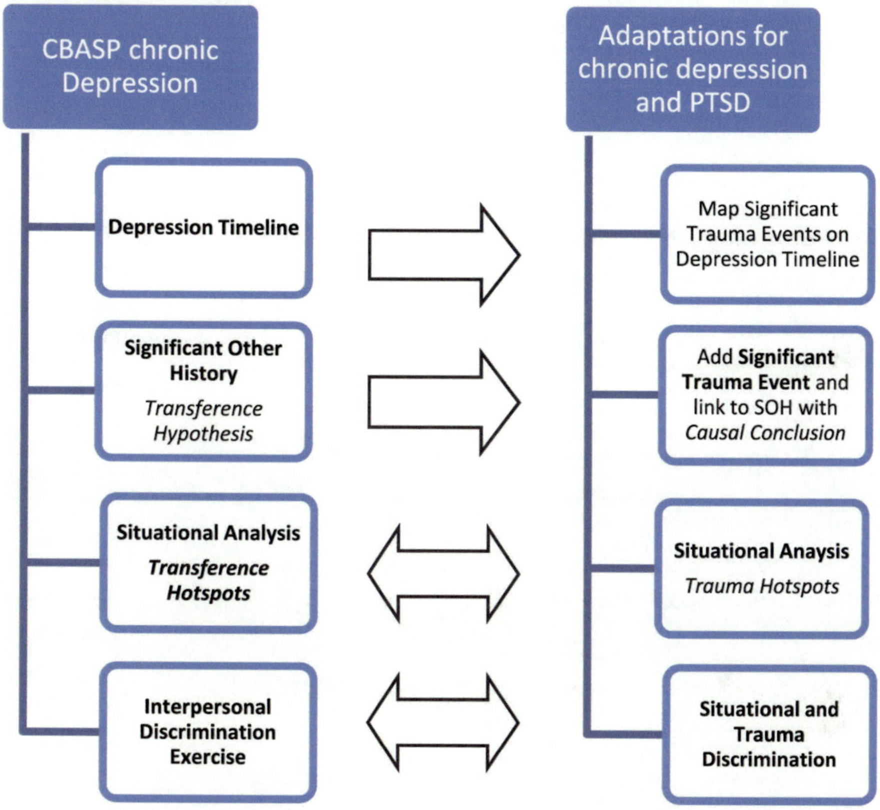

Note: Schematic shows CBASP procedures used to treat depression (left), as well as the parallel adaptations at each stage to accommodate PTSD symptoms (right).

Figure 1. Adaptations to CBASP for Co-existing PTSD and MDD

10. Results

Both the measure for depression (BDI-II), $t(11)=6.28$, $p=.00$ and for PTSD (PCL-C), $t(11)=6.99$, $p=.01$ evidenced a significant reduction at the end of treatment. The results can be seen in figure 2. There was a greater reduction in the mean BDI-II score than for PCL-C scores. Mean depression fell with mild depressive range. Mean scores on the PCL-C were higher overall and showed less reduction compared to the BDI-II. There was a significant reduction, however, even though mean PCL-C scores continued to show symptom expression for PTSD.

We were particularly interested in the Hypothesized change from concrete/preoperational cognitive processes to formal operational cognitive processes over the course of CBASP treatment. As expected, there was no significant change in sensorimotor or dialectic/systemic cognitive orientations at the end of treatment. However, there was a significant reduction in the frequency ratings for preoperational cognitions, $t(11)=8.20, p=.00$. Additionally, there was a moderate increase in the production of formal operational cognitions at the end of CBASP treatment, $t(11)=2.08$, p=.06 . These findings can be seen in figure 3.

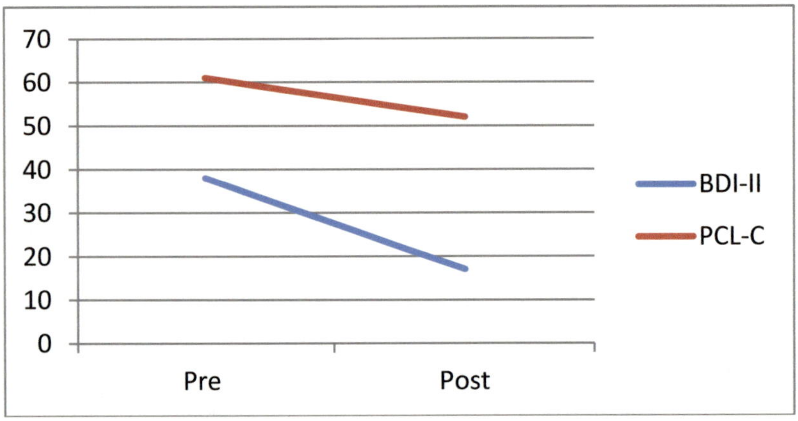

Figure 2. CBASP 24 individual sessions (N=12)

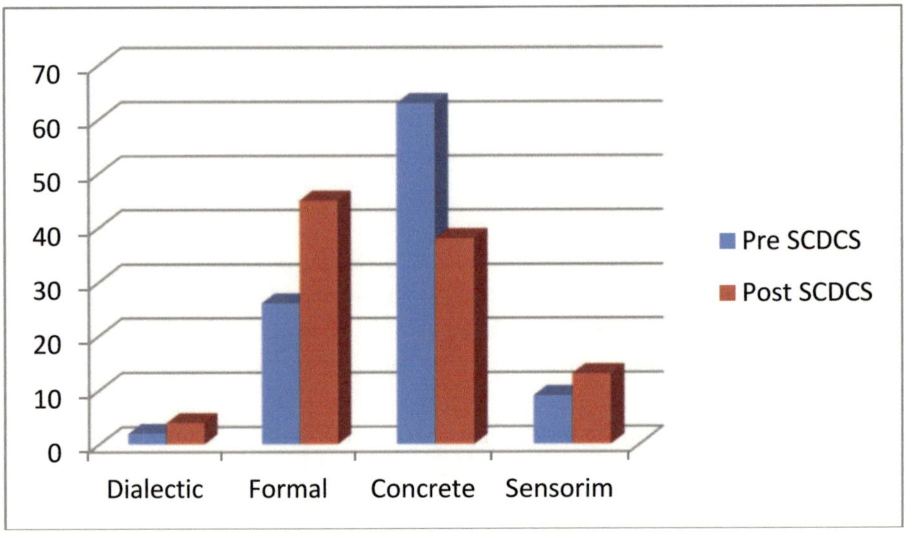

Note: Standard Cognitive Developmental Classification System (SCDCS)

Figure 3. CBASP - Cognitive-Affective Change 24 sessions (N=12)

11. Limitations and future research

This study was conducted as a preliminary investigation of the feasibility of adaptation to the CBASP method to accommodate co-morbid PTSD when working with chronically depressed patients. This was a small, homogenous sample of middle aged veterans who were not able to utilize first line trauma-focused treatments and our results may not generalize to other age, gender or cultural groups. Although there were significant results in terms of symptom reduction, the effect size is small. Future controlled research is needed on a larger, heterogeneous sample to see if these results can be replicated. It would be essential to compare co-morbid groups who receive CBASP and CBASP that has been adapted for co-existing PTSD/MDD to determine added benefits of the adapted model.

12. Summary and conclusions

In this chapter, we proposed the use of an adapted CBASP model treatment of chronic depression with co existing posttraumatic stress disorder. Given the high rate of co-occurrance and significant symptomatic interaction we propose that with specific adaptations CBASP provides an active therapeutic environment that can accommodate the patient's traumatic memories and link them to interpersonal avoidance patterns that exacerbate depressive mood. The techniques of Situational Analysis and Interpersonal Discrimination Exercises assist the patient to make clearer distinctions between historical traumatic events and their current interpersonal life.

The effectiveness of CBASP in the treatment of co-morbid PTSD and chronic MDD is being studied in veteran populations at several VA Healthcare Systems in the United States due to the significant number of treatment refractory cases that require maintenance mental health care. There are also a high ratio of young veterans returning from multiple deployments in Iraq and Afghanistan that are diagnosed with chronic forms of depression and PTSD [8]. The increased burden of delivery of effective mental health services is by no means isolated to veteran populations. Natural disasters, interpersonal violence, and increased familial stressors appear to be omnipresent over the past several years placing children and adults at risk for the chronic psychiatric conditions such as MDD and PTSD. Finding efficacious methods for early intervention and improving our service delivery system are becoming more important than ever. The potential benefits of a transdiagnostic perspective in the adaptation of CBASP to patients with chronic depressive co-morbidities, potentiates a reduction in the rate of refractory treatments outcomes.

Author details

Todd K. Favorite
University of Michigan Dept. of Psychiatry, Ann Arbor VA Healthcare System, USA

Todd Vance
University of Virginia Dept. of Psychiatry, Salem VA Healthcare System, USA

13. References

[1] Cicchetti,D., & Barnett, D. (1991). Attachment organization in maltreatment pre-schoolers. *Developmental and Psychopathology*, 3, 397-411.

[2] Bonanno, G. A., Brewin, C. R., Kaniasty, K. & La Greca, A. M, (2010). Weighing the costs of disaster: Consequences, risks, and resilience in individuals, families, and communities. *Psychological Science in the Public Interest, 11(1),* 1-49.

[3] McCullough, J.P. Jr. (2000) *Treatment for Chronic Depression: Cognitive Behavioral Analysis System of Psychotherapy.* The Guilford Press: New York, NY.

[4] Nemeroff, C.B., Heim, C.M., Thase, M.E., Klein, D.N., Rush, A.J., Schatzberg, A.F., Ninan, P.T., McCullough, J.P., Weiss, P., Dunner, D.L., Rothbaum, B.O., Kornstein, S.G., Keitner, G., & Keller, M.B. (2003). Differential responses to psychotherapy versus pharmacotherapy in the treatment of patients with chronic forms of major depression and childhood trauma. Proceedings of the National Academy of Sciences, 100, 14293-14296.

[5] Wiersma, J.E., Van Schaik, DJF, van Oppen, P., McCullough, Jr., J.P, Schoever, R.A., Dekker, J.J. et al. (2008). Treatment of chronically depressed patients: A multisite randomized controlled trial testing the effectiveness of CBASP for chronic depressions versus usual secondary care. *Biological Medical Central Psychiatry, 8,* 1-13.

[6] Foa, E.B., & Rothbaum, B.O. (1998). Treating the trauma of rape: Cognitive-Behavioral therapy for PTSD, New York: Guilford Press.

[7] Valenstein M, Austin K, Khanuja K, McCarthy JF, Owen RE, Blow FC (2004). Specialty Care for Veterans with Depression in the VHA: 2002 National Registry for Depression (NARDEP) Report. Serious Mental Illness Treatment Research and Evaluation Center.

[8] Hoge, C.W., Auchterlonie, J.L., Milliken, C.S.(2006). Mental health problems, use of mental health services, and attrition from military service after returning from deployment to iraq or afghanistan. *JAMA*, 295, 9, 1023-1032.

[9] Chermack, S.T., Zivin, K., Valenstein M., Ilgen ,M., Austin K.L., Wryobeck J., Blow, F.C. (2008). The Prevalence and Predictors of Mental Health Treatment Services in a National Sample of Depressed Veterans. Medical Care. 46(8):813-820.

[10] Gerrity, M.S., Corson, K., & Dobscha, S.K. (2007) Screening for posttraumatic stress disorder in VA primary care patients with depression symptoms. *Journal of General Internal Medicine, 22,* 1321-1324.

[11] Campbell, D.G., Felker, B.L., Liu, C., Yano, E.M., Kirchner, J.E., Chan, D., Rubenstein, L.V., & Chaney, E.F. (2007). Prevalence of depression-PTSD comorbidity: Implications for clinical practice guidelines and primary care-based interventions. *Journal of General Internal Medicine, 22,* 711-718.

[12] Kessler, R.C, Sonnega, A., Bromet, E., Hughes, M., Nelson,C.B.(1995). Posttraumatic Stress Disorder in the National Comorbidity Survey, *Arch Gen Psychiatry*. 52(12):1048-1060.

[13] American Psychiatric Association (2000) *Diagnostic and statistical manual of mental disorders, fourth edition, text revision.* Washington, DC, American Psychiatric Association.

[14] Cochran, S.V., Rabinowitz, F.E. (2003) Gender-sensitive recommendations for assessment and treatment of depression in men. *Professional Psychology: Research and Practice*, 34(2), 132-140.

[15] Magovcevic, M., Addis, M.E. (2008) The masculine depression scale: Development and psychometric evaluation. *Psychology of Men & Masculinity*, 9(3), 117-132.

[16] Yehuda, R., Giller, E.L., Southwick, S.M., Lowy, M.T., Mason, J.W. (1991). Hypothalamic-pituitary-adrenal dysfunction in posttraumatic stress disorder. *Biol Psychiatry*. 15;30(10):1031-48.

[17] Rauch, S., Favorite, T., Giardino, N., Porcari, C., Martis, B., Liberzon, I. (2009). Relationship between anxiety, depression, and health satisfaction among veterans with PTSD. *Journal of Affective Disorders*, 2010;121(1-2):165-8.

[18] Briere, J. (2002) Treating adult survivors of severe childhood abuse and neglect: Further development of an integrative model. In J.E.B. Meyers, L. Berliner, J. Briere, C.T. Hendrix, T. Reid, & C. Jenny (Eds.) (2002) *The APSAC handbook on child maltreatment, 2nd Edition.* Newbury Park, CA: Sage Publications.

[19] Kessler, R.C., Berglund, P., Delmer, O., Jin, R., Merikangas, K.R., & Walters, E.E. (2005a). Lifetime prevalence and age-of-onset distributions of DSM-IV disorders in the National Comorbidity Survey Replication. *Archives of General Psychiatry, 62(6)*: 593-602.

[20] Herman, J. L. (1992) *Trauma and Recovery*. Basic Books.

[21] Resick, P.A., Nishith, P., Griffin, M.G. (2003) How well does cognitive-behavioral therapy treat symptoms of complex PTSD? An examination of child sexual abuse survivors within a clinical trial. *CNS Spectr.* 8(5), 340-355.

[22] Brady, K.T., Killeen, T.K., Brewerton, T., & Lucerini, S. (2000) Comorbidity of psychiatric disorders and posttraumatic stress disorder. *Journal of Clinical Psychiatry, 61 (suppl 7)*, 22-32.

[23] McCullough, J.P. Jr. (2008) The cognitive behavioral analysis system of psychotherapy: A value-added strategy for chronic depression. *Psychiatric Times*, 25 (10),

[24] McCullough, J.P., Jr. (2006). Treating chronic depression with disciplined personal involvement: CBASP. Springer-Verlag: New York, LLC

[25] Monson, C.M., Schnurr, P.P., Resick, P.A., Friedman, M.J., Young-Xu, Y., & Stevens, S.P. (2006) Cognitive Processing Therapy for veterans with military-related Posttraumatic Stress Disorder. *Journal of Consulting and Clinical Psychology, 74*, 898-907.

[26] Ivey, A.E., Rigazio-DiGilio, S.A. (1991). The standard cognitive-developmental classification system. In A.E. Ivey, *Developmental strategies for helpers: Individual, family and network interventions* (pp.301-306). Pacific Grove, CA: Brooks/Cole.

Chapter 12

Group Intervention for Chronic Depression and PTSD

Todd K. Favorite and Kayla J. Conrad

Additional information is available at the end of the chapter

http://dx.doi.org/10.5772/51226

1. Introduction

In this chapter, we propose the use of the Cognitive Behavioral Analysis System for Psychotherapy as a group modality in the treatment of co-morbid chronic depression and posttraumatic stress disorder. CBASP has been found to be effective for the treatment of chronic depression and the functional impairments often associated with this disorder (i.e., pessimism, sense of failure, lack of satisfaction, guilt, sense of punishment, self-hate, self-accusations, irritability, social withdrawal, indecisiveness, work inhibition, sleep disturbance, loss of appetite, weight loss, somatic preoccupation, and loss of libido, etc.). [1,2,3,4,5,6]. Although large studies such as Klien et al. [6,7,8] have focused on individual treatment for which it was developed, CBASP has been shown to be feasible as a group treatment in U.S., Canada, and in Germany. Clinical application of group CBASP in the U.S., thus far, has focused on combat veterans, who have been shown to be particularly vulnerable to Posttraumatic stress disorder (PTSD) and chronic depression [9]. We will outline the nature of these often chronic, co-existing symptoms and then present the rationale. For group CBASP interventions with co-morbid population.

The rationale for developing a group protocol for CBASP is based on a number of variables. For example, group involvement for chronically depressed patient reduces social isolation which limits opportunities to experience social interaction and new learning. In addition, interactions among patients with similar symptoms and experiences may create opportunities for validation, belonging, and the generation of hope that may not be as strong in individual psychotherapy. Group interactions also provide an in-vivo learning environment that maximizes interpersonal exposure and enhances social skill development. We have found that peer modeling has a positive impact on attendance as well as increased compliance with assignments and in session participation. Finally, within the VA Healthcare

System where we have treated combat veterans, the provision of. Group psychotherapy allows greater access to treatment for growing numbers of veterans seeking help.

The rationale for developing a group format for this established, evidence-based treatment for chronic depression stems, in part, from the need for greater access to treatment for increasingly numbers of veterans returning from combat with PTSD and MDD symptoms. Group methodologies have been shown to be very effective in working with homogeneous populations, both in terms of cultural characteristics and symptom presentation [10]. In fact, veterans share a distinct military culture and as such report a "bond" and increased sense of cohesion with the experiences of each other than they do with most civilians [11]. Utilizing this commonality to enhance a sense of social connection and support as well as counteract patterns of interpersonal avoidance may improve treatment outcomes for this frequently treatment resistant population.

In a meta-analysis of 48 group therapy studies of depression treatment, McDermut, Miller, Brown [12] found that patients treated in group modalities reported a significant reduction in depressive symptoms when compared to 85% of untreated patients. In studies exploring the benefits of culturally relevant intervention strategies, Ginder and Smith [13] found that when group interventions with homogeneous cultural groups, they were four times more effective than groups that were culturally nonspecific.

2. Problem statement

2.1. Co-morbid MDD and PTSD

Veterans often present with a co-morbid symptom presentation, and co-morbid symptom expression has demonstrated poorer treatment outcomes across psychopathologies [14,15]. The co-morbidities of chronically depressed individuals include anxiety disorders and substance dependence, somatic and physiological disorders and include a range of personality disorders [16,17]. Understanding how these various symptom structures and clinical presentations relate, and developing effective strategies for addressing clinical concerns is paramount, if we hope to effectively treat patients with co-morbid depression and PTSD.

We are focusing on the co-occurrence of chronic depression and chronic posttraumatic stress disorder (PTSD), because it represents the most common co-occurring symptom set for males (48%) and females (49%) of any Axis I disorders, with the exception of PTSD and alcohol abuse for males (51%) [18]. This co-morbidity has also become increasingly critical to our understanding of the etiology of chronic depression from a developmental perspective. For the patient presenting with early onset chronic depression we can typically find a developmental profile of maltreatment in the form of emotional abuse or neglect, physical abuse or neglect, and sexual abuse [19]. However, interpersonal maltreatment is not the only childhood traumatic experience occurring within the context of family and caregiver relationships, individuals are also subject to a range of losses or "psychological insults" [20], such as warfare, sociopolitical stressors, and environmental disasters. These stressors often have a negative impact on individuals' views of themselves, others, and their world [20].

The foundational derailment of secure attachments and normative cognitive-affective development produces negative self-other attributions and an enhanced fear response toward unfamiliar or threatening environmental stimuli. Behaviorally, this is manifested in a predominantly avoidant coping strategy, which, in turn, increases the strength of the fear structure [21]. Chronic depressive trajectories of late onset or adult traumatic events have received less attention in the literature and yet represent approximately 8% of the chronically depressed adult population. For instance, over 50% of military veterans diagnosed with PTSD carry a diagnosis of depression lasting for two or more years with no evidence of depressive disorder prior to their military duty [22,9]. This co-morbid PTSD/chronically depressed population has a high treatment refractory rate for both antidepressant medication and psychosocial interventions [23].

PTSD is a chronic often disabling disorder that affects approximately 6.8% of the U.S. population with a lifetime prevalence of 3.6% for males, and 9.7% for females [18]. In the Veterans Health Study [22] it was shown that 31% of the over 2,000 veterans sampled, had experienced significant depressive symptoms with 54% of these depressed veterans evidencing one or more psychiatric co-morbidity, predominantly PTSD. Additionally, 88% had medical co-morbidities such as hypertension, heart disease, diabetes, and degenerative joint disease. The lifetime prevalence of Major Depressive Disorder in patient populations such as combat veterans who have a diagnosis of PTSD has been reported to be as high as 68%[24]. Large community sample co-morbidity research has demonstrated that individuals who have PTSD are 3-5 times more likely to develop Major Depressive Disorder over their lifetime [18]. There is a complex interaction among neurobiological and psychosocial factors that involve the overactivation of the hypothalamic-pituitary-adrenal axis [25]. While the empirical literature has begun to outline the interaction of these two disorders, most of the treatment literature focuses on effective interventions with either MDD or PTSD alone. This presents a gap in our understanding about how to treat patients with co-morbid chronic depression/PTSD.

That we are treating interacting disorders rather than two separate or sequential disorders complicates both treatment and the evidence base of the treatment modality, which is based on data from single diagnosis samples. Regarding the complexity of treatment, the clinician has, in the case of PTSD, the treatment goal of reducing patients' trauma symptoms when their motivation is poor and their coping strategies (i.e., avoidance, substance abuse, anger) are maladaptive and entrenched. When treatment for chronic depression is linked to that of PTSD, treatment can be compromised and derailed by the expression of trauma symptoms that may undermine the patient's sense of safety and trust and reduce treatment adherence.

As clinicians working in the Veterans Administration HealthCare System, we have noted that when these disorders co-occur, patients report greater symptom distress, treatment interventions can become highly problematic, and/or patients become treatment refractory [23]. Although first-line PTSD treatments, such as Prolonged Exposure Therapy (PE) and

Cognitive Processing Therapy (CPT) for non-comorbid PTSD report a remission of acute depressive symptoms when PTSD symptoms are actively addressed, some chronically depressed patients find it difficult to engage in and complete trauma focused therapies that activate traumatic memories and require adherence to between-session imaginal and in-vivo exposures. This problem may be reflected in a 23% drop-out rate for civilians receiving trauma-focused therapy and as high as 30% dropout for veterans with PTSD. Many of these veterans had co-occurring disorders, including MDD [24].

3. Application area

3.1. CBASP group application

The adaption of CBASP to a group treatment maintains the core structure and principles of the individual treatment while expanding on behavioral skill development and behavioral activation. The structure of the CBASP group follows the outline provided below, which provides for pretreatment screening and education, treatment measures and co-construction of the *transference hypothesis,* which is generalized to the impact on the group environment rather than specifically on the therapist as in individual CBASP treatment.

3.2. Pre-treatment interview

Screening and Baseline measures

- Interview and differential diagnosis MINI v6,
- Significant Other History (SOH), *Transference Hypothesis*
- Beck Depression Inventory -II
- CBASP Interpersonal Questionnaire (CIQ)
- Depression Timeline
- Interpersonal Impact Inventory (IMI)
- Interpersonal Inventory of Problems (IIP)

3.3. Session structure

- Check-in (mood and activity level) 10 minutes
- Presentation of Coping Questionnaire * 50 minutes
- New learning, i.e., behavioral skills, 20 minutes
- Consolidation of new learning 10 minutes
- Assignment and troubleshooting

*Each member is responsible for 3 CQs each week.

3.4. Session 1-6 initial phase

Primary focus is on the development of Situational Analysis using the Coping Questionnaire:

- Situational "slice of time"

- Development of narrative (beginning, mid, end points, behavioral focus)
- Identify situational interpretations or "reads"
- Actual Outcome=Desired Outcome
- Remediation of interpretations and development of Action Interpretations
- Generalization of learning

Introduction of Behavioral Activation - Daily monitoring sheet and identification of depressant vs. antidepressant behaviors

3.5. Sessions 6-10 early treatment

Continued review of Situational Analyses, and Future Situational Analyses with focus on developing new behavioral skills.

- Active listening/communication skills
- Assertiveness
- Emotion Regulation skills
- Monitoring and incremental increase antidepressant activities
- Role plays to practice new interpersonal behaviors generated in group, i.e., *"let's try that out and see how it works"*

3.6. Session 10-12 mid- treatment

Situational Analyses and Future Situational Analyses with focus on:

- Interpersonal Impact Inventory (IMI)
- Identification of interpersonal "hot spots" related to Significant Other History *transference hypothesis* for each group member.
- Focus on behavioral manifestation of *transference hypothesis* in interpersonal life.
- Link behaviors to circumplex – role play alternative behaviors, and cognitions that mediate interpersonal "pulls."
- Review the impact of behaviors on achieving Desired Outcomes

3.7. Session 12-18 mid-treatment

Situational Analyses and Future Situational Analyses with focus on:

- Improving behavioral skills, i.e., behavioral activation, communication, assertiveness, emotion regulation
- Complete Interpersonal Discrimination Exercise (IDE) based on Situational Analyses
- Generalization and consolidation of new learning

3.8. Session 18-24 late treatment

CBASP skills are being practiced weekly:

- Situational Analysis and Future SAs
- Interpersonal interactions and behavioral skills: Behavioral Activation, Active Listening, Assertiveness, Emotion regulation
- Interpersonal Discrimination Exercise based on situational "hotspots"

3.9. Sessions 24-28 termination and relapse prevention

- Review of basic principles of learning theory and the issues related to extinction trial
- Individualized behavioral practice plan, identification of roadblocks, supports, and contacts
- Group feedback of individual gains, areas of vulnerability, and role in the group
- Establish future meeting dates and support contacts

4. Research course

4.1. Method

In a study conducted at the Ann Arbor Veterans Healthcare System, 52 male veterans, aged 55-66 with PTSD and MDD were treated using CBASP group therapy for 28 weeks [26]. A comparative sample of 45 male veterans, aged 49-62, were treated with a supportive therapy for the same number of sessions. There was exclusion criteria for psychosis/schizophrenia, bipolar disorder, and active substance abuse. In each of these group therapy conditions, chronic depression was the primary diagnosis, PTSD was secondary. All participants were on antidepressant medications and dosage was unchanged during the group intervention. Symptom measurement, using the BDI-II [27] and the PSTD Checklist-C [28] were given to all therapy participants at the beginning and end of treatment. These measures were again given at 1 month and 6 month follow-up.

4.2. Research results

Data was collected and analyzed using SPSS version 18. Group data was compared using paired t-test. There was a significant improvement in the CBASP group, $t\ (51) = 5.12$, $p< .004$ for depression and PTSD symptoms $t\ (51) =3.24$, $p<.05$, as compared to no significant change in the supportive treatment group $t\ (44) = 1.15$, *ns* (Figure 1).

The CBASP group was measured at the end of 1 month post treatment and again after 6 months post treatment to assertain the durability of the effects of treatment. The results of the treatment sessions and follow up measures on the BDI-II and PCL-C are seen in Figure 2. Depression symptoms demonstrated increase at 1 month and 6 month follow–up assessment compared to end of treatment level. The PCL-C continued to drop at 1 month and then showed a increase at 6 months. The increase for both the BDI-II and PCL-C during the follow up phase were that was nonsignificant.

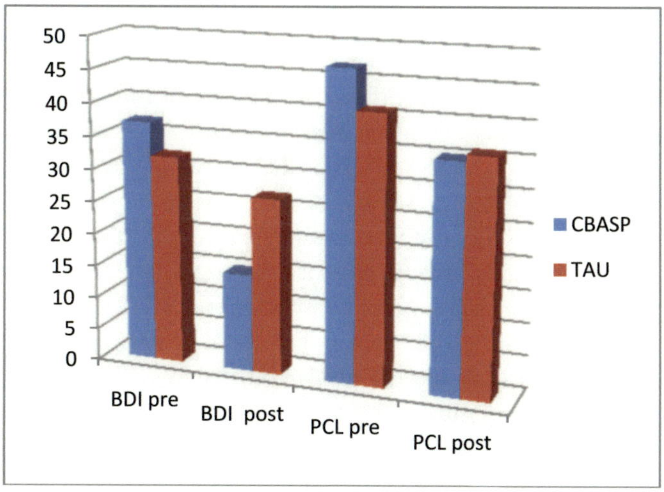

Note: CBASP group N=52 and TAU group N=45. BDI=Beck Depression Inventory–II, PCL-C= PTSD Checklist-Civilian.

Figure 1. CBASP and TAU Pre and Post scores on BDI-II and PCL-C

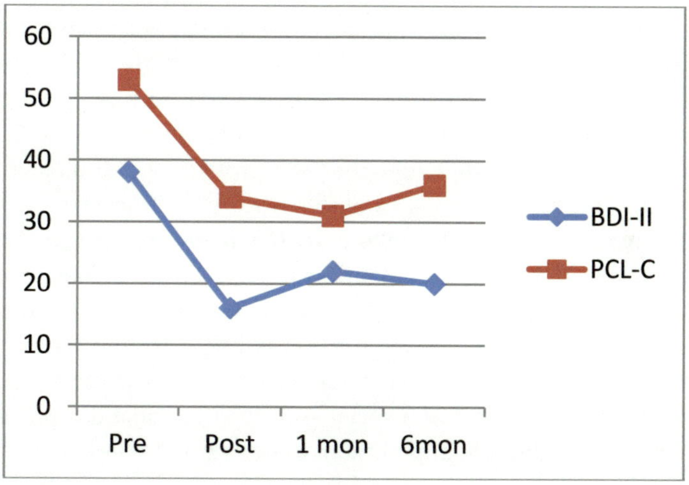

Figure 2. CBASP mean scores on BDI-II and PCL-C (N=52)

Figure 2 CBASP session scores on BDI-II and PCL-C with 1 and 6 months follow up.

5. Limitations and future research

The conclusions drawn from this sample of male veterans with chronic depressive disorders and co-morbid PTSD, demonstrates the feasibility of CBASP as a treatment for co-morbid MDD/PTSD with significant reductions in depression and PTSD symptoms compared to treatment as usual. The lack of randomization, absence of a control condition, and a relatively small effect size represent some of the limitations in this study. Nevertheless, the results suggest that using group CBASP to address co-morbid chronic depression and PTSD provides a feasible means of addressing the complexities of these co-occurring disorders.

The direction of future research is focused on dismantling of the CBASP method to identify the relative power of the active mechanisms within the model as well as their interrelationship and impact on outcome. In addition, we are actively exploring different configurations and dosages of the group method to determine the most effective delivery system. This includes explore the added benefit of parallel individual CBASP sessions as well as providing twice weekly group sessions to see if these agumentations provide significant additive effects to weekly, group only sessions. We believe that it is essential to provide termination phase sessions that are paced to the patients' learning aquisition and consolidation. This may necessiate spread out session at the end of group treatment, with the expectation that this might minimize the extinction effect and symptom relapse.

6. Conclusions

CBASP group therapy shows promise in the facilitation of cognitive, emotional, and behavioral change by providing the opportunity for patients to process reactions with other group members who share similar life experiences. Pilot studies have shown CBASP to be feasible and effective in a group format [29] whether alone or in combination with individual therapy. In this chapter we have focused on culturally specific application for group CBASP to treat outpatients in US Veteran Administration Medical Centers; however, CBASP group is being studied in heterogeneous groups and inpatient applications in Canada, Germany the U.S. and UK. Data from this research will serve to inform clinicians as to relative effectiveness of this methodology within a group context, but will begin to address questions about CBASP's therapeutic mechanisms and their role in promoting reduction in the symptoms of chronic depression. Beyond the potential advantages of CBASP groups in terms of greater treatment access and cost-effectiveness, there are the nonspecific factors such as enhanced social support, normalization of symptoms, and interpersonal skill development within a social context that make it a powerful foundation for behavioral change and a durable impediment to depression relapse.

Author details

Todd K. Favorite and Kayla J. Conrad
University of Michigan, Dept. of Psychiatry, Ann Arbor VA Healthcare System, Michigan USA

7. References

[1] Schramm, E., Zobel, I., Dykierek, P., Kech, S., Brakemeier, E-L., Külz, A., Berger, M. (2011). Cognitive behavioral analysis system of psychotherapy versus interpersonal psychotherapy for early-onset chronic depression: A randomized pilot study. *Journal of Affective Disorders, 129,* 109-116.

[2] McCullough, J.P., Jr., Lord, B.D., Conley, K.A. & Martin, A.M. (2010). A method for conducting intensive psychological studies with early-onset chronically depressed patients. *American Journal of Psychotherapy, 64,* 317-338.

[3] McCullough, J. P. Jr. & Penberthy, J.K. (2011). Cognitive Behavioral Analysis System of Psychotherapy for chronic depression. In Springer, W.W., Allen, R. & Beevers, C.G. (Eds.). *Treatment of Depression in Adolescents and Adults: Clinician's Guide to Evidence-Based Practice*. Hoboken, NJ: Wiley & Sons. Chapter 5, pp. 183-220.

[4] Wiersma, J.E., Van Schaik, DJF, van Oppen, P., McCullough, Jr., J.P, Schoever, R.A., Dekker, J.J. et al. (2008). Treatment of chronically depressed patients: A multisite randomized controlled trial testing the effectiveness of CBASP for chronic depressions versus usual secondary care. *Biological Medical Central Psychiatry, 8,* 1-13.

[5] Blalock, J.A., Fouladi, R.T., Cinciripini, P.M., Markowitz, C., Klein, .N., Rothbaum, .O., Arnow, B.A., Manber, R., Riso, L.P., Sui, D., McCullough, Jr., J.P. *(April, 2008).* Cognitive and behavioral mediators of combined pharmacotherapy and psychotherapy of chronic depression. *Cognitive Therapy and Research, 32,* 197-211.

[6] Klein, D.N., Schwartz, J.E., Santiago, N.J., Vivian, D., Vocisano, C., Castonguay, L.G., Arnow, B.A., Blalock, J.A., Markowitz, J.C., Rothbaum, B.O., & McCullough, Jr. J.P. (2003). Therapeutic alliance in depression treatment: Controlling for prior change and patient characteristics. *Journal of Consulting and Clinical Psychology, 71,* 997-1006.

[7] Nemeroff, C.B., Heim, C.M., Thase, M.E., Klein, D.N., Rush, A.J., Schatzberg, A.F., Ninan, P.T., McCullough, J.P., Weiss, P., Dunner, D.L., Rothbaum, B.O., Kornstein, S.G., Keitner, G., & Keller, M.B. (2003). Differential responses to psychotherapy versus pharmacotherapy in the treatment of patients with chronic forms of major depression and childhood trauma. Proceedings of the National Academy of Sciences, 100, 14293-14296.

[8] Santiago, NJ, Klein, DN, Vivian, D, Arnow, BA, Blalock,JA, Kocsis, JH, Markowitz, JC, Manber, R, Riso, LP, Rothbaum, BO, Rush, AJ, Thase, ME, McCullough. JP, Jr. (2005). The therapeutic alliance and CBASP-specific skill acquisition in the treatment of chronic depression. *Cognitive Therapy and Research, 29,* 803–817.

[9] Hoge, C.W., Auchterlonie, J.L., Milliken, C.S.(2006). Mental health problems, use of mental health services, and attrition from military service after returning from deployment to iraq or afghanistan. *JAMA,* 295, 9, 1023-1032.

[10] Sue, S., Zane, N. (2009). The role of culture and cultural techniques in psychotherapy: A critique and reformulation. *Asian American Journal of Psychology,* 1, 3-14.

[11] Reger, M.A., Etherage, J. R., Reger, G.M., Gahm, G.A (2008).Civilian Psychologists in an Army Culture: The Ethical Challenge of Cultural Competence. Military Psychology Special Issue: Clinical Military Psychology Ethics. 20, (1), 21-35.

[12] McDermut, W., Miller, I.W., Brown, R.A. (2001). The Efficacy of Group Psychotherapy for Depression: A Meta-analysis and Review of the Empirical Research. *Clinical Psychology: Science and Practice,* 8, 98–116.

[13] Griner, D., Smith, T.B. (2006). Culturally adapted mental health intervention: A meta-analytic review. *Psychotherapy: Theory, Research, Practice, Training,* 43, 531-548.

[14] Keitner, G.I., Ryan, C.E., Miller, I.W., Kohn, R. & Epstein, N.B. (1991). Twelve month outcomes of patients with major depression and comorbid psychiatric or medical illness (chronic depression). *American Journal of Psychiatry,* 148, 345-350.

[15] Rohde, P., Lewinsohn, P.M., & Seeley, J.R. (1991). Comorbidity of unipolar depression: II. Comorbidity with other mental health disorders in adolescents and adults. *Journal of Abnormal Psychology*, 100, 214-222.

[16] Kaye, A.L., McCullough, J.P., Roberts, W.C., McCune, K.J., Hamptom, C., & Kornstein, S.G. (1994). Differentiating affective and characterological DSM-III-R psychopathology in non-treatment, community unipolar depressives. Depression, 2, 80-88.

[17] McCullough, J.P. (1996). The importance of diagnosing comorbid personality disorder with patients who are chronically depressed. *Depressive Disorders: Index and Reviews*, 1 (1), 16-17.

[18] Kessler, R.C, Sonnega, A., Bromet, E., Hughes, M., Nelson,C.B.(1995). Posttraumatic Stress Disorder in the National Comorbidity Survey, *Arch Gen Psychiatry.* 52(12):1048-1060.

[19] Cicchetti,D., & Barnett, D. (1991). Attachment organization in maltreatment pre-schoolers. *Developmental and Psychopathology*, 3, 397-411.

[20] Bonnano, Brewin, Kaniasty, & La Greca (2010). Weighing the Costs of Disaster: Consequences, Risks, and Resilience in Individuals, Families, and Communities Psychological Science in the Public Interest,11: 1-49.

[21] Foa, E.B., & Rothbaum, B.O. (1998). Treating the trauma of rape: Cognitive-Behavioral therapy for PTSD, New York: Guilford Press.

[22] Valenstein M, Austin K, Khanuja K, McCarthy JF, Owen RE, Blow FC. (2004). Specialty Care for Veterans with Depression in the VHA: 2002 National Registry for Depression (NARDEP) Report. Serious Mental Illness Treatment Research and Evaluation Center.

[23] Chermack ST, Zivin K, Valenstein M, Ilgen M, Austin KL, Wryobeck J, Blow FC. (2008). The Prevalence and Predictors of Mental Health Treatment Services in a National Sample of Depressed Veterans. Medical Care. 46(8):813-820.

[24] Rauch, S., Favorite, T., Giardino, N., Porcari, C., Martis, B., Liberzon, I. (2009). Relationship between anxiety, depression, and health satisfaction among veterans with PTSD. *Journal of Affective Disorders,* 2010;121(1-2):165-8.

[25] Yehuda, R., Giller, E.L., Southwick, S.M., Lowy, M.T., Mason, J.W. (1991). Hypothalamic-pituitary-adrenal dysfunction in posttraumatic stress disorder. *Biol Psychiatry*. 15;30(10):1031-48.

[26] Favorite, T.K., Messina, M., Smith, E., Porcari, C. (2009). Group Cognitive Behavioral Analysis System for Psychotherapy in the Treatment of Chronic Comorbid PTSD and Depression. Association for Behavioral and Cognitive Therapies, 41st Annual Convention, New York, NY

[27] Beck A.T., Steer, R.A., Brown, G.K. (1996). Manual for the Beck Depression Inventory-II. San Antonio, TX: Psychological Corporation.

[28] Norris, F.H., Hamblen, J.L. (2004). Standardized self-report measures of civilian trauma and PTSD. In J.P. Wilson, T.M. Keane & T. Martin (Eds.), *Assessing psychological trauma and PTSD* (pp. 63-102). New York: Guilford Press.

[29] Favorite,T.K., Sayegh,L. (2010). Cognitive Behavioral Analysis System of Psychotherapy (CBASP): Adapted to group therapy for outpatients. World Congress of Behavioral and Cognitive Therapies, Boston, MA

Chapter 13

Depression, Vascular Conditions and Chronicity

Adrie Seldenrijk, Nicole Vogelzangs, Patricia van Oppen,
Brenda Penninx and Anneke van Schaik

Additional information is available at the end of the chapter

http://dx.doi.org/10.5772/51623

1. Introduction

In recent years, the association between depression and cardiovascular disease has been studied extensively (Nicholson *et al.* 2006; Van der Kooy *et al.* 2007). Cardiovascular disease (CVD) refers to those conditions that affect the heart and blood vessels, including amongst others coronary heart disease, cerebrovascular disease, and peripheral artery disease. According to the World Health Organisation, cardiovascular disease now is the primary cause of death around the world. Depressive disorders enhance the development of CVD by both behavioural and biological pathways. They may contribute to unhealthy lifestyle habits that increase cardiovascular risk, such as smoking, low physical activity, and unhealthy diet. Also, this psychiatric condition is associated with activation of the immune system, blood coagulation, hyperactivity of the physiological stress system (e.g. hypothalamic pituitary adrenal axis), and other biological mechanisms which are thought to be involved in de development and progression of CVD. As these behavioural and biological factors are more continuously present in persons with chronic depression, it can be assumed that the risk of developing CVD is even higher in chronically depressed subjects, although this has not been clearly demonstrated yet. The first aim of this Chapter is to summarize what is known about the association between depression and vascular conditions. An overview of the literature will be given and a more detailed description of recent findings from a large Dutch cohort study on depression and anxiety (Seldenrijk *et al.* 2010; Seldenrijk *et al.* 2011b; Vogelzangs *et al.* 2010) will be presented. The second aim is to discuss the relevance of reviewed findings for chronic depression.

2. Depression and vascular comorbidity

2.1. Existing evidence on association between depression and CVD

A recent meta-analysis (Nicholson *et al.* 2006) has reviewed prospective cohort studies that reported on the association between depression and coronary outcomes in healthy populations and in coronary heart patients. Twenty-one studies in healthy populations were identified that investigated the incidence of myocardial infarction or fatal coronary heart disease over a mean follow-up period of 10.8 years. It was shown that depression was associated with an 81% increased risk of new coronary events. Studies using clinical measures of depression reported a higher risk than those using symptom scales. Another meta-analysis (Van der Kooy *et al.* 2007), which additionally included cerebrovascular disease outcomes, has shown an even more distinct difference between the effect sizes of clinical depression versus depressive symptoms in association with subsequent CVD (risk ratio of 2.54 versus 1.39, respectively). The authors suggest that this difference may indicate a dose-response relationship between depressed mood and the development of CVD. The meta-analysis by Nicholson and colleagues also identified thirty-four prognostic studies that investigated the association between depression and coronary or all cause mortality in coronary heart patients over a mean follow-up period of 3.2 years (Nicholson *et al.* 2006). Crude results indicated that depressed patients had an 80% higher risk to die during the follow-up compared with non-depressed patients. Results from studies that also adjusted for confounding indicate that 88% of the associations were independent from major coronary risk factors. Although the high risk estimates may be inflated due to incomplete and biased reporting of adjustment, these meta-analytic data provide evidence for depression as a risk factor in the development and course of CVD. In addition, (Carney & Freedland, 2009) have reviewed the literature in order to identify subtypes of depression which are associated with the highest risk of cardiac events in coronary heart patients. They discuss existing evidence from several large clinical trials, such as ENRICHD, MIND-IT, and SADHART. The authors conclude that in particular patients who are unsuccessfully treated for depression following an acute coronary syndrome were found to be at risk for cardiac morbidity or mortality.

This paragraph has illustrated the now large body of literature relating depression to clinical end-points of CVD based on e.g. general practice or hospitalization records. However, the emergence of modern imaging techniques has enabled to study pre- or subclinical cardiovascular outcomes. By examination of subclinical CVD, the temporal sequence and the pathophysiological pathways of the associations might be better understood.

2.2. Arteries and subclinical CVD

Detailed information on different aspects of the cardiovascular burden throughout the body can be obtained using non-invasive methods. Before an overview is given of the research regarding depression and subclinical CVD markers, we will first give some background information on the function and structure of human arteries, and the changes that reflect subclinical disease.

2.2.1. Function and structure of arteries

The arterial tree has a conduit and a cushioning function. The first refers to its delivery of oxygenized blood to bodily organs and tissue, and the second to the converting of an intermittent, pulsatile flow to a more continuous blood flow. With respect to the composition of the arterial wall, three layers or 'tunica' can be distinguished from the inside to the outside: the intima, the media, and the adventitia (Zarins & Glagov, 2004). The tunica intima is made up of endothelial cells and subendothelial connective tissue. The endothelium, being in direct contact with the blood flow, forms a permeability barrier and thrombo-resistant lining, thereby supporting the artery's conduit function. The tunica media is a thick layer that predominantly consists of elastic fibres and smooth muscle cells. These components are essential for elasticity and contractility, the characteristics needed for cushioning. The adventitia, the outer layer of the arterial wall, is composed of supportive and nutritive tissue, including collagen (a protein that makes up connective tissue) bundles, fibroblasts, and small blood vessels.

2.2.2. *Vascular disease processes*

Although changes in the structure and function of arterial walls to some extent reflect adaptive processes that are related to age and blood pressure, they also mark 'subclinical' pathophysiological processes which lead to CVD. Two separate, but overlapping conditions that affect medium and large arteries are *athero*sclerosis and *arterio*sclerosis (Mackey *et al.* 2007). Atherosclerosis primarily compromises the conduit functioning of an artery, but is also associated with increased stiffness. Atherosclerosis starts in the intima and includes focal thickening, the formation of athērōmata (literally: tumors full gruel-like matter). Those atheromatous plaques are built up from fatty substances, cholesterol, cellular waste products, calcium and fibrin, and cause the arteries to narrow and be less flexible. Atherosclerosis therefore can (partially) block the oxygen-rich blood supply, leading to ischemic events. Arteriosclerosis, or hardening of the arteries, impairs the cushioning function, and along the line increases the risk of endothelial damage, i.e. atherosclerosis. Arteriosclerosis starts in the media en includes decreasing levels of elastin and increased amounts of collagen and calcium, which leads to arterial stiffening.

2.2.3. *Subclinical CVD markers*

One of the ways to measure subclinical atherosclerosis is by calculating the ankle-brachial index (ABI). The ABI is based on potential differences between systolic pressures in arteries of the lower legs and the arms. This measure is used to screen for peripheral arterial disease, but a low ABI (≤0.90; indicative of limited blood flow to the legs) has also been recognized as an indicator of systemic atherosclerosis (Newman *et al.* 1993). Other markers of subclinical atherosclerosis are carotid intima-media thickness (CIMT) and coronary or aortic calcification. CIMT can be measured after visualizing the innermost two layers of the arterial wall by using ultrasonography. Calcification of the coronary arteries or aorta can be identified in 3D images of the heart using electron beam computed tomography. These atherosclerosis markers have shown a predictive value for future incident cardiovascular events (Fowkes *et al.* 2008; Greenland *et al.* 2007; Lorenz *et al.* 2007). Arteriosclerosis also can be detected using various markers of arterial stiffness or endothelial dysfunction (Anderson, 2006). Arterial stiffness can be locally measured using ultrasonography, e.g. by calculating the carotid distensibility coefficient (DC). The DC gives the relative change in cross-sectional area (diameter) per unit of pressure. A measure to estimate aortic stiffness is to analyze pulse waves or contours, derived by applanation tonometry. The arterial pressure waveform consists of a forward wave which is created by ejection and a backward wave caused by reflection (e.g. at bifurcations). The central augmentation index (AIx) estimates the percentage of augmented late systolic pressure due to arterial stiffness. Indicators of arterial stiffness have shown capable of predicting future cardiovascular events (Adji *et al.* 2011; Laurent *et al.* 2006).

2.3. Existing evidence on association between depression and subclinical CVD

Studies investigating the association between depression and the ABI have yielded conflicting results. One prospective study used low ABI amongst other measures to define incident peripheral arterial disease in a middle-aged population and found moderate or high levels of depressive symptoms to be associated with an 20% and 44% increased risk (Wattanakit *et al.* 2005). In contrast, two studies found no association between depressed mood and low ABI among older men and women. This lack of a significant association might have been due to a low prevalence of depressive disorder (3%) in the population-based Rotterdam Study (Tiemeier *et al.* 2004) or to a relatively small sample size (n=167) in the other study which was carried out in patients with peripheral arterial disease and controls (Arseven *et al.* 2001). Literature on the association between depression and other markers of subclinical atherosclerosis shows a similar inconclusiveness as the ABI research. Some studies – based on middle-aged or older individuals – have shown a positive association between depression and CIMT(Chen *et al.* 2006; Elovainio *et al.* 2005; Paterniti *et al.* 2001; Stewart *et al.* 2007; Tiemeier *et al.* 2004; Whipple *et al.* 2009), whereas other studies have found no association (Jones *et al.* 2003; Matthews *et al.* 1998; Narita *et al.* 2008; Rice *et al.* 2009; Seldenrijk *et al.* 2011a; Spitzer *et al.* 2008). Likewise, depression has been associated with coronary or aortic calcification in some (Agatisa *et al.* 2005; Hamer *et al.* 2010; Matthews *et al.* 2010; Tiemeier *et al.* 2004), but not in other (Diez Roux *et al.* 2006; O'Malley *et al.* 2000) studies. An interesting observation with respect to chronicity of depression is that the positive findings for depression and calcification were particularly found for long-term poor mental health as indicated by recurrent depressive episodes or repeatedly measured depressive symptoms.

Studies investigating the association between depression and arteriosclerosis have used a variety of indexes for vascular function (Lavoie *et al.* 2010; Oulis *et al.* 2010; Paranthaman *et al.* 2010; Rajagopalan *et al.* 2001; Rybakowski *et al.* 2006; Sherwood *et al.* 2005; Tiemeier *et al.* 2003). Irrespective of these different outcome measures, all studies unanimously have shown depressed individuals to have impaired endothelial function or increased arterial stiffness. The association may be influenced by psychiatric characteristics, such as chronicity of symptoms, but evidence for this idea is still meager. In older diabetic women, recurrent but not single episode depression was associated with endothelial dysfunction (Wagner *et al.* 2009). In initially severely depressed women, successful antidepressant treatment was followed by a restoration of vascular function (Oulis *et al.* 2010). Additionally, preliminary evidence from a case-control study (Paranthaman *et al.* 2012) suggests that non-response to antidepressant monotherapy in late-life is related to increased endothelial dysfunction (n=31) and CIMT (n=45).

These observations are indicative of an association between depression and subclinical CVD. However, for both atherosclerosis and arteriosclerosis, there are still doubts on the generalizability of the observations since sample sizes of existing studies often were small, and many studies were performed in older or diseased populations. In a large Dutch cohort study some of these limitations could be overcome. This study addresses both depression and anxiety, since these are highly concurrent disorders (Kessler *et al.* 2005) with partially overlapping symptoms (Hiller *et al.* 1989).

2.4. Netherlands Study of Depression and Anxiety (NESDA)

2.4.1. Sample

NESDA is an ongoing longitudinal cohort study to examine the prevalence, course and consequences of depressive and anxiety disorders. In order to represent various health care settings and stages of psychopathology, participants were recruited from community (19%), primary care (54%) and outpatient psychiatric clinics (27%). Participants were men and women, aged 18-65 years at the baseline assessment in 2004-2007. Individuals with remitted and current depressive or anxiety disorders, as well as healthy controls were included. Details of the study rationale, recruitment strategy and methods are described elsewhere (Penninx *et al.* 2008). Based on NESDA baseline and 2-year follow up data, associations between depression, anxiety and several vascular conditions have been investigated in large samples (see flow chart, figure 1). The methods and results of three publications (Seldenrijk *et al.* 2010; Seldenrijk *et al.* 2011b; Vogelzangs *et al.* 2010) are being described below.

2.4.2. Methods

The assessment included amongst others a blood draw, a medical examination, administration of several written questionnaires concerning, e.g., mood state, lifestyle, and medical history, a psychiatric interview, and an interview regarding somatic health aspects. Diagnoses of depressive disorders (major depression, dysthymia) and anxiety disorders (generalized anxiety disorder, panic disorder, agoraphobia, social phobia) were established using the DSM-IV based Composite International Diagnostic Interview. In addition, clinical characteristics of these disorders were assessed. Severity of symptoms was measured with the 30-item Inventory of Depressive Symptomatology self-report version and the 21-item Beck Anxiety Inventory. Duration of symptoms was assessed using the Life Chart method (Lyketsos *et al.* 1994), after which the percentage of time with symptoms during the past few years was computed. Psychoactive medication use was assessed based on drug container inspection of all drugs used in the past month and classified according to the WHO Anatomical Therapeutic Chemical classification. Psychoactive medication included selective serotonin reuptake inhibitors (SSRIs), tricyclic antidepressants (TCAs), other antidepressants and benzodiazepines.

The presence of CVD at the baseline assessment was adjudicated using standardized algorithms considering self-report and medication use based on drug container inspection.

CVD included stroke and coronary heart disease, i.e. angina pectoris, myocardial infarction, percutaneous transluminal coronary angioplasty and coronary artery bypass grafting. Cardiovascular surgery was based on self-report alone, whereas other reported CVD conditions were only considered present when self-report was supported by the use of medication. Subclinical atherosclerosis was indicated by the ABI, measured using a Doppler ultrasound at the baseline assessment. In line with recommendations from the Ankle Brachial Index Collaboration, three groups of increased cardiovascular risk were distinguished: low ABI (0.90 or less) and mildly low ABI (ranging 0.90 to 1.11), but also high ABI (greater than 1.40) (Fowkes *et al.* 2008). ABI analyses were conducted in subjects without known CVD. Two year after baseline, 87.1% of the NESDA sample took part in a follow-up visit. A subsample of these participants was then recruited for additional cardiovascular measurements, including two different indicators of arterial stiffness (Seldenrijk *et al.* 2011b). The carotid DC was measured using M-mode ultrasound scanning. In addition, the central AIx was estimated by using radial pulse wave analysis.

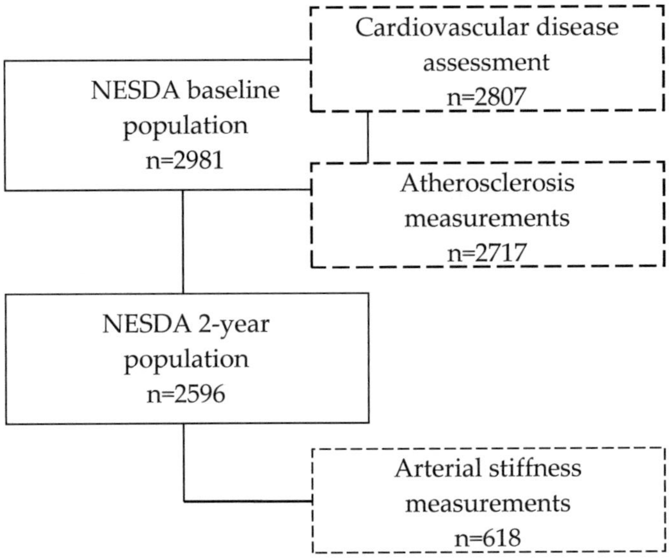

Figure 1. Flow chart of study population per vascular outcome

2.4.3. *Results*

The prevalence of CVD in the NESDA baseline population was 5.6%. First, depressive and anxiety disorders were analyzed separately. After adjustment for sociodemographics and lifestyle factors, people with a current depression (odds ratio of 1.6) and those with a current anxiety disorder (odds ratio of 2.2) showed increased likelihood of having CVD as compared with those who never had a depressive or anxious episode. When combining the presence or absence of both psychiatric conditions in one categorical variable, only people with a current anxiety disorder with or without co-morbid depression more often had coronary heart disease. The adjusted odds were 2.7 for subjects who only had a diagnosis of anxiety disorder and 3.5 for those who also had a co-morbid depressive disorder. No significant association was found between depression or anxiety and stroke, nor between remitted diagnoses and CVD. Of the psychiatric characteristics, severity of depressive or anxiety symptoms was positively associated with coronary heart disease in a dose-response manner. No significant associations were found for duration of psychiatric symptoms prior to baseline or use of psychotropic medication.

The prevalence of a low ABI was 2.2% in the CVD-free baseline population. People with a current diagnosis of depression or anxiety disorder almost 3-times more often had a low ABI as compared with controls. This increased likelihood in currently depressed or anxious was independent of sociodemographic factors, hypertension, diabetes and lifestyle factors. No increased risk was found for those with remitted diagnoses of depression or anxiety disorders. Possible explanations for this are decreased reliability of remitted diagnoses because of their retrospective character and that they indicate less severe exposure to psychological distress, the current group more frequently including chronic and relapsing cases. Psychiatric characteristics, such as severity and duration of depressive or anxiety symptoms prior to baseline, or the use of antidepressant medication, did not further differentiate the risk of low ABI in depressed and anxious subjects. No association was found between depression or anxiety and mildly low (prevalence 35.7%) or high (prevalence 2.5%) ABI.

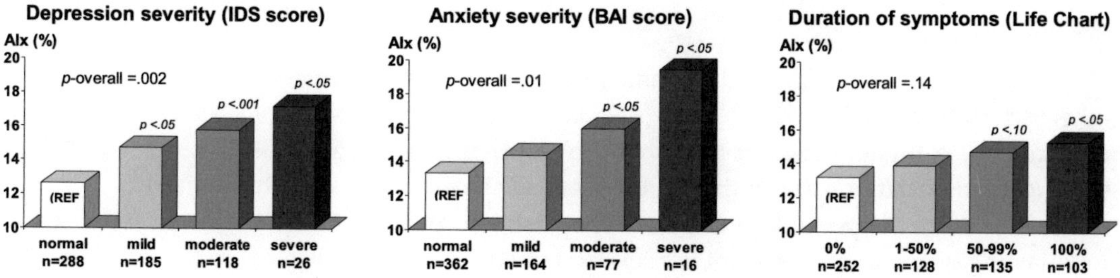

Figure 2. Association between symptom severity or duration and central arterial stiffness (AIx in %)

People with a current depressive or anxiety disorder at the NESDA 2-year assessment showed an increased central arterial stiffness as compared with controls. Again, those who had suffered from a depressed or anxious episode in the past but were currently recovered, did not differ from controls with respect to arterial stiffness. In addition to earlier mentioned explanations (i.e. reliability, chronicity), this could also imply that arterial status returns to normal when people recover from depression or anxiety. Evidence for a dose-response relationship was provided in our observations of an increased AIx in subjects who were longer or more severely exposed to depressive or anxiety symptoms over time (see fig. 2). No significant associations were found for carotid DC, although the duration of depressive and anxiety symptoms tended to be associated with a higher carotid artery stiffness. To rule out the possibility that observed associations were driven by subjects with known CVD or diabetes, or using antihypertensive or lipid-modifying medication, analyses were repeated without those cases and results remained similar. After exclusion of participants with suspected cardiovascular health, those using TCAs or combined serotonin/noradrenaline reuptake inhibitors (SNRIs) showed significantly increased AIx.

3. Summary and relevance for chronic depression

At this point in time there is a paucity of research that directly compares chronic versus non-chronic depression in association with the development of CVD. This paragraph summarizes the evidence regarding an association between depression and vascular conditions as presented above. In addition, inferences are made on the relevance of the reviewed evidence for a chronically depressed population.

Meta-analytic data have shown that depression increases one's risk to develop CVD (Nicholson *et al.* 2006; Van der Kooy *et al.* 2007) and to have an unfavourable course of CVD with more cardiac events and higher mortality rates (Nicholson *et al.* 2006) (see paragraph 2.1). Included studies that investigated clinical depression showed larger effect sizes than those using symptom lists. This may suggest that a more sustained exposure to psychological distress results in a dose-response effect on cardiovascular outcomes. Although the studies in these meta-analyses had no primary focus on chronic depression, it can thus be argued that chronically depressed patients have a particularly increased cardiovascular risk. A literature review of studies in coronary heart patients has supported this idea for depression as a prognostic factor: patients with treatment resistant depression more than responders were at risk for an unfavourable course of CVD (Carney & Freedland, 2009).

The mostly cross-sectional studies that investigated depression in relation to subclinical atherosclerosis are still inconclusive (see paragraph 2.3). Some studies failed to provide evidence for a higher cardiovascular risk in depression. However, other studies did find significant associations for either subclinical atherosclerosis or arteriosclerosis. Certain observations are of special interest, since they seem to point out that people suffering from long-lasting or treatment resistant depression constitute a distinctly high-risk group. Studies that demonstrated depression to be associated with a higher prevalence of aortic or coronary calcification found this either in participants who repeatedly reported high depressive symptoms (Hamer *et al.* 2010), or in those with recurrent depressive episodes (Agatisa *et al.* 2005; Matthews *et al.* 2010). Also with respect to CIMT and endothelial function, a gradient has been shown across groups, with non-depressed control subjects having the best vascular structure or function, antidepressant non-responders worse and responders in-between (Paranthaman *et al.* 2012).

Based on our studies (Seldenrijk *et al.* 2010; Seldenrijk *et al.* 2011b; Vogelzangs *et al.* 2010), it can be concluded that people with a current depressive or anxiety disorder have a higher likelihood of coronary heart disease and peripheral atherosclerosis and increased central arterial stiffness (see paragraph 2.4.3). No significant associations were found for remitted disorders. Psychiatric characteristics that in some way differentiated the CVD risk were severity of symptoms (coronary disease, central arterial stiffness) and duration of symptoms (arterial stiffness). In all three studies, a current diagnosis of depression or anxiety was associated with an increased likelihood of vascular conditions. No significant associations were found for subjects with remitted disorders. Since emotional distress likely exerts its effects on the arteries in a cumulative manner, people who chronically suffer from a psychiatric condition, such as depressive disorder, can be considered a high risk population. One explanation for the divergence between current and remitted diagnoses is that the group with current psychopathology also includes people who are chronically affected by, or frequently relapse into, depressive or anxious episodes. As compared with a remitted diagnosis, a current diagnosis thus might indicate a more sustained exposure to psychological distress. Our study on arterial stiffness (Seldenrijk *et al.* 2011b) did provide more direct support for a cumulative effect: the higher the percentage of time affected by depressed or anxious symptoms, the stiffer one's arteries were. Although depression was not significantly associated with CVD independent of anxiety in (Vogelzangs *et al.* 2010), it was demonstrated that participants with both current anxiety and depression carried the highest risk of having coronary heart disease. The additive effect of different psychiatric conditions (e.g. panic disorder and depression) on vascular health previously had been described by (Gomez-Caminero *et al.* 2005). These individuals who suffer from both depression and anxiety at the same time might well define a chronically depressed population. This hypothesis is supported by prospective data from the NESDA cohort, which indicated that a chronic course of depressive disorder is predicated by having a co-morbid anxiety disorder (Penninx *et al.* 2011). In line with this, other studies (e.g. (Fava *et al.* 2008)) have found that depressed patients with high levels of anxiety are less likely to respond to treatment.

As mentioned before, the observations discussed are not without inconsistencies. Some studies did not find significant associations between depression and subclinical atherosclerosis. Likewise, our own studies provided no evidence for an association between depression and stroke or carotid arterial stiffness, nor did we find an effect of the duration of depressive symptoms on some vascular outcomes. These discrepancies across studies could be due to differences in populations and in vascular outcome measures. At a younger age, the prevalence of clinical CVD is not very high, and the range of aberrant subclinical values is not wide. As a consequence, associations are hard to be detected. Linked to this point, a differential impact (i.e. rate and severity) of aging across the arterial tree might also partially explain the discrepant findings. It has been demonstrated that subclinical atherosclerosis probably does not affect all arterial beds in a uniform and contemporaneous manner (DeCara, 2011). This may be due to differential composition of the vascular wall (elastic versus muscular arteries) as well as the location of the arteries in the body.

The association between chronic depression and CVD has also received support from other lines of research. First, it has been suggested that specific subtypes of depression may be partly caused by CVD or cardiovascular risk factors. Some evidence exists that these subtypes are more chronic in course. One of the primary criteria of a 'vascular depression' (Alexopoulos *et al.* 1997) is clinical or subclinical evidence of cerebrovascular impairment. Another potential characteristic of this depression subtype is a late first onset of someone's first depressive episode. Patients with vascular depression seem to be less likely to respond to antidepressant treatment (Navarro *et al.* 2004; Patankar *et al.* 2007). Likewise, the metabolic syndrome has been investigated as a prognostic factor for the course of depressive disorder. Metabolic syndrome is a combination of cardiovascular risk factors (Mottillo *et al.*

2010), including abdominal obesity, lipid abnormalities, hypertension, and hyperglycaemia. Based on a community sample of older persons, (Vogelzangs *et al.* 2011) found that depressed subjects with metabolic syndrome ('metabolic depression') were almost 3-fold more likely to have persistent or recurrent depression. In addition, depression and more specifically treatment resistant depression has been associated with inflammation (Miller *et al.* 2009). Since inflammation is considered one of the important mechanisms that enhance the development of CVD (Willerson & Ridker, 2004), individuals who are nonresponsive to antidepressant treatment may have a higher likelihood of future cardiovascular events. Furthermore, specific types of antidepressant medications (e.g. TCAs and SNRIs) have been associated with unfavourable side-effects on metabolism, sympathetic activity and the immune system (Licht *et al.* 2012; van Reedt Dortland *et al.* 2010; Vogelzangs *et al.* 2012). Although the prospective nature of some evidence suggests that active ingredients of the antidepressants might be responsible (Licht *et al.* 2012), it also is likely that patients who use these antidepressants differ from non-users or SSRI users by having more severe and more chronic psychopathology.

4. Possible implications

The above reviewed epidemiological evidence seems to indicate that chronic depression can be considered a cardiovascular risk factor. The question now arises of how this knowledge may be useful in clinical practice. First, modification of the risk factor would be expected to have beneficial effects on vascular health. Apart from the challenge this by definition means in chronic depression, it is still unknown whether successful treatment of depression indeed leads to improvement in cardiovascular morbidity and mortality. As for now, randomized controlled trials in CVD-free populations have not yet been carried out. Some trials (SADHART, (Glassman *et al.* 2002); ENRICHD, (Berkman *et al.* 2003); MIND-IT, (van Melle *et al.* 2007)) did investigate the effects of antidepressant psychotherapy or pharmacotherapy on cardiovascular morbidity and mortality in coronary patient populations. Although these studies have shown that depression is treatable in coronary patients, no significant differences were found in medical end-points between intervention and control groups. However, (Carney & Freedland, 2007) have pointed out that future studies are still needed to reinvestigate this issue with more effective therapies and in larger, sufficiently powered samples.

Until we know how the associations between depression and (subclinical) CVD come about in terms of physiological pathways, the best advice appears to be to focus on general cardiovascular risk reduction in high-risk populations. With respect to pharmacologic treatment in chronically depressed patients, extra caution taken by psychiatrists potentially could prevent the occurrence of some cardiovascular events. Before and during the start of treatment with especially TCAs and SNRIs, it now is common practice to screen for CVD by measuring blood pressure and performing an ECG in patients with cardiovascular risk factors and in elderly patients. In view of the available evidence as discussed in the former paragraphs, there are reasons to belief that a broader range of people might benefit from more active cardiovascular screening. For some subgroups (such as older patients with a chronic depression or with both depressive and anxiety disorders) regular measurements of blood pressure, cholesterol and glucose levels could be incorporated as a matter of standard practice. In addition, because of the increased prevalence of (subclinical) CVD in this population, extra attention to a healthy lifestyle appears an important aspect of the treatment of depressed patients. As to the primary target of cardiovascular risk intervention, the American Heart Associations has stated:

> "Adoption of healthy life habits remains the cornerstone of primary prevention, including the avoidance of tobacco (including second-hand smoke), healthy dietary patterns, weight control, and regular, appropriate exercise. An important role of healthcare providers is to support and reinforce these public health recommendations for all patients." (Pearson *et al.* 2002)

Regarding exercise, some inspiring observations for the improvement of both mental and vascular health have recently been published: physical activity reduces the risk of CVD events (Hamer *et al.* 2011) and positively influences depressive complaints (Carek *et al.* 2011; Hoffman *et al.* 2011). The reinforcing and supporting role thus also fits professionals in the field of chronic depression, particularly since a tendency to ignore cardiovascular symptoms and taking action from it might be inherent in serious mental illnesses.

Author details

Adrie Seldenrijk, Nicole Vogelzangs, Patricia van Oppen,
Brenda Penninx and Anneke van Schaik
Department of Psychiatry, Vrije Universiteit, Amsterdam, Netherlands

5. References

Adji, A., O'Rourke, M.F. & Namasivayam, M. (2011). Arterial stiffness, its assessment, prognostic value, and implications for treatment. *Am J Hypertens.* 24(1):5-17.

Agatisa, P.K., Matthews, K.A., Bromberger, J.T., Edmundowicz, D., Chang, Y.F. & Sutton-Tyrrell, K. (2005). Coronary and aortic calcification in women with a history of major depression. *Arch.Intern.Med* 165(11):1229-1236.

Alexopoulos, G.S., Meyers, B.S., Young, R.C., Campbell, S., Silbersweig, D. & Charlson, M. (1997). 'Vascular depression' hypothesis. *Arch.Gen.Psychiatry* 54(10):915-922.

Anderson, T.J. (2006). Arterial stiffness or endothelial dysfunction as a surrogate marker of vascular risk. *Can.J Cardiol.* 22 Suppl B:72B-80B.

Arseven, A., Guralnik, J.M., O'Brien, E., Liu, K. & McDermott, M.M. (2001). Peripheral arterial disease and depressed mood in older men and women. *Vasc.Med* 6(4):229-234.

Berkman, L.F., Blumenthal, J., Burg, M., Carney, R.M., Catellier, D., Cowan, M.J., Czajkowski, S.M., DeBusk, R., Hosking, J., Jaffe, A., Kaufmann, P.G., Mitchell, P., Norman, J., Powell, L.H., Raczynski, J.M. & Schneiderman, N. (2003). Effects of treating depression and low perceived social support on clinical events after myocardial infarction: the Enhancing Recovery in Coronary Heart Disease Patients (ENRICHD) Randomized Trial. *JAMA* 289(23):3106-3116.

Carek, P.J., Laibstain, S.E. & Carek, S.M. (2011). Exercise for the treatment of depression and anxiety. *Int J Psychiatry Med* 41(1):15-28.

Carney, R.M. & Freedland, K.E. (2007). Does treating depression improve survival after acute coronary syndrome? Invited commentary on... Effects of antidepressant treatment following myocardial infarction. *Br.J Psychiatry* 190:467-468.

Carney, R.M. & Freedland, K.E. (2009). Treatment-resistant depression and mortality after acute coronary syndrome. *Am J Psychiatry* 166(4):410-417.

Chen, C.S., Chen, C.C., Kuo, Y.T., Chiang, I.C., Ko, C.H. & Lin, H.F. (2006). Carotid intima-media thickness in late-onset major depressive disorder. *Int J Geriatr.Psychiatry* 21(1):36-42.

DeCara, J.M. (2011). Carotid intima-media thickness and risk for coronary heart disease. *Current Cardiovascular Imaging Reports* 2(5):350-355.

Diez Roux, A.V., Ranjit, N., Powell, L., Jackson, S., Lewis, T.T., Shea, S. & Wu, C. (2006). Psychosocial factors and coronary calcium in adults without clinical cardiovascular disease. *Ann.Intern.Med.* 144(11):822-831.

Elovainio, M., Keltikangas-Jarvinen, L., Kivimaki, M., Pulkki, L., Puttonen, S., Heponiemi, T., Juonala, M., Viikari, J.S. & Raitakari, O.T. (2005). Depressive symptoms and carotid artery intima-media thickness in young adults: the Cardiovascular Risk in Young Finns Study. *Psychosom.Med* 67(4):561-567.

Fava, M., Rush, A.J., Alpert, J.E., Balasubramani, G.K., Wisniewski, S.R., Carmin, C.N., Biggs, M.M., Zisook, S., Leuchter, A., Howland, R., Warden, D. & Trivedi, M.H. (2008). Difference in treatment outcome in outpatients with anxious versus nonanxious depression: a STAR*D report. *Am J Psychiatry* 165(3):342-351.

Fowkes, F.G., Murray, G.D., Butcher, I., Heald, C.L., Lee, R.J., Chambless, L.E., Folsom, A.R., Hirsch, A.T., Dramaix, M., deBacker, G., Wautrecht, J.C., Kornitzer, M., Newman, A.B., Cushman, M., Sutton-Tyrrell, K., Fowkes, F.G., Lee, A.J., Price, J.F., d'Agostino, R.B., Murabito, J.M., Norman, P.E., Jamrozik, K., Curb, J.D., Masaki, K.H., Rodriguez, B.L., Dekker, J.M., Bouter, L.M., Heine, R.J., Nijpels, G., Stehouwer, C.D., Ferrucci, L., McDermott, M.M., Stoffers, H.E., Hooi, J.D., Knottnerus, J.A., Ogren, M., Hedblad, B., Witteman, J.C., Breteler, M.M., Hunink, M.G., Hofman, A., Criqui, M.H., Langer, R.D., Fronek, A., Hiatt, W.R., Hamman, R., Resnick, H.E., Guralnik, J. & McDermott, M.M. (2008). Ankle brachial index combined with Framingham Risk Score to predict cardiovascular events and mortality: a meta-analysis. *JAMA* 300(2):197-208.

Glassman, A.H., O'Connor, C.M., Califf, R.M., Swedberg, K., Schwartz, P., Bigger, J.T., Jr., Krishnan, K.R., van Zyl, L.T., Swenson, J.R., Finkel, M.S., Landau, C., Shapiro, P.A., Pepine, C.J., Mardekian, J., Harrison, W.M., Barton, D. & Mclvor, M. (2002). Sertraline treatment of major depression in patients with acute MI or unstable angina. *JAMA* 288(6):701-709.

Gomez-Caminero, A., Blumentals, W.A., Russo, L.J., Brown, R.R. & Castilla-Puentes, R. (2005). Does panic disorder increase the risk of coronary heart disease? A cohort study of a national managed care database. *Psychosom.Med* 67(5):688-691.

Greenland, P., Bonow, R.O., Brundage, B.H., Budoff, M.J., Eisenberg, M.J., Grundy, S.M., Lauer, M.S., Post, W.S., Raggi, P., Redberg, R.F., Rodgers, G.P., Shaw, L.J., Taylor, A.J. & Weintraub, W.S. (2007). ACCF/AHA 2007 clinical expert consensus document on coronary artery calcium scoring by computed tomography in global cardiovascular risk assessment and in evaluation of patients with chest pain: a report of the American College of Cardiology Foundation Clinical Expert Consensus Task Force (ACCF/AHA Writing Committee to Update the 2000 Expert Consensus Document on Electron Beam Computed Tomography) developed in collaboration with the Society of Atherosclerosis Imaging and Prevention and the Society of Cardiovascular Computed Tomography. *J.Am.Coll.Cardiol.* 49(3):378-402.

Hamer, M., Ingle, L., Carroll, S. & Stamatakis, E. (2011). Physical Activity and Cardiovascular Mortality Risk: Possible Protective Mechanisms? *Med Sci.Sports Exerc.*

Hamer, M., Kivimaki, M., Lahiri, A., Marmot, M.G. & Steptoe, A. (2010). Persistent cognitive depressive symptoms are associated with coronary artery calcification. *Atherosclerosis* 210(1):209-213.

Hiller, W., Zaudig, M. & von Bose, M. (1989). The overlap between depression and anxiety on different levels of psychopathology. *J Affect.Disord.* 16(2-3):223-231.

Hoffman, B.M., Babyak, M.A., Craighead, W.E., Sherwood, A., Doraiswamy, P.M., Coons, M.J. & Blumenthal, J.A. (2011). Exercise and pharmacotherapy in patients with major depression: one-year follow-up of the SMILE study. *Psychosom.Med* 73(2):127-133.

Jones, D.J., Bromberger, J.T., Sutton-Tyrrell, K. & Matthews, K.A. (2003). Lifetime history of depression and carotid atherosclerosis in middle-aged women. *Arch.Gen.Psychiatry* 60(2):153-160.

Kessler, R.C., Chiu, W.T., Demler, O., Merikangas, K.R. & Walters, E.E. (2005). Prevalence, severity, and comorbidity of 12-month DSM-IV disorders in the National Comorbidity Survey Replication. *Arch.Gen.Psychiatry* 62(6):617-627.

Laurent, S., Cockcroft, J., Van, B.L., Boutouyrie, P., Giannattasio, C., Hayoz, D., Pannier, B., Vlachopoulos, C., Wilkinson, I. & Struijker-Boudier, H. (2006). Expert consensus document on arterial stiffness: methodological issues and clinical applications. *Eur Heart J* 27(21):2588-2605.

Lavoie, K.L., Pelletier, R., Arsenault, A., Dupuis, J. & Bacon, S.L. (2010). Association between clinical depression and endothelial function measured by forearm hyperemic reactivity. *Psychosom.Med* 72(1):20-26.

Licht, C.M., Penninx, B.W. & de Geus, E.J. (2012). Effects of Antidepressants, but not Psychopathology, on Cardiac Sympathetic Control: A Longitudinal Study. *Neuropsychopharmacology* .

Lorenz, M.W., Markus, H.S., Bots, M.L., Rosvall, M. & Sitzer, M. (2007). Prediction of clinical cardiovascular events with carotid intima-media thickness: a systematic review and meta-analysis. *Circulation* 115(4):459-467.

Lyketsos, C.G., Newman, A.B., Cwi J, Heithoff K & Eaton WW (1994). The Life Chart Interview: a standardized method to describe the course of psychopathology. *International Journal of Methods in Psychiatric Research* 4:143-155.

Mackey, R.H., Venkitachalam, L. & Sutton-Tyrrell, K. (2007). Calcifications, arterial stiffness and atherosclerosis. *Adv.Cardiol.* 44:234-244.

Matthews, K.A., Chang, Y.F., Sutton-Tyrrell, K., Edmundowicz, D. & Bromberger, J.T. (2010). Recurrent major depression predicts progression of coronary calcification in healthy women: Study of Women's Health Across the Nation. *Psychosom.Med* 72(8):742-747.

Matthews, K.A., Owens, J.F., Kuller, L.H., Sutton-Tyrrell, K. & Jansen-McWilliams, L. (1998). Are hostility and anxiety associated with carotid atherosclerosis in healthy postmenopausal women? *Psychosom.Med* 60(5):633-638.

Miller, A.H., Maletic, V. & Raison, C.L. (2009). Inflammation and its discontents: the role of cytokines in the pathophysiology of major depression. *Biol Psychiatry* 65(9):732-741.

Mottillo, S., Filion, K.B., Genest, J., Joseph, L., Pilote, L., Poirier, P., Rinfret, S., Schiffrin, E.L. & Eisenberg, M.J. (2010). The metabolic syndrome and cardiovascular risk a systematic review and meta-analysis. *J Am Coll.Cardiol.* 56(14):1113-1132.

Narita, K., Murata, T., Hamada, T., Kosaka, H., Sudo, S., Mizukami, K., Yoshida, H. & Wada, Y. (2008). Associations between trait anxiety, insulin resistance, and atherosclerosis in the elderly: a pilot cross-sectional study. *Psychoneuroendocrinology* 33(3):305-312.

Navarro, V., Gasto, C., Lomena, F., Torres, X., Mateos, J.J., Portella, M.J., Masana, G. & Marcos, T. (2004). Prognostic value of frontal functional neuroimaging in late-onset severe major depression. *Br.J Psychiatry* 184:306-311.

Newman, A.B., Siscovick, D.S., Manolio, T.A., Polak, J., Fried, L.P., Borhani, N.O. & Wolfson, S.K. (1993). Ankle-arm index as a marker of atherosclerosis in the Cardiovascular Health Study. Cardiovascular Heart Study (CHS) Collaborative Research Group. *Circulation* 88(3):837-845.

Nicholson, A., Kuper, H. & Hemingway, H. (2006). Depression as an aetiologic and prognostic factor in coronary heart disease: a meta-analysis of 6362 events among 146 538 participants in 54 observational studies. *Eur.Heart J* 27(23):2763-2774.

O'Malley, P.G., Jones, D.L., Feuerstein, I.M. & Taylor, A.J. (2000). Lack of correlation between psychological factors and subclinical coronary artery disease. *N.Engl.J Med* 343(18):1298-1304.

Oulis, P., Kouzoupis, A., Kyrkou, K., Masdrakis, V.G., Georgiopoulos, G., Karapoulios, E., Georgiou, S., Karakatsanis, N.A., Lykka, M., Papadimitriou, G.N., Papamichael, C. & Stamatelopoulos, K. (2010). Reversal of increased arterial stiffness in severely depressed women after 6-week antidepressant treatment. *J Affect.Disord.* 122(1-2):164-166.

Paranthaman, R., Greenstein, A., Burns, A.S., Heagerty, A.M., Malik, R.A. & Baldwin, R.C. (2012). Relationship of endothelial function and atherosclerosis to treatment response in late-life depression. *Int J Geriatr.Psychiatry* .

Paranthaman, R., Greenstein, A.S., Burns, A.S., Cruickshank, J.K., Heagerty, A.M., Jackson, A., Malik, R.A., Scott, M.L. & Baldwin, R.C. (2010). Vascular function in older adults with depressive disorder. *Biol Psychiatry* 68(2):133-139.

Patankar, T.F., Baldwin, R., Mitra, D., Jeffries, S., Sutcliffe, C., Burns, A. & Jackson, A. (2007). Virchow-Robin space dilatation may predict resistance to antidepressant monotherapy in elderly patients with depression. *J Affect.Disord.* 97(1-3):265-270.

Paterniti, S., Zureik, M., Ducimetiere, P., Touboul, P.J., Feve, J.M. & Alperovitch, A. (2001). Sustained anxiety and 4-year progression of carotid atherosclerosis. *Arterioscler.Thromb.Vasc.Biol* 21(1):136-141.

Pearson, T.A., Blair, S.N., Daniels, S.R., Eckel, R.H., Fair, J.M., Fortmann, S.P., Franklin, B.A., Goldstein, L.B., Greenland, P., Grundy, S.M., Hong, Y., Miller, N.H., Lauer, R.M., Ockene, I.S., Sacco, R.L., Sallis, J.F., Jr., Smith, S.C., Jr., Stone, N.J. & Taubert, K.A. (2002). AHA Guidelines for Primary Prevention of Cardiovascular Disease and Stroke: 2002 Update: Consensus Panel Guide to Comprehensive Risk Reduction for Adult Patients Without Coronary or Other Atherosclerotic Vascular Diseases. American Heart Association Science Advisory and Coordinating Committee. *Circulation* 106(3):388-391.

Penninx, B.W., Beekman, A.T., Smit, J.H., Zitman, F.G., Nolen, W.A., Spinhoven, P., Cuijpers, P., de Jong, P.J., van Marwijk, H.W., Assendelft, W.J., van der, M.K., Verhaak, P., Wensing, M., de, G.R., Hoogendijk, W.J., Ormel, J. & van, D.R. (2008). The Netherlands Study of Depression and Anxiety (NESDA): rationale, objectives and methods. *Int J Methods Psychiatr.Res* 17(3):121-140.

Penninx, B.W., Nolen, W.A., Lamers, F., Zitman, F.G., Smit, J.H., Spinhoven, P., Cuijpers, P., de Jong, P.J., van Marwijk, H.W., van der, M.K., Verhaak, P., Laurant, M.G., de, G.R., Hoogendijk, W.J., van der, W.N., Ormel, J., van, D.R. & Beekman, A.T. (2011). Two-year course of depressive and anxiety disorders: results from the Netherlands Study of Depression and Anxiety (NESDA). *J Affect.Disord.* 133(1-2):76-85.

Rajagopalan, S., Brook, R., Rubenfire, M., Pitt, E., Young, E. & Pitt, B. (2001). Abnormal brachial artery flow-mediated vasodilation in young adults with major depression. *Am J Cardiol.* 88(2):196-8, A7.

Rice, S.C., Zonderman, A.B., Metter, E.J., Najjar, S.S. & Waldstein, S.R. (2009). Absence of relation between depressive symptoms and carotid intimal medial thickness in the Baltimore Longitudinal Study of Aging. *Psychosom.Med* 71(1):70-76.

Rybakowski, J.K., Wykretowicz, A., Heymann-Szlachcinska, A. & Wysocki, H. (2006). Impairment of endothelial function in unipolar and bipolar depression. *Biol Psychiatry* 60(8):889-891.

Seldenrijk, A., van Hout, H.P., van Marwijk, H.W., de Groot, E., Gort, J., Rustemeijer, C., Diamant, M. & Penninx, B.W. (2011a). Carotid atherosclerosis in depression and anxiety: associations for age of depression onset. *World J Biol Psychiatry* 12(7):549-558.

Seldenrijk, A., van Hout, H.P., van Marwijk, H.W., de Groot, E., Gort, J., Rustemeijer, C., Diamant, M. & Penninx, B.W. (2011b). Depression, anxiety, and arterial stiffness. *Biol Psychiatry* 69(8):795-803.

Seldenrijk, A., Vogelzangs, N., van Hout, H.P., van Marwijk, H.W., Diamant, M. & Penninx, B.W. (2010). Depressive and anxiety disorders and risk of subclinical atherosclerosis Findings from the Netherlands Study of Depression and Anxiety (NESDA). *J Psychosom.Res* 69(2):203-210.

Sherwood, A., Hinderliter, A.L., Watkins, L.L., Waugh, R.A. & Blumenthal, J.A. (2005). Impaired endothelial function in coronary heart disease patients with depressive symptomatology. *J Am Coll.Cardiol.* 46(4):656-659.

Spitzer, C., Volzke, H., Barnow, S., Krohn, U., Wallaschofski, H., Ludemann, J., John, U., Freyberger, H.J., Kerner, W. & Grabe, H.J. (2008). Association between depression and subclinical carotid atherosclerosis in patients with Type 1 diabetes. *Diabet.Med* 25(3):349-354.

Stewart, J.C., Janicki, D.L., Muldoon, M.F., Sutton-Tyrrell, K. & Kamarck, T.W. (2007). Negative emotions and 3-year progression of subclinical atherosclerosis. *Arch.Gen.Psychiatry* 64(2):225-233.

Tiemeier, H., Breteler, M.M., van Popele, N.M., Hofman, A. & Witteman, J.C. (2003). Late-life depression is associated with arterial stiffness: a population-based study. *J Am Geriatr.Soc.* 51(8):1105-1110.

Tiemeier, H., van Dijck, W., Hofman, A., Witteman, J.C., Stijnen, T. & Breteler, M.M. (2004). Relationship between atherosclerosis and late-life depression: the Rotterdam Study. *Arch.Gen.Psychiatry* 61(4):369-376.

Van der Kooy, K., van, H.H., Marwijk, H., Marten, H., Stehouwer, C. & Beekman, A. (2007). Depression and the risk for cardiovascular diseases: systematic review and meta analysis. *Int J Geriatr.Psychiatry* 22(7):613-626.

Van Melle, J.P., De Jonge, P., Honig, A., Schene, A.H., Kuyper, A.M., Crijns, H.J., Schins, A., Tulner, D., van den Berg, M.P. & Ormel, J. (2007). Effects of antidepressant treatment following myocardial infarction. *Br.J Psychiatry* 190:460-466.

Van Reedt Dortland, A.K., Giltay, E.J., van, V.T., Zitman, F.G. & Penninx, B.W. (2010). Metabolic syndrome abnormalities are associated with severity of anxiety and depression and with tricyclic antidepressant use. *Acta Psychiatr.Scand.* 122(1):30-39.

Vogelzangs, N., Beekman, A.T., Boelhouwer, I.G., Bandinelli, S., Milaneschi, Y., Ferrucci, L. & Penninx, B.W. (2011). Metabolic depression: a chronic depressive subtype? Findings from the InCHIANTI study of older persons. *J Clin.Psychiatry* 72(5):598-604.

Vogelzangs, N., Duivis, H.E., Beekman, A.T., Kluft, C., Neuteboom, J., Hoogendijk, W.J., Smit, J.H., De Jonge, P. & Penninx, B.W.J.H. (2012). Association of depressive disorders, depression characteristics and antidepressant medication with inflammation. *Translational Psychiatry* .

Vogelzangs, N., Seldenrijk, A., Beekman, A.T., van Hout, H.P., de, J.P. & Penninx, B.W. (2010). Cardiovascular disease in persons with depressive and anxiety disorders. *J Affect.Disord.* 125(1-3):241-248.

Wagner, J., Tennen, H., Mansoor, G. & Abbott, G. (2009). Endothelial dysfunction and history of recurrent depression in postmenopausal women with Type 2 diabetes: a case-control study. *J Diabetes Complications* 23(1):18-24.

Wattanakit, K., Williams, J.E., Schreiner, P.J., Hirsch, A.T. & Folsom, A.R. (2005). Association of anger proneness, depression and low social support with peripheral arterial disease: the Atherosclerosis Risk in Communities Study. *Vasc.Med* 10(3):199-206.

Whipple, M.O., Lewis, T.T., Sutton-Tyrrell, K., Matthews, K.A., Barinas-Mitchell, E., Powell, L.H. & Everson-Rose, S.A. (2009). Hopelessness, depressive symptoms, and carotid atherosclerosis in women: the Study of Women's Health Across the Nation (SWAN) heart study. *Stroke* 40(10):3166-3172.

Willerson, J.T. & Ridker, P.M. (2004). Inflammation as a cardiovascular risk factor. *Circulation* 109(21 Suppl 1):II2-10.

Zarins, C.K. & Glagov, S. (2004). Pathophysiology of human atherosclerosis, *in* R. W. Hobson II, S. E. Wilson and F. J. Veith (ed.), *Vascular surgery; principles and practice*, Marcel Dekker, Inc, New York, USA.

Section 5

Challenging the Stigma of Serious Mental Illness

Chapter 14

A Journey Through Schizophrenia

Susan L. Renes

Additional information is available at the end of the chapter

http://dx.doi.org/10.5772/53225

1. Introduction

Schizophrenia rolls in like a slow fog, becoming imperceptibly thicker as time goes on. At first, the day is bright enough, the sky is clear; the sunlight warms your shoulders. But soon, you notice haze beginning to gather around you, and the air feels not quite so warm. After awhile, the sun is a dim lightbulb behind a heavy cloth. The horizon has vanished into a gray mist, and you feel a thick dampness in your lungs as you stand, cold and wet, in the afternoon dark. (Saks, 2007, p. 35).

The positive and negative symptoms and the prodromal, acute, and residual phases of schizophrenia are described in this chapter using the personal accounts of Elyn Saks and other professionals who have made public their personal struggles with schizophrenia. Psychologists, psychiatrists, and other professionals have disclosed their stories in the professional literature and their own biographies. These professionals believe there is a need for the general public and those with serious mental illnesses to hear stories of those who are leading successful lives after surviving the fire of the illness and its treatment (Bassman, 1997; Baxter, 1998; Breeding, 2008; Deegan, 1993; Deegan, 2003; Freese, Knight, & Saks, 2009). The successes reported by these professionals are not anomalies. Longitudinal studies report a large number of people with schizophrenia seeing improvement in their condition over time (Davidson, Schmutte, Dinzeo, & Andres-Hyman; 2008; Ellison, Russinova, Massaro, Lyass, 2005; Siebert, 2005). These individuals also make the case for the need of those with schizophrenia and other mental illnesses to be heard by professionals who offer understanding, hope, and support and listen with an understanding heart rather than from an uncaring, objective perspective (Brooks, 2011; Chadwick, 2006; Deegan, 1993; Frese et al., 2009; Frese & Davis, 1997).

2. Prodromal phase

Saks is the Associate Dean, Chaired Professor of Law, Psychology, and Psychiatry & Behavioral Sciences at the University of Southern California Gould School of Law; Adjunct

Professor of Psychiatry at the University of California, San Diego, School of Medicine; and Assistant Faculty, the New Center for Psychoanalysis. Saks began to notice changes in her behavior at age eight. She became very obsessive about lining up the shoes in her closet before she could go to bed at night. She kept her bedroom light on until all the books on the shelves were organized just right. At times, she would wash her hands one, two and, three times to make sure they were clean. These noticeable changes might have been preceded by even earlier events that went unnoticed. Ms. Saks developed a fear that someone was lurcking outside her window at night. Ms. Saks became fearful of being alone, the darkness, and the nighttime. She began to recognize her limitation in controlling her fears and emotions. Delusional perceptions are very common in the early stages of schizophrenia (Fanous & Kenler, 2008; Gourzi, Katrianous & Beratis, 2002; Maddux & Winstead, 2012; Maxmen, Ward, & Kilgus, 2009). Saks describes her sense of hopelessness when trying to influence her environment and organize it; thus the title for her book, *The Center Cannot Hold: My Journey Through Madness.*

Carol North (1987) is currently the Chair in Crisis Psychiatry and Professor in the Departments of Psychiatry and Surgery/Division of Emergency Medicine/Section on Homeland Security at The University of Texas Southwestern Medical Center in Dallas. She is also Director of the Program in Trauma and Disaster at the VA North Texas Health Care System. She was only six years old when she found herself seeing frightening hallucinations of killer bees, murderers, and potential kidnappers on her way to school every day. When she heard voices talking to her in school, it did not occur to her that others did not hear the voices, too. Later those voices became very intrusive, so loud in fact that she often wondered if others could hear them, too. Gene Deegan, Psy.D. (2003), a Research Fellow at the Center for Psychiatric Rehabilitation, Boston University was diagnosed with "ambulatory schizophrenia" (p. 369) at age 17 but it was not until the time of his college graduation the he felt his sense of identity disintegrating with unusual sensations and terrible anxiety causing him to believe his very existence was precarious at best.

The majority of individuals who suffer from schizophrenia first experience prodromal or early symptoms such as social withdrawal, impaired functioning, flat affect, unusual perceptions, odd thinking, rambling speech, or preoccupation with overvalued thoughts (Gourzi, Katrianous & Beratis, 2002; Maddux & Winstead, 2012; Maxmen et al., 2009). Approximately one-fourth of those suffering from schizophrenia first experience an abrupt onset (referred to the acute phase) experiencing delusions, hallucinations, disorganized speech, or grossly disorganized or catatonic behavior. For those who experience prodromal symptoms following an acute phase, these symptoms are referred to as the residual phase. During these prodromal or residual phases, individuals are generally looked on as odd or referred to as "strange".

3. Diagnostic criteria

According to Kaplan (2008), a Swiss psychiatrist, Eugene Blueler, first used the term schizophrenia in 1908, as a description for a condition first described by a German psychiatrist, Emil Kraeplin, who referred to the condition as dementia praecox. Blueler defined schizophrenia as a disease best understood as a type of alteration of thinking and feeling and relating to the external world (Kuhn, 2004). Today, both the American Psychiatric Association's (2000) *Diagnostic and Statistical Manual of Mental Disorders*, 4th edition, text revised (DSM-IV-TR), and the World Health Organization's (1993) *International Classification of Diseases*, 10th revision (ICD-10) include in their descriptions the positive symptoms of delusions, hallucinations, disorganized speech, disorganized or catatonic behavior, and the negative symptoms of flat affect, reduced speech, lack of ability to experience joy or pleasure, lack of interest in forming relationships, and lack of ability to become motivated. To receive a diagnosis of schizophrenia, the DSM-IV-TR requires three diagnostic criteria be met: (a) two or more of the following characteristics present for a significant period of time for at least a month: delusions, hallucinations, disorganized speech (manifesting from a formal thought disorder), disorganized or catatonic behavior, or negative symptoms; (b) social or occupational dysfunction that is significantly below what was seen prior to the onset of the disturbance, and (c) of significant duration: i.e. continuous signs persisting for at least six months.

The DSM-IV-TR contains five sub-classifications of schizophrenia: (a) paranoid type (delusions or auditory hallucinations are present, but thought disorder, disorganized behavior, or affective flattening are not); (b) disorganized type (a thought disorder and flat affect are present together), (c) catatonic type (almost immobile or movement that is agitated and without purpose, (d) undifferentiated type (psychotic symptoms but the paranoid, disorganized, or catatonic symptoms are not met), and (e) residual (positive symptoms are present but only at a low intensity). The ICD-10 describes two additional subtypes: (a) post-schizophrenic depression: (depression arising in the aftermath of a schizophrenic illness with possible schizophrenic symptoms still present, and (b) simple schizophrenia (development of negative symptoms of schizophrenia with no psychotic episodes.

4. Acute phase

The acute phase of schizophrenia usually manifests during adolescence or early adulthood, a time when social interactions and identity development can be seriously affected by the symptoms of schizophrenia. Many of those suffering from schizophrenia find they are less able to engage in social interactions after the onset of the disease, intensifying their anxiety (Lysaker & Lysaker, 2010). Elyn Saks (2007) describes her experience:

Place yourself in the middle of the room. Turn on the stereo, the television, and a beeping video game, and then invite into the room several small children with ice cream cones. Crank up the volume on each piece of equipment, then take away the children's ice cream. Imagine these circumstances existing every day and night of your life. (p. 229).

Saks received the diagnosis of chronic paranoid schizophrenia with acute exacerbation following involuntarily admission to the Yale Psychiatric Institute (Saks, 2007). However, from the late 70s to early 80s, following graduation from Vanderbilt, Saks attended Oxford University, returning to the United States in 1982. While at Oxford Saks experienced both the positive and negative symptoms of schizophrenia. After arriving in England, she found it difficult to interact with others increasing her isolation; she found herself depressed along with feelings of self-hatred and a sense of paranoia. When the positive symptoms of schizophrenia appeared, she believed her neighbors were listening in on her conversations, that entities in the sky were going to harm her, and believed she was being commanded to harm herself. Hospitalization led her to employ the services of a psychoanalyst. The relationship with the psychoanalyst and her regimented schedule allowed her to develop friendships and engage more frequently in social interactions. Saks completed her degree at Oxford despite recurrent psychotic episodes.

Saks remained in England the year following her graduation, returning to the United States following admission to Yale Law School. Unfortunately, she had to leave behind the friends she had made, the routine she had developed, and the relationship with her psychoanalyst. Two weeks after classes began, Saks experienced visual hallucinations, psychotic thoughts, and disorganized speech. During a study session with her students, she invited them to accompany her to the roof of the library where she engaged in behavior that concerned those around her.

Carol North (1987) continued hearing voices into her adolescence but also began to experience visual hallucinations: colored lines wove around and moved occasionally in sync with the normal sounds of someone sneezing or a door slamming, eventually creating the illusion of seeing sounds. The voices did not explain to her what she was experiencing. Convinced she was on the verge of something big, she awoke one night to the sounds of someone calling her name and saw Jesus standing next to her bed. While in college, her hallucinations continued, resulting in the first of many hospitalizations.

Frederick J. Frese, Ph.D., a psychologist who has worked extensively with patients and families who are consumers of mental health, was diagnosed with schizophrenia at age 25. Frese (2000) writes, "When you are going into a schizophrenic break, in your mind you are behaving in a proper manner, but generally you also pick up from others that they are having problems with the way in which you are acting" (Frese, p.1417). His description of his second psychotic break shows an example of what he describes above, an individual believing he or she is behaving in a proper manner.

The Sunday before I was to fly with them to Nashville, I experienced my second psychotic break, while attending a religious service at the large Jesuit Gesu Church. For some reason during the service, without invitation, I proceeded to the altar. I began to assist the priest as he said the Mass. After this admittedly bizarre behavior, I passed out. While I was unconscious, someone apparently arranged for me to be taken to Milwaukee's large public psychiatric hospital. When I awoke, I found I was strapped down to a bed in another padded, psychiatric seclusion room. I was very delusional. (Frese, 2010, p. 377).

5. The path and the stumbling blocks to recovery

A description of schizophrenia based on a discussion of the symptoms of the disorder would be incomplete without a discussion of the recovery processes and what these individuals view as significant in both helping and hindering this recovery process. Fortunately, the professionals discussed in this chapter, Frese, Saks, North and Degan, along with Wendy Walker Davis (Frese & Davis, 1997), Ron Bassman (1997), Al Siebert (1994), and Pat Deegan (1993) have brought their stories forward. The common themes in their stories of recovery and the common roadblocks to those recoveries provide valuable insights for those working in the mental health field.

5.1. Stigma

Many of the professionals cited in this chapter (Bassman, 1997; Deegan, 1993; Frese, 2000; Frese et al., 2009; Saks, 2007) discuss in their professional writings the significance of the stigma associated with schizophrenia. These professionals have described this stigma as a very serious matter, the consequences of the stigma sometimes worse than the symptoms of the disorder. How many mental health professionals and non-professionals are afraid to even discuss recovery because the resulting stigma would be harmful to them? Many who do disclose their experiences are told they do not, in fact, have schizophrenia, but were misdiagnosed. With the symptoms of schizophrenia and the stigma both entities to overcome, how has this stigma manifested itself in the lives of those who have chosen to go public?

Link and Phelan (2001) define the stigma associated with mental illness in terms of the labeling, stereotyping, loss of status, and discrimination that can occur when one group exercises power over another. Ritsher and Phelan (2004) discuss the concept of internalized stigma, that often results in inner psychological harm and the authors see this internalized stigma as resulting in the belief that one does not belong in any social groups. The stigma associated with a mental illness affects the individual's self-esteem and adaptive social functioning outside the family, and influences the willingness of outpatients to take the medications that their psychiatrists prescribe (Link & Phelan, 2001; Lysaker, Tsai, Yanos, & Roe, 2008; Perlick, 2001; Ritsher & Phelan, 2004). Furthermore, family members are also affected by the stigma. They experience a type of stigma just from being the relative of a person with schizophrenia. Because the wellbeing of family influences the individual with schizophrenia, the family's response to the stigma can affect the person with the illness.

Pat Deegan (1993) was told at 17 that she had a disease like diabetes and if she continued taking neuroleptic medications, she might be able to cope. Rather than being seen as a precious human being, Deegan describes being told she was a schizophrenic, with family and friends referring to her as "a schizophrenic" (p. 9). Saks (2008) believes she was given a grave prognosis that she describes as a death sentence; she would never live or work on her own. Frese et al. (2009) discuss the pessimistic view of recovery that permeates the mental health profession and Frese and Davis (1997) describe how the limitations put on the person with the illness by professionals and others eventually become the limitations of the person themselves. It becomes a common practice to encourage individuals to lower their expectations regarding potential personal accomplishments and to assume a full life is just not possible. Ronald Bassman (1997) writes:

Having experienced both sides of the treatment model, I have the dubious privilege of seeing the discrimination, stigmatization, and devaluation that permeate both the mass media and the mental health system. I see good professionals unwittingly underestimating potential and overvaluing diagnosed weaknesses while inadvertently limiting precious hope; in so doing, they make it difficult for other much-needed recovered role models to come forward. (p. 240).

5.2. Recovery

What are the components of recovery that many of these professionals agree on? What have researchers uncovered that appears to significantly influence the recovery from schizophrenia in a positive way? First, is the belief put forth by many that recovery is a process, not a destination that will occur after a long series of events (Deegan, 1993; Frese et al., 2009; Frese & Davis, 1997). Symptoms often require continual management, but it is possible to manage symptoms effectively and live happy, successful lives. Bassman (Frese et al, 2009) lists the factors of continuing to have hope, safe havens, natural supports, belief in himself, family reconciliation, and meaningful work as significant factors. Deegan (1993) admits using the hospital when she needs to, taking medications, receiving support from friends, work, physical exercise, and time in nature as ways she manages her symptoms. Feeling empowered in a recovery process that is strength based, with peer support, that works to reduce stigma, exhibits respect from professionals, includes an educational component, and allows a place for hope to reside are all factors that seem to repeat themselves in the writings of those who are recovering (Cavelti, Beck, Kvrgic, Kossowsky, & Vauth, 2012; Frese, et al., 2009, Freese, 2000). The important role that meaningful work can play should not be overlooked (Ellison et al., 2005; Honkonen, Stengård, Virtanen, & Salokangas; 2007; Tandon, Nasrallah, & Keshavan; 2010; Ventura et al., 2011). Eack, Greenwald, Hogarty, and Keshavan (2010) and Tandon et al. (2010) view cognitive work as helpful with Tandon et al. seeing family psychoeducation, social skills training, and active community involvement as significant as well.

6. Summary

What we offer those who experience the symptoms of schizophrenia should be based on not only an accurate understanding of schizophrenia, but an appreciation of what is possible in the recovery of that disorder; and an appreciation of what supports the likelihood that an individual experiencing these symptoms will be limited not by internalized or externalized stigma, a treatment team caught in the limitations of the diagnosis, or a vacant and seemingly uncaring environment that can develop from family, friends, and professionals who see only limitations and not possibilities. The mental health field owes a debt of gratitude to the professionals who have come forward with their stories, telling what was required for them to overcome not only the illness but many times overcoming the people treating the illness as well. May the mental health field use these experiences from those who have been both doctor and patient to improve the quality of treatment to those who must respond to schizophrenia, viewed as one of the most challenging of mental illnesses.

Author details

Susan L. Renes*
School of Education, University of Alaska Fairbanks, Fairbanks, Alaska, USA

7. References

Baxter, E.A. (1998). The turn of the tide. *Psychiatric Services, 49*(10), 1297-1298.

Bassman, R. (1997). The mental health system: Experiences from both sides of the locked doors. *Professional Psychology: Research And Practice, 28*(3), 238-242. doi:10.1037/0735-7028.28.3.238

Breeding, J. (2008). To see or not to see: "Schizophrenia" and the possibility of full recovery. *Journalistic of Humanistic Psychology, 48*(4), 489-504. doi: 10.1177/0022167808316942

Beck, A. T., Rector, N. A., Stolar, N., & Grant, P. (2009). Overview of schizophrenia. In A. T. Beck, N. A. Rector, N. Stolar, & P. Grant, *Schizophrenia: Cognitive Theory, Research, and Therapy* (pp. 1-29). New York, NY: Guilford Publications.

Cavelti, M., Beck, E., Kvrgic, S., Kossowsky, J., & Vauth, R. (2012). The role of subjective illness beliefs and attitude toward recovery within the relationship of insight and depressive symptoms among people with schizophrenia Spectrum Disorders. *Journal Of Clinical Psychology, 68*(4), 462-476. doi:10.1002/jclp.20872

Deegan, G. (2003). Discovering recovery. *Psychiatric Rehabilitation Journal, 26*(4), 368-376.

Deegan, P. E. (1993). Recovering our sense of value after being labeled mentally ill. *Journal of Psychosocial Nursing & Mental Health Services, 31*(4), 7-11.

Eack, S. M., Greenwald, D. P., Hogarty, S. S., & Keshavan, M. S. (2010). One-year durability of the effects of cognitive enhancement therapy on functional outcome in early schizophrenia. *Schizophrenia Research, 120*(1-3), 210-216. doi:10.1016/j.schres.2010.03.042

Ellison, M.L., Russinova, Z., Massaro, J., & Lyass A. (2005). People with schizophrenia employed as professionals and managers: Initial evidence and exploration. *Schizophrenia Research, 76*(1), 123–125. doi: 10.1016/j.schres.2004.09.023

Fanous, A.H., & Kendler, K.S. (2008). Genetics of clinical features and subtypes of shizophrenia: A review of the recent literature. *Current Psychiatry Reports, 10,* 164-170.

Frese, F. J. (2010). On the impact of being diagnosed with schizophrenia. *Journal Of Mental Health, 19*(4), 376-378. doi:10.3109/09638237.2010.492419

Frese. F.J. (2000). Practicing psychologists and schizophrenia: A view from both sides. *Journal of Clinical Psychology, 56*(11), p1413-1426.

* Corresponding Author

Frese, F., Knight, E. L., & Saks, E. (2009). Recovery from schizophrenia: With views of psychiatrists, psychologists, and others diagnosed with this disorder. *Schizophrenia Bulletin, 35*(2), 370-380. doi:10.1093/schbul/sbn175

Frese, F. J., & Davis, W. (1997). The consumer–survivor movement, recovery, and consumer professionals. *Professional Psychology: Research And Practice, 28*(3), 243-245. doi:10.1037/0735-7028.28.3.243

Gourzis, P., Katrianous, A., & Beratis, S. (2002). Symptomatology of the initial prodromal phase in schizophrenia. *Schizophrenia Bulletin, 28*(3), 415-429.

Honkonen, T., Stengård, E., Virtanen, M., & Salokangas, R. R. (2007). Employment predictors for discharged schizophrenia patients. *Social Psychiatry & Psychiatric Epidemiology, 42*(5), 372-380. doi:10.1007/s00127-007-0180-5

Kaplan, R. M. (2008). Being Bleuler: The second century of schizophrenia. *Australasian Psychiatry, 16*(5), 305-311. doi:10.1080/10398560802302176

Kuhn R. (2004). Eugen Bleuler's concepts of psychopathology. *History of Psychiatry, 15,* 361-366.

Link, B. G., & Phelan, J. C. (2001). Conceptualizing stigma. *Annual Review Of Sociology, 27*(1), 363 - 385.

Lysaker, P.H., & Lysaker, J.T. (2010). Schizophrenia and alterations in self-experience: A comparison of 6 perspectives. *Schizophrenia Bulletin, 36*(2), 331-340. doi: 10.1093/sch bul/sbn077

Lysaker, P.H., Tsai, J., Yanos, P., & Roe, D. (2008). Associations of multiple domains of self-esteem with four dimensions of stigma in schizophrenia. *Schizophrenia Research, 98,* 194-200. doi:10.1016/j.schres.2007.09.035

Maxmen, J.S., Ward, N.G., & Kilgus, M. (2009). *Essential psychopathology & its treatment* (3rd ed.). New York: W.W. Norton & Company.

North, C. (1987). *Welcome, silence: My triumph over schizophrenia.* New York, NY: Simon and Schuster.

Perlick, D. (2001). Special section on stigma as a barrier to recovery: Introduction. *Psychiatric Services, 52*(12), 1613-1614. doi: 10.1176/appi.ps.52.12.1613

Ritsher, J.B., & Phelan, J.C. (2004). Internalized stigma predicts erosion of morale among psychiatric outpatients. *Psychiatry Research, 129,* 257–265.

Saks, E.R. (2007). *The center cannot hold: My journey through madness.* New York, NY: Hyperion.

Saks, E.R. (2008). A professor's story: Going public after tenure. *The American Prospect,* A4-A5. Retrieved from http://prospect.org/article/professors-story

Siebert, A. (2000). How non-diagnostic listening led to a rapid "recovery" from paranoid schizophrenia. Journal of Humanistic Psychology, 40(1), 34-58.

Tandon, R., Nasrallah, H. A., & Keshavan, M. S. (2010). Schizophrenia, "Just the Facts" 5. Treatment and prevention Past, present, and future. *Schizophrenia Research, 122*(1-3), 1-23. doi:10.1016/j.schres.2010.05.025

Ventura, J., Subotnik, K. L., Guzik, L. H., Hellemann, G. S., Gitlin, M. J., Wood, R. C., & Nuechterlein, K. H. (2011). Remission and recovery during the first outpatient year of the early course of schizophrenia. *Schizophrenia Research, 132*(1), 18-23. doi:10.1016/j.schres.2011.06.025